WITHDRAWN

Materials Management Systems

MATERIALS MANAGEMENT SYSTEMS

A Modular Library

ROBERT GOODELL BROWN, MA, PE, FAPICS, FOR
President, Materials Management Systems, Inc.

A WILEY-INTERSCIENCE PUBLICATION

JOHN WILEY & SONS,   New York • London • Sydney • Toronto

Copyright © 1977 by John Wiley & Sons, Inc.

All rights reserved. Published simultaneously in Canada.

No part of this book may be reproduced by any means,
nor transmitted, nor translated into a machine language
without the written permission of the publisher.

This publication is designed to provide accurate and authoritative information in regard to the
subject matter covered. It is sold with the understanding that the publisher is not engaged in
rendering legal, accounting, or other professional service. If legal advice or other expert
assistance is required, the services of a competent professional person should be sought.

*From a Declaration of Principles jointly adopted by a Committee of the American Bar
Association and a Committee of Publishers.*

Library of Congress Cataloging in Publication Data:
Brown, Robert Goodell.
   Materials management systems.

   Includes index.
   1. Materials management. 2. Materials
management—Data processing. I. Title.

TS161.B76   6585.7′028′54   77-8281
ISBN 0-471-11182-1

Printed in the United States of America

10 9 8 7 6 5 4 3 2 1

Preface

This book is written for the industrial engineer, inventory control manager, production planning manager, systems analyst, or operations research specialist who is working to improve the planning and control systems for materials management. The company or corporation division could have only a few hundred employees or could be among the largest in the world.

The reader is presumed to know something about the operations of his company and the environment in which production planning, inventory control, forecasting, physical distribution, and materials management operate. That is, you should be able to recognize a problem you have when it is discussed here. It is not the purpose of this book to describe why companies operate the way they do, but rather to help solve the problems you already know you have.

The primary focus of much of the work covered here is on service parts for equipment and machinery and on packaged consumer products, especially those products that are distributed through many field warehouses. Some of the material is also applicable to the assembly of customized capital equipment or to purchased materials. The industries in which these concepts have evolved include the following.

1. Manufacturing: food, textiles, apparel, pharmaceuticals, paint, machinery, instruments.
2. Wholesaling: durable and nondurable goods.
3. Retailing: building materials, hardware, general merchandise, food, automotive parts.

Fortune, Business Week, the *Wall Street Journal,* and *Barron's* are concerned with the economics of aggregate inventories and production by whole industries. Management of an individual enterprise struggles to cope with short-term reactions to inflation, recession, competition, shortages, and regulation, and to head toward long-term goals of survival, profit, and growth. This book is concerned with the control systems that make it possible to implement management's current policies as they deal with the flow of materials. Some of the topics covered are necessarily directed to quite small details of record-keeping and decisions about individual products and materials. But these microscopic decisions make corporate sense only when there is a clear delineation of the aggregate consequences of alternative strategies and tactics, expressed in terms that relate to the corporation.

This book is intended as a reference for the design of improved systems of planning and control, probably on a computer. The development continually emphasizes the relationships between management policy and day-to-day operations.

During the past two dozen years I have worked intensively with several American and European corporations, government agencies, and commercial enterprises. In the course of developing, evaluating, documenting, and implementing systems for them, I have also evolved a large suite of computer programs that are being used actively to control the flow of their materials. This book is a result of that library of programs. It is in no sense, however, a user's manual or a detailed exposition on the tricks to make the programs efficient and economical. Rather it is a reference manual to the principles underlying the algorithms that have been implemented.

To build a house, a hospital, or an office complex, the contractor needs detailed plans and specifications. The materials management systems library of programs, users' manuals, and narrative documentation constitute the specifications for systems that a great many different kinds of companies can use to build improved materials management systems. The formal definition of the building blocks for these systems is recorded, for clarity and precision, in APL, specifically APL*Plus®, an enhanced version of Iverson's notation supported by Scientific Time Sharing Corporation. Users have come to realize that where there is a discrepancy between the formal definition in APL and the narrative, the APL version is official—we know that it works.

The architects and engineers who design buildings and prepare specifications for the builder use a great deal of their own experience as well as published reference material from handbooks and catalogs. The concepts of strengths of material, for example, might be illustrated by a sketch of a typical truss. This book is intended to be that sort of a reference handbook—to explain why one would choose a particular alternative and how each of the techniques is derived. The emphasis is on making the proper choices from the state of the art to fit particular operating environments.

A big advantage to writing the formal definition of the system modules in

PREFACE

APL is that this particular realization is executable, so that the concepts can be tested in the real environment. For the developer this means that there is a chance for Murphy's Law to bring to light unforeseen attributes of the environment, which can be incorporated into the system definition easily. Hence the system, when finally specified, is complete and relevant.

How should you treat the APL formal definition? If you are interested in it as a package that you can use in operations, consult Scientific Time Sharing Corporation for access and user documentation for their Library 777. The primary intent of the book is to give you enough information so that you can develop your own application for selected techniques. I have tried to give you the essential information in unambiguous form when it is hard to discover. You will, of course, have to work out the systems, procedures, formats, and file structures to meet the needs of your system.

One advantage of having an executable realization of the formal definition is that you can quickly try many alternatives in your own situation to see at first hand what works best, before undertaking to develop a complete system. Library 777 offered by Scientific Time Sharing Corporation can be of considerable help during the investigation stage to sort out the practical implications of competing concepts.

This executable realization of the formal definition means that the user can implement the proposed system on a pilot basis, to gain assurance that it really does work in his environment. In the course of the pilot operations he also gets a chance to train the users so they can exploit better tools effectively. Clearly he also gets the benefit of the improvement quickly, at least in the pilot area, and has a factual basis for projecting the payout of a complete system design and implementation.

The final operational system will usually be implemented in some other language, on a computer already used for other applications in the company. Part of the reason for such an implementation is the interactions between the forecasting, production planning, scheduling, distribution, and inventory control systems, and the other accounting, engineering, purchasing, and order entry systems of the company. Another explicit reason for implementing in another language is often the aspirations of the company's data processing department, who see any outside service as competition, especially to be feared if it is effective.

Once the specifications of the features a particular user wants are complete and operationally verified, they are unambiguous so that the time and effort to do the systems analysis and programming is drastically reduced compared with projects that start from scratch. Conversion to an APL system is quite easy. Scientific Time Sharing Corporation has such an implementation in its public Library 777. Even though the same language is used, there are essential differences between the implementation and the formal definition on which this book is based. The algorithms are the same, but file design differs and in some cases the code runs faster. Conversion to APLSV on another computer is also nearly mechanical. Implementations have been made in COBOL, FORTRAN, RPG, BASIC, PL/I, and probably other languages, on all sorts and sizes of computers. A small company could even make use of the formal definition to set up primarily manual systems to gain some of the benefits from modern methods.

Out of necessity for completeness some of the concepts covered in this book have appeared in the literature before. Some of the concepts that have been recently developed but have not been widely published include the following:

1. Master/satellite concepts of physical distribution.
2. Structured basis for choosing among alternative strategies for computing statistical safety stocks and for stratifying the inventory.
3. Decision rules for "fair share" allocation and rebalancing field stocks.
4. Special forecasting techniques for demand when equipment population is known, new product introduction, promotions, and assortments.
5. Structure of the design assumption in alternative rules for computing the lot quantities, with pragmatic rules of thumb for choosing the right rule in a given operating environment.
6. Automatic and conversational master scheduling, with provision for both net change and regeneration, and the ability to explore the capacity and materials availability for tentative schedules without disturbing the official schedule.
7. Explosion with phantom bills of materials and effectivity dates for engineering changes.
8. Techniques for managing the replenishment of stocks for items with "lumpy" demand.
9. Believable daily priority lists for shop floor control.
10. Marketing intelligence to improve the simple descriptive statistical forecasts, with provision for incorporating a known backlog of scheduled orders.

My aim is to help the reader see the fundamental structure of a materials management control system, with a range of options available in each part. The selection among the strategic options must take account of the larger policy alternatives and decisions by all levels of corporate management, especially the marketing and financial objectives.

Not only is there a formal statement of the design assumptions for each

PREFACE

technique, but the library can be used to investigate the sensitivity to key assumptions. The fact that the particular realization of the formal definition can be executed on full-scale inventories gives both the designer and the manager insights into whether a more elegant rule or method is likely to produce significant results, making it worthwhile to implement and maintain it. The consequences of selection among all sorts of alternatives can be evaluated in the aggregate, for live data about actual company operations. The reports can be expressed in concrete terms, to help management make informed judgments about the relevance of a particular recommended approach.

Are these methods better than what you are doing now? How much better? Don't take my word for it, try it out in your own environment. This book is concerned with why the methods should be an improvement.

The concepts presented here are the results of more than 30 years of professional experience in designing and implementing materials management systems for commercial, industrial, and government enterprises throughout the United States and Europe. In addition, each year I have conducted intensive short courses, and graduate courses in several universities, typically involving some 2000 student-days a year.

There are also some pragmatic comments on how to run a company, based not only on my outside view as a consultant, but also from my experience as vice-president for operations services for the Curtiss Wright Corporation, as a director of Scientific Time Sharing Corporation, and as president of Materials Management Systems, Inc.

The data base used for the examples has been modified to protect actual customer data or to make specific points. All exhibits have been produced from actual working programs. There are no "mock-ups."

Section I is an overview of the entire scope of the book, with brief glimpses of the major operating tools. This should help set the framework in which the next three sections develop structured building blocks for forecasting, inventory management, and production planning. Chapter 12 is a break in the flow to bring together some of the notions of forecasting and inventory management into simple systems. Section V deals with complete materials management systems, with special emphasis on the neglected area of physical distribution. The systems architecture can do no more than hint at the variety of ways in which the fundamental concepts can be put together into an operating system.

Scientific Time Sharing Corporation has generously provided computer time with which to do this development. Jim Russell has been most helpful with constructive criticism, especially in the area of manufacturing practice.

Nancy Wier of McKinsey & Company has gone through a draft of the manuscript with a very fine-tooth comb and has identified many areas of obscurity and inaccuracy. She helped enormously by focusing attention on the areas that needed additional work before publication.

Sam Spink and Warren Daley of OMC Parts and Accessories Division have had exceptional vision in supporting a major project to develop an integrated materials management system based on this formal definition. Among a great many people there who have helped, Larry Lewis and John Dredge have continually made practical suggestions for improving the practicality of the approach.

ROBERT GOODELL BROWN

Norwich, Vermont
July 1977

Contents

Section 1 OVERVIEW OF THE SYSTEM 1

    1 The Action System, 5
    2 The Planning System, 19
    3 The Requirements System, 35
    4 The Strategic System, 53

    Summary   Levels of Systems, 67

Section 2 FORECASTING 73

    5 Statistical Forecast Models, 77
    6 Revising the Forecast, 107
    7 Marketing Intelligence, 123
    8 Forecast Errors, 136

    Summary   The Best Forecast, 158

Section 3 INVENTORY MANAGEMENT 161

    9 Stratification, 163
    10 Safety Stock Strategies, 173
    11 Lot Quantity Decision Rules, 202
    12 Inventory Control, 241

    Summary   Why Have Decision Rules? 262

Section 4 PRODUCTION PLANNING 265

13 Master Schedule, 269
14 Explosion, 298
15 Shop Floor Control, 316

Summary Computers and People, 327

Section 5 PHYSICAL DISTRIBUTION 329

16 Regional Control, 333
17 Central Control, 346

Summary Why Have Inventory? 370

Appensix A   File Structure, 373
Appendix B   Bibliography, 390
Appendix C   Glossary, 393
Appendix D   Tables of Probability Functions, 418

INDEX 431

SECTION **I**

Overview of the System

On a warm September afternoon at the beginning of the school term, Professor Einar Hille came into Room 101 in Leet Oliver Memorial Hall and wrote on the blackboard, "The real numbers are a complete ordered field." As the dozen graduate students dutifuly took down that graffito he turned to the class and said, "Gentlemen, we will spend the rest of this term in a course in the theory of real variables to develop an understanding of the meaning for those three words."

That has always seemed to me to be a good way to start an exposition, with a summary of where one is going. Materials management systems can't be described by quite such an elegant epigram, but Exhibit I.1 will help to organize thoughts about the types of systems we are concerned with in this book.

The materials management system can be organized into four main blocks or modules:

1. The action system produces daily instructions to the shop people about what to make, to the stockroom about what to pick, to the traffic department about what to ship. The primary intent of a planning and control system is to get instructions to the people who can act on them.
2. The planning system develops the production and purchasing schedules to ensure that the right materials are available at the right time in sufficient quantities to meet customers' requirements.
3. The strategy system sets up planning targets for the inventory levels at which the planning system should aim, with proper lot sizes where appropriate, and different management objectives for different strata of the inventory.
4. The requirements system provides a forecast of requirements by item, by location, or by time period, to reflect some combination of a firm backlog of scheduled orders, marketing intelligence about changes, a statistical projection from past demand, and dependent demand for subordinate items.

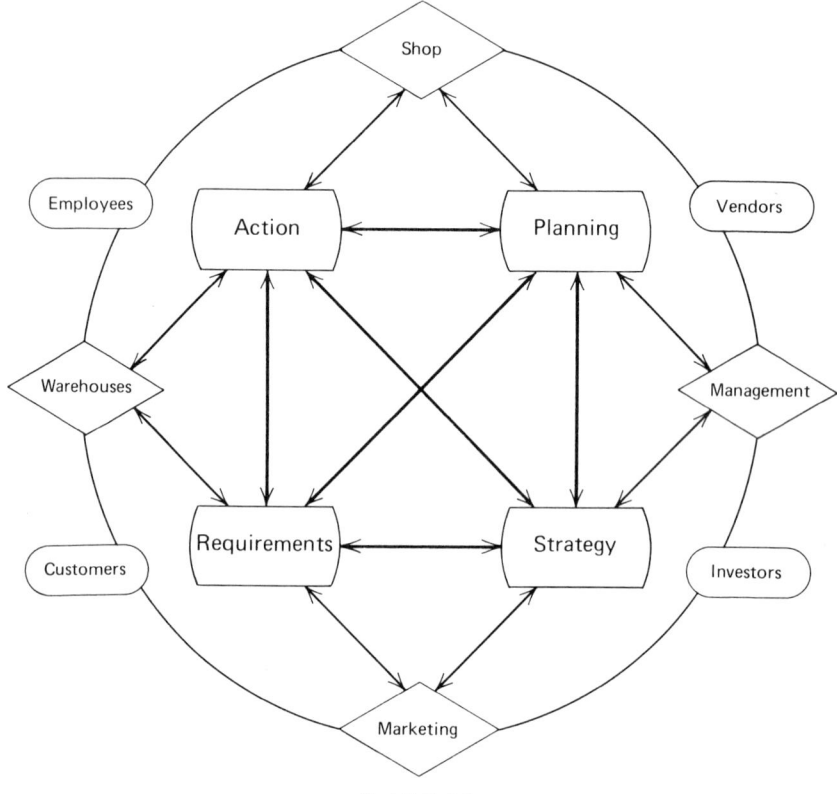

Exhibit I.1

Each of these elements uses information provided by most of the other elements, and in turn produces results that will be used by others. The four systems are the concern of this book. However, the materials management system has to work in an operating environment: requirements come from order entry in the field warehouses and from marketing plans. Inventory strategy is affected by marketing objectives and by top management objectives for the corporation. The way that the master schedule is developed for a production plan must take account of capacity and labor availability, which both come from the current plant operations and from management plans. The action system sends instructions both to the producing part of the company and to the field.

Even these parts of the company are not wholly self-contained. There are ultimately people involved: employees, vendors, investors, and customers, and those people interact with each other.

Exhibit I.1 is misleading. These modules do not interact directly. Just as the telephone company provides elaborate switching systems in central

OVERVIEW OF THE SYSTEM

offices to permit subscribers to talk to each other, a good materials management system operates through a common data base, shown in the center of Exhibit I.2.

Not only does information flowing between any pair of systems in the materials management system pass through the central file, but information to and from the order entry, purchasing, accounting, and engineering systems can also pass through this same data base. This structure makes it very convenient to use the formal definition of the materials management system on a pilot basis in a live environment, where simple programs pass data back and forth from the APL*Plus files to the files of other systems already in operation.

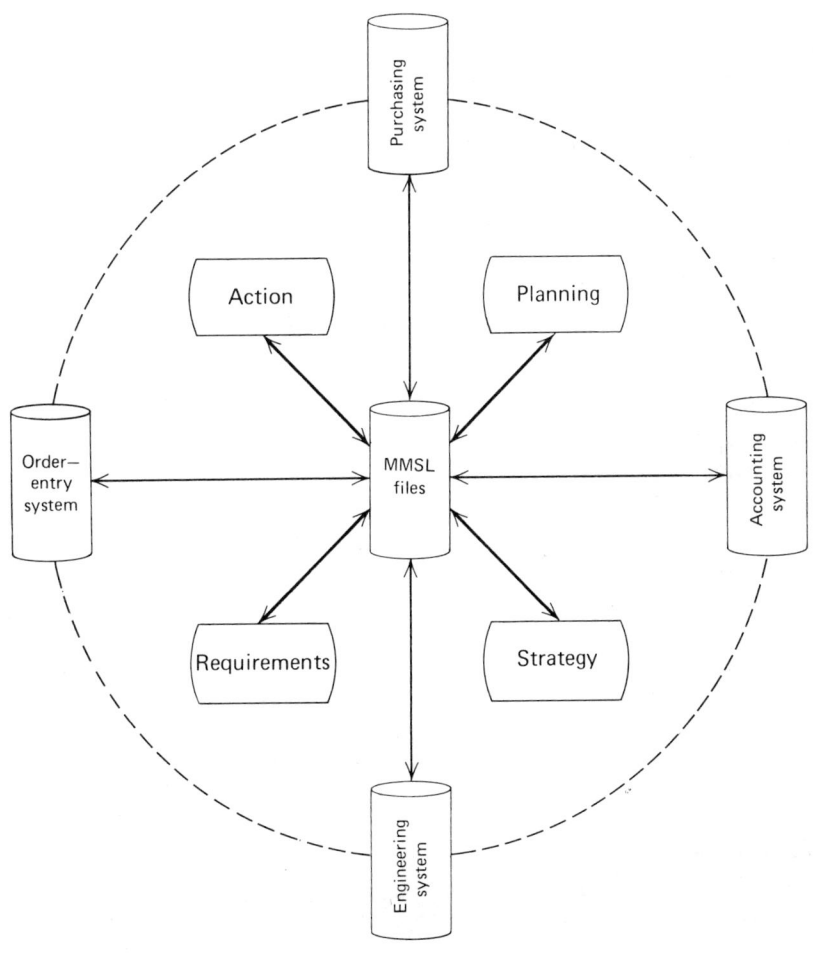

Exhibit I.2

One can even go further. If a company already has a good forecasting system, for example, we can "move" the requirements box in Exhibit I.2 out to the dotted circle, and consider it as a system in the environment instead of a new system. So long as the proper information flows from systems on the dotted circle into the MMSL data base, it does not matter whether any of the materials management modules are operating as an executable realization of the formal definition, or are already implemented in the normal environment of the company.

The four chapters in this section exhibit typical reports from the various systems of the materials management system:

1. Action system.
2. Planning system.
3. Requirements system.
4. Strategy system.

The intent of these exhibits is to set the stage for the detailed work to follow. The environment is generally a company that makes equipment, so that it includes purchase of raw materials, various manufacturing operations, assembly, and distribution of the product through field warehouses. Some of the parts and materials may have requirements as service parts, and may be distributed in kits. The same environment applies to several types of packaged consumer products, such as pharmaceuticals, food, apparel, cosmetics, and even toys. In some of these companies the numerical values of costs, volumes, lead times, and numbers of steps in the process are quite different from the values shown in the exhibits, but the underlying logical structure is the same.

John Hamner at Caterpillar once remarked to me, "If a normal person were planning to build a house, he'd probably specify a bathroom and a powder room. But I believe, Bob, that you'd tell the architect to give you two bathrooms, just leave the tub out of one of them." It is that sort of common structure to the materials management system that we want to bring out in this book.

So don't worry if the examples don't match your company exactly. Don't worry if you already have some of the work done and in operation. Look for the features that may be worth considering as an addition or an extension to what your present system does. The library has enough modules that somewhere in that pile there is likely to be a pony. The structure of the design of the library allows you to mix and mingle these modules at will, like building from an Erector set.

CHAPTER **1**

The Action System

One of the principal features of an effective control system is a great deal of feedback, connecting one part of the system with another. Hence there is no real "beginning" or "end" to the system. (We see later that there is a hierarchy of "insides" and "outsides" for different parts of the system.) One might start anywhere to describe a complex system; here we start with the action that takes place because of the planning decisions. We do have to stop at the point where people get some form of report with information to help them choose among alternative courses of action. The administrative supervision and control techniques that get people actually to do something are outside the scope of this book.

There is a fundamental concept underlying all these reports. They do not in general give direct orders to do this or that. Rather they tend to display several options, with information about the consequences of choosing among them. People on the shop floor, in the shipping department, and in the stockroom have access to other local information that cannot be programmed, and some of it may be relevant to the decision. If people know the relative advantages of different courses of action, they can take local conditions and preferences into account. Where people have little insight into the implications of their work, the company can be quite inefficient. It is also a mistake to go to the other extreme and dictate detailed action from the top down. The scope of choices is of course limited when the consequences affect others. But if within that scope the choices don't affect the rest of the organization, then encourage people to use their own judgment.

If a person's judgment is good, and if he can learn from making mistakes, he is a candidate for advancement. Even if he is not ready for advancement, a person who is given some freedom is likely to build factors into his decisions that in the long run are good for the corporation. And he will be happier if he isn't told what to do, by the numbers.

This is a personal philosophy. There are those who disagree, even to the point of dictating the color of an employee's shirt and the style of his home life. There may even be workers who prefer to be told exactly what to do. That is a different style from the one that colors the development of the systems and procedures described here.

The action module can be separated into two parts. The first has to do with the way that products are distributed from the producing plant (or vendor source) among the field warehouses. The second is concerned with the progress of work through the manufacturing process.

1.1 DISTRIBUTION

The finished products of a company may be carried in stock at each of several warehouses. These products may be assembled machinery, service parts and supplies, packaged consumer goods, and the like. If your products are shipped directly to the customer from the factory, you can skip to the next section. There are many products, like instruments and materials handling equipment, for which the variety of the final product is so great that each one is built to order and shipped directly. That is not our concern at the moment, although it is later.

For reasons that are discussed in detail in Chapter 17, one warehouse is designated as a "master" warehouse, and the other locations as "satellites." Every product has one, and only one, master warehouse, but the location of that master may be different for different items. The master warehouse is usually next to the plant for manufactured products. For purchased material it may be near the source, or in the center of the market. There is an exception to the rule of only one master: for products made in several different plants, each source might have as associated master warehouse, but then the country is divided into territories and regions so that there is only one master within a territory, with perhaps several satellites. Bricks and paint, for example, cannot profitably be carted very far from the point of manufacture.

The master location is really a logical concept rather than a physical one. The "master warehouse" may be part of a location that is also a "satellite." The function of the satellite is to fill orders from customers in that region. The master warehouse holds a national safety stock to assure continued service at all satellites. The master warehouse issues stock for distribution to satellites. If the satellite is in the same building, it may simply transfer inventory from one paper account to another. There are also systems, discussed in Chapter 16, where the national safety stock is not held in any one place but is distributed directly from the source to the field. Another modification to be considered later is that all material stocked in the field is shipped directly from the vendor to the distribution center without passing

DISTRIBUTION

through a central warehouse. For the present, consider that products from the factory do come into a central place, which serves as a master warehouse for the whole country, and may or may not have as associated satellite function to serve local customers.

The products are shipped from the master warehouse to the satellites in trucks or rail cars. The shipping schedule may be fixed, with a predetermined route, or may be on demand, whenever there is something that needs to be shipped.

The first decision problem is what to load onto the next truck going to a particular destination. Exhibit 1.1 is an example of a kind of report that helps the traffic planner determine whether a truck is needed now, and what to put on it if it is.

This sort of report can be prepared for any selected source and for one or more destinations, in this case from the Master warehouse to New York. The example shows 15 lines that could be shipped. The "fair share" quantities show what New York is entitled to, taking account of stock on hand, safety stock targets, lead times, and forecasts of requirements. When there are package modules or maximum limits, the quantity to ship may be rounded to less than the total fair share, and the balance may be shown in subsequent shipments on the list.

The latest ship date is computed from the stock status at New York, both on hand and in transit, considering transit time, and planned safety stock. The report is organized in sequence by latest ship date—most urgent at the top. The weight and cube information helps the planner make up an actual shipment.

For example, he might reason as follows: item number 1, the extension, should go today, and the second item, the windshield, within a couple of weeks. The first seven items would just about make up a truckload, and if they are all shipped now, another shipment to New York would not be required for about 10 weeks. At that time the priorities and fair shares of the other products may change. The point is that all 15 products have enough stock today in the master warehouse to cover New York's requirements through Christmas. If they aren't shipped now, they are still in the finished goods inventory. Of course, there may be additional products that crop up on the priority list by early October. A different mix can be made up then.

1.11 Allocation

Next let's look at some of the planning tools that might help the planner to decide what the fair shares and shipping quantities are. Exhibit 1.2 shows

SOURCE: 100 MASTER
15 LINES TO SHIP.

DESTINATION: 300 NEW YORK, NY

LINE NO	PART NO	DESCRIPTION	QUANTITY FAIR SHARE	TO SHIP	SHIP BEFORE	WEIGHT POUNDS	CUMULATIVE	SIZE CUBIC FEET	CUMULATIVE
1	36-168-388	EXTENSION	17	17	8/04/76	187	187	13	13
2	41-037-913	WINDSHIELD	855	855	8/16/76	2,479	2,666	180	192
3	44-100-824	ADAPTOR	2,440	2,440	9/10/76	3,904	6,570	293	485
4	41-182-643	SHROUD	539	539	10/01/76	3,881	10,451	280	765
5	40-028-167	ADAPTOR	3,897	3,897	10/18/76	8,573	19,025	624	1,389
6	49-029-897	ADAPTOR	1,395	1,395	10/18/76	3,766	22,791	279	1,668
7	50-655-961	DISPLAY	105	105	10/18/76	934	23,726	67	1,735
8	40-696-973	IGNITION	572	572	10/29/76	801	24,526	55	1,790
9	36-183-917	SHROUD	132	132	11/01/76	1,267	25,794	91	1,881
10	49-341-925	PRIMER	57	57	11/03/76	256	26,050	19	1,900
11	44-683-325	GASTANK	29	29	11/08/76	493	26,543	35	1,935
12	44-004-679	HOURMETER	282	282	12/21/76	1,241	27,784	90	2,025
13	44-008-530	IGNITION	103	103	12/21/76	81	27,865	6	2,031
14	35-026-478	ADAPTOR	1,444	1,444	12/21/76	2,744	30,609	188	2,219
15	41-031-505	ADAPTOR	86	86	12/21/76	249	30,858	18	2,237

ACTION: CHANGE, SHIP, NEXT = S
SHIP THROUGH LINE NUMBER = 7

Exhibit 1.1

37-01-1906   HOME UNIT | FILE INDEX = 1
ALLOCATION TO 100 DAYS SUPPLY BEYOND ORDER POINT.

SOURCE		DESTINATION		COST	FAIRSHARE	QUANTITY	SHIP BY
MASTER	100	BROADVIE	110	0	42	36	9/28/76
		ATLANTA,	300	3	6	6	12/01/76
		LOS ANGE	500	9	97	96	9/02/76
		DENVER,	400	5	126	120	9/08/76
TOTAL					271	258	

39-10-3209   FOUNTAIN | FILE INDEX = 2
ALLOCATION TO 84 DAYS SUPPLY BEYOND ORDER POINT.

SOURCE		DESTINATION		COST	FAIRSHARE	QUANTITY	SHIP BY
MASTER	100	BROADVIE	110	0	905	96	10/05/76
		NEW YORK	200	4	329	240	9/22/76
		LOS ANGE	500	9	505	504	9/13/76
TOTAL					1,739	840	

EXCESS AT		PIECES	DOLLARS	MONTHS
DENVER,	400	12	145.20	0.0
TOTALS		12	145.20	

37-62-1981   FURNACE | FILE INDEX = 3
ALLOCATION TO 50 DAYS SUPPLY BEYOND ORDER POINT.

SOURCE		DESTINATION		COST	FAIRSHARE	QUANTITY	SHIP BY
MASTER	100	BROADVIE	110	0	33	24	9/20/76
		ATLANTA,	300	3	41	36	9/13/76
		LOS ANGE	500	9	41	36	9/14/76
TOTAL					115	96	

EXCESS AT		PIECES	DOLLARS	MONTHS
NEW YORK	200	51	9,024.22	0.3
TOTALS		51	9,024.22	

Exhibit 1.2

the allocations for three products. The allocation may have been triggered because there was a receipt from source, or because there was a demand transaction at some satellite location, reducing the available stock there. If there was no increase in stock from a delivery, and no decrease by filling customer demand, a product is not allocated. Products that aren't included in the shipment list today disappear from the file. If they weren't urgent enough to ship yesterday, and there has been no change in status, they can't be urgent today.

In the first case, the master warehouse has enough to send to each of four satellites. Large fair shares are rounded to integral multiples of packages of 12, but Atlanta, which gets only six, gets individual pieces. The shipment to Los Angeles is most urgent, and the small shipment to Atlanta isn't very urgent at all, since there is a great deal of this product already there.

For the other two products, the fair shares are quantities sufficient to bring available stock to 84 and 50 days' supply above order point. Broadview's share is 905 pieces of the fountain, but there is a maximum shipment limit never to be exceeded of 100, which is rounded to 96 because of the module quantity (pallets of 12). For both of the latter two products one of the satellites already has more than the fair share, and the excess is reported in pieces, dollar value, and months of supply. The cost column is not significant in this case because all shipments are made from the master warehouse to the satellites.

Another way of allocating the same three products is shown in Exhibit 1.3. (Chapter 17 discusses additional criteria for allocation.) Any excess stock at satellites is available to be sent to some other location. The quantities of the latter two products from each source are again computed to bring available stock to 85 and 53 days' supply above order point for all locations. But Denver and New York can serve as source locations now. The relative amounts to be sent to each destination are computed by the transportation algorithm of linear programming, to ensure that freight costs are minimized, using the costs (in cents per pound) shown in the cost column. In the case of the middle product in Exhibit 1.3, it would be best to send the nine pieces from Denver to Los Angeles now, because that costs only four cents per pound. If the remaining 500 pieces are still needed, they can be shipped from the master warehouse later. Similarly for the bottom product, a dozen pieces should be sent to Atlanta from the master warehouse now; the other three dozen available in New York at a higher cost, can be sent later if still needed.

When there isn't enough stock in the system even to cover order points at the satellites, there is provision for recomputing safety factors to get the maximum possible service out of the stock that is available.

DISTRIBUTION

```
37-01-1906      HOME UNIT | FILE INDEX = 1
ALLOCATION TO 100 DAYS SUPPLY BEYOND ORDER POINT.

SOURCE          DESTINATION         COST  FAIRSHARE  QUANTITY  SHIP BY

MASTER    100   BROADVIE  110         0       42        36     9/28/76
MASTER    100   ATLANTA,  300         3        6         6    12/01/76
MASTER    100   LOS ANGE  500         9       97        96     9/02/76
MASTER    100   DENVER,   400         5      126       120     9/08/76

TOTAL                                        271       258


39-10-3209      FOUNTAIN | FILE INDEX = 2
ALLOCATION TO 85 DAYS SUPPLY BEYOND ORDER POINT.

SOURCE          DESTINATION         COST  FAIRSHARE  QUANTITY  SHIP BY

MASTER    100   BROADVIE  110         0      934        96    10/05/76
MASTER    100   NEW YORK  200         4      337       240     9/22/76
MASTER    100   LOS ANGE  500         9      506       504     9/13/76
DENVER,   400   LOS ANGE  500         4        9         9     9/13/76

TOTAL                                      1,786       849


37-62-1981      FURNACE | FILE INDEX = 3
ALLOCATION TO 53 DAYS SUPPLY BEYOND ORDER POINT.

SOURCE          DESTINATION         COST  FAIRSHARE  QUANTITY  SHIP BY

MASTER    100   BROADVIE  110         0       59        48     9/20/76
MASTER    100   ATLANTA,  300         3       13        12     9/13/76
MASTER    100   LOS ANGE  500         9       60        60     9/14/76
NEW YORK  200   ATLANTA,  300         4       45        36     9/13/76

TOTAL                                        177       156
```

Exhibit 1.3

1.12 Performance Measurement

Management should be kept aware of how the system is doing, for comparison with the strategic plans for production, service, and investment.

A report produced once a day (Exhibit 1.4) summarizes for every warehouse in the system how many products are stocked there, the value (at standard cost) of stock on hand and in transit, the dollar value of back-ordered demand, and the number of items on back order. The "on order" column for satellite locations means stock in transit from the master to that location. The same column for the master warehouse is the stock on order

PERFORMANCE

MONDAY, AUGUST 23, 1976
EASTERN DAYLIGHT TIME 17:18:07

WHICH ITEMS = ALL
ALL 713 ITEMS WILL BE USED.
LOCATIONS TO BE INCLUDED = ALL
6 LOCATIONS WILL BE USED.

LOCATION	ITEMS	ON HAND	ON ORDER	$ BACKORD	ITEMS B/O
MASTER	699	4,075,837	1,124,470	25	1
INDIANAPOLIS, IN	699	62,172	112,374	99,503	377
NEW YORK, NY	339	98,266	153,120	12,287	64
ATLANTA, GA	346	119,151	194,154	12,286	58
DENVER, CO	346	151,517	203,542	15,046	56
LOS ANGELES, CA	341	111,835	134,670	12,730	51
TOTAL	2770	4,618,779	1,922,329	151,879	607
ELAPSED TIME	1M 30.470S				
CPU TIME	9.344S				

Exhibit 1.4

from vendors or in production on firm schedules. One report on its own doesn't tell much of a story, but a succession of these reports can quickly spot any trends in performance.

A computer specialist might be tempted to program the system to show a track record, for convenience. It could be done quite easily. But I commend to your attention the fact that when a manager has to look at a report every day, and physically move a pencil to transcribe the data from the report to a continuing graph or table (depending on management style), that few seconds give an opportunity to think about what the figures mean. Of course, if the boss has his secretary do the posting, he'd better have a secretary who thinks and calls attention to unusual phenomena. With such a secretary, who needs a boss? I hate to disappoint all you zealots in computer technology, but from time to time throughout this book there will be occasions when I do ask the user to think about what is going on. (See 13.6.)

1.2 PRODUCTION CONTROL

The second major part of the action module is directed toward control over the flow of work through a manufacturing process. If all your products are purchased, or if the production process is extremely simple (or established

PRODUCTION CONTROL

as a definite flow of work), then this particular part of the system may not be of much interest. But for products that are made in a job shop, with several operations, the reports displayed here can be of enormous value in getting the right things done at the right time.

It is rather astonishing how many different kinds of production process would qualify for the "job shop" idea that is relevant here. Of course the typical job shop does general machining and assembly of products with a high degree of variety of specifications. But commercial printing, pharmaceutical manufacturing, custom packaging, and photographic film all have elements in the typical process that can use these concepts.

The work sheet shown in Exhibit 1.5 is an example of a priority report that can be issued every morning to each superintendent or foreman in the plant. The list is printed in sequence by the latest start date (in the rightmost column), with the most urgent job first. That latest start date is computed in the planning module to allow a reasonable time for all subsequent operations and still get the job done on schedule.

DEPARTMENT   350   MR GORHAM   FRIDAY, JUNE 25, 1976

PART NUMBER	ORDER REFERENCE	GOOD QUANTITY	OPERATIONS SEQUENCE	NAME	STANDARD HOURS	WORK CENTER	LATEST START
33-28-2343	10162		10	ASSEMBLE B	17325.00	1001	6/15/76
39-82-5503	10174	18,000	10	ASSEMBLE	9 900.00	2150	6/18/76
33-28-2343	10180	4,000	10	ASSEMBLE B	2000.00	1001	6/21/76
33-28-2343	10162		20	MOUNT GEAR	3465.00	1002	6/22/76
33-28-2343	10162		30	FINAL ASSE	3465.00	1050	6/24/76
39-82-5503	10192		10	ASSEMBLE	10270.00	2150	6/24/76
36-32-6386	10163	4,000	10	ASSEMBLE	4000.00	2100	6/25/76
33-28-2343	10197	4,162	10	ASSEMBLE B	2081.00	1001	6/28/76
33-28-2343	10180		20	MOUNT GEAR	400.00	1002	6/28/76
33-28-2343	10180		30	FINAL ASSE	400.00	1050	6/30/76
36-32-6386	10181	2,000	10	ASSEMBLE	2000.00	2100	7/01/76
33-28-2343	10214	4,096	10	ASSEMBLE B	2048.00	1001	7/05/76
33-28-2343	10197		20	MOUNT GEAR	416.20	1002	7/05/76
39-82-5503	10209	15,489	10	ASSEMBLE	7744.50	2150	7/05/76
33-28-2343	10232	6,064	10	ASSEMBLE B	3032.00	1001	7/06/76
33-28-2343	10197		30	FINAL ASSE	416.20	1050	7/07/76
37-56-4105	10164	2,000	10	SOLDER JOI	200.00	3000	7/07/76
36-32-6386	10198	3,894	10	ASSEMBLE	3894.00	2100	7/08/76
39-82-5503	10244	116,79	10	ASSEMBLE	5839.50	2150	7/09/76
33-28-2343	10249	5,553	10	ASSEMBLE B	2776.50	1001	7/12/76
33-28-2343	10214		20	MOUNT GEAR	409.60	1002	7/12/76
33-28-2343	10232		20	MOUNT GEAR	606.40	1002	7/13/76
33-28-2343	10266		10	ASSEMBLE B	2709.50	1001	7/13/76
37-56-4105	10182		10	SOLDER JOI	243.10	3000	7/13/76
39-82-5503	10226	14,704	10	ASSEMBLE	7352.00	2150	7/13/76
33-28-2343	10214		30	FINAL ASSE	409.60	1050	7/14/76
33-28-2343	10232	–	30	FINAL ASSE	606.40	1050	7/15/76
36-32-6386	10215	3,710	10	ASSEMBLE	3710.00	2100	7/15/76

Exhibit 1.5

The jobs to be done are identified by part number and order reference number. For example, the first and third jobs on the list are for the same part number 33-28-2343, but have different reference numbers, indicating that they have different priorities. The first lot must start operation 10 by 6/15/76, and the second lot of the same product needn't start operation 10 until 6/21/76.

A value in the "good quantity" column indicates that previous operations have been completed. For example, order reference 10180 is now at operation 10, with 4000 pieces to be made. it goes through operations 20 and 30 in the same department, but they needn't start until 6/28/76 and 6/30/76, respectively.

The operation name, standard hours of direct work, and work center designation can be printed to help the superintendent plan his work.

Here is another example of the basic philosophy of giving the man on the spot information about what is wanted, what the freedom for choice is, and then leaving him with the final decision of what to do.

The first job can't be started, although it is the most urgent, because the previous operations haven't been completed. However, I would expect that an aggressive superintendent would find out where that job is and make effective use of the informal communications network to get it pulled ahead smartly.

Some foremen might like to "save a setup" by combining orders 10198 and 10215 for part number 36-32-6386. That is all right provided the urgent work is being done. But this work sheet was issued on June 25, and there are seven lines on the report that should already have started, three of which have material completed through earlier operations. Those jobs should be started first, before anyone worries about saving a setup. The report can be controlled from the office by not listing work that doesn't need to start until July, to provide still further limits on the scope of choice. But when work has been released deliberately by the planning system in advance of need to build a stabilization stock, then the man in the shop can be encouraged to use his own judgment in running lots together, picking the easy jobs, or assigning the good jobs to Charlie.

1.2 Reporting Progress

The foreman or dispatcher marks actual progress on his work sheet throughout the day. The intent is to issue a new work sheet every day. At the end of the day, the work sheets are turned in to be posted to the data base so that a new work sheet can be generated on the basis of current status.

PRODUCTION CONTROL

Several kinds of progress can be reported.

1. A lot can finish the operation for which it is scheduled, and yield as a good quantity the scheduled quantity. For that the workman has only to enter an "F."
2. The operation can be completed, but with some scrap loss, so that the order is closed short; this can be indicated by a "C" with a note of the good quantity that is available to the next operation.
3. Part of the scheduled quantity could have been completed, with the balance still due to be completed later. A "P," with a note of the

```
REF,OPN = 10187
PROG = F

REF,OPN = 10188
PROG = L

REF,OPN = 10189
PROG = F

REF,OPN = 10189
NOT A VALID ORDER.

REF,OPN = 10191
PROG = F

REF,OPN = 10211
PROG = F

REF,OPN = 10204
PROG = F

REF,OPN = 10221 2
PROG = F

REF,OPN = 10222 2
PROG = F

REF,OPN = 10223 2
PROG = C
QUANTITY = 1000000

REF,OPN = 10224 2
PROG = F

REF,OPN = 10225 2
PROG = F
```

Exhibit 1.6

quantity available for the next operation, will effectively split the lots into two sublots (which should come together later).
4. There are operations on the list for production planning and quality control as well as the more traditional process route steps. In some of these cases the planner might want to mark his work sheet with "L" for completing the last operation.

21 ORDERS REPORTED AS CLOSED SHORT

PART NO	REFERENCE	ORIG QTY	GOOD QTY	OPERATION
36-32-6386	10163	4,147	4,000	1
37-56-4105	10164	2,479	2,000	1
39-91-0374	10165	31,164	30,000	1
33-65-3387	10166	757	750	1
39-82-5503	10174	18,841	18,000	1
37-22-6605	10175	15,676	15,000	1
33-28-2343	10180	4,297	4,000	1
36-32-6386	10181	4,013	2,000	1
39-91-0374	10183	3,675	3,000	1
32-47-0389	10185	60,477	60,000	1
38-84-7072	10187	1,093,131	900,000	1
32-72-7100	10188	789,704	750,000	1
34-36-4115	10189	886,937	800,000	1
32-47-0389	10160	37,702	35,000	1
32-47-0389	10167	29,520	25,000	1
37-56-4105	10199	2,361	2,000	1
38-84-7072	10204	1,202,714	1,000,000	1
34-36-4115	10223	1,076,791	1,000,000	1
37-22-6605	10227	8,005	8,000	1
35-45-5678	10280	117	100	1
87-65-4321	10281	132	100	1

9 ORDERS COMPLETED THE LAST OPERATION

PART NO	REFERENCE	ORIG QTY	GOOD QTY	YIELD	SCHED DATE
36-51-5186	10172	16,592	16,592	100.00	6/29/76
38-84-7072	10221	1,285,414	1,285,414	100.00	7/05/76
34-36-4115	10223	1,076,791	1,000,000	92.87	7/05/76
32-72-7100	10222	961,330	961,330	100.00	7/05/76
37-22-6605	10175	15,676	15,000	95.69	6/29/76
39-82-5503	10174	18,841	18,000	95.54	6/29/76
32-47-0389	10185	60,477	60,000	9 .21	7/05/76
35-45-5678	10289	37	37	100.00	6/30/76
87-65-4321	10290	45	45	100.00	6/30/76

STORE LIST IN FILE = DIRECTORY
COMPONENT = LAST
DUPLICATE. REPLACE IT? Y

Exhibit 1.7

PRODUCTION CONTROL

See Chapter 15 for a discussion of the varying needs of engineering, accounting, manufacturing, and production planning for including or excluding various kinds of operations in the process routing.

A clerk can post the progress to the data base through a conversational program as shown in Exhibit 1.6. The particular job is identified by the reference number. If more than one operation was completed in the same day, the operation sequence number is also provided. But if the progress was just to complete the scheduled operation, the operation sequence number need not be supplied. The computer asks for "Progress = " and then waits for a code letter, F, C, P, or L. Note in one case the reference number was not a valid open order. When the progress code is "C" for closed short, the computer then asks for the good quantity completed.

When all of the progress has been posted, the computer prepares various summaries of the activity. Two are shown in Exhibit 1.7. The first identifies any orders that were posted with a "C" for closed short, so that the planner can scan the list to see that they are reasonable and retrieve information for yield analysis. The second report summarizes all production that has been completed, with a comparison of the original schedule quantity and the final good quantity, converted into gross yield ratios. The schedule data of completion is also printed, as a check on whether work is being completed very much ahead of, or behind, schedule.

As part of the retrieval concept, which is covered in detail in Chapter 9, the list of items that have completed the last operation is stored in a special directory, which can be used to trigger the allocation computations about how much of the product to ship to each location.

CHAPTER **2**

The Planning System

A person trying to drive from the Blackstone Hotel on the south side of Chicago's Loop to either Minneapolis or Seattle must first reach the Kennedy Expressway. Even if he plans to fly from O'Hare Airport to either city, he starts by reaching the expressway. The action modules exhibited in Chapter 1 have to do with the current situation and immediate goals, such as turning corners and stopping for the lights and traffic jams. In this chapter we turn to the question of planning for the longer range, such as which city to aim for, and whether to drive or fly. Now that there is an indication that features are possible for a materials management system that will make it operate satisfactorily for any given set of immediate goals, let us look at the means for establishing those goals.

The basic elements of a production plan are rather simple. We need to know what we have, what we are already committed to get, what we plan to use, and what level of stock we would like to maintain.

2.1 LOCATION STATUS

One possible report of status for a given product is tabulated in three lines for each location; see Exhibit 2.1. There are columns for each planning period at fortnightly intervals starting from the date at which stock was posted, 7/01/76 in this case. The top line gives a forecast of the total requirements for the furnace at that location for each period. The details of how to get that forecast are displayed in Chapter 3, and the techniques are covered thoroughly in Section 2. The second line shows the amounts that are expected to be allocated to that location, to arrive sometime within the indicated planning period. Broadview has 200 pieces now in transit to it, and another 43 are likely to be received in the period ending 10/21/76. The bottom line shows the planned availability. Broadview starts out with a net back order of 14 pieces today, but if the 200 in transit are received and 18 are sold during the period ending 7/15/76, then the stock on hand at the

37-62-1981   FURNACE   FILE INDEX = 3

	7/01/76	7/15/76	7/29/76	8/12/76	8/26/76	9/09/76	9/23/76	10/07/76	10/21/76
LOCATION: BROADVIEW, IL 110									
FORECAST: SS =		18	18	33	37	31	28	28	26
ALLOCATION: IT =	200								43
AVAILABLE: OH =	⁻14	168	150	117	80	49	21	⁻7	10
LOCATION: ATLANTA, GA 300									
FORECAST: SS =	21	47	48	46	46	44	43	45	48
ALLOCATION: IT =									
AVAILABLE: OH =	117	70	22	⁻24	⁻70	⁻114	⁻157	⁻202	⁻250
LOCATION: NEW YORK, NY 200									
FORECAST: SS =	14	19	19	20	21	20	20	20	21
ALLOCATION: IT =	180								
AVAILABLE: OH =		161	142	122	101	81	61	41	20
LOCATION: LOS ANGELES, CA 500									
FORECAST: SS =	19	32	33	32	32	30	30	32	34
ALLOCATION: IT =	216								
AVAILABLE: OH =	84	268	235	203	171	141	111	79	45

Exhibit 2.1

end of that period is projected to be 168 pieces. The first column of the first row shows the planned safety stock, as a check against the availability going below safety stock or even into back order.

The situation revealed for this furnace is not particularly good. Atlanta is going to run short by 8/12, whereas New York will have stock past 10/21. But in the short run, through the end of July, all locations are in reasonably good shape. Before there is actually a problem, a great many planning decisions and actions may be taken, so that the situation will change. At least one can get a current picture of what the problems may be, in order to decide whether to change plans. Wouldn't it be nice if in Chicago traffic one could see far enough ahead to decide whether to go out Congress Street or up Michigan Avenue to Ohio Street, in order to reach the Kennedy Expressway?

2.2 MASTER SCHEDULE

The master schedule for any manufactured product or purchased material is a plan, period by period, of the amounts of new product to be available to stock. The essential ingredients of a master schedule are illustrated in Exhibit 2.2 for a breaker that is used both as a service part and as a subordinate part of one or more larger assemblies.

The level code 2 indicates that there are two higher levels of assembly—

```
42-070-845      BREAKER     | FILE INDEX = 566    LEVEL CODE 2
MINIMUM STOCK TARGET = 28723.   AS OF  6/30/76  STOCK ON HAND = 123533
SCHEDULING RULE: FIXED LOT QUANTITY
```

PERIOD ENDING	DIRECT REQUIREMENTS	DEPENDENT REQUIREMENTS	FIRM ORDERS	NOTIONAL ORDERS	PROJECTED AVAILABILITY
7/14/76	14,973				79,837
7/28/76	14,973				64,864
8/11/76	11,495				53,369
8/25/76	10,547				42,822
9/08/76	8,574				34,248
9/22/76	7,095	8,255			18,898
10/06/76	6,409	7,600			4,889
10/20/76	5,496			36,000	35,393
11/03/76	5,633	7,600			22,160
11/17/76	6,136	10,600			5,424
12/01/76	6,265			36,000	35,159
12/15/76	7,947				27,212

Exhibit 2.2

MASTER SCHEDULE   21

this breaker goes into some subassembly (which would have level code 1) which in turn goes into a final product (level code 0) which has no other assembly usage. The heading tells us that the strategic modules (Chapter 4) have set a minimum stock target of 28,723, but as of 6/30/76 there are 123,000 pieces in stock. In Chapter 13 we deal with each of several rules for generating a master schedule. This item is planned to have new production scheduled in fixed lot quantities of 36,000 pieces each.

For convenience in displaying a long schedule on a single sheet of paper, the two-week periods are listed down the page. In some periods there are direct requirements, such as for service parts or OEM scheduled backlog. There are also dependent requirements exploded from the master schedules for higher levels of assembly. At the time when this report was prepared there were no firm orders in the file and two notional orders. There is plenty of stock on hand to cover the projected requirements. The rightmost column, projected availability, shows the stock that is expected to be on hand at the end of each planning period, starting with present stock on hand, subtracting both direct and dependent requirements, and adding new production.

A "firm" order is any manufacturing lot or purchase order to which a reference number has been assigned. These quantities are scheduled to arrive in stock at the end of a lead time from the time when they were generated. "Notional orders" are quantities that appear in the master schedule, but which will not be needed until more than a freeze period from now. Because subordinate parts and materials are needed earlier than the completion of a subassembly, the master schedule must extend to a planning horizon past the normal lead time.

The master schedule, with notional orders, can be exploded and offset to generate dependent requirements on all the subordinates used to make the items. Notional orders, however, can be changed in the next planning cycle. They serve two purposes: to generate requirements that may fall within a lead time for subordinates, and to give information to other parts of the system about what is likely to come. In general, notional orders are due more than a lead time into the future. They can be changed, depending on the rule used for master scheduling, every time the master schedule is regenerated. A notional order due in the period now just past the lead time can be made firm by assigning a unique reference number to it. Then the rules change about shifting either the quantities or due dates as requirements and stock status change. The details of these rules are covered in Chapter 13.

2.21 Order Status

For a variety of reasons the planner may want to see all existing open orders for selected products. If finished stock is too large, some open orders should be cancelled, reduced in quantity, or deferred. Conversely, if there is a shortage, some lots may have to be scheduled for earlier delivery, exploiting the ability of the manufacturing process to do a reasonable number of jobs in less than standard lead time.

For purchased material, the open orders show purchase requisitions that have been issued, with the quantity, schedule and need dates, and where the order now stands, in terms of both the operations sequence number in the process routing and the number of days required to complete the remaining operations.

In the pharmaceutical industry it is occasionally necessary to review lots in progress as the FDA issues new instructions about formulation or what can be sold in various markets.

If there are too many small lots in process, production planning might cancel some of them and combine the quantities into one of the existing lot numbers.

Exhibit 2.3 illustrates a situation in which one of the three firm orders, not required for more than a lead time, is cancelled. It can be reissued later on another planning cycle.

2.22 Pegged Requirements

A very important aspect of the planning process, which makes it anything but automatic, is to check the availability of materials and manufacturing capacity. it is nedessary to know if finished product cannot be made in time to meet the customer demand date. Sometimes part of the requirements can be met, but not all of them. For an item used as a subordinate in many different assemblies, a change in the schedule for one or two of its parents may help to resolve the problem. (When we come to scheduled backlog and marketing intelligence in Chapters 6 and 7, part of the interaction between the production scheduling process and requirements generation will be the feasibility of the schedule that results from a given set of requirements.)

"Pegged requirements" simply show the source of the elements of the dependent demand for any item. The bracket shown in Exhibit 2.4, is used on seven different parent items, one apiece on some of them and three apiece on others. The time when the bracket is needed may be offset by one to four planning periods (two to eight weeks) depending on the way the parent item is assembled.

MASTER SCHEDULE

The report shows one line for each parent, with the contribution to dependent demand from their notional orders. For example, 87-65-4321 is scheduled to run 45 units every two weeks, which generates a requirement for 45 brackets every two weeks. The parent item 39-91-0374 is scheduled to run 247 per period, but the quantity of three brackets each results in a dependent requirement of 741 brackets.

The first requirement of 1000 for part number 37-56-4105 is scheduled for the period ending 9/08/76, but because of the offset, the brackets are required in the preceding period in order to be available by the right time in the assembly process.

If the dependent requirements on this item present a problem, then one can work back to the schedules of some of the parent items, make net changes to the schedule, check the materials and capacity again, and continue until the schedule is satisfactory. Then the tentative schedule can replace the official schedule as the basis for generating new firm orders at all levels of assembly.

2.23 Exception Action

The need date for any lot is computed on the basis of current actual requirements and stock status, in each planning cycle, as a true expression of when the material is needed to satisfy all requirements. The schedule date is the date when the lot is scheduled by the planner, for a variety of reasons. One fundamental concept is that of the "freeze period." A freeze period is generally of the same length as a lead time, but it has a different connotation in a time-phased, net-requirements planning system. The full ramifications are covered in Chapter 13. For the present, however, the freeze period means that any firm order due within the freeze period will not have the quantity changed. It can even be locked so that the schedule date won't be changed automatically. The planner can, of course, change any date or quantity. Production due beyond the freeze period can be changed both in quantity and timing as requirements change.

As a particular consequence of this usage, if a new replenishment lot is really needed within the freeze period, the schedule date is set automatically at the end of the freeze period. Otherwise a quantity that had been due within the freeze (probably zero) would be changed, and that goes against the definition. These are the "short-dated" orders.

During successive planning cycles if stock status or requirements change, even firm orders may have to be expedited. If so the need date changes, but the schedule date can be locked to remain where it was.

A "hot list" of exceptions can highlight those lots where the need has

EDITORDS

THURSDAY, AUGUST 5, 1976
EASTERN DAYLIGHT TIME 19:58:35

WHICH ITEMS = TEST
TEST FOR INCLUSION = OVERCOVER
ALL ITEMS WILL BE TESTED.

PART NUMBER	FILE INDEX	LOCK SCHED	1 REFERENCE NUMBER	2 ORIGINAL QUANTITY	3 GOOD QUANTITY	4 SCHEDULE DATE	5 NEED DATE	6 NOW AT OP SEQ	7 DAYS REMAINING
32-216-331	3		16654	4,800	4,800	10/08/76	10/08/76	1	140
			17285	1,200	1,200	2/08/77	2/08/77	1	140
			17315	2,734	2,734	9/22/76	7/07/76	1	65

REFERENCE NUMBER TO CHANGE = 17285

EDIT: FIELDS, SPLIT, DROP, NEXTREF = D

REFERENCE NUMBER TO CHANGE =
SCHEDULE IS NOT NOW LOCKED.
LOCK IT? N
FILE REVISIONS? Y

Exhibit 2.3

32-47-0389   BRACKET   FILE INDEX = 12

                                  E X T E N D E D   R E Q U I R E M E N T S   B Y   P E R I O D
PART NO   QUANTITY EACH OFFSET 8/11/76 8/25/76 9/08/76 9/22/76 10/06/76 10/20/76 11/03/76 11/17/76 12/01/76

87-65-4321   1   4   45   45   45   45   45   45   45   45   45
35-45-5678   1   4   37   37   37   37   37   37   37   35   33
39-91-0374   3   1   741   741   741   741   741   741   741   741
37-56-4105   3   1   3000   3000   3000   3000   3000   3000   3000   3000
33-28-2343   3   2   2358   2358   2358   2358   2358   2358   2358   2358   2358
30-47-4646   1   3   4   539
37-01-1906   1   4

TOTAL DEPENDENT DEMAND   2440   6181   6181   6181   6181   6181   7671   6183   6716
DIRECT DEMAND ON THIS ITEM   119   388   133   133   136   612   1367   145   143

FIRM OPEN REPLENISHMENT ORDERS
NEW NOTIONAL ORDER SCHEDULE

Exhibit 2.4

HOTLIST

FRIDAY, JUNE.25, 1976
EASTERN DAYLIGHT TIME 18:15:20

WHICH ITEMS = ALL
ALL 29 ITEMS WILL BE USED.
MINIMUM DAYS DIFFERENCE IN DUE DATES = 10

PART NO	DESCRIPT	INDEX	LEVEL	REF NO	GOOD QTY	NEED DATE	SCHEDULE	DAYS REM
33-28-2343	MOTOR 0.5	7	1	10162	34,650	5/23/76	7/13/76	15
39-91-0374	HEAT EXCHA	10	1	10165	30,000	5/22/76	7/13/76	7
33-65-3387	HUMIDIFIER	11	1	10286	2,658	1/02/76	8/25/76	15
32-47-0389	BRACKET	12	2	10219	114,733	6/30/76	7/19/76	10
				10237	215,374	6/25/76	7/20/76	10
				10254	251,246	6/30/76	7/26/76	10
				10271	315,810	6/23/76	7/27/76	13
30-72-6859	FAN	13	2	10220	66,000	7/04/76	7/19/76	2
				10238	66,000	7/06/76	7/20/76	2
				10255	84,674	7/10/76	7/26/76	2
				10272	112,853	7/02/76	7/27/76	5

Part Number	Description			Item #	Quantity	Date 1	Date 2	
38-84-7072	STOVE BOLT	15	3	10221	1,285,414	6/10/76	7/05/76	2
32-72-7100	NUT 1/4 IN	16	3	10222	961,330	6/13/76	7/05/76	2
34-36-4115	WASHER	17	3	10223	1,000,000	6/12/76	7/05/76	2
36-51-5186	TAP	19	2	10224	17,363	6/19/76	7/19/76	13
				10242	9,446	6/21/76	7/20/76	13
				10259	11,780	6/23/76	7/26/76	13
				10276	14,166	6/21/76	7/27/76	16
				10172	16,592	5/29/76	6/29/76	13
				10190	16,460	6/05/76	7/05/76	11
				10207	17,273	6/12/76	7/12/76	11
39-82-5503	HOUSING	22	2	10244	116,79"	6/13/76	7/20/76	7
				10278	56,717	6/18/76	7/27/76	10
				10192	20,540	6/21/76	7/05/76	7
37-22-6605	BEARING	23	2	10210	11,431	6/26/76	7/12/76	12
				10245	27,936	6/19/76	7/20/76	12
				10279	23,941	6/25/76	7/27/76	15

ELAPSED TIME 2M 29:58S
CPU TIME   27S

Exhibit 2.5

crept up on the schedule. All the lots shown in Exhibit 2.5 have a current need date that is at least 10 days earlier than the current schedule date. The items are identified by part number, a short verbal description, a file index number (key to the retrieval system), and level code, to indicate whether the problem stems directly from customer requirements or depends on the master schedules of higher levels of assembly.

The orders are identified by reference number, with the current good quantity in production and the schedule and need dates. The number of days remaining to complete the rest of the steps in the manufacturing process is also shown for information.

In some of these cases the schedule does not have to be changed. In others a change to a parent item might alleviate problems for several subordinates. Note that it does no good to reschedule a subordinate—that leaves the requirements right where they were. It also means that all the other subordinates may be available, as work in process inventory, but the parent assembly can't be built and shipped to customers. A reschedule of the parent item warns the customer about probable delays in delivery and ensures that all subordinates are properly coordinated with that schedule. Chapter 13 has more on this, much more.

The hot list can also identify jobs where the need date is later than the schedule date, which could be pushed back.

2.3 SUMMARY REPORTS

Whereas the planners are concerned with the master schedules for individual products, components, parts, and materials, various levels of management want a summary of the consequences of the current plans, to check that corporate objectives for inventory investment are being met.

The budget shown in Exhibit 2.6 has much the same format as the schedule for an individual item. In this case, however, the quantities shown in the table are all reported in standard cost, accumulated over all the items used to generate the report.

The safety stock objective is the national safety stock that is provided at the master warehouse to ensure that the satellites can continue to receive material as they sell what they have, and thus provide service to the customers.

"Working stock" is a term that will be encountered in the strategic modules (see Chapter 11). Essentially it is the component of the inventory investment created because products are bought or manufactured in lot quantities. The value, on the average, aggregated over an inventory of many

SUMMARY REPORTS

REQUIREMENTS, PRODUCTION, AND STOCK
REPORTED IN TOTAL COST

SAFETY STOCK   = $2,352,641.40
WORKING STOCK = $461,945.84
STOCK ON HAND = $3,707,228.83

PERIOD ENDING	DIRECT REQUIREMENTS	DEPENDENT REQUIREMENTS	FIRM ORDERS	NOTIONAL ORDERS	PROJECTED AVAILABILITY
8/16/76	537,876	7,332	38,066		3,200,087
8/30/76	456,165	4,301	45,441		2,785,062
9/13/76	481,793	1,255	271,427		2,573,440
9/27/76	178,283	823	44,963		2,439,297
10/11/76	560,438	2,693	67,582		1,943,747
10/25/76	472,556	85,417	69,597		1,455,371
11/08/76	551,348	42,194	22,304	1,809,577	2,693,711
11/22/76	192,795	12,084	18,819	383,830	2,891,480
12/06/76	174,709	9,550	9,493	168,210	2,884,924
12/20/76	150,602	10,809	3,265	156,308	2,883,086
1/03/77	155,509	15,440	1,942	168,432	2,882,511
1/17/77	171,406	9,743	1,253	160,141	2,862,757
1/31/77	169,586	15,442	1,859	172,445	2,852,033
2/14/77	167,782	19,216	619	169,948	2,835,602
2/28/77	165,347	16,313	223	218,520	2,872,685
3/14/77	205,156	21,665	965	244,913	2,891,742
3/28/77	202,626	24,703	1,141	218,232	2,883,785
4/11/77	218,657	20,526	297	237,352	2,882,251
4/25/77	222,795	21,160		207,808	2,846,104
5/09/77	231,171	25,736	2,795	258,844	2,850,836
5/23/77	235,084	23,497	3,009	251,828	2,847,092
6/06/77	239,469	18,857	670	300,966	2,890,402
6/20/77	244,404	16,155		249,927	2,879,770
7/01/77	192,617	36,720		230,194	2,880,627
7/18/77	275,484		250	298,531	2,903,925

Exhibit 2.6

HEADCOUNT

FRIDAY, AUGUST 20, 1976
EASTERN DAYLIGHT TIME 10:21:40

WHICH ITEMS = ALL
ALL 713 ITEMS WILL BE USED.
SCHEDULE: OFFICIAL, TENTATIVE = 0
SCHEDULE RECORDED AT 2 WEEKS PER PERIOD.
NUMBER OF PERIODS TO REPORT = 10
HOURS PER PERSON PER PLANNING PERIOD = 75
INCLUDE DEPARTMENT NUMBER(S) = ALL
7 DEPARTMENTS TO BE REPORTED.

FORECASTS REVISED AS OF   7/31/76

STOCK POSTED AS OF   8/04/76

DEPT	GRADE	8/18/76	9/01/76	9/15/76	9/29/76	10/13/76	10/27/76	11/10/76	11/24/76	12/08/76	12/22/76
320	A										
321	A										
324	B										
324	C	9		2	7	1	4	12	2		10
324	D		6	18	5	9	15	190	68	41	23
325	B		1				1				
325	C		1			1	6	17	3	2	2
325	D										
325	G		1				1				
326	B										
326	C	3	2	7	2	4	9	44	17	9	8
326	D	2	1				1	5	5	1	2
341	A						2	1			
341	B										
342	B	2	4	4	2	3	53	35	6	5	6
342	D										
TOTAL		16	16	32	16	17	91	304	102	60	53

ELAPSED TIME 2M 07.093S
CPU TIME   19.996S

Exhibit 2.7

items, will be half the sum of the lot quantities for the individual items. In this case, it is reported at standard cost.

Stock on hand includes finished goods that may be in the field or in transit to field warehouses.

There are several firm orders currently scheduled to be completed by the end of the year. The bulk of the notional orders begins to build up in November. The projected availability is the estimated stock on hand as of the end of the period.

Incidentally, I believe this is another instance where the manager should involve himself in a little work, by transcribing these summary reports as they are issued once a month to a "slanted chart," to be described in Chapter 13. The mechanical work of transcribing the information forces him to compare this month's budget elements with budgets prepared earlier for the same periods. These slanted charts can be extremely powerful devices for detecting changes in requirements early enough to still have some options in coping with the shortages or excesses.

2.31 Labor Required

A different sort of summary report, for production management, indicates the numbers of people required for each planning period, listed by production department and labor grade (Exhibit 2.7). Instead of extending the work content in dollars as delivered, this report shows the number of people, at an average number of standard hours per direct labor person, required for the period in which that work is scheduled, at each step of the manufacturing process.

It can be seen that there will be a great deal of work required in November. But some of that work can be released now to anticipate the peak and build up a stabilization stock.

Note that as part of the philosophy of management, the formal materials management planning system does not automatically reschedule work to try to meet capacity according to some theoretical mathematical model, which would probably achieve the correct answer, with arbitrary precision, for a problem you don't have.

Professor Seward once looked over my shoulder in an engineering laboratory and remarked, "Brown, I don't know about those last 17 decimal places . . . but the first one is wrong."

By involving experienced people who can take various risks and incorporate their own subjective judgment, the system is likely to get an accurate, if not precise, answer to the correct problem. The elegance of formal planning models can be of great convenience in carrying out the arithmetic to

SUMMARY REPORTS

evaluate the consequences of alternative courses of action, but the decision is still basically a matter of human judgment. An experienced person, who knows the room available in which to maneuver and is willing to take some risks, can usually do a much better job than a formal computer system. The advantage of the computer is that it can display complete and current information about the situation and the alternatives, so that the person making the decision has better information.

2.32 Work in Process

Still another way of looking at the current production plans that can help the planner see problems is a matrix display of where work in process currently is, and where it is scheduled to be performed. This has to do with that first line in Exhibit 1.5, where the most urgent job to be started in Department 350 had not completed its operations in other departments.

The report in Exhibit 2.8 has one column for each department in which

```
         WORKLOAD

FRIDAY, AUGUST 20, 1976
EASTERN DAYLIGHT TIME 10:19:38

WHICH ITEMS = ALL
ALL 713 ITEMS WILL BE USED.
STOCK STATUS POSTED AS OF    8/04/76
USE WHICH DUE DATE: SCHEDULE NEED = S
REPORT WORK DUE TO START AFTER = 100176
AND DUE TO START BEFORE = 103076
THE WINDOW IS  4.14 WEEKS LONG.
```

HOURS BY DEPARTMENT

IN↓	DO→	324	325	326	341	342	TOTAL
	320	874	10	229		71	1183
	321						
	324	2					2
	325	1774	1212	86		96	3168
	326	9618		2558		433	12610
	341	92	46	38	165	11	352
	342	2868	305	645	1	2070	5888
TOTAL		15229	1573	3556	166	2681	23204

```
ELAPSED TIME     1M 39.233S
CPU TIME            11.420S
```

Exhibit 2.8

work is scheduled to be done. This report elides the time dimension and reports all work due to start within a window sepcified by the user (in this case about four weeks).

As an example, Department 326 will have about 13,000 hours of work to do during October, much of which is now in the department.

CHAPTER **3**

The Requirements System

It must be evident by now that the classification of various programs into one or another of the four "systems" is quite arbitrary. Some of the exhibits could just as well have been displayed in connection with a different system. For example, the dependent demand on subordinate items is really part of the requirements to be covered by production, but it is generated in the process of exploding master schedules for the parent items. There are usually many wasys of classifying any set of tangible things or concepts. The purpose of a classification scheme is to show some of the kinds of order that are present, not to exclude an object from another set. The Linnaean binomial system of nomenclature in biology is meant to show the genus and species of plants and animals, as they are related to other plants and animals. But people would probably still think of a whale as a fish or a bat as a sort of bird.

It should be equally clear that the four systems are not integral units, to be adapted or rejected as a whole. If some features have appeal they can be used, and other features can be modified to suit the environment. It is the purpose of this book to help display the range of choices possible and the derivation of each, so that the user can make informed choices to get the type of system that best suits his need.

The requirements system includes a variety of devices for accumulating a record of the requirements to be filled. There are generally four possible sources of these requirements:

1. Dependent demand on subordinate parts and materials results from exploding downward the master schedule for parent assemblies and products. In some cases the parent "item" doesn't exist as such, in the sense that it would be built for stock. It might be defined by a synthetic bill of materials, like an automobile that had 60% four-door and 40% two-door body; 30% six-cyclinder and 70% eight-cylinder engine; and 40% a tape deck installed at the factory.

2. A scheduled backlog of requirements booked by customers for delivery in the future is a second sort of requirement, common in the OEM suppliers, but also common even in companies that think of themselves primarily as consumer packaged goods manufacturers. Firm requirements may be known in advance from subsidiary and affiliated divisions, especially for overseas factories, or from some dealers.
3. The statistical forecast, projected from past demand, can be very useful in many kinds of service parts and products that go into a market with a large number of customers or users, and where the technology is mature enough to be able to define a market.
4. Marketing intelligence provides for overriding the statistical forecast for economic, competitive, marketing, and regulatory changes in the environment, and for extending the probable volume of orders in the backlog beyond the horizon where orders are booked.

We have already introduced the concept of dependent demand in Chapter 2, and will see a great deal more of it in Chapter 14. This chapter exhibits typical reports concerned with statistical forecasts, the backlog, and marketing intelligence, to give the general flavor of the variety of options that can be developed for generating requirements.

3.1 REQUIREMENTS REPORT

Requirements may be generated at regular intervals such as calendar months, weeks, fortnights, or four-week accounting periods. Minor variations are required in some of the programs to accommodate one reporting interval instead of another. For purposes of consistency, and to illustrate probably the most common environment, the examples given throughout the book are based on calendar months. There is some reason for the choice of a month rather than a week as the forecasting interval. In many manufacturing companies the lead times are many months long, and a monthly interval gives sufficient precision. In some of the simpler manufacturing processes with very short lead times and important differences from week to week because of promotions, such as for cosmetics, a weekly forecasting interval would be preferable. The difference between 12 calendar months and 13 four-week periods would be simply to accommodate the accounting systems already in operation.

A typical forecast report, which displays all of the information on the file, would include potentially all four sources of requirements: the statistical forecast model, marketing intelligence, scheduled demand, and dependent demand. In the case of the carburetor illustrated in Exhibit 3.1, there is a subtotal for the net forecast, which implies emphasis on the forecast as distinct from scheduled backlog and dependent demand, which are in a sense known in advance. The forecasts are recorded by month for each location. The master warehouse record in many instances is treated as a national record summed over all stocking locations. However, a forecast by item is also required for each of the locations in which it is stocked. Sometimes the people reviewing a forecast report feel more comfortable if they can see some history to judge whether the current forecast is plausible. By now, however, there is a reasonably common appreciation of the fact that there are many, many techniques of forecasting that can extract more information from past history than a person can by inspection. The real role of personal judgment and experience is reflected in the marketing intelligence.

Forecasts are almost always displayed on a rolling basis—extending a year into the future at all times. Some reports that are more oriented to marketing and accounting budgets can be abstracted on the basis of the current fiscal year, but for production planning and control, one must be able to see past the lead time late in a fiscal year as well as early in the year.

3.2 BACKLOG

The backlog of scheduled orders may be the primary source of demand in some industries, especially those that build customized capital equipment, like boilers, forklifts, and electronic instruments, or primary materials like chemicals and metals. Even among manufacturers of service parts and consumer products, there are often significant requirements for other divisions and for export to affiliated plants overseas. The information for each customer order must identify the item and the customer, the quantity and time wanted, and probably other information, like a purchase order number or reference number. Exhibit 3.1 shows scheduled demand in five months, which might have come from one or more customers.

It may also be convenient at times to get a summary by part number of the status of open orders for a certain customer (Exhibit 3.2). For different purposes one might want the list arranged by date due, part number, or reference number. For a planning system to be really handy for the user, there must be provision for the user to decide at the last moment how he wants a report arranged, depending on the question he is trying to answer.

The "user field" is for special features of the application. For example, if the items were standard paper products (bags, cups, plates, and so on) the user field could identify imprint copy, pattern, and colors. other users may record purchase order numbers or other information.

44-796-500   CARBURETOR | FILE INDEX = 693

LOCATION: MASTER

	7/76	8/76	9/76	10/76	11/76	12/76	1/77	2/77	3/77	4/77	5/77	6/77	TOTAL
STAT MODEL	60	53	41	31	22	17	22	27	42	54	66	69	504
MKT INTELL	5	4	5	3	2	2							21
NET FCST	65	57	46	34	24	19	22	27	42	54	66	69	525
SCHED DEM	801	928	1222	1420	1379								5750
TOTAL REQ	866	985	1268	1454	1403	19	22	27	42	54	66	69	6275
	7/75	8/75	9/75	10/75	11/75	12/75	1/76	2/76	3/76	4/76	5/76	6/76	TOTAL
HISTORY													

LOCATION: INDIANAPOLIS, IN

	7/76	8/76	9/76	10/76	11/76	12/76	1/77	2/77	3/77	4/77	5/77	6/77	TOTAL
STAT MODEL	5	5	4	3	3	2	3	3	4	5	6	6	49
NET FCST	5	5	4	3	3	2	3	3	4	5	6	6	49
TOTAL REQ	5	5	4	3	3	2	3	3	4	5	6	6	49
	7/75	8/75	9/75	10/75	11/75	12/75	1/76	2/76	3/76	4/76	5/76	6/76	TOTAL
HISTORY	3	3	4	3	3	1	2	2	5	4	5	5	40

LOCATION: DENVER, CO

	7/76	8/76	9/76	10/76	11/76	12/76	1/77	2/77	3/77	4/77	5/77	6/77	TOTAL
STAT MODEL	6	5	5	4	3	2	3	3	4	5	6	7	53
NET FCST	6	5	5	4	3	2	3	3	4	5	6	7	53
TOTAL REQ	6	5	5	4	3	2	3	3	4	5	6	7	53
	7/75	8/75	9/75	10/75	11/75	12/75	1/76	2/76	3/76	4/76	5/76	6/76	TOTAL
HISTORY	4	1	5	1	1	1	1	1	4	2	9	6	35

LOCATION: LOS ANGELES, CA

	7/76	8/76	9/76	10/76	11/76	12/76	1/77	2/77	3/77	4/77	5/77	6/77	TOTAL
STAT MODEL	19	17	13	10	7	5	6	8	13	16	20	21	155
NET FCST	19	17	13	10	7	5	6	8	13	16	20	21	155
TOTAL REQ	19	17	13	10	7	5	6	8	13	16	20	21	155
	7/75	8/75	9/75	10/75	11/75	12/75	1/76	2/76	3/76	4/76	5/76	6/76	TOTAL
HISTORY	12	7	15	4	5	1	3	3	13	8	26	23	120

LOCATION: NEW YORK, NY

	7/76	8/76	9/76	10/76	11/76	12/76	1/77	2/77	3/77	4/77	5/77	6/77	TOTAL
STAT MODEL	30	26	20	14	10	8	10	14	22	28	34	35	251
MKT INTELL	3	1	2	1	1	1							9
NET FCST	33	27	22	15	11	9	10	14	22	28	34	35	260
TOTAL REQ	33	27	22	15	11	9	10	14	22	28	34	35	260
	7/75	8/75	9/75	10/75	11/75	12/75	1/76	2/76	3/76	4/76	5/76	6/76	TOTAL
HISTORY	19	15	28	5	7	3	6	7	25	17	33	27	192

Exhibit 3.1

SHOWBACKLOG

FRIDAY, JUNE 25, 1976
EASTERN DAYLIGHT TIME 16:35:56

CUSTOMER NUMBER(S) = 1034
SORT ON FIELD NUMBER = 2
PRINT AT THE TERMINAL? YES
ALIGN THE PAPER WHEN KEY BARD UNLOCKS.

CUSTOMER = 1034

PART NO	QUANTITY	DUE DATE	USER FLD
32-62-4530	589	7/13/76	1753
30-72-6859	680	7/13/76	1319
32-72-7100	702	7/13/76	1448
32-37-7745	530	7/13/76	1083
32-62-4530	931	8/22/76	1694
30-47-4646	756	8/22/76	1742
30-72-6859	935	8/22/76	1166
32-72-7100	911	8/22/76	1535
32-37-7745	672	8/22/76	1479
32-62-4530	847	9/07/76	1769
30-47-4646	459	9/07/76	1679
32-47-0389	8	9/07/76	1716
30-72-6859	384	9/07/76	1633
32-72-7100	763	9/07/76	1450
32-62-4530	527	10/14/76	1525
30-47-4646	533	10/14/76	1577
32-47-0389	384	10/14/76	1044
30-72-6859	520	10/14/76	1440
32-72-7100	263	10/14/76	1157
32-62-4530	92	11/02/76	1617
30-47-4646	219	11/02/76	1314
32-47-0389	67	11/02/76	1491
32-37-7745	831	11/02/76	1513
32-74-9969	48	11/02/76	1056
32-62-4530	654	12/13/76	1713
30-47-4646	50	12/13/76	1738
32-47-0389	418	12/13/76	1722
32-37-7745	35	12/13/76	1668
32-74-9969	737	12/13/76	1285
32-47-0389	687	1/28/77	1095
30-72-6859	679	1/28/77	1295
32-72-7100	416	1/28/77	1179
32-37-7745	54	1/28/77	1814
32-74-9969	329	1/28/77	1641

ELAPSED TIME   2M 06:58S
CPU TIME   38S

Exhibit 3.2

3.3 AGGREGATE FORECASTS

Although production planning and control must have detailed forecasts listed by product and location for various management analyses and reports, it may be more pertinent to accumulate the individual forecasts into groups, such as product lines, sales territories, or inventory classes.

Exhibit 3.3 was prepared for 630 different end items that fall into six product lines. The forecasts include only the statistical model, not marketing intelligence, the backlog, or internal usage for dependent demand. The forecasts are accumulated in standard cost (one might have selected selling price or cubic feet) and include only the headquarters location.

Although forecasts for individual items are normally extended to a planning horizon that is reasonable in view of the freeze periods and lead times, there are times when management wants to see the current estimate of longer trends. The report shown has extended forecasts to two years, as a statistical model. Obviously if marketing intelligence and scheduled backlog are not recorded that far in the future, they cannot be included in the report.

3.4 MARKETING INTELLIGENCE

Marketing intelligence is purely subjective judgment, based on unorganized, semiquantitative sources of information. In an industry that gets a firm backlog of orders for the next few months, the marketing intelligence may be a marketing plan or objective of what backlogs can be expected to be farther in the future. Much as it may surprise some readers there are companies that issue a dictum from the top to the marketing department saying what the level of sales is jolly well going to be next year. Marketing intelligence is one way of recording in the files what that directive amounts to, but a system of management controls outside the scope of this book would be required to ensure that the actual sales do follow the Chairman's plan. A good materials management system can ensure that products are produced economically to cover the forecast. If the goods aren't sold, they wind up in inventory. Chapter 13 has some comments on a technique of accounting for inventory investment that makes it quite clear what part of an organization generated the inventory, or any piece of it.

In the consumer products companies, there are other reasons for marketing intelligence, such as new product introduction, promotions, competitive action, and the state of the economy. Sometimes government regulations have a bearing on changes in the demand for individual products.

AGGREGATE FORECASTS AFTER POSTING MAY DEMAND.

FORECASTS INCLUDE: MODEL
FORECASTS WEIGHTED BY TOTAL COST
ITEMS GROUPED ACCORDING TO PRODUCT LINE
LOCATIONS: INDIANAPOLIS, IN

TIMES SCALE FACTOR 0.001

GROUP	ITEMS	JUN 4.31	JUL 4.45	AUG 4.45	SEP 4.31	OCT 4.45	NOV 4.31	DEC 4.02	JAN 4.45	FEB 4.02	MAR 4.45	APR 4.31	MAY 4.45	TOTAL
8	39	28	30	29	23	20	19	19	25	21	24	24	27	288
		31	34	32	26	24	23	23	29	25	27	27	31	333
512	470	345	342	295	270	321	296	210	214	224	305	323	349	3,494
		359	356	310	283	335	310	223	228	237	319	337	363	3,660
256	73	51	48	56	44	94	84	66	80	37	50	41	51	704
		53	49	58	46	96	85	68	82	39	52	42	52	720
768	2	1	1	1	2	3	3	2	2				-1	14
				1	1	2	2	2	1			-1		7
16	29	11	10	10	10	10	9	9	11	11	14	14	13	132
		12	11	10	10	10	10	9	11	12	15	14	14	139
11018	7	2	-1	2		8	9	8	12	2	3	3	1	51
		1		1	1	7	7	7	11	1	2	2		37
T O T	630	440	433	396	351	459	421	317	348	299	398	406	442	4,709
		457	451	414	369	477	439	334	366	315	416	423		4,920

Exhibit 3.3

STATISTICAL FORECAST MODEL

One point of departure for reviewing individual forecasts for reasonableness is to compare the current forecast with history (Exhibit 3.4).

When there are seasonal patterns to the demand, the cumulative sales from the beginning of the fiscal year (shown as the second line in each row) may be more informative than the month-by-month data. The first three pairs of rows show history for up to three years. The third pair shows the current fiscal year to date. The last two pairs of each row show the current forecast. Inspection of the cumulative totals for each year indicates the trend, and for intermediate months gives one a rough feeling for the percent that will be sold by any particular month.

3.5 STATISTICAL FORECAST MODEL

The statistical forecasts analyze the history of past demand, looking for level, trend, and seasonal patterns. Section II, and especially Chapter 5, are devoted to alternative techniques for getting good statistical forecasts. There are limits to the practical accuracy that can be achieved in forecasts for individual products. Usually several different statistical techniques if properly applied will achieve just about the same accuracy. Big differences in the accuracy usually have been found to result from using a technique incorrectly rather than from any inherent limitation to the technique itself. One source of improper use is to use the wrong model—omitting trends that are present or forcing the seasonal pattern to follow a profile that doesn't really represent the market. Sometimes the problem has resulted from poor initial conditions, for example, setting a trend to zero for a new product in a growing market simply because there wasn't any history from which to estimate the trend.

Through a considerable evolution of practice over the past quarter century there are now some versatile techniques for finding the right forecast model and the right initial conditions.

Years ago it seemed to be reasonable to involve the user in the selection of the correct forecast model. It rapidly became apparent, however, that the factors to be taken into account were several orders of magnitude more complex than most users were accustomed to handling. Hence we have now taught the computer to make the same sorts of judgments, quickly and consistently.

The informed user can still exercise a great deal of control in forcing particular models if he wants to. Chapter 5 deals with the techniques and procedures.

Perhaps of even more interest, however, are the techniques that have been evolved for setting up an initial forecast for new products that have no his-

39-10-3209	FOUNTAIN FILE INDEX = 2 LOCATION: NEW YORK, NY											
	NOV	DEC	JAN	FEB	MAR	APR	MAY	JUN	JUL	AUG	SEP	OCT
1974 MO HIST AC												
1975 MO HIST AC			154 154	100 254	80 334	79 413	43 456	29 485	17 502	12 514	49 563	183 746
1976 MO HIST AC	165 165	265 430	249 679	187 866	148 1014	138 1152	227 1379	192 1571				
1976 MO FCST AC									157 1728	151 1879	160 2039	199 2238
1977 MO FCST AC	223 223	255 478	211 689	238 927	210 1137	235 1372	234 1606	204 1810	234 2044	221 2265	226 2491	272 2763

37-62-1981	FURNACE FILE INDEX = 3 LOCATION: NEW YORK, NY											
	NOV	DEC	JAN	FEB	MAR	APR	MAY	JUN	JUL	AUG	SEP	OCT
1974 MO HIST AC												
1975 MO HIST AC			24 24	30 54	46 100	34 134	31 165	44 209	22 231	34 265	35 300	31 331
1976 MO HIST AC	35 35	30 65	36 101	22 123	32 155	20 175	48 223	57 280				
1976 MO FCST AC									42 322	46 368	42 410	47 457
1977 MO FCST AC	45 45	48 93	47 140	50 190	53 243	53 296	60 356	65 421	60 481	63 544	58 602	64 666

Exhibit 3.4

FORECAST ERRORS

tory. "Short history" in the sense referred to in Exhibit 3.5 means anything with less than six months of demand history, and this includes new products scheduled to be released to the market several months from now; thus the history available, in one sense, may correspond to a negative number of months. The forecast is needed now, of course, to plan production to have goods available when the product is released, but the forecast during the first lead time is forced to be zero.

The seasonal patterns, and even trends, can be scaled from a similar product that has already been on the market simply by giving a reference to the item. When an existing product is extended to be stocked at additional locations, the obvious reference item is the same product on a national basis, from the master warehouse record. For brand-new products, where there is no history, marketing estimates can be plugged in as the base level, to be used in scaling the selected profiles from the reference item.

There have been a great many improvements in the state of the art in materials management systems since World War II, with elegant dynamic lot size models, MRP, theoretical optimum cost safety stocks, and techniques of forecasting. Each has contributed to the improvement of materials management, especially when applied to an operating environment that actually had the problem solved. The single biggest contribution to improvement over inventory management during that time has not been so much any theoretical technique as it has been the measurement of the forecast errors as a basis for setting safety stocks and planning targets (Chapter 10).

Today forecasting techniques are about as accurate as can be expected in any company. There isn't much hope that a magic formula or procedure will dramatically improve the accuracy. But many companies have tremendous opportunity for reducing investment and improving service in field stocks by basing safety stocks on a measurement of the errors actually experienced, in contrast to the naive methods of setting safety stocks as so many weeks of supply.

3.6 FORECAST ERRORS

The proper measure of forecast error is the standard deviation (see Chapter 8) rather than the mean absolute deviation (MAD) that has been popularized by IBM and its imitators, established a long time ago because of limitations in data processing capacity. For products with a respectable history, the standard deviation can be measured from the product's own history. But for new products there is no history.

```
WHICH ITEMS = ALL
ALL 713 ITEMS WILL BE USED.
LOCATIONS TO BE INCLUDED = ALL
6 LOCATIONS WILL BE USED.
MAXIMUM NUMBER OF TERMS IN THE MODEL = 13
MAXIMUM NUMBER OF MONTHS OF HISTORY = 36

FORECASTS REVISED AS OF    5/31/76

SET SMOOTHING RATE AUTOMATICALLY? YES
FOR ITEMS WITH SHORT HISTORY:
    SCALE SEASONAL MODELS? N
    USE PLUGGED LEVEL? N
```

50-317-404	31-062-414	49-063-710		
34-064-240	34-192-754	40-193-005	46-195-903	39-196-746
46-001-132	32-198-518	41-002-459	38-199-544	38-200-216
44-201-627	41-202-709	47-203-281	44-204-372	31-205-310
35-207-776	32-210-297	39-212-520	36-213-151	44-214-833
44-004-679	41-217-986	48-218-002	42-220-490	44-221
37-090-455	47-091-452	33-420-687	38-005-934	3˙ ˙-517
50-223-123	38-224-189	47-006-519	32-007-03⁵	
38-009-008	39-010-067	42-226-126	38-2²˙	31-723-246
47-230-424	36-452-145	35-231-898	˙ ˙-547	47-727-487
36-233-452	33-234-665	47-012-9˙	˙-076-961	41-731-173
44-092-931	32-238-432	38-˙˙	40-734-302	47-735-890
40-242-081	39-014-654	/08	41-739-526	31-573-331
48-453-667	47-467-7˙	/42-308	37-744-645	34-745-155
50-483-658	44-0˙	31-748-409	42-749-168	33-750-985
42-249-222	˙ ˙3	38-753-322	43-754-641	40-281-422
36-016-7˙˙	˙0-079	36-757-491	41-050-415	37-759-658
45-0˙	˙-182-643	36-183-917	35-288-460	31-764-117
	43-079-651	35-080-803	39-767-255	36-768-243
˙49	44-770-851	47-186-456	48-772-902	35-773-759
˙˙7-023	50-190-751	36-774-9˙8	36-775-375	50-776-745
˙9-777-766	40-778-642	34-779-103	37-077-200	
34-752-354	36-181-015	39-758-253	48-274-577	36-094-909
32-355-032	33-078-629	35-184-970	41-780-863	48-781-931
43-782-291	37-707-683	32-280-241	32-784-830	50-785-190
48-786-765	41-787-033	50-788-376	41-278-362	35-789-193
45-188-707	32-791-549	46-792-777	32-793-708	32-794-883
36-795-994	42-258-018	44-796-500	49-797-748	47-271-106
39-279-455	43-144-398			

```
27 ITEMS HAD NO HISTORY.
THERE WERE 10 ITEMS LOCKED AS NO SMOOTHING.
PUT THEIR FILE INDEX NUMBERS INTO FILE = DIRECTORY
COMPONENT = LOCKED
THE FILE NOW HAS 4 RECORDS.

ELAPSED TIME        17M 26.537S
CPU TIME             1M 14.136S
```

Exhibit 3.5

```
            VARLAW

     TUESDAY, AUGUST 3, 1976
     EASTERN DAYLIGHT TIME 15:14:25


     FORECASTS REVISED AS OF   5/31/76

     WHICH ITEMS = ALL
     ALL 713 ITEMS WILL BE USED.
     LOCATIONS TO BE INCLUDED = 200
     1 LOCATIONS WILL BE USED.

     THE VARIANCE LAW IS   <MSE =   2.466 × LEVEL* 1.596>.

     ELAPSED TIME      2M 55.034S
     CPU TIME             11.138S
```
Exhibit 3.6

It is well established that in any inventory there is a very consistent model that relates the standard deviation (or its square, the variance) to the forecast level. This relationship is called a variance law. It can be inferred from the records for items that have had enough history to fit a model. The parameters of the law for a particular application can be stored. Then when new items with short history are implemented, the variance law can be used to establish an initial estimate of the standard deviation.

There are two common forms of the variance law. The one illustrated in Exhibit 3.6 says that the variance for any item is proportional to the 1.6 power of the forecast level. An alternative form of the law says that the variance is represented by some polynomial expression of the forecast. In industries with heavy promotions from time to time that briefly raise the level of demand by a large factor, the variance law can be used to estimate the safety stocks required during the promotion, even when there is no history for that sort of promotion.

3.7 REVISING THE FORECASTS

The forecasts are revised at regular intervals—either by calendar months or by specified numbers of weeks between revisions—on the basis of actual demand recorded during the past period. The system for recording demand has to be able to separate demand to be used in building a statistical forecast from withdrawals for scheduled backlog, or for dependent demand, or transfers from one stocking location to another. The process of revision moves the origin in time for planning the future ahead one period, and modifies the coefficients in the statistical model slightly on the basis of the difference between the most recent forecast and the actual demand recorded. Chapter 6 displays the basis for this smoothing and provides some examples of the way the user can get an appreciation of what is going on.

The process of revising the forecasts also serves to check on the forecasts and alert the users to special situations in which the marketing intelligence group should consider what the probable cause and remedy of the problem are.

One flag is the "demand filter," (Exhibit 3.7) which reports any actual demand that is outside a reasonable spread from the forecast, based on the current value of the standard deviation. These differences, if significant, can usually be traced either to a keypunch error or to the recording of demand for forecasting that should have been a withdrawal for internal usage or to fill the scheduled backlog.

```
                FORECAST

       FRIDAY, JUNE 25, 1976
       EASTERN DAYLIGHT TIME 16:10:59

       HAVE YOU POSTED CURRENT DEMAND? YES
       DEMAND BEING POSTED THROUGH  6/30/76

                     DEMAND FILTER TRIPS
        PART      INDEX   WHSE    MIN      MAX  ACTUAL = CORRECTED

       33-59-2650   26    100      0       106   154  =
       34-86-5174   27    100     -7        95   115  =
       87-65-4321   29    400    -24        58    90  =

              SUMMARY OF FORECAST RECORDS PROCESSED

       CODE 1: NORMAL PROCESSING                         29
               TOTAL NORMAL ITEMS                        29
               TOTAL ITEMS PROCESSED                     29

       THERE WERE 12 SKU'S WITH TRACKING SIGNAL TRIPS.
       WAREHOUSE 100 ITEMS: FILE = TRACK
       CREATE A NEW FILE? YES
       COMPONENT = WHSE100
       WAREHOUSE 110 ITEMS: COMPONENT = WHSE110
       WAREHOUSE 300 ITEMS: COMPONENT = WHSE300
       WAREHOUSE 400 ITEMS: COMPONENT = WHSE400
       WAREHOUSE 200 ITEMS: COMPONENT = WSHE200
```

Exhibit 3.7

EVALUATING MARKETING INTELLIGENCE 49

A second sort of exception report is the "tracking signal" which detects a consistent bias in the forecasts, with too many positive errors in a row indicating that the demand is rising faster than the forecasts can adapt. There are many sorts of action that management can take to improve the forecasts when these tracking signals are reported. Therefore the item identification is stored in a directory for retrieval in other sorts of reports. Chapter 8 deals at length with what to do, and why, when there is a tracking signal report.

3.8 EVALUATING MARKETING INTELLIGENCE

Marketing intelligence allows people a considerable sense of fun and power in manipulating the forecasts to make them add up to whatever the boss indicates he wants. That is fine so long as the actual demand materializes at that level. But we need assurance that demand is actually occurring at the forecast rate.

Exhibit 3.8 compares the actual demand for each item (by part number and stocking location) with both the statistical model and the net forecast that includes marketing intelligence. The two differences can be normalized by the standard deviation as a sort of unit of measure about how close one would expect the forecast to be for this particular item.

Consider, for example, part number 37-62-1981 in warehouse 100. The actual demand last month was 344, as compared with a statistical model of 283 and a net forecast of 312. The actual was higher than either forecast, but the marketing intelligence reduced the error. Since the track record has been for a standard deviation of 33 units either way, the difference between 344 and 283 is 1.83 standard deviations, whereas the difference between 344 and 312 is only 0.96 standard deviations. The reduction in error due to the marketing intelligence is 0.87 (actually 0.869) standard deviations, reported as an index of improvement in the rightmost column of the table.

Note that the items are listed by descending value of improvement—the last item increased the forecast error by more than one standard deviation. The user may specify his own index of merit, but there are strong reasons for presenting the report this way. Highlighting the best performance at the top of the list gives credit where credit is due for the improvements in forecast error. The middle of the list shows insignificant changes that might say, "Save your breath to cool your tea. Don't waste effort in reviewing forecasts if the changes are going to be small."

At the bottom of the list are the opportunities to learn more about promotions, competition, marketing plans, the economy, and government regulation, in order to take better account of these factors in future. The listing

APPROXIMATELY 33 SKU'S HAD MARKETING INTELLIGENCE THIS MONTH.
PRINT AT THE TERMINAL? YES
ALIGN THE PAPER.

EVALUATION OF MARKETING INTELLIGENCE

PART NUMBER	WAREHOUSE CODE	ACTUAL DEMAND	FORECASTS MODEL	FORECASTS NET	STANDARD DEVIATION	NORMALIZED MODEL	NORMALIZED NET	IMPROVE-MENT
37-62-1981	100	344	283	312	33	1.83	0.96	869
36-32-6386	400	125	146	124	17	-1.26	0.06	570
33-28-2343	300	192	252	209	38	-1.56	-0.44	560
32-62-4530	300	161	208	172	44	-1.07	-0.25	410
32-47-0389	300	34	42	35	9	-0.91	-0.11	39*
32-62-4530	400	307	421	359	80	-1.43	-0.65	389
37-01-1906	300	33	47	40	10	-1.44	-0.72	360
33-65-3387	200	109	242	201	57	-2.33	-1.61	359
30-47-4646	400	177	246	207	56	-1.23	-0.53	348
33-28-2343	200	84	138	115	37	-1.46	-0.84	310
37-36-0819	100	762	560	631	239	0.85	0.55	298
33-65-3387	300	43	123	102	41	-1.96	-1.44	257
37-62-1981	300	67	96	83	26	-1.11	-0.61	248
39-10-3209	100	676	338	428	389	0.87	0.64	231

37-56-4105	400	55	114	94	47	-1.26	-0.83	214
39-91-0374	100	242	155	171	152	0.57	0.47	105
39-10-3209	400	38	131	125	60	-1.55	-1.45	50
87-65-4321	100	115	43	42	44	1.65	1.68	-23
35-45-5678	100	118	114	113	18	0.22	0.28	-55
36-32-6386	100	317	317	372	191	0.00	-0.29	-144
39-91-0374	500	57	31	26	28	0.93	1.10	-178
33-65-3387	100	676	787	875	193	-0.57	-1.03	-227
32-47-0389	100	230	274	305	58	-0.76	-1.30	-268
37-56-4105	100	577	696	775	130	-0.92	-1.52	-304
37-01-1906	100	92	105	125	30	-0.43	-1.09	-329
33-28-2343	100	762	888	989	152	-0.83	-1.50	-333
39-91-0374	400	78	59	49	21	0.88	1.35	-465
30-47-4646	100	1066	1084	1247	172	-0.10	-1.05	-473
37-62-1981	200	57	48	42	12	0.74	1.24	-495
32-62-4530	100	964	1078	1215	132	-0.86	-1.90	-517
37-36-0819	400	173	177	151	37	-0.11	0.59	-537
32-47-0389	200	94	82	68	20	0.59	1.28	-692
36-32-6386	300	115	113	93	17	0.12	1.27	-1152

ELAPSED TIME   5M 03:56S
CPU TIME   3:08S

Exhibit 3.8

must not, under any circumstances, be interpreted as, "Aha. I caught you. The computer would have done better than you did." That attitude, if perceived, is a sure way to cut off communications about vital information about the marketplace that can be supplied only by human judgment.

It appears to take a company two to three years to learn to use this feedback of evaluation effectively. However, once the organization has learned, new individuals can enter and leave the group and make significant contributions quickly. It does not take a person as long to learn in an established group, as it did for the group itself to learn the first time.

SECTION 4

The Strategic System

One of the fundamental requirements for a control system is feedback that compares actual status with plan, in order to produce an error signal that can be trapped to make changes that will return the environment nearer to the target. There are feedback loops at many levels in a materials management system. Some are quite local and internal, such as the way the forecase error is used to smoothe the forecast coefficients each period. Others relate to the interaction of the materials management system with the external corporate environment, like the evaluation of marketing intelligence, and the performance in terms of stock status and service. If the feedback is fully damped, so that error signals tend always to drive the system state back toward the target, the system can survive all sorts of rude shocks, delays, and noise.

One has to be very careful, of course, about undamped reactions that can set off a series of larger and larger oscillations. A real danger of some theories of inventory control is that no one can possibly analyze the nature of the feedback loops, and there might be hidden sources of instability. It is not so much that one knows that a particular technique is wrong as it is that one doesn't know for sure that it won't lead to trouble. The fact that the formal definition of the intended system can be used in the real environment with live data affords some assurance that the region of instability, if there is one, is not part of normal operations.

A fundamental concept of cybernetics, or the science of control, is that the control system must have at least as many possible states as the environment it intends to control. That has been a stumbling block for some of the packaged applications on the market. IBM's PICS package might have been the ideal control system when it was first developed, but does it really apply to a market with a broader definition than "all large manufacturers of postage meters based in Stamford, Connecticut"? In many of these applications packages there aren't enough alternative states to be able to accommodate a wider variety of companies and product lines that the case used for the original development.

This book stresses options and choices that tend to ensure that the control system will have the requisite variety to match the environment in which it is used. Furthermore, as actual operating experience indicates the need for additional variety, the modular structure of the library permits one rapidly to develop and evaluate additional alternatives.

There are some choices that relate to individual items, either as products or by stocking locations. The stratification of the inventory to permit these alternatives is covered in Chapter 9. There are choices that depend on the environment, by which the user selects some modules in preference to others or manages certain parts of the inventory with different techniques than used for other parts. These choices are stressed in the chapters dealing with techniques. The examples in this first section have revealed some of the options for specifying report formats and the retrieval of special sets of items to answer on-off management questions. Those specifications can be left until the user has a question that he wants answered. The normal routine reports sometimes seem to be special cases of free-form management reports originally designed to answer specific questions.

This chapter is an overview of the strategic kinds of options concerned primarily with stratification of the inventory, and with alternative safety stock strategies. Implicit in the analysis is also the choice of replenishment lot quantities, but the details for that subject are left for Chapter 11.

4.1 STRATIFICATION

The "stock" of an item refers to the number of pieces of material on hand. An "inventory" usually can be taken to mean a whole list of items; if we mean the amount of money or space tied up by that inventory, we usually use the phrase "inventory investment." A single company may have several different inventories. There has always been an obvious, if not clear, distinction among raw materials, work in process, finished goods, stock in transit, and field stocks. That is one dimension along which stocks can be classified. There are also such distinctions as make/buy, trim/functional, current/noncurrent, competitive/noncompetitive. Any of these attributes, and others, can be used in classifying items to create an inventory for a particular purpose.

Usually there aren't more than about a dozen meaningful classifications with significant numbers of items, but for particular decisions or reports, items can be retrieved according to any of several characteristics or combinations of characteristics. For that reason the "part number" as such doesn't really have to be significant. Attempts to set up significant part numbering systems get hung up on the fact that all the possible classifica-

SAFETY STOCKS 55

tions can't be defined in advance, because it isn't possible to know what questions will be raised. Therefore the basic concept of the design of a materials management data base (see Appendix A) is that any field in any record, or combination of fields, can be used to define an ad hoc classification any time it is known why a particular set of items should be grouped together.

One way of classifying an inventory is by the distribution by value, or ABC listing. For each item the current annual forecast is extended by some appropriate measure like selling price, standard cost, cubic feet, or profit. The entire inventory is then sorted into descending sequence on the product. At the top of the list a relatively few Class A items account for 50% of the total value of the whole inventory. Because there are so few items, each one can receive special attention. Because they represent so much value, it is worth putting effort into the management of these items.

The last half of the list typically accounts for perhaps only 5% of the total value. These Class C items should be treated robustly and simply. The two-bin system of replenishment described in Chapter 12 can be quite effective. Because there are so many items in this group, simpler control techniques save control costs. Because the total value of all the items together is so small, minor inaccuracies in the results of simple control can't possibly have important consequences. To be sure, one doesn't want to hold up the shipment of a half-million dollar boiler for lack of a penny's worth of cotter pins. It would be far better to spend $5 on a year's supply of cotter pins and not run short of them. One should not get trapped into spending $10 for a control system that will enable him to operate with only $3 worth of cotter pins in stock.

The ABC listing shown in Exhibit 4.1 first prepares a summary, with aggregate numbers of items and value, listed by semidecade class intervals. The middle section reports some parameters of a log-normal distribution that can be used to estimate quickly the consequences of alternative courses of action for the whole inventory. Then, to identify the items where special control should be exercised, the Class A items are listed in descending sequence of importance. Usually one or two pages is all that is needed to include half the total volume of sales, profit, investment, or space.

4.2 SAFETY STOCKS

There are several places where safety stocks are needed to ensure service to customers and to allow orderly production with adequate lead times. The safety stock, in pieces, for any item is the product of the standard deviation of forecast errors, and a safety factor. The forecasting system generates a

DISTRIBUTION BY ANNUAL VALUE OF TOTAL COST

CLASS INTERVAL	NUMBER OF ITEMS	TOTAL VALUE	CUMULATIVE PERCENTAGES		
			ALL ITEMS	ACTIVE ITEMS	VALUE
100,000.00	6	811,863.07	0.86	0.91	15.42
31,622.78	25	1,297,002.46	4.43	4.73	40.05
10,000.00	98	1,603,099.80	18.43	19.66	70.49
3,162.28	199	1,128,352.95	46.86	50.00	91.92
1,000.00	190	364,560.88	74.00	78.96	98.85
316.23	78	52,829.98	85.14	90.85	99.85
100.00	36	7,006.08	90.29	96.34	99.98
31.62	13	759.82	92.14	98.32	100.00
10.00	5	107.76	92.86	99.09	100.00
3.16	3	22.08	93.29	99.54	100.00
1.00	1	1.65	93.43	99.70	100.00
0.32	1	0.54	93.57	99.85	100.00
0.00	44		99.86		100.00
TOTALS	699	5,265,607.07			

AVERAGE VALUE PER ITEM PER YEAR = 8,039.09

LOGNORMAL DISTRIBUTION:

PARAMETER SIGMA 1.61
STANDARD RATIO 5.00
J-FACTOR 3.65

MEDIAN ITEM   2,200.96
MEDIAN VALUE   29,363.17

THERE ARE 17 ITEMS WITH VALUE EXCEEDING 50000
PRINT AT THE TERMINAL? YES
ALIGN PAPER.

ITEM		WAREHOUSE	VALUE	CUMUL VALUE
47-012-930	BINTAG	200	177,922.61	177,922.61
38-027-275	ADAPTOR	200	159,043.33	336,965.95
42-070-845	BREAKER	200	140,569.69	477,535.64
49-029-897	ADAPTOR	200	116,033.34	593,568.98
40-028-167	ADAPTOR	200	115,710.67	709,279.64
36-094-909	HOUSING	200	102,583.43	811,863.07
35-026-478	ADAPTOR	200	94,710.31	906,573.38
40-068-388	IGNITION	200	74,587.12	981,160.50
33-078-629	BUSHING	200	70,628.54	1,051,789.04
49-030-061	ADAPTOR	200	68,079.83	1,119,868.87
40-696-973	IGNITION	200	67,010.80	1,186,879.67
33-076-961	SHORT	200	66,942.08	1,253,821.76
41-182-643	SHROUD	200	57,515.95	1,311,337.70
33-162-316	WINDSHIELD	200	57,386.48	1,368,724.18
44-100-824	ADAPTOR	200	57,064.16	1,425,788.34
45-059-213	WINDSHIELD	200	52,967.47	1,478,755.81
36-183-917	SHROUD	200	51,356.98	1,530,112.79

Exhibit 4.1

measurement of the standard deviation, item by item. The reason for using the standard deviation rather than the forecast itself (as in setting safety stock at six weeks of supply) is that some items can be forecast better than others. Everyone knows the products that are almost impossible to forecast, implying a relatively large standard deviation. These items justify a large safety stock to ensure service if the forecast can't be made more accurate, and that might be a characteristic of the business you are in. But think for a moment of all the other items in the inventory that don't leap to your mind, the ones that aren't problems. One reason those items are not problems is that the standard deviation of forecast errors is reasonably low. Hence those items don't need as much safety stock to ensure a given level of service; under a policy of providing a set number of weeks of supply, the stock exists anyhow.

The safety factor is a dimensionless number, computed item by item, to balance the investment in safety stocks against one or more appropriate measures of service. Chapter 10 deals in some detail with the derivations of six alternative decision rules, illustrates the difference in their effects in typical inventories, and gives some guidelines for choosing among them. The choice of a decision rule for a given inventory class is a strategic choice, usually made when the system is first specified and then forgotten. It might be appropriate to choose different decision rules for different inventory classes.

The other management choice is tactical. For selected samples, or for the whole inventory, one can report the effect on investment and service of choosing different values of a "management policy variable" for a given decision rule. The definition and implications of the management policy variable are different for the six alternative rules to be discussed. In the case illustrated in Exhibit 4.2, the management policy variable is the number of shortages per item per year, and the table reports the consequences of choosing values from 0.1 (one shortage every 10 years) to 0.5 shortages per year. The particular rule is one that will maximize the dollar demand filled from stock for a given aggregate inventory investment.

There are four measures of service:

1. Number of shortage occurrences in a year, or the number of times that a back order would exist if the replenishment order arrived at the end of the normal lead time. Alternatively this value can be interpreted as the number of times that frozen schedules have to be short-dated to get material early enough to satisfy all the demand.

2. Value of back orders on an annual basis is a measure of the seriousness of shortages if expediting can't avert them. The particular strategic

THE PRESENT INVENTORY HAS THESE CHARACTERISTICS:

THE 200 ITEMS IN THIS RECORD:
	AMOUNT	VALUE
SALES	540,220	$1,749,705.86
LOTS ORDERED	801	$19,395.70

CUSTOMER SERVICE

	SHORTAGES	PERCENT SERVICE
DEMAND TRANSACTIONS	908.74	99.83 o/o *OF TRANSACTIONS*
SHORTAGE OCCURRENCES	58.96	92.64 o/o *OF RECEIPTS*
VALUE BACKORDERED	4,682.59	99.73 o/o *OF SALES*
AVERAGE DURATION	12.79 *DAYS PER SHORTAGE.*	

INVENTORY INVESTMENT (DOLLARS)
SAFETY STOCK	$48,572.82
WORKING STOCK	112,416.22
THEORETICAL ON HAND	160,989.04
STD. DEV. OF ON HAND	10,023.50
ACTUAL ON HAND	299,558.91
THEORETICAL ON ORDER	972,635.91
ACTUAL ON ORDER	1,595,983.36

INVESTIGATE ORDER QUANTITY STRATEGIES? NO

THE CODES FOR THE SAFETY STOCK STRATEGIES ARE:
  1 = *FILL THE SPECIFIED FRACTIONS OF DEMAND FROM STOCK.*
  2 = *MAXIMIZE DOLLAR DEMAND FILLED FROM A GIVEN INVENTORY.*
  3 = *SET SAFETY STOCK AS SPECIFIED NUMBERS OF SIGMAS.*
  4 = *SET SAFETY STOCK AS SPECIFIED TIME SUPPLIES.*
  5 = *MINIMIZE SHORTAGE OCCURENCES FOR A GIVEN INVENTORY.*
  6 = *MINIMIZE TRANSACTION SHORTAGES FOR A GIVEN INVENTORY.*

CODE FOR DECISION RULE = 2
POLICY VARIABLE IS THE NUMBER OF SHORTAGES PER ITEM PER YEAR.
EXTREME VALUES = .1 .5

POLICY VARIABLE	SAFETY STOCK DOLLARS	SHORTAGE OCCUR. ITEMS/YR	BACKORDER DEMAND DOL/YR	SHORTAGE DURATION DA/SHORT	TRANSACT SHORTS NO/YR
0.100	67138	19.3	1267	10.26	242
0.138	62069	27.0	1857	11.74	356
0.190	56639	37.6	2734	13.30	525
0.263	51016	51.8	3996	13.16	774
0.362	45018	70.7	5859	13.27	1140
0.500	38844	95.1	8513	12.73	1662
CURRENT	48573	59.0	4683	12.79	909

Exhibit 4.2

choice of a decision rule illustrated says that for a given investment, this measure is lower than for any other possible decision rule.
3. Shortage duration is actually derived from the size of the back order, and is an indication of how long, one the average, back orders would exist provided material arrives at the end of the specified lead time.
4. Transactions short converts the number of pieces short for each item into customer lines that could not be filled, on the basis of the average number of pieces per customer line order.

Somewhere in that list, or in an equivalent table for a different range of values for the management policy variable, there is a combination of measures of service and of investment in safety stocks that will satisfy management. That value of the policy variable is the one that can be implemented to set safety stocks for individual items. The values of the policy variables should be reviewed for each major inventory class at least annually at budget time, to reflect current management thinking about service and investment. The choices can be reviewed more often for selected classes of products. Although the policy variable values may change only from year to year, the safety factors, and hence safety stocks, for individual litems will be recomputed probably monthly or quarterly to reflect changes in forecast, forecast errors, costs, lead times, and other factors that go into the computation.

When it comes to implementing the strategic choice, a code for one of the six decision rules can be posted to individual item records, so that it is conceivable that different decision rules would be used for six different classes of the inventory. That is not likely, of course, because some of the decision rules available are clearly a great deal better than the others. But all six are available so that the user can convince himself whether there is a difference, and how big it is.

The set of items processed at one time (Exhibit 4.3) can be defined virtually without limit, because any set of items can be retrieved according to any definable set of characteristics indicated by information in the data base about the item.

The current values for policy values associated with all six strategies for safety stock, plus the carrying charge used in computing one of several alternative economical order quantities (controlled item by item) can be displayed for the record and changed if necessary. It is common to find that one decision rule is chosen for computing the national safety stock and a different decision rule—a different strategic choice—for safety stocks at the field distribution warehouses. The consequences of the choice are summarized at the end of the analysis.

DECISION

TUESDAY, AUGUST 3, 1976
EASTERN DAYLIGHT TIME 17:30:00

DISPLAY OR CHANGE POLICY VARIABLES? N

WHICH ITEMS = ALL
ALL 713 ITEMS WILL BE USED.
LOCATIONS TO BE INCLUDED = 100 200
2 LOCATIONS WILL BE USED.

RECOMPUTE REPLENISHMENT LOT QUANTITIES? YES

655 PARTS HAD ANNUAL USAGE $5,265,476.66
WORKING STOCK IS $411,866.74, OR .94 MONTHS OF SUPPLY.
2818 REPLENISHMENT ORDERS GENERATED PER YEAR.

MASTER WAREHOUSE

	LOCATION:	MASTER	
SAFETY STOCKS:	*LOW*	*IMPLEMENTED*	*HIGH*
INVENTORY INVESTMENT $	590,523	692,942	771,961
MONTHS OF SUPPLY	1.35	1.58	1.76
BACKORDERS/YR $	653,674	515,340	441,999
PERCENT FILLED	87.59	90.21	91.61
SHORTAGE OCCURRENCES	228	171	137
PERCENT OF LOTS	8.10	6.08	4.88

SATELLITE LOCATIONS

	LOCATION:	INDIANAPOLIS, IN	
SAFETY STOCKS:	*LOW*	*IMPLEMENTED*	*HIGH*
INVENTORY INVESTMENT $	179,712	205,953	225,625
MONTHS OF SUPPLY	0.43	0.49	0.54
BACKORDERS/YR $	53,564	38,166	29,265
PERCENT FILLED	98.93	99.24	99.42
SHORTAGE OCCURRENCES	422	322	260
PERCENT OF LOTS	14.98	11.44	9.22

58 ITEMS WERE REJECTED BECAUSE OF NON-POSITIVE SALES OR COSTS.
PUT THEIR INDEX NUMBERS INTO FILE = DIRECTORY
COMPONENT = COSTS
REPLACE IT? YES

ELAPSED TIME	4M 31.694S
CPU TIME	51.084S

Exhibit 4.3

PART NUMBER	ANNUAL USAGE	CONVERS FACTOR	NO LOC	INVENTORY INVESTMENT IN MONTHS				
				WORKING	NATL SS	REGIONAL	THEORET	ONHAND
44-004-679	4,612		4	0.4	1.4	0.8	2.6	4.8
32-007-035	25,338		4	0.4	1.4	0.7	2.5	4.7
44-008-530	26,295		5	0.5	1.5	0.8	2.7	4.9
47-012-930	4,877		4	0.5		0.8	1.4	3.8
47-467-719	17,489		2	0.7	1.2	0.7	2.5	4.3
44-100-824	16,249		5	0.4	1.3	0.9	2.5	4.7
35-026-478	22,600		4	0.4	1.0	0.9	2.3	4.5
38-027-275	29,737		5	0.4	0.7	0.9	2.0	4.3
40-028-167	24,881		4	0.4	0.8	1.0	2.2	4.3
49-029-897	18,887		5	0.4	0.8	1.0	2.2	4.4
49-030-061	11,210		4	0.4	1.2	1.0	2.7	4.5
41-031-505	7,570		5	0.4	1.3	1.0	2.7	4.6
49-341-925	3,059		4	0.6	1.8	1.1	3.5	5.2
47-805-263	11,721		2	0.6			0.6	6.6
48-115-916	1,383		4	1.3		0.8	2.1	4.0
41-037-913	6,617		5	1.1	0.6	1.4	2.5	5.6
45-059-213	9,440		4	0.7	1.5	1.0	2.3	4.5
50-655-961	2,038		5	0.5	1.1	0.6	2.6	4.8
33-162-316	12,123		3	0.4	1.1	0.6	2.0	4.5
41-164-588	7,257		4	0.7		0.8	2.6	4.7

ID	Count							
40-068-388	24,036	2	0.4	1.0	0.9	2.3	5.2
44-683-325	942	5	0.5	1.6	0.6	2.7	4.9
36-168-388	1,225	4	1.0	1.0	0.7	2.7	4.4
34-694-846	1,889	5	0.8		0.7	1.6	2.3
40-696-973	25,530	5	0.3	0.8	0.4	1.6	4.0
42-070-845	443,748	2	0.5		0.8	1.3	3.3
42-071-955	102,813	2	0.4	1.4	0.7	2.5	5.7
36-074-565	75,333	4	1.4		1.8	3.2	1.9
33-076-961	5,524	4	1.0		1.4	2.4	3.7
47-180-523	1,239	5	0.9		0.8	1.8	3.8
41-182-643	4,321	4	0.4	1.2	0.9	2.4	4.4
36-183-917	2,482	4	0.4	1.2	0.7	2.3	4.8
35-080-803	9,943	4	1.0		1.4	2.4	3.9
37-077-200	6,036	3	0.1	0.4	0.9	0.6	9.5
36-181-015	847	4	0.6	1.6	0.9	3.2	49.7
33-078-629	12,415	4	0.5	0.6	0.8	2.0	6.7
35-184-970	3,643	5	0.5	1.4	1.1	2.7	16.9
47-271-106	3,442	2	0.9			2.1	14.0
42-047-513	4,751	2	0.3		0.1	0.3	9.7
43-144-398	5,158	5	0.2	0.1		0.4	7.9
49-257-621	4,570	2	0.2			0.2	9.8
TOTAL			0.6	0.5	0.8	1.9	4.2

Exhibit 4.4

The results can be interpreted by management more clearly when they are summarized in relative terms, location by location. An indication of the sensitivity to the value chosen for the policy variables is given by showing what the investment and service would have been if the policy variable were 0.5 and 1.5 times the value actually used.

Safety stock investment is shown both in dollars and in months of supply. But note that the months of supply is a result—the safety stocks are computed item by item, evaluated, added together, and finally compared to the sales forecast. This is quite different from specifying that the safety stock for each item shall be so many months of supply.

Service is measure both in terms of the value that would be back ordered if replenishment always takes the standard lead time, and in the number of replenishment lots that might have to be expedited to provide essentially perfect service. Back orders are expressed in dollars and interpreted as a percentage of the dollar value of the forecast. Expediting actions are expressed both as absolute numbers of events and as a percent of all the replenishment lots generated in a year.

4.3 FEEDBACK

The performance report (Exhibit 1.4) gives a current snapshot of the actual inventory investment and service that can be compared with the intention from the policy variables implemented (Exhibit 4.3).

To get a clearer picture of the status versus intent for individual items (aggregated across all stocking locations), a list of the intended theoretical inventory versus the current actual on hand can be tabulated in units, dollars, months of supply, or even pounds and cubic feet (Exhibit 4.4). The theoretical inventory includes the following.

1. Working stock that derives from the planned lot sizes for replenishment orders.
2. National safety stock normally held at the master warehouse to ensure service to the satellites with minimum disruption of production schedules.
3. Regional stocks, which include both a normal allowance for stock in transit from the source to the satellites, and the regional safety stocks budgeted to give a certain level of service.

One executive had to confess that his new control system gave him more information than he could digest. He appreciated the ability to control

FEEDBACK

ITEM : 37-01-1906   HOME UNIT FILE INDEX = 1

LOCATION	USAGE		FORECAST	ON HAND	
	PAST 12	PAST 6	NEXT 12	UNITS	MONTHS
MASTER	213	213	1052	424	3.63
BROADVIEW, IL	278	122	8	55	71.00
ATLANTA, GA	445	236	647	49	1.00
LOS ANGELES, CA	286	151	424	70	2.13
DENVER, CO	353	144	582	132	2.91
TOTAL	1362	653	1661	730	5.66

ITEM : 39-10-3209   FOUNTAIN FILE INDEX = 2

LOCATION	USAGE		FORECAST	ON HAND	
	PAST 12	PAST 6	NEXT 12	UNITS	MONTHS
MASTER			10832	2536	4.12
BROADVIEW, IL	5723	3577	3923	43	1.62
DENVER, CO	769	299	1405	19	0.14
NEW YORK, NY	1832	1141	2477	221	1.42
LOS ANGELES, CA	2156	1102	3091	593	3.01
TOTAL	10480	6119	10896	3412	4.79

ITEM : 37-62-1981   FURNACE FILE INDEX = 3

LOCATION	USAGE		FORECAST	ON HAND	
	PAST 12	PAST 6	NEXT 12	UNITS	MONTHS
MASTER			3489	426	1.47
BROADVIEW, IL	1219	741	486	⁻14	⁻0.35
ATLANTA, GA	869	416	1342	117	1.12
NEW YORK, NY	402	215	598		
LOS ANGELES, CA	651	345	953	84	1.17
TOTAL	3141	1717	3379	613	2.21

Exhibit 4.5

almost everything in sight, but he personally didn't have time to understand how to use all the controls. Still, he did not want to turn the system over to his subordinates entirely, with no visibility.

Exhibit 4.5 is a report designed to give a snapshot that this executive could scan quickly to see if there are problems and at least identify where they lie. Then he could use his staff meeting to get more details of what the problem is and to ensure that the people on the working level are taking effective action to correct the situation.

All the report shows, for each product by location, is a crude record of usage in the past 12 months and the past six months, as a basis for getting a feeling about the forecast and the trend. The computer's record of the forecast for the next year is also shown, including the statistical model, marketing intelligence, scheduled backlog, and even dependent demand. The current inventory position is reported both in units and in months of supply. It takes only seconds to find two problems on that page, and a quick check can be made to ensure that something is done about them.

Summary: Levels of Systems

The classification of modules of a materials management system according to action, planning, requirements, and strategy tends to bring together analyses and reports that apply to similar parts of the corporate organization, as well as activities that tend to have similar cycles of operation.

For example, most of the "action" reports are essentially run every day to reflect current status. The "planning" reports are developed once a week, or once every other week in typical organizations. For many manufacturing industries the requirements can be forecast once a month, although as we noted above, when there are significant promotions, or very short lead times, a shorter interval may be appropriate. The strategic choices of decision rules generally tend to be made once and for all, with a review of management policy variables on an annual or quarterly basis, but the current policy is applied in recomputing lot quantities and safety factors every time the forecast is reviewed.

Another taxonomy may also be helpful in distinguishing design criteria for different parts of a system, which we can think of as the "level" of the application. Every major system is made up of bits and pieces at different levels in this sense. The levels are not necessarily chronological in the sequence of implementation, but rather relate to a scheme put forward by Stafford Beer for the identification of a hierarchy of control actions for any organization or organism. We deal here with only three levels, which seem to apply to formal decisions relating to materials management. The fourth level involves questions such as whether to develop new products, and the fifth level is concerned with questions such as whether to merge with Occidental Petroleum or take over Sir Hugh Frazer. These latter two levels are outside the scope of this book.

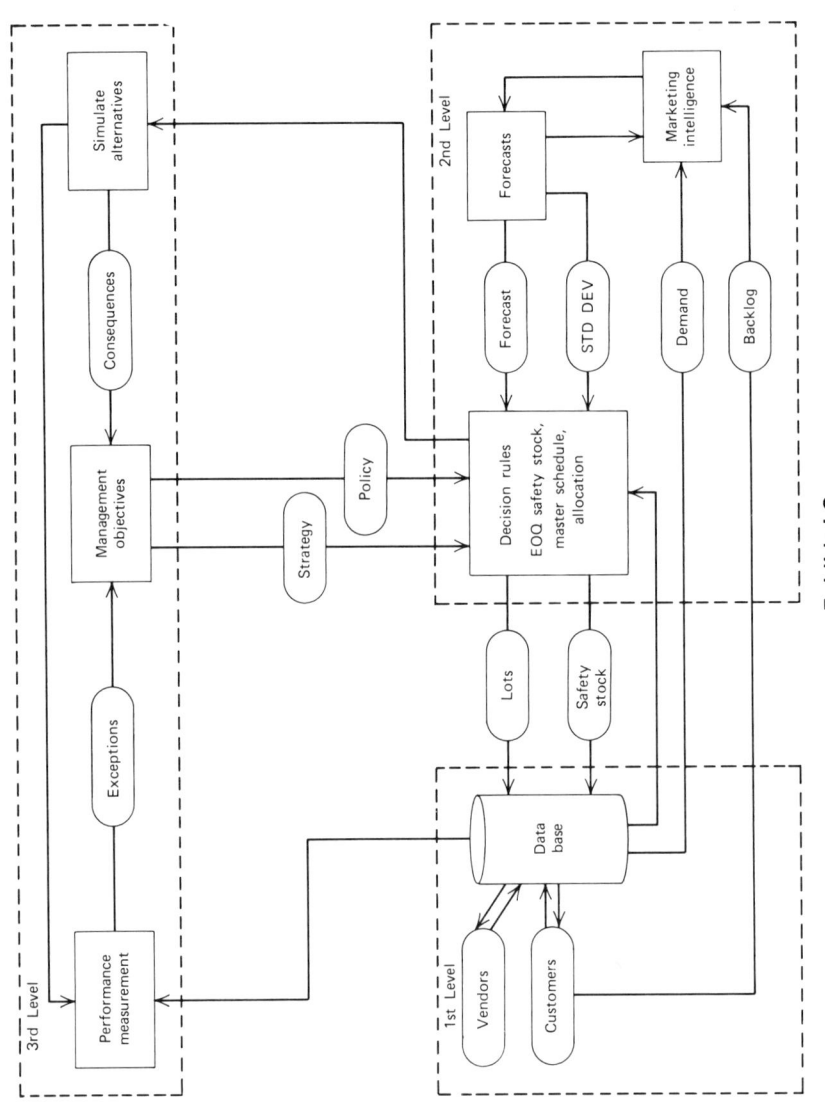

Exhibit I.3

FIRST-LEVEL SYSTEMS

The "first-level" part of a system has to do primarily with the transactions that post the files in the data base, where there is a continual rate of activity, high volume of information, and in general not much question about the logical foundation. For example, a demand transaction reduces inventory balances and increment the history in any system, whether it is for the corner grocery or General Motors. There is almost always a unique "right" answer as the result of posting a transaction. Thus the people in a first-level system tend to be clerks, who can be trained and supervised. The primary concern in developing first-level systems is with data processing efficiency, to handle large volumes of information accurately and economically. It is the sort of business IBM and the other hardware vendors are good at, and interested in. Many of the "action" system operations are essentially first level in nature.

SECOND-LEVEL SYSTEMS

The essential purpose of the second-level parts of a total system is to answer questions, for example, when to procure more stock, how much to get, where to send the received material, and when to schedule production. Implicit in these operations is a formal basis for decisions or a decision rule (often involving a square root).

The duty cycle tends to be less frequent than for the first-level system, and therefore some delays can be tolerated. It might be disastrous if the order-entry system did not keep up with the flow of paper, but a few days' delay in revising the forecast will not have a detectable impact on the operations.

With each decision rule there is an exchange curve that trades some measure of capital investment (usually in inventory) for something with the dimensions of an operating expense, such as setup cost, or the expense of expediting. One consequence of the choice of a value for the policy variable shows up on the balance sheet, and tends to be of interest to the financial executives of the business. The other consequence shows up in the P&L statement and is of more direct concern to operating people in production and marketing. Hence the actual level at which the firm is to operate is the result of a negotiation between different organizations. The formal analyses of consequences make it possible to display the anatomy of one's assumptions, as John Magee has so happily phrased it, so that both sides make an informed choice.

There are alternative design assumptions to a second-level system, requiring different strategic choices among decision rules. Thus there is not a single "right" answer as there is in a first-level system.

For the most part the information required is already in the data base, and the options and choices can be supplied by middle management, who are in a position to take some risks. There is a legitimate basis for an honest difference of opinion, and the analyses of the system help evaluate the consequences but don't specify the One Best Way that Frederick Taylor was so fond of espousing.

First-level formal control systems for management were already rife by the end of World War II on unit record equipment. Second-level systems came into operation during the 1950s and 1960s as the result of the application of wartime experience with operations research to industrial problems. Materials management and especially inventory control were a fertile area for exploration and contribution by the operations research professionals.

The planning and requirements operations of the materials management are typically second-level types of applications.

THIRD-LEVEL SYSTEMS

The third level is where management's corporate objectives mesh with the routine operations of the materials management system. The major input is guidance in the strategic selection among alternative decision rules, and current policy setting the exchange of capital investment for operating expense.

It is still, however, somewhat awkward to try to get a meaningful answer from executives to questions such as, "What carrying charge should we use?," or, "What is the right level of customer service?" Hence part of the third-level system must be a simulation capability that displays the consequences of the possible choices among alternatives, expressed in terms that management can understand, often at the aggregate level of the balance sheet and the P&L statement. This is the sort of inventory management that is routinely reported in *Fortune* and the *Wall Street Journal*.

Simulating alternatives and making strategic and tactical choices can be an empty exercise unless the loop is closed and actual operating conditions are monitored and compared with the plan. Once management develops a sense of trust in the system it may be possible to increase their productivity by exception reports, but in some cases a fair amount of detail is still wanted. In my own automobile, for example, I have a manual gearshift and

THIRD-LEVEL SYSTEMS

gages that tell me the rpms, the oil temperature, and the rate of battery charge. I simply don't trust Detroit's "idiot lights," nor do I want my choice of gear for an icy curve with a reverse crown made by someone several years ago and far away.

The unambiguous right answers in first-level systems tend to be similar for all industries everywhere in the world. In the second-level decision rules most companies in the same industry will make similar choices of strategy, and competition may force similar tactical choices of policy. The third-level systems, which only recently have gained acceptance in American industry, tend to be quite personal in nature.

The way in which the alternatives are presented must match the personal style of the executives making the decisions. If a vice-president for production in a shoe company were to move to the position of vice-president for marketing in a cosmetics company, he would probably still use most effectively similar presentations of information about alternatives. The new vice-president of production in the shoe company could conceivably have quite a different style, which would require modifications to at least the appearance of the third-level system. An advantage of developing the formal definition of the system in a high-level language like APL is that it is exceptionally easy to modify the system quickly in response to needs of the users.

A materials management system can be built for a very wide variety of operating environments if there are enough possible states of the control system. The modular design described in this book works in that direction. Good control requires feedback at all levels, and an explicit part of the design and architecture is the consideration of the feedback, both at a technical level and between routine operations at the management level.

Throughout the book there are many, many options for executing various components of systems at all levels. In addition, there are important aids to help you choose among those options to get a system that works well in your environment. These aids to selection are of three general types:

1. Programmed decisions, such as the choice of a particular forecast model, where the criteria are complex and the statistical theory for making the right decision is easier to incorporate into a computer program than to teach people.
2. Recommendations, such as the strategic selection among safety stock and lot size decision rules. Here there are good ground rules for preferring one over another, and this book concentrates on explaining and illustrating years of research in a way that helps a practical person see what is relevant in his case.

72　SUMMARY: LEVELS OF SYSTEMS

3. Simulations, as in the case of the tactical choices of management policy variables. These ancillary third-level programs display immediately the consequences of alternative choices in terms that a responsible manager should be able to interpret in his environment.

Thus not only is there the requisite variety to have the system match your environment, but also an integral part of the system is a meta-system to help you customize the application to the real environment.

SECTION **II**

Forecasting

There are very few industries in which a materials management system can wait for a firm order for its product before planning to get the materials and manufacturing capacity to produce it, and still deliver in time to satisfy the customer. The building industry seems to be an exception.

Thus one needs a forecast of requirements that are to come. Some of the requirements may be represented by the backlog of open orders. Even so, orders are not always booked early enough to allow for the acquisition of long-lead-time materials. There are two approaches to forecasting that can be nicely balanced through the appropriate feedback of results.

One is a "descriptive" approach to forecasting, which uses a history of previous demand to look for patterns that can be extrapolated into the future. In the stock market, this approach is sometimes called "technical."

The other is an "explanatory" approach, which seeks to understand the basic reasons why rates of demand change. In the stock market the analogous approach is called "fundamental."

A blend of the two approaches can provide an excellent basis for generating the total requirements that must be covered by the production schedule.

In the schematic diagram shown in Exhibit II.1 "descriptive statistical forecast" may use any reasonable technique to analyze demand history, item by item. It produces two sorts of outputs. First consider the "long-range summary" report, which might, like Exhibit 3.3, show the current forecasts for each period, extending well past the current planning horizon. The report can be aggregated by any attribute of the inventory, such as ABC classification, product line, region, or commodity group.

A group of people, the marketing intelligence group, reviews these reports in the light of other information about the market, the product line, and marketing plans. The nature of the review depends on the kind of a market that management sees. Hence the format and organization of the reports may change to meet these needs. Chapter 7 deals at some length with the way that a marketing intelligence group can review the current forecasts and make changes which are recorded in the data base, to be available in any forecast report.

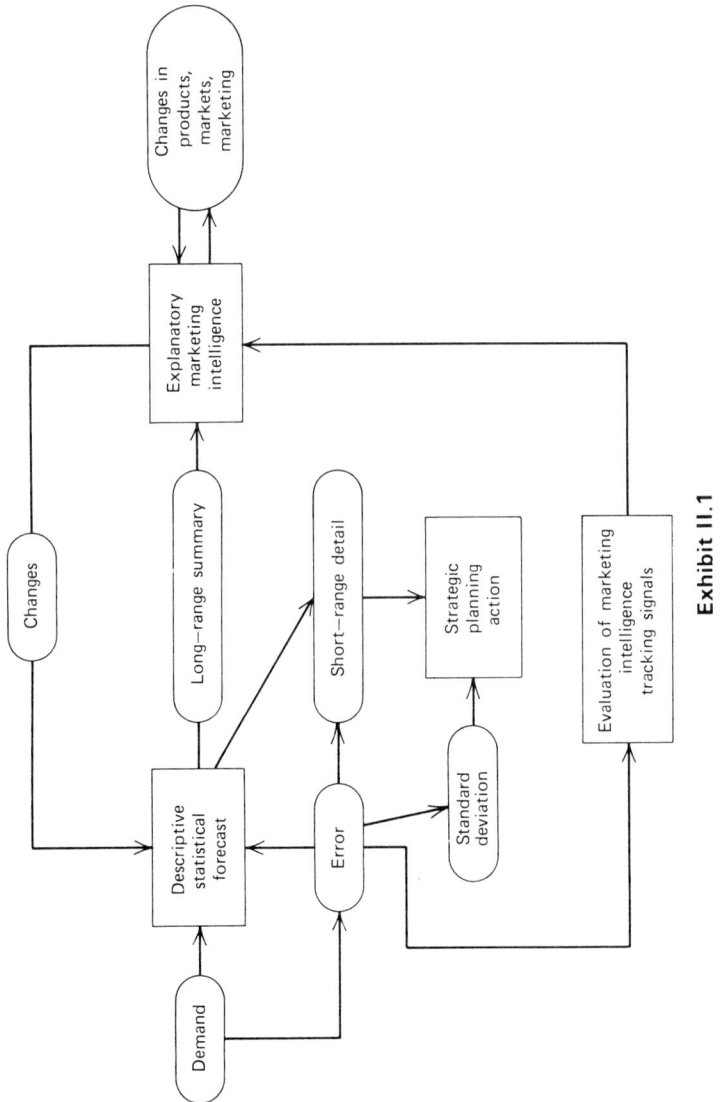

Exhibit II.1

FORECASTING

In particular, the effects of these changes are reflected in the short-range detailed forecasts, like Exhibit 3.1, that are used in other parts of the materials management system for planning how to cover requirements.

The principal driving force for the whole requirements system is current demand, shown at the left of Exhibit II.1. It obviously is used in generating the statistical forecasts (as we shall see in Chapters 5 and 6), but it is also compared with the most recent forecast to generate an error signal.

All control systems need feedback, and the error signals (discussed in Chapter 8) provide the necessary correction to make the statistical forecasts adapt to changes in demand patterns.

The standard deviation of the distribution of forecast errors is an essential factor in inventory planning (to be covered in Section III, especially Chapter 10).

Feedback also controls the blending of statistical and marketing forecasts through the evaluation of marketing intelligence and the action taken when the system trips a tracking signal.

CHAPTER 5

Statistical Forecast Models

We start by examining the sorts of demand, or surrogates for demand, that can be effectively forecast, and give some indication of the circumstances under which one might want to use one or another. Then there is the question of how often to revise the forecast and why; in the examples used throughout the book the interval is a calendar month, but some applications use one, two, or four weeks. The meat of this chapter is an examination of the classes of models that can be used to describe time series, with some reasons for expecting to use one type rather than another. Recently some rather powerful automatic techniques have been developed by which a computer program can examine each time series in turn and select the best model. Finally, consider the special problems of establishing a forecast model for new items that have no demand history.

5.1 WHAT TO FORECAST

It might seem obvious that one wants to forecast customer demand—the quantity that the customers would want if it were available to be delivered in each time period. Some companies do not record demand, but only shipments or orders. Shipments represent the quantities shipped when stock was available and hence may show abnormal low periods during a shortage, followed by abnormal high periods when production catches up with the back orders. Orders are sometimes recorded in the period received, instead of in the period when the customer expects to get the material. If service is fairly good, shipments follow demand closely. If most demand is for immediate shipment, orders are also close to demand. But even if there have been severe shortages, or long intervals between order entry and shipment, the available records represent demand.

The forecasting procedures to be described do adapt to changing conditions, and do measure the errors in the forecast. If the data used do not exactly match demand the forecast isn't as accurate as it conceivably might be. But since the forecasting system measures the errors, adequate provisions for safety stock are made. As the data become better, the forecasts improve and the safety stock is reduced. Start now with a good forecast rather than waiting for the necessary effort before you get any useful forecast.

Forecasts are needed for each product (part number) at a national level for production planning and purchasing. They are also needed at the regional level to control the distribution of products to the field warehouses. Throughout this book we refer to a "stockkeeping unit" (SKU) as a part number at a warehouse. Each part number represents as many different SKUs as there are locations stocking it.

Demand for a part number can be forecast, and then that forecast prorated among SKUs based on the historical percentage of demand by region. Experiments have shown, however, that another alternative is preferable. The forecast for each region is based on the region's own history, and national demand is forecast separately based on the total of all demand. The national forecast for the product is about the same in either case. If every region uses a stable percentage of the national total, the regional forecasts will be the same both ways. However, usually there are different trends, and possibly even seasonal patterns by region, which can be reflected only by forecasts based on local information. Note that the national forecast is the key to controlling how much stock there is in the system; the regional forecasts are primarily used to control how to split up that pie.

Typically the forecasts are developed for individual products and SKUs, but in some industries there are different bases for forecasting. In the case of custom-made capital equipment like boilers and electronic instruments, there isn't an identifiable end "product"—every order is for a different configuration of more or less standard components. There are two approaches that can be used in these cases. (*a*) Forecast at the level of the standard components, and let the products be assembled to order at short notice from adequate stocks (the "modular bill of materials"). (*b*) Set up a synthetic product for each product line, and forecast that. This "product" is never built, but it represents possible configurations. The requirements for subordinate parts are based on percentages obtained from the history of usage.

A special case of the synthetic product is the assortment of consumer goods, such as shoes, apparel, or silverware. The consumer need is for a pair of shoes that fit, in the right price range, with some general considerations of style, col r, and type. But there are a great many SKUs on the market that satisfy that consumer need. The consumer need is stable and can be forecast, if the right assortment can be identified. The demand for all

WHAT TO FORECAST

SKUs in that assortment is equal to the market need, but with a great deal of substitutability. If the total forecast is right, then within wide ranges it doesn't matter much how individual styles within the assortment are planned, so long as there is a reasonable variety but not too wide a choice.

Assortments must be defined "from the outside in," from the consumer's point of view. Typically most manufacturers think of "inside out" product lines, based on the way the product is made, not the way the consumer uses it to fill a need. As an example, flatware (spoons, knives, forks, and so on) would naturally be grouped both by the manufacturer and the consumer according to pattern. But what of ashtrays, vases, anchovy unwinders, and picture frames? It was a real breakthrough when the vice-president of marketing at a large Eastern company suddenly exclaimed, "Those are all $25 wedding gifts." Forecast the total sales of $25 wedding gifts, decide on a reasonable variety of items, prorate the total in any reasonable way, and the customer will buy from what you have made available. You can substitute a candy dish this year for the ashtray of last year, but the total market for $25 wedding gifts goes on and on and on.

Along the same line are the options and accessories that go along with products, such as the tape deck and CB radio for a car, special recorders for a testing device, and type of starting engine or hydraulic drive on a Diesel tractor. Here one knows quite a bit about the forecast, or production plan, for the prime product. Historical data can show the typical percentage of each accessory bought, and those percentages can be forecast and applied to the prime product production plan. In the automotive market it used to be that radios were much more popular at the beginning of each model year when the Joneses bought their latest model. The bargain hunters at the end of the model year didn't want as many accessories. But even that sort of seasonal pattern can be recognized and forecast in the model of installation rates.

Still another instance is the requirements for service parts on aircraft, office copiers, and computers. The "customer" is a technical representative. The requirement is generated by the equipment as used in the field. But in many of these industries there are excellent current statistics on not only how many machines there are but also how they are being used. All aircraft operations and flying hours are logged carefully, under government regulation, and IBM and Xerox base their billing on the actual metered use of leased machines. Failure rates can be expressed as pieces used per 1000 machine months in the field. These failure rates can be forecast and applied to management production plans for new installations, in order to get the parts forecast. In some instances it has even been possible to get an initial estimate of the failure rate from the type of part. Analysis of past usage of large numbers of parts that have functionally similar uses show that there is a predictable pattern of failure that can be used as an initial estimate for new parts.

Air conditioners and apparel sold by mail order afford still another problem of what to forecast. It is part of the marketing strategy in both industries to send out more units than will ultimately be bought, so that there will be net returns of salable merchandise. The return rate depends, of course, on how many units have been shipped and on characteristic time lags. A forecast of returns can be netted out from the forecast of shipments to get an estimate of the requirements for new production; this can be quite crucial late in the selling season.

There are similar phenomena in the return of leased equipment to offset production requirements for new manufacture. In all these cases it seems more effective to forecast demand and returns separately, using the models and techniques appropriate to each, and then net the production requirements. A naive forecast of net outflow may overlook some valuable information.

One last comment on what to forecast: there are some series where the rate of growth is inherently exponential (as are most things related to the population or the government). In those cases the series should be transformed first by taking logarithms. Forecast in logarithmic terms and then get the final forecast by taking antilogs.

5.2 SAMPLING INTERVAL

Forecasts are revised periodically. Throughout this book we use the calendar month in the examples, since this is common to so many industries. There are some industries where it is appropriate to revise the forecast every week, every two weeks, or every four weeks. There is no important difference between 12 calendar months a year and 13 four-week accounting periods except for convenience in interfacing with existing accounting and reporting practice. The forecasts will generate the same requirements in either case. (As we shall see in a bit, the 12 months do not have to be of equal length, and could represent four-week, four-week, five-week periods.)

A forecast should be revised every week or every other week when there is important information that can be distingusished by weeks. For example, consumer promotions may start in the third week of one month and last through the second week of the next. Unless real information about requirements is available on a weekly basis, there is no important gain or loss from revising the forecast every week or every month. As a rule of thumb the length of the sampling interval, between revisions of the forecast, should not be less than about a tenth of the typical lead time, and there are some

MODELS OF TIME SERIES

advantages to revising the forecast at least three times per lead time. Within that broad range, any convenient calendar reporting interval will do.

The reason for the limit of 10 revisions per lead time is just common sense—with long lead times one can't react much to finer information. The reason for the limit of at least three revisions per lead time is also that typically one can react more smoothly if there are several gradual changes rather than one big change. Neither limit is hard and fast. There are companies with lead times of three days which can revise the forecast once a month, and companies with lead times of 27 months which also revise the forecasts every month. In the latter case, however, I would certainly not propose to revise the forecast every week.

5.3 MODELS OF TIME SERIES

As a basis for discussion of the concepts involved with statistical forecasting from discrete time series, we can use the four series tabulated in Exhibit 5.1. Each of these is a month-by-month history spanning six years, representing demand. The four patterns are somewhat different.

Exhibits 5.2 to 5.4 plot three of the series so that you can get a visual impression of the pattern of demand that has occurred in the past.

5.31 Level and Trend

The statistical model of the pattern of demand may include any of several terms. The level represents the current rate of deseasonalized demand. The trend represents the rate at which that level is moving upward or downward (or possibly sideways when the value of the trend is 0). In the early days of the development of computer techniques for forecasting there was considerable emphasis on deciding between "horizontal" and "trend" models. The reason was not because one got a better forecast, but because of the limitations of the computer a quarter century ago. If there wasn't any apparent trend, then the space and computing time saved by having only a "horizontal" model were considerable. With modern computers, however, this is no longer a consideration.

All models now include trend, which may be zero. Consider the following argument. A large trend will clearly affect the forecast in the future, and will be considered significant by any statistical test. A zero trend is clearly not significant and has no effect on the forecast, whether or not it is included in the model. A very small trend won't have much effect on the forecast, and some other very small trend passes the threshold at which trends are considered significant. Statistical tests set the second threshold

PROMOTE

YR	JAN	FEB	MAR	APR	MAY	JUN	JUL	AUG	SEP	OCT	NOV	DEC	TOT
1971	186	258	216	210	57	204	185	12	106	207	71	240	1952
1972	263	152	335	249	107	177	183	61	196	195	183	256	2357
1973	235	131	333	219	113	196	144	9	171	189	125	164	2029
1974	137	215	257	200	33	190	179	34	187	171	136	175	1914
1975	208	141	164	181	129	87	231	54	166	267	79	194	1901
1976	293	227	257	276	50	135	92	4	67	148	57	331	1937
	1322	1124	1562	1335	489	989	1014	174	893	1177	651	1360	12090

SEASONAL

YR	JAN	FEB	MAR	APR	MAY	JUN	JUL	AUG	SEP	OCT	NOV	DEC	TOT
1971	772	811	950	811	623	525	406	772	1336	1099	1029	762	9896
1972	755	795	1007	745	564	624	403	755	1379	1168	1026	846	10067
1973	755	797	1073	733	723	648	478	861	1382	1200	1158	818	10626
1974	865	854	1104	910	763	660	512	945	1514	1309	1127	819	11382
1975	810	856	1233	822	856	753	559	959	1301	1233	1187	945	11514
1976	943	932	1207	932	753	705	621	1016	1494	1302	1195	848	11948
	4900	5045	6574	4953	4282	3915	2979	5308	8406	7311	6722	5038	65433

SQUARE

YR	JAN	FEB	MAR	APR	MAY	JUN	JUL	AUG	SEP	OCT	NOV	DEC	TOT
1971	60	60	60	190	190	190	60	60	60	190	190	190	1500
1972	60	60	60	190	190	190	60	60	60	190	190	190	1500
1973	60	60	60	190	190	190	60	60	60	190	190	190	1500
1974	60	60	60	190	190	190	60	60	60	190	190	190	1500
1975	60	60	60	190	190	190	60	60	60	190	190	190	1500
1976	60	60	60	190	190	190	60	60	60	190	190	190	1500
	360	360	360	1140	1140	1140	360	360	360	1140	1140	1140	9000

TREND

YR	JAN	FEB	MAR	APR	MAY	JUN	JUL	AUG	SEP	OCT	NOV	DEC	TOT
1971	71	159	81	102	92	116	128	97	78	132	105	116	1277
1972	133	130	165	145	141	127	151	146	147	150	185	148	1768
1973	143	143	188	154	168	160	156	144	159	171	180	126	1892
1974	118	209	174	169	152	181	197	180	191	186	209	156	2122
1975	178	196	151	183	224	154	247	214	204	258	205	189	2403
1976	244	263	222	255	208	202	202	213	179	222	218	282	2710
	887	1100	981	1008	985	940	1081	994	958	1119	1102	1017	12172

Exhibit 5.1

lower than the first. By the time the trend is small enough to be considered insignificant, it has ceased to have any appreciable effect on the forecast. Therefore you might as well allow all statistical forecast models to include a trend. If it is not significant the values computed will be so small as to get virtually the same effect as a horizontal model. The extra cost of computing an unnecessary trend is somewhat less than the costs of the statistical tests to decide that it isn't necessary.

MODELS OF TIME SERIES

5.32 Polynomials

In my earlier book *Smoothing, Forecasting and Prediction of Discrete Time Series* I showed how it was theoretically possible to include higher-order polynomials, such as "triple smoothing." Although it is mathematically correct, and physically desirable in tracking ballistic missiles, any polynomial model higher than an ordinary straight line is operational nonsense for forecasting demand. If your history shows a growth curve that isn't linear and that you expect to continue, then take logarithms before forecasting rather than using higher order polynomials.

5.33 Seasonal Cycles

Some of the series shown in the examples have regular seasonal cycles. The fact that demand is consistently low in June and July and consistently high in September and October can be used to advantage in forecasting demand next June, July, September, and October. (One marketing specialist once told me, "Of course may demand is seasonal. Look at that. It's been high

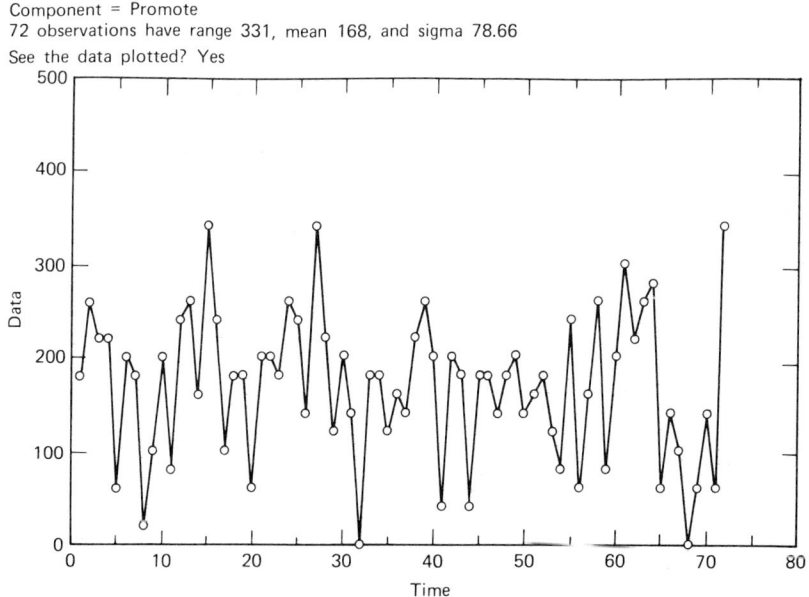

Exhibit 5.2

Component = Seasonal
72 observations have range 1111, mean 908.8, and sigma 258.2

See the data plotted? Yes

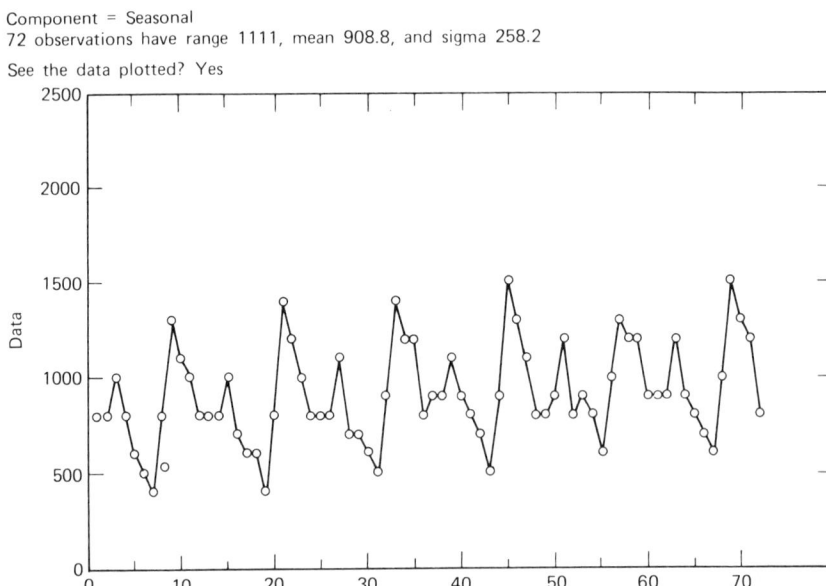

Median = 856
Range (excluding extremes) = 1088

Exhibit 5.3

every May for the last year." Usually one would want a little more evidence that a seasonal cycle will repeat itself in future years.)

5.331 Correlation. One indication of a consistent seasonal pattern is the serial correlation, as in Exhibit 5.5. The correlation coefficient must lie between 1 (absolutely related) and -1 (absolutely opposite). In Exhibit 5.5A, for the "seasonal" data, there are large peaks every 12 observations. The fact that the coefficient is nearly 1 for lags of 12 months means that if a given month's demand is on one side of the long-term average, say, below, then demand 12 months later is almost certainly going to be on the same side of the average. There is also some tendency for demand to be on the same side of the average at lags of six months, which is not suprising for consumer goods that typically have a peak demand in spring and another in autumn. However, demand in pairs of months three to four months apart are somewhat likely to be on opposite sides of the average.

Exhibit 5.5B shows that for the "trend" series there is no special tendency for demand to be on the same, or opposite, sides of the average for any lag. Hence there is probably no seasonal pattern that could be used. (Note that

MODELS OF TIME SERIES

the raw data, because of the very evident long-term trend, tend to be on the same side of the average for half the length of the series.)

5.332 Base Indices. There are essentially two techniques for representing seasonal cycles. One is the "base index" approach, where there is a factor for each period of the year (12 for monthly forecast revisions) that expresses the typical level of demand in a particular month compared to the long-term average.

Exhibit 5.6 shows these ratios for each of the 12 months of the year. The middle column is averaged over all six years and would normally be used in forecasting. The side columns show the variation from year to year, in terms of the year when the ratio was smallest for each month and the year when it was largest.

The lower display graphs the way that forecasts of the total demand for the whole season would be generated in terms of the percent done in the

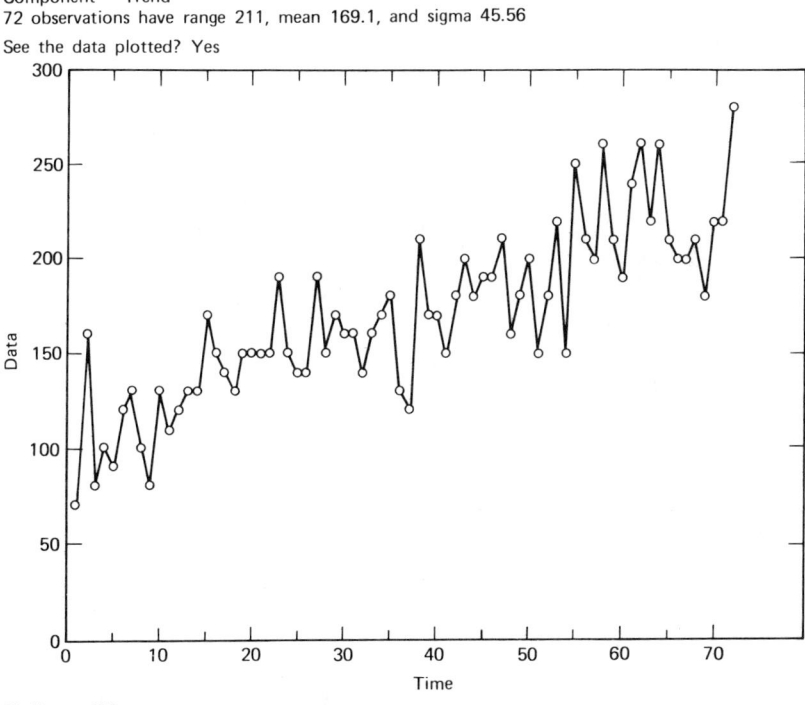

Exhibit 5.4

Component = Seasonal
72 observations have range 1111, mean 908.8, and sigma 258.2
Obs/cycle = 12
The level = 786.2, the trend = 3.36

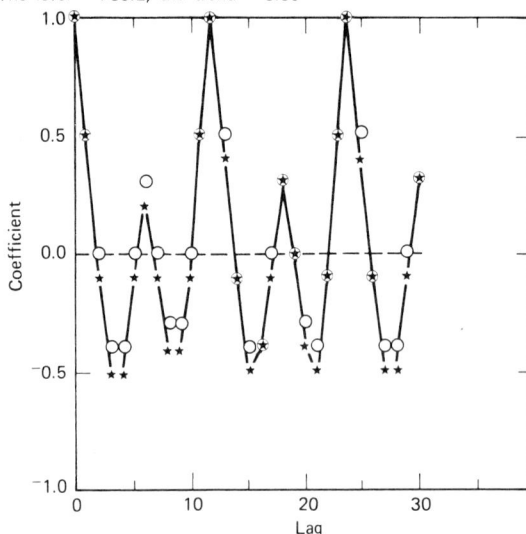

Legend: o = Raw data, * = residuals from centered moving average
Exhibit 5.5A

Component = Trend
72 observations have range 211, mean 169.1, and sigma 45.56
Obs/cycle = 12
The level = 103.6, the trend = 1,821

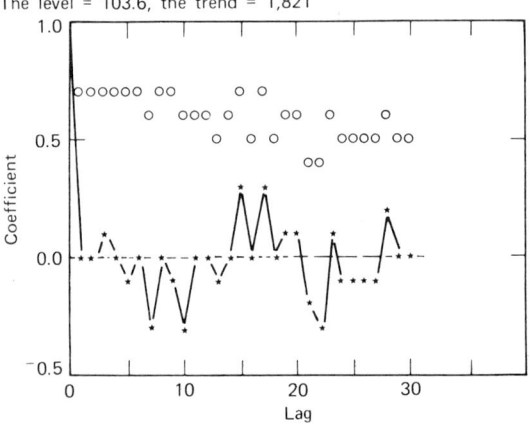

Legend: o = Raw data, * = residuals from centered moving average
Exhibit 5.5B

Plot of the Forecast Each Period to the End of the Season

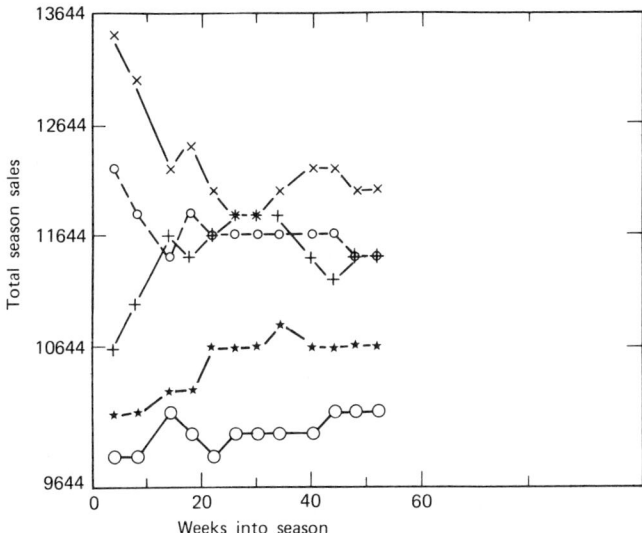

Component = Seasonal.
72 observations have range 1111, mean 908.8, and sigma 258.2.
Observations/season = 12.
The level = 786.2, the trend = 3.36.
Ratios of period data to a centered moving average:

Period	Minimum	Average	Maximum
1	0.861	0.917	0.965
2	0.899	0.941	1.008
3	1.182	1.219	1.286
4	0.830	0.916	1.003
5	0.684	0.787	0.887
6	0.658	0.719	0.787
7	0.480	0.543	0.614
8	0.892	0.967	1.001
9	1.351	1.533	1.661
10	1.260	1.327	1.405
11	1.166	1.215	1.265
12	0.825	0.909	0.973

Season	Symbol	Actual Sales	Forecast Min	Forecast mean	Forecast Max
2	○	10067	9644	9866	10067
3	*	10626	10067	10509	10816
4	○	11382	11382	11636	12174
5	+	11514	10658	11443	11826
6	×	11948	11821	12255	13405

Exhibit 5.6

prior year, as of each month in the season. If the lines were perfectly flat, then the first forecast would agree with the final total. In most cases, the forecasts for the year based on the first two or three months can be quite different from the actual total. This is the primary disadvantage to seasonal forecasting with base indices. Early in the season, when one still has some options in commitments for coverage, the forecasts are quite unstable. Late in the year, the percent done is quite dependable, but by that time it is too late to change production commitments for this season.

Base index numbers do have appeal in that people can readily understand how they work. They do work reasonably well, provided the demand in the low part of the cycle is still a very large number. However, when the expected demand in the low part of the cycle is on the order of the "noise" in the data (the unpredictable random perturbations), the ratios become very unstable. The variance of the reciprocal of a random variable is proportional to the square of the variance of the variable itself. Thus when demand is very low, squaring the variance greatly magnifies the variation in the forecast.

There is one place, however, where a base index makes a lot of sense. That is to represent the known variation introduced by the number of effective selling days in each month. A month with more selling days should be expected to develop larger demand than a short month. Furthermore there is no error of estimating the ratios from statistical data. The calendar is exactly known well in advance, so there is no amplification of the noise.

The calendar can be expressed in ratios, working days, weeks, or any other convenient unit. The computer can convert the data supplied to total 52 weeks per year and then apply suitable ratios to store a calendar, in effective weeks per month, as shown in Exhibit 5.7. In use, data for the current month are "normalized" to a standard month of 4.3333 weeks before the forecasting process. Then the forecast, in units per standard month, is adjusted for each future month by the calendar index ratio for that month.

```
       CALENDAR
WEDNESDAY, AUGUST 4, 1976
EASTERN DAYLIGHT TIME 14:13:24


ACTION = D
                JUN    JUL    AUG    SEP    OCT    NOV    DEC    JAN    FEB    MAR    APR    MAY
WEEKS/MONTH     4.31   4.45   4.45   4.31   4.45   4.31   4.02   4.45   4.02   4.45   4.31   4.45

ACTION = E
NOTHING FILED.

ELAPSED TIME    22.857S
CPU TIME         0.107S
```

Exhibit 5.7

MODELS OF TIME SERIES

5.333 Fourier Series. An alternative representation of seasonal patterns has the advantage of being very stable, even to the point of representing net returns when necessary. It is also harder for people to comprehend what is going on. In the six successive parts of Exhibits 5.8 to 5.10, the 12 months are represented by the dark dots. Points are plotted at 48 intervals, to give some continuity to the graph, but only the heavy dots would be used for forecasting at monthly intervals. Nyquist has proved that with 12 observations per cycle, no more than six frequencies are ever required.

Figure 5.8 top shows the fundamental sine wave that goes through one complete cycle in 12 observations. Each successive graph adds the effect of another sine wave, with a pair of coefficients that control the phase angle and amplitude of a sine wave that goes through one more complete cycle in a 12-month year.

Figure 5.10 bottom shows the profile that has been developed with all six possible frequencies, expressed by 11 coefficients. (The twelfth one is theoretically present but in all cases it is zero, so it can be omitted from the expressions.)

The French mathematician Fourier proved in 1822 that any series that shows periodic oscillations, of whatever pattern, can be represented by a sufficient series of sine waves. For example, the fundamental pitch of a musical instrument is governed by the frequency of the slowest sine wave used to represent the sound vibrations. The characteristic overtones that enable one to distinguish a violin from an oboe, both playing middle C, can be represented by several sine waves of higher and higher frequencies. With a sampled-data series, like demand at regular intervals throughout the year, Nyquist's theorem says how many terms are sufficient—one pair for each frequency up to half the number of samples in a cycle.

The Fourier models used quite widely for statistical forecasting now are not intended for people to compute, but can easily be programmed on a computer. The biggest advantage is that the forecast is stable at all parts of the cycle. The effective correction for each month of the year is based on information from all months. This averaging process reduces the sensitivity to random fluctuations in one particular month of the year. The base index approach is far more susceptible to these random fluctuations.

5.34 Fitting a Model

The process of finding the values of the coefficients in the model to represent a particular series is illustrated in Exhibit 5.11. The series itself is listed in the leftmost column of the table. Then the rest of the columns are standard fitting functions: the first, all 1's, represent the level of demand. The next, starting at −71 down to 0 for the most recent observation,

Coefficients
□:
162.2 ⁻109.7

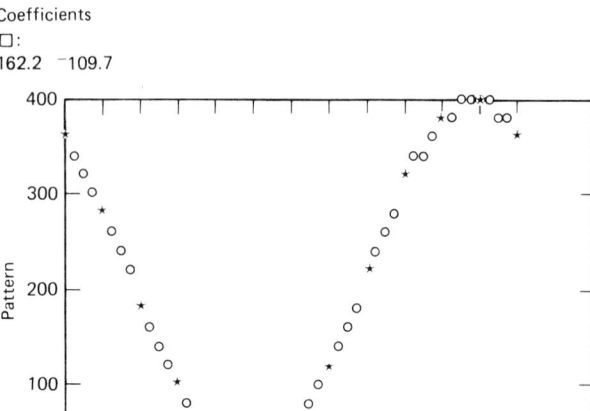

Plot another pattern? Yes

Coefficients
□:
162.2 ⁻109.7 ⁻222.3 ⁻115.8

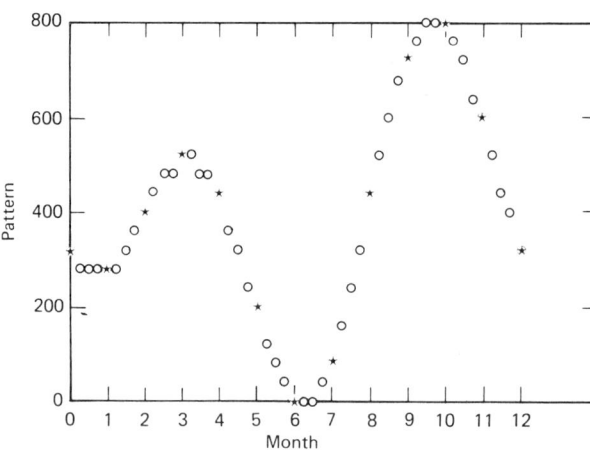

Exhibit 5.8

Plot another pattern? Yes

Coefficients
☐:
162.2 ⁻109.7 ⁻222.3 ⁻30.04 39.52 85.37 ⁻27.44

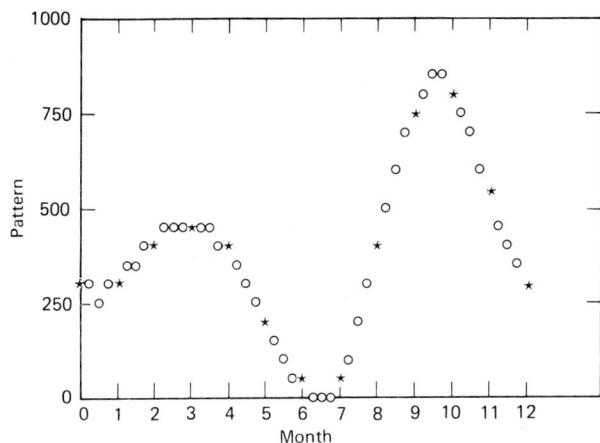

Plot another pattern? Yes

Coefficients
☐:
162.2 ⁻109.7 ⁻222.3 ⁻115.8 ⁻30.04 39.52

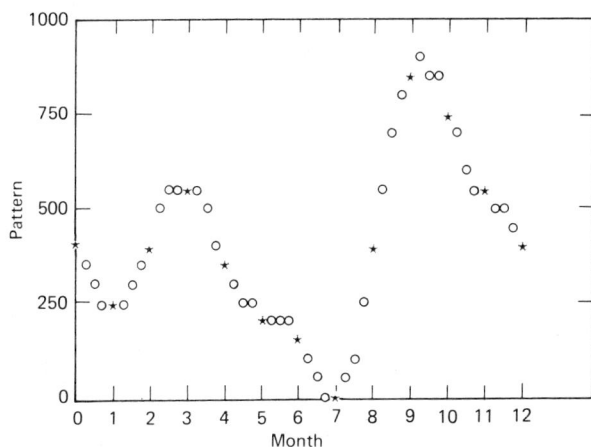

Exhibit 5.9

Coefficients
☐:
162.2 ⁻109.7 ⁻222.3 ⁻115.8 ⁻30.04 39.52 85.37 ⁻27.44 ⁻47.66 5.771

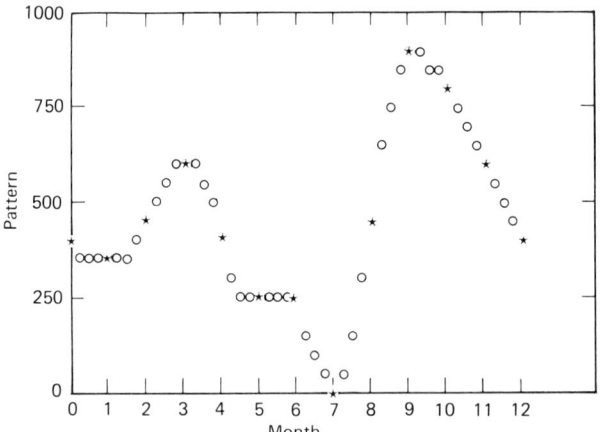

Plot another pattern? Yes

Coefficients
☐:
162.2 ⁻109.7 ⁻222.3 ⁻115.8 ⁻30.04 39.52 85.37 ⁻27.44 ⁻47.66 5.771 ⁻33.37

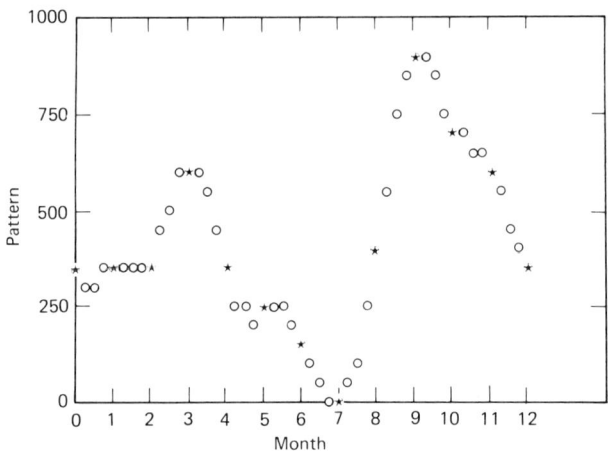

Exhibit 5.10

COMPONENT = PROMOTE
NUMBER OF TERMS = 10

SERIES   FITTING FUNCTIONS

186	1	⁻71	0.866	0.500	0.5	0.866	0	1	⁻0.5	0.866
258	1	⁻70	0.500	0.866	⁻0.5	0.866	⁻1	0	0.5	⁻0.866
216	1	⁻69	0.000	1.000	⁻1.0	0.000	0	⁻1	1.0	0.000
210	1	⁻68	⁻0.500	0.866	⁻0.5	⁻0.866	1	0	⁻0.5	0.866
57	1	⁻67	⁻0.866	0.500	0.5	⁻0.866	0	1	⁻0.5	⁻0.866
204	1	⁻66	⁻1.000	0.000	1.0	0.000	⁻1	0	1.0	0.000
185	1	⁻65	⁻0.866	⁻0.500	0.5	0.866	0	⁻1	⁻0.5	0.866
12	1	⁻64	⁻0.500	⁻0.866	⁻0.5	0.866	1	0	⁻0.5	⁻0.866
106	1	⁻63	0.000	⁻1.000	⁻1.0	0.000	0	1	1.0	0.000
207	1	⁻62	0.500	⁻0.866	⁻0.5	0.866	⁻1	0	⁻0.5	0.866
71	1	⁻61	0.866	⁻0.500	0.5	⁻0.866	0	⁻1	⁻0.5	⁻0.866
240	1	⁻60	1.000	0.000	1.0	0.000	1	0	1.0	0.000
263	1	⁻59	0.866	0.500	0.5	0.866	0	1	⁻0.5	0.866
152	1	⁻58	0.500	0.866	⁻0.5	0.866	⁻1	0	⁻0.5	⁻0.866
335	1	⁻57	0.000	1.000	⁻1.0	0.000	0	⁻1	1.0	0.000
249	1	⁻56	⁻0.500	0.866	⁻0.5	⁻0.866	1	0	⁻0.5	0.866
107	1	⁻55	⁻0.866	0.500	0.5	⁻0.866	0	1	⁻0.5	⁻0.866
177	1	⁻54	⁻1.000	0.000	1.0	0.000	⁻1	0	1.0	0.000
183	1	⁻53	⁻0.866	⁻0.500	0.5	0.866	0	⁻1	⁻0.5	0.866
61	1	⁻52	0.500	⁻0.866	⁻0.5	0.866	1	0	⁻0.5	⁻0.866
196	1	⁻51	0.000	⁻1.000	⁻1.0	0.000	0	1	1.0	0.000
195	1	⁻26	0.500	⁻0.866	⁻0.5	⁻0.866	⁻1	0	⁻0.5	0.866
183	1	⁻25	0.866	0.500	0.5	0.866	0	⁻1	⁻0.5	⁻0.866
256	1	⁻24	1.000	0.000	1.0	0.000	1	0	1.0	0.000
235	1	⁻23	0.866	0.500	0.5	0.866	0	1	⁻0.5	0.866
131	1	⁻22	0.500	0.866	⁻0.5	0.866	⁻1	0	⁻0.5	⁻0.866
164	1	⁻21	0.000	1.000	⁻1.0	0.000	0	⁻1	1.0	0.000
181	1	⁻20	⁻0.500	0.866	⁻0.5	⁻0.866	1	0	⁻0.5	0.866
129	1	⁻19	⁻0.866	0.500	0.5	⁻0.866	0	1	⁻0.5	⁻0.866
87	1	⁻18	⁻1.000	0.000	1.0	0.000	⁻1	0	1.0	0.000
231	1	⁻17	⁻0.866	⁻0.500	0.5	0.866	0	⁻1	⁻0.5	0.866
54	1	⁻16	⁻0.500	⁻0.866	⁻0.5	0.866	1	0	⁻0.5	⁻0.866
166	1	⁻15	0.000	⁻1.000	⁻1.0	0.000	0	1	1.0	0.000
267	1	⁻14	0.500	⁻0.866	⁻0.5	⁻0.866	⁻1	0	⁻0.5	0.866
79	1	⁻13	0.866	⁻0.500	0.5	⁻0.866	0	⁻1	⁻0.5	⁻0.866
194	1	⁻12	1.000	0.000	1.0	0.000	1	0	1.0	0.000
293	1	⁻11	0.866	0.500	0.5	0.866	0	1	⁻0.5	0.866
227	1	⁻10	0.500	0.866	⁻0.5	0.866	⁻1	0	⁻0.5	⁻0.866
257	1	⁻9	0.000	1.000	⁻1.0	0.000	0	⁻1	1.0	0.000
276	1	⁻8	⁻0.500	0.866	⁻0.5	⁻0.866	1	0	⁻0.5	0.866
50	1	⁻7	⁻0.866	0.500	0.5	⁻0.866	0	1	⁻0.5	⁻0.866
135	1	⁻6	⁻1.000	0.000	1.0	0.000	⁻1	0	1.0	0.000
92	1	⁻5	⁻0.866	⁻0.500	0.5	0.866	0	⁻1	⁻0.5	0.866
4	1	⁻4	⁻0.500	⁻0.866	⁻0.5	0.866	1	0	⁻0.5	⁻0.866
67	1	⁻3	0.000	⁻1.000	⁻1.0	0.000	0	1	1.0	0.000
148	1	⁻2	0.500	⁻0.866	⁻0.5	⁻0.866	⁻1	0	⁻0.5	0.866
57	1	⁻1	0.866	⁻0.500	0.5	⁻0.866	0	⁻1	⁻0.5	⁻0.866
331	1	0	1.000	0.000	1.0	0.000	1	0	1.0	0.000

Exhibit 5.11

represent the trend in that level. (Note that there is a break in the table, to get it all on one page. It should be easy, however, to see how the missing figures would be generated.) The next pair of columns represent a cosine wave and a sine wave, displaced one from the other by three observations, and going through one cycle per 12 observations. The next pair of columns skips every other value, and hence is a cosine and sine wave going through two cycles per 12 months. Successive columns to the right are generated by skipping additional values, to make them go through more cycles per year, but they are still essentially the sine waves shown in Exhibits 5.8 to 5.10. For computational convenience we represent the two coefficients by a cosine and a sine, rather than the phase angle and amplitude, but one pair of characteristics can always be computed from the other.

The coefficients in the model are found by any standard multiple regression program for fitting the series to the fitting functions. The "least-squares" process ensures that the sum of the squares of the differences between this profile and the actual series will be smaller than for any other set of coefficients with these fitting functions. Since the fitting functions are orthogonal—not correlated with each other—we can add more terms as necessary to represent the model, without having to recompute previous values of the coefficients.

The list of values of the fitting functions is a table of program constants that can be generated once and stored.

The coefficients in the model can be used at any time to generate the forecast for the future. Exhibit 5.12 shows the coefficients, in the leftmost column, with values of the fitting functions extending into future time. In this exhibit time runs from left to right, rather than down the page as in Exhibit 5.11. To get a forecast multiply each coefficient by the values of the fitting function for each of the time periods in which you want a forecast. The results of that multiplication are shown in the second part of the display. Then the forecast for each future period is just the column sum, as shown in the vector labeled "totals."

This is the way that the statistical forecast, shown in Exhibit 3.1, is computed at any time: the matrix multiplication of a vector of coefficients which are special to a given item and a universal table of fitting functions for the periods for which a forecast is to be developed.

Exhibit 5.13 uses the same coefficients, but sets some of the "small" values to zero, effectively removing them from the model. Are the two forecasts significantly different from each other?

5.4 MODEL SELECTION

The foregoing discussion showed what a forecast model is and how the coefficients are computed and used to generate a forecast. In this section we

COEFS

157.600	
−0.291	
32.900	
46.200	
−7.290	
−0.937	
−11.403	
−14.820	
32.540	
57.810	

FITTING FUNCTIONS

	1	2	3	4	5	6	7	8	9	10	11	12
	1.000	1.000	1.000	1.000	1.000	1.000	1.000	1.000	1.000	1.000	1.000	1.000
	1.000	2.000	3.000	4.000	5.000	6.000	7.000	8.000	9.000	10.000	11.000	12.000
	0.866	0.500	0.000	−0.500	−0.866	−1.000	−0.866	−0.500	0.000	0.500	0.866	1.000
	0.500	0.866	1.000	0.866	0.500	0.000	−0.500	−0.866	−1.000	−0.866	−0.500	0.000
	0.500	−0.500	−1.000	−0.500	0.500	1.000	0.500	−0.500	−1.000	−0.500	0.500	1.000
	0.866	0.866	0.000	−0.866	−0.866	0.000	0.866	0.866	0.000	−0.866	−0.866	0.000
	0.000	−1.000	0.000	1.000	0.000	−1.000	0.000	1.000	0.000	−1.000	0.000	1.000
	−1.000	0.000	1.000	0.000	−1.000	0.000	1.000	0.000	−1.000	0.000	1.000	0.000
	−0.500	−0.500	1.000	−0.500	−0.500	1.000	−0.500	−0.500	1.000	−0.500	−0.500	1.000
	0.866	0.866	0.000	−0.866	−0.866	0.000	0.866	0.866	0.000	−0.866	−0.866	0.000

MULTIPLICATION

	1	2	3	4	5	6	7	8	9	10	11	12
	157.60	157.60	157.60	157.60	157.60	157.60	157.60	157.60	157.60	157.60	157.60	157.60
	−0.29	−0.58	−0.87	−1.16	−1.45	−1.75	−2.04	−2.33	−2.62	−2.91	−3.20	−3.49
	28.49	16.45	0.00	−16.45	−28.49	−32.90	−28.49	−16.45	0.00	16.45	28.49	32.90
	23.10	40.01	46.20	40.01	23.10	0.00	−23.10	−40.01	−46.20	−40.01	−23.10	0.00
	−3.65	3.64	7.29	3.65	−3.64	−7.29	−3.65	3.64	7.29	3.65	−3.64	−7.29
	−0.81	−0.81	0.00	0.81	0.81	0.00	−0.81	−0.81	0.00	0.81	0.81	0.00
	0.00	11.40	0.00	−11.40	0.00	11.40	0.00	−11.40	0.00	11.40	0.00	−11.40
	−14.82	0.00	14.82	0.00	−14.82	0.00	14.82	0.00	−14.82	0.00	−14.82	0.00
	−16.27	−16.27	32.54	−16.27	−16.27	32.54	−16.27	−16.27	32.54	−16.27	−16.27	32.54
	50.06	50.06	0.00	−50.06	−50.06	0.00	50.06	−50.06	0.00	50.06	−50.06	0.00

TOTALS

1	2	3	4	5	6	7	8	9	10	11	12
223.42	161.38	257.58	206.84	66.76	159.61	148.13	23.91	133.79	180.78	105.44	200.85

Exhibit 5.12

FCSTCALC
COEFFICIENTS = 157.6 0 32.9 46.2 0 0 -11.403 -14.82 32.54 57.81

COEFS   FITTING FUNCTIONS

		1	2	3	4	5	6	7	8	9	10	11	12
157.600		1.000	1.000	1.000	1.000	1.000	1.000	1.000	1.000	1.000	1.000	1.000	1.000
0.000		1.000	2.000	3.000	4.000	5.000	6.000	7.000	8.000	9.000	10.000	11.000	12.000
32.900		0.866	0.500	0.000	-0.500	-0.866	-1.000	-0.866	-0.500	0.000	0.500	0.866	1.000
46.200		0.500	0.866	1.000	0.866	0.500	0.000	-0.500	-0.866	-1.000	-0.866	-0.500	0.000
0.000		0.500	-0.500	-1.000	-0.500	0.500	1.000	0.500	-0.500	-1.000	-0.500	0.500	1.000
0.000		0.866	0.866	0.000	-0.866	-0.866	0.000	0.866	0.866	0.000	-0.866	-0.866	0.000
-11.403		0.000	0.000	0.000	1.000	0.000	-1.000	0.000	1.000	0.000	-1.000	0.000	1.000
-14.820		1.000	-1.000	1.000	-1.000	1.000	-1.000	1.000	-1.000	1.000	-1.000	1.000	-1.000
32.540		-0.500	-0.500	1.000	-0.500	-0.500	1.000	-0.500	-0.500	1.000	-0.500	-0.500	1.000
57.810		0.866	-0.866	0.000	0.866	-0.866	0.000	0.866	-0.866	0.000	0.866	-0.866	0.000

MULTIPLICATION

	1	2	3	4	5	6	7	8	9	10	11	12
	157.60	157.60	157.60	157.60	157.60	157.60	157.60	157.60	157.60	157.60	157.60	157.60
	0.00	0.00	0.00	0.00	0.00	0.00	0.00	0.00	0.00	0.00	0.00	0.00
	28.49	16.45	0.00	-16.45	-28.49	-32.90	-28.49	-16.45	0.00	16.45	28.49	32.90
	23.10	40.01	46.20	40.01	23.10	0.00	-23.10	-40.01	-46.20	-40.01	-23.10	0.00
	0.00	0.00	0.00	0.00	0.00	0.00	0.00	0.00	0.00	0.00	0.00	0.00
	0.00	0.00	0.00	0.00	0.00	0.00	0.00	0.00	0.00	0.00	0.00	0.00
	0.00	0.00	0.00	-11.40	0.00	11.40	0.00	-11.40	0.00	11.40	0.00	-11.40
	-14.82	14.82	-14.82	14.82	-14.82	14.82	-14.82	14.82	-14.82	14.82	-14.82	14.82
	-16.27	-16.27	32.54	-16.27	-16.27	32.54	-16.27	-16.27	32.54	-16.27	-16.27	32.54
	50.06	-50.06	0.00	50.06	-50.06	0.00	50.06	-50.06	0.00	50.06	-50.06	0.00

TOTALS

1	2	3	4	5	6	7	8	9	10	11	12
228.17	159.13	251.16	203.55	71.05	168.64	154.62	23.40	129.12	179.24	111.48	211.64

Exhibit 5.13

MODEL SELECTION

deal with the question of how many of the possible terms to have in the model. The minimum number of terms is two, for level and trend. The maximum number is 13, for level and trend, and six pairs of seasonal coefficients, except that the last member of the last pair is always zero and therefore can be omitted. The possible numbers of terms in a model are 2, 4, 6, 8, 10, 12, and 13. (Note that with weekly forecast revision there would be more terms.) Which number should we use for a given series? Several program products on the market have implemented the adaptive smoothing, with Fourier series, on the basis of my 1963 book. They have "left that decision up to the customer," especially since it takes a good deal of computer time to simulate the different possibilities for each series. The decisions not only can be programmed, but can be made highly automatic and efficient to reach better decisions than users usually can, since the same logic can be applied to all series in a very short time.

Exhibits 5.14 to 5.16 deal with each of the sample series. The first step in analyzing the data is to form a moving average of 12 successive observations. The moving average is then moved back so that the value is assigned to the middle of the 12 months. The idea is that if there is any secular trend, there are six months after the average with the trend in one direction, and six months before with the trend in the opposite direction. The effects of trend average out over that year.

The centered moving average is subtracted from the raw data. The residual difference then has no effect of trend (or of level for that matter). Differences corresponding to the same month in successive years are grouped together, as they would be for a base index. The asterisk shows the average of these differences over all the years available, six years in these examples. The large circle indicates the largest difference for that month in any year and the small circle shows the smallest difference for that month in any year.

In Exhibit 5.14 the range between the circles representing extremes from year to year is much smaller than the range between the highest average (for September) and the smallest average (for July). The contribution to variation in the data that can be attributed to months is much larger than the contribution due to years. Hence one would conclude that the series does have a seasonal pattern, and that the pattern repeats consistently from year to year.

Contrast the graph in Exhibit 5.15. In the second case, although there is some "profile" indicated by the line joining the asterisks, the range from high to low is somewhat less than the range for a given month from year to year. February, on the average, is somewhat high. But in some years February was very high and in other years February was low. Hence the knowledge that the month we are trying to forecast is February won't help

Differences from a 12-Point Centered Moving Average

Component = Seasonal
72 observations have range 1111, mean 908.8, and sigma 258.2
Obs/cycle = 12
The level = 786.2, the trend = 3.36
Plot the profile? Yes
Differences from a 12-point centered moving average

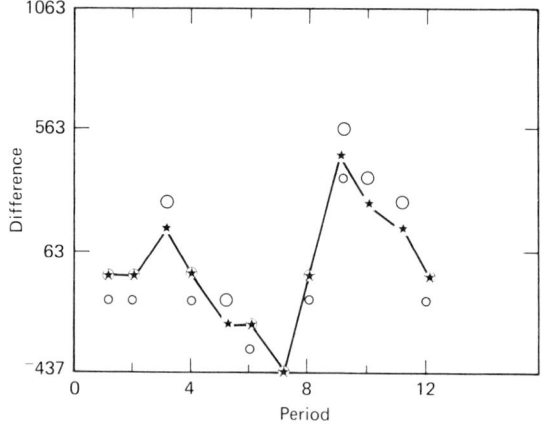

Model Terms	Seasonal Amplitude	Standard Deviation
2		346.390
4	195.557	288.136
6	250.125	131.485
8	49.841	122.613
10	89.520	78.819
12	48.342	60.126
13	33.590	47.954 ←

Exhibit 5.14

much—we don't know whether next February will be one of the high or low ones.

This analysis is purely subjective, to try to help the reader form an accurate mental image of what the computer programs do. The real analysis is shown in the table below the graph. There is a row in the table for each of the seven possible numbers of terms in the model. (If the forecasts were revised every week, every two weeks, or every four weeks, there would be more lines in the table, because there are larger numbers of frequencies that can be distinguished up to the Nyquist frequency.) The middle column of the table is the amplitude of the seasonal frequency that

MODEL SELECTION

was added to get that number of terms. For example, the amplitude of the fundamental frequency (one cycle per year) in Exhibit 5.14 is 196—the square root of the sum of the squares of the coefficients of the cosine and the sine wave at that frequency. Adding the sine wave that goes through two cycles per year adds an amplitude of 250, and so on. The rightmost column is a measure of the standard deviation of the residual differences between the raw data and the model with the specified number of terms.

In general we would like to pick a model that gives us the smallest standard deviation. In Exhibit 5.14 that is a 13-term model, which reduces the standard deviation to only 48 from 346 for a nonseasonal model.

Differences from a 12-Point Centered Moving Average

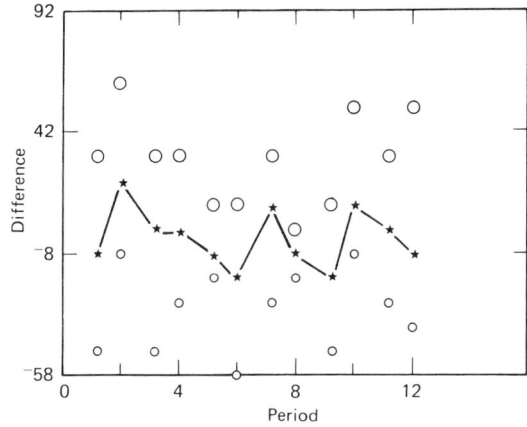

```
Component = Trend
72 observations have range 211, mean 169.1, and sigma 45.56
Obs/cycle = 12
The level = 103.6, the trend = 1.821
Plot the profile? Yes
Differences from a 12-point centered moving average
```

Model Terms	Seasonal Amplitude	Standard Deviation
2		26.577 ←
4	3.726	26.691
6	3.788	26.802
8	9.325	25.357
10	8.667	24.010
12	5.857	23.548
13	1.590	23.682

Exhibit 5.15

There is an exception, however. The amplitude must be large enough to be significant. In Exhibit 5.15 the absolute minimum standard deviation is 23.548 for a 12-term model. But the amplitude of the sine wave is only 5.9 for the last frequency added to the model. The amplitude is likely to be spurious. The rule used to accept a model is that the amplitude must be at least half as large as the standard deviation that would be achieved if the terms were included. The amplitude 5.9 is less than half of 23.5, so we reject the 12-term model, and start moving up the table. In all cases the seasonal amplitudes are too small to be taken seriously, so we are left with the two-term model. That is, this series is judged to be nonseasonal, although there is a slight "profile."

In Chapter 12 we consider some special techniques of inventory control for items with "lumpy" demand. Lumpy demand is defined as a series where the standard deviation, after fitting the best possible model, is still larger than the level. In these cases the model is set with one term only, for the average.

Exhibit 5.16 shows a series where the 12-term model gives the lowest standard deviation, but the amplitude for the fifth frequency is too small, so we move back up to the 10-term model, which has almost as small a standard deviation, and a clearly significant amplitude.

Any time you see that the analysis has selected a 10-term model, it is a clear indication of some quarterly phenomenon, often a promotional calendar or a bonus scheme, or a four-, four-, five-week calendar that you didn't take into account in the effective weeks per month. The reason is the 10-term model includes a level, a trend, and four pairs of seasonal terms. The fourth pair has a large amplitude. But the fourth frequency is a sine wave that goes through four cycles per year, or quarters. In the example in Exhibit 5.16 there is some sort of a strong fundamental frequency, on which is superimposed a quarterly cycle.

5.5 SCREEN FOR OUTLIERS

Sometimes when the analysis classifies the demand as "lumpy," it may be caused by one or two months of exceptional demand in the history. A strike, followed by exceptional shipments, or inclusion of a special export or government order that should have been treated as a scheduled backlog will increase the standard deviation of the residual differences. It is a good idea to screen the history for these outliers, looking for instances where the actual demand in one or more months is more than four standard deviations away from the model, evaluated in past time. If such outliers are detected, you may want to modify the record of history more fairly to reflect normal

SYSTEM PROCEDURES   101

Component = Promote
72 observations have range 331, mean 168, and sigma 78.66
Obs/cycle = 12
The level = 183, the trend = ⁻0.3578
Plot the profile? Yes
Differences from a 12-point centered moving average

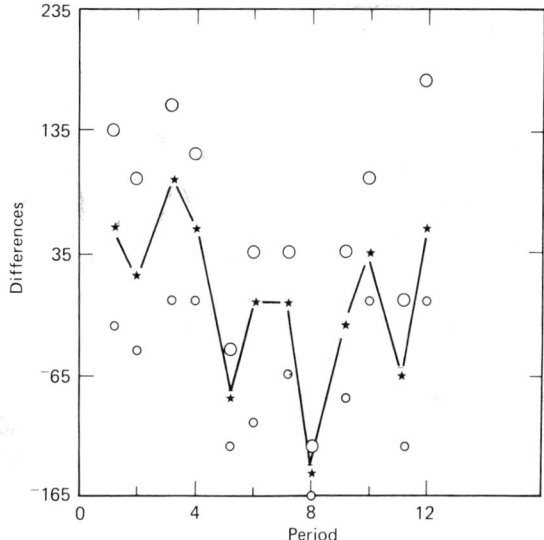

Model Terms	Seasonal Amplitude	Standard Deviation
2		101.874
4	57.396	84.826
6	7.552	85.739
8	18.571	84.812
10	66.401	48.009 ←
12	11.699	47.090
13	3.234	47.352

Exhibit 5.16

patterns of demand. The demand history used as a basis for statistical forecasting should be a reasonable representation of normal usage. It is not necessarily the same thing as actual sales as recorded for accounting and auditing purposes. As we have seen in Section I, and will see more in Chapter 7, there are several other sources of significant demand aside from that portion of the sales that are to be forecast from a statistical model. Therefore if abnormal history is adjusted and the models are fit again, often a reasonable adjustment will eliminate a fair number of the "lumpy" items. It is unusual to get rid of all of them, and hence we need some special techniques for controlling the inventory of such items.

5.6 SYSTEM PROCEDURES

The discussion so far has been directed at the general principles of what a model is, how it is used, and the rationale programmed to make an automatic determination of the number of terms to be included. The program to process demand history and find the model, with the initial values of the coefficients, was illustrated in Exhibit 3.5. Note that one of the questions was "Maximum number of terms in the model =," which provides the user with an opportunity to override the automatic selection and deliberately use simpler models. Another question is "Maximum number of months of history =," which allows the user to fit a model only to recent history, even though there is more information on the file.

Exhibit 5.17 is a flow chart indicating the major choices and options that can be considered in fitting a model to a time series. The basic loop starts at the top, checks to see if there is another item to be processed, and exits when the end of the list is reached. The first decision is whether the item has any history posted. If there is no history on the file, we post an exception counter and branch by SW6. It is possible to use a "plugged level" to set up an initial forecast. There is provision for locking an item out so that there is no smoothing. If that flag is encountered in the item master record, another exception counter is posted, and control passes to the beginning of the loop. One common use of locked smoothing is for subordinate materials and parts that have assembly usage only, that is, no direct demand. Since all of the demand is generated as dependent demand by the explosion process (Chapter 14), it can bypass forecasting entirely.

When we find an item that has history and is to be forecast, the next check is on the date at which the product is identified for discontinuation. That limits the forecast horizon. Each item can have a different forecast horizon, depending on its lead time and level code, but if the item is flagged to be discontinued within the ordinary horizon, the horizon is automatically moved forward, so that forecasts will not be generated past the discontinue date.

Now we look at the amount of history. If there are 12 or more months of history, the least-squares fit and analysis of the number of terms (Exhibit 5.11) proceeds automatically. The exception is that with only 24 months of history, the model is limited to a maximum of four terms—only the fundamental cycle is allowed. With more than 36 months of history, any of the seven possible models could be chosen.

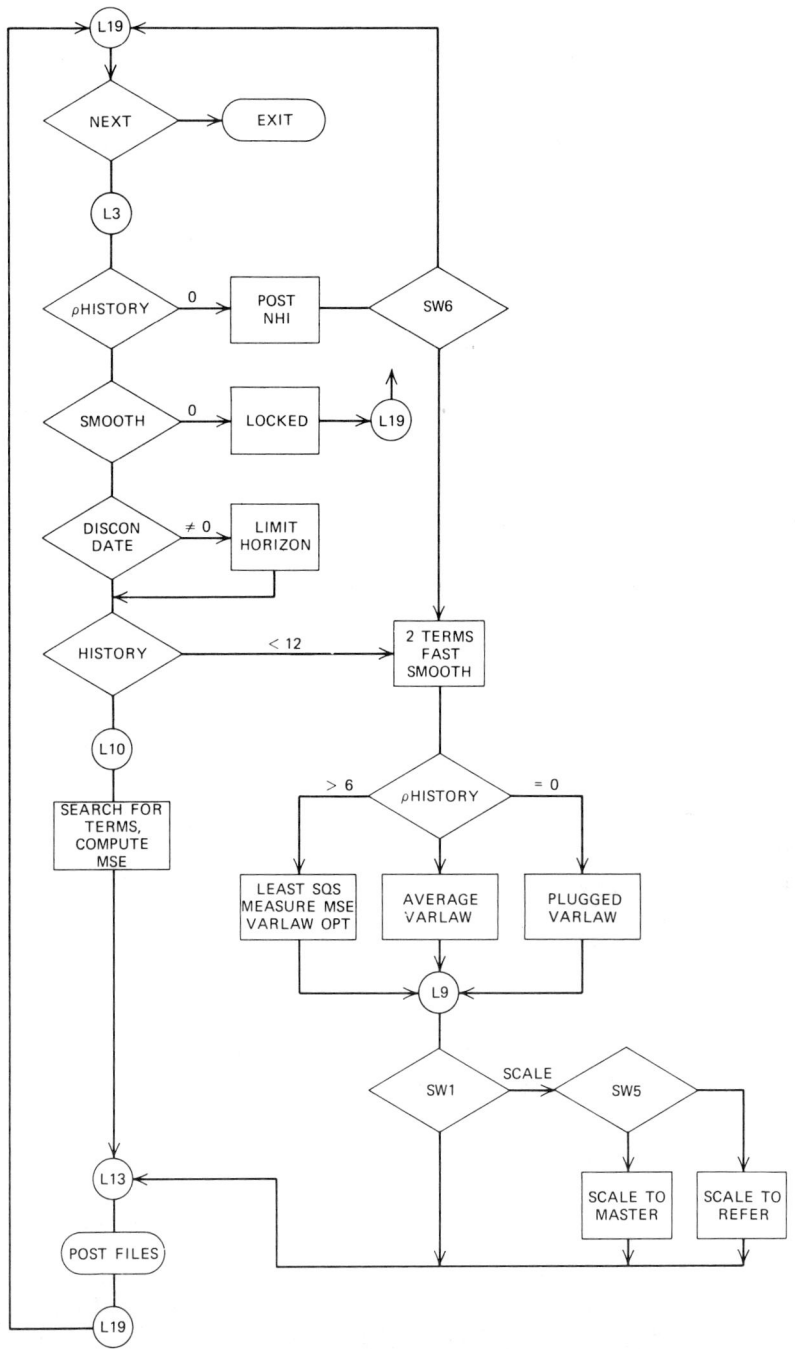

Exhibit 5.17

When there are fewer than 12 months of history, the first step is to force a two-term (nonseasonal) model. With 7 to 11 months of history, the level and trend are computed by a least-squares fit. The mean square error (variance) is measured from the residuals between the data and the model (see Chapter 8 for a discussion of forecast errors), but the measured mean square error can be overridden if the user has elected to use the variance law, which assigns a value for the mean square error that is typical of the whole inventory for items with that level of demand.

If there are from 1 to 5 months of history, the level is taken as the average of the data, the trend is set to zero, and the mean square error is determined from the variance law.

An exception to the "no history" branch, just after junction L3, is when the user has "plugged" an average into the item master record, as for a new item, which can be used to set up a forecast. In that case the level is set equal to the plugged value, the trend is zero, and the mean square error is taken from the variance law.

After point L9, there are three possible routes, all of which apply to items with less than 11 months of history. The switch SW1 can bypass any scaling entirely. If some form of scaling has been selected, then SW5 determines whether the reference item is the master location for the SKU or a general reference item.

Scaling implies that the item does belong to a product family that is known in advance to have a seasonal pattern, represented by more than two terms. The level of demand for the new item has been established by a least-squares line, the average, or a plugged value. The computer can retrieve the coefficients for the reference item from the data base and adjust all the coefficients in the model in proportion to the ratio of the level for the item being implemented to the level of the reference item.

The general reference item will select any item in the file. But sometimes a product is stocked at a new satellite location, where there is no history. In that case the obvious reference is the master warehouse location for the same product, which has the national forecast. In either case the seasonal profile is taken from the national forecast of the reference item.

5.7 NEW ITEMS

When new items are to be set up for materials management there may be no history at all. For a brand-new product, we need a forecast today to start the manufacturing plan, but the product won't be on the market for several months, so there can't possibly be any demand to be recorded as history for several months. In the item master record there is provision for storing the effectivity date, which can be well in the future. In this case, a plugged level

42-258-018	PUMP											
	LEVEL	TREND	3	4								
MASTER	82.50	3.86	27.39	3.71								
INDIANAPOLIS, IN	6.97	0.25	1.60	0.33								
ATLANTA, GA	6.10	0.30	2.60	0.38								
NEW YORK, NY	23.17	1.09	8.74	0.78								
DENVER, CO	46.26	2.23	14.45	2.22								

COEFFICIENTS TO BE CHANGED =

32-793-708	SHIPPER											
	LEVEL	TREND	3	4	5	6	7	8	9	10		
MASTER	34.12	0.80	9.44	-1.01	-4.29	-0.44	-1.10	-2.89	-3.13	-0.80		
INDIANAPOLIS, IN	0.11	-0.32	0.99	-0.31	-2.75	-0.35	-1.46	-1.09	-1.73	-1.75		
ATLANTA, GA	6.10	0.21	1.59	-0.98	0.19	-0.44	-0.31	-0.33	-0.34	0.55		
NEW YORK, NY	27.81	0.90	6.76	2.30	-1.83	0.35	0.58	-1.47	-1.16	0.40		

COEFFICIENTS TO BE CHANGED =

46-792-777	SHIPPER											
	LEVEL	TREND	3	4	5	6						
MASTER	28.80	0.77	5.97	4.36	-1.02	3.33						
INDIANAPOLIS, IN	1.93	-0.10	0.38	0.71	-0.93	1.07						
LOS ANGELES, CA	7.22	0.24	1.48	0.85	-0.14	0.49						
NEW YORK, NY	19.64	0.63	4.11	2.80	0.05	1.77						

COEFFICIENTS TO BE CHANGED =

32-791-549	GEAR											
	LEVEL	TREND	3	4	5	6	7	8	9	10	11	12
MASTER	159.00	3.24	27.77	14.99	9.99	45.50	-0.84	-16.22	-1.55	10.68	29.26	-16.32
INDIANAPOLIS, IN	25.59	-1.08	9.54	-5.47	-4.00	15.06	-9.59	-5.16	-6.21	5.09	15.75	-8.16
LOS ANGELES, CA	133.40	4.32	18.21	20.46	13.97	30.44	8.73	-11.07	7.74	5.59	13.50	-8.16

COEFFICIENTS TO BE CHANGED =

Exhibit 5.18

can be provided. The mean square error is obtained from the variance law. The smoothing rate is locked as a "don't smooth" item, since there will be no more information until the product hits the market. The final step in processing a forecast model for these items is to plug the initial months with zeros until the release date. The forecast beyond the release date becomes a realistic picture of what we expect to sell, but we don't want the model to project demand for months before the product actually gets to the market.

See Chapter 7 on marketing intelligence for estimating the quantity needed to fill the pipeline for a new product.

When all the processing has been done to set up forecast models for a group of products, one can inspect the coefficients as in Exhibit 5.18.

For four successive items the numbers of terms selected range from 4 (simple seasonal) to 12 (nearly the most complex profile). The same number of terms is provided in the model for every location, although the values of the coefficients do not need to be in any relation from one location to another. Thus there can be different trends, different seasonal patterns, and different levels of demand for the same product in different regions.

Once the values of the coefficients are stored in the data base, then the statistical forecasts can be computed and reported as in Exhibit 3.1.

If forecasts are provided from the user's own system the file space can be reduced, since it is not necessary for other applications to distinguish among marketing intelligence and scheduled demand, nor is it necessary to store the coefficients and the history.

CHAPTER **6**

Revising the Forecast

Forecasts are revised periodically, such as once a month or once a week, to take account of current information about demand. The process is one of recomputing values for the coefficients in the model. Since the forecast is computed for time into the future from "now," one part of the revision is simply to move the origin in time forward one period. For example, if last month the level was 100 and the trend five per month, this month we would expect the level to be 105 (and the trend still to be five). The other part of the revision modifies the coefficients slightly to take account of the forecast error. If there was no error, the coefficients stay the same, and hence the forecast for a given period is the same as it was the last time it was computed. If the demand was above the forecast, then the coefficients are modified slightly to raise all future forecasts, and conversely if demand was below forecast.

It is not necessary to proceed as described in Chapter 5 to compute the values of the coefficients by a least-squares fit of the model to all of the history. And yet one wants the forecast to be a least-squares fit to that history.

All the techniques of revising a statistical forecast in vogue for repetitive demand forecasting are weighted least-squares computations. That is, the simple least-squares fit of a model to data computes coefficients so that the differences between the data and the resulting forecasts, when squared and added over all observations, will be as small a sum as possible. In a weighted least-squares scheme, the squared differences are assigned different weights, depending on how long ago the observation was, and one wants the sum of the weighted squares to be as small as possible.

All statistical forecasts are simply descriptions of what has already happened. The forecast is a model of past demand, evaluated at a future time. Thus it is impossible for a statistical forecast to predict changes in the pattern of the series before they occur. We deal in Chapter 7 with marketing intelligence to anticipate changes in the pattern. Attempts to evaluate one technique of forecasting against another may be futile—there will be differences, to be sure, but those differences represent more characteristics of the time series used in the test than they do the forecasting technique. If the model chosen properly represents the significant variation in the past (i.e., including trends when they are present and seasonal profiles when necessary) then the resulting forecasts will be good representations of future demand only when the time series continues to exhibit those characteristics.

Exhibit 3.7 shows the appearance at the terminal of the forecasting revision process with demand filter trips (Chapter 8) and tracking signals. Exhibit 3.8 illustrates the evaluation of marketing intelligence.

6.1 WEIGHTS USED IN SMOOTHING

There are many different techniques of "smoothing," or of revising the coefficients in the model in response to new demand information. They can be characterized by the difference in the pattern of weights assigned to the squared differences for which the sum is to be minimized.

1. Uniform weights reduce to simple least squares where the same weight is assigned to the error in each past observation. For a simple horizontal model, this generates the common moving average forecast.
2. Exponentially declining weights assign importance to past errors rather like compound interest. If the weight on the current observation is 1, the weight on the preceding one might be 0.9, the one behind that $0.9 \times 0.9 = 0.81$, and so on. The weights decline with age, so that the forecast is more representative of current demand and less influenced by old demand.
3. Adaptive weights, suggested by Derek Trigg in England and C. S. van Dobben de Bruyn in Holland, are a modified form of the exponential weights in which the single constant is modified each period in proportion to some measure of the forecast error. One difficulty with this scheme is that the feedback relationships are compounded and so far it has not been possible to analyze the stability of the system—one simply doesn't know whether there is an unstable region and where it might be.
4. Norbert Wiener proved during the early 1940s that there exists an optimum set of weights for any stationary time series. Peter Winters in the 1950s proposed a method of simulation to find what those weights are (the method suffers from the fact that unless one has a very long series, the sampling error of the experiments is much larger than the phenomenon being sought). George Box at Wisconsin and Gwilym Jenkins at Imperial College in London have developed a mathematically rigorous method for finding both the best model and the optimum set of weights for revising the coefficients. Their method works extremely well

for process control, for which it was originally conceived at ICI, but suffers in demand forecasting from the fact that with the relatively short historical records available, it generally reduces to simple exponential smoothing.
5. Jeff Harrison at Warwick and Colin Stevens, a consultant, in England have developed a Bayesian scheme for inferring continually what the model and the weights would be. Exponential smoothing, adaptive weights, and the Box–Jenkins technique are all special cases of their Bayesian approach. The technique requires about two years of history to settle into a good forecast, and it has remarkable properties of being able to distinguish among a variety of perturbations, which might be ignored if only a transient pulse, but which should be incorporated in the model if there is a permanent step change in the demand pattern.

In the Materials Management System library at the present time the forecasting methods use a simple exponentially declining series of weights. This choice is not because these forecasts are in any sense optimum, but they do work in practice. It has seemed appropriate to devote an equal amount of development effort to all other parts of the system to achieve a balanced result for running the business, rather than to strive for the ultimate perfection in forecasting at any cost, and have no way of using the results in practice. However, since the system is highly modular it would not take much effort to develop an executable realization of the formal definition of any other technique, add it to the library, and have it as an alternative for users who see an advantage to another technique.

Very precise measurements of alternatives do show differences in accuracy—or more properly, in precision—of the forecasts. The end result in terms of the total inventory investment required to produce and distribute products and achieve a desired level of service is hardly distinguishable among techniques. Provided one uses the right model and any reasonable set of weights, and measures the resulting error as a basis for setting the right safety stocks, the operating results from one technique are very much like another. The uncontrolled factors, like productivity, yield, missing records, and unplanned promotions, will have far more to do with the investment and customer service achieved than the difference among good techniques.

As standard features of the Materials Management Systems library there are two weights available. They are expressed in terms of a discount rate, which is 0.9 for normal smoothing and 0.75 for fast smoothing. Normal smoothing is used when the model was fitted to at least a year of history, and fast smoothing can be automatically assigned for shorter historical bases.

The user can also override the choice and assign smoothing rates in any way he chooses.

The effect of normal smoothing is to respond to random variations in the data about the way a 19-month simple moving average would respond. The effect of fast smoothing is to respond about the way that a seven-month moving average would respond. In both cases the measure of response is the variance introduced by noise, rather than the elapsed time to get through the transient reaction to a step change in the underlying demand pattern.

6.2 SMOOTHING CALCULATIONS

The process of revising the coefficients is illustrated in Exhibit 6.1. The previous set of coefficients is listed in the leftmost column. These coefficients represent the square wave illustrated in Exhibit 5.1. The next five columns carry out the process of moving the origin in time from one month to the next. Mathematically the process is to multiply the vector of coefficient values by a transition matrix. However, since most of the elements of that matrix are zero, the computational effect is to take pairs of values of the coefficients, with the nonzero pairs of elements from the transition matrix. The coefficients in the first column are multiplied by the first multiplier and the coefficients in the second column by the second multiplier, and the results added together to get the forecasts listed under "rolled forward." Since the trend was zero, the level (and the trend) stay the same. The particular nonzero coefficients that are affected only get signs changed, but for some of the other frequencies they would also get values modified.

The "smoothing" process uses the smoothing vector shown in the next

Exhibit 6.1

```
           SMOOTHING
COEFFICIENTS = 125 0 0 0 43.3333 -75.05555 0 0 0 0 0 0 21.6667
FAST SMOOTHING? NO
ERROR = 50
```

OLD COEFS	IN PAIRS		MULTIPLIERS		ROLLED FORWARD	SMOOTHING VECTOR	CORR-ECTION	NEW COEFS
125.000	125.000	0.000	1.00E0	1.00E0	125.000	1.43E⁻2	0.717	125.717
0.000	125.000	0.000	0.00E0	1.00E0	0.000	5.40E⁻5	0.003	0.003
0.000	0.000	0.000	8.66E⁻1	5.00E⁻1	0.000	1.43E⁻2	0.717	0.717
0.000	0.000	0.000	⁻5.00E⁻1	8.66E⁻1	0.000	2.01E⁻4	0.010	0.010
43.333	43.333	⁻75.056	5.00E⁻1	8.66E⁻1	⁻43.333	1.43E⁻2	0.717	⁻42.616
⁻75.056	43.333	⁻75.056	⁻8.66E⁻1	5.00E⁻1	⁻75.056	9.34E⁻5	0.005	⁻75.051
0.000	0.000	0.000	0.00E0	1.00E0	0.000	1.43E⁻2	0.717	0.717
0.000	0.000	0.000	⁻1.00E0	0.00E0	0.000	5.40E⁻5	0.003	0.003
0.000	0.000	0.000	⁻5.00E⁻1	8.66E⁻1	0.000	1.43E⁻2	0.717	0.717
0.000	0.000	0.000	⁻8.66E⁻1	⁻5.00E⁻1	0.000	3.11E⁻5	0.002	0.002
0.000	0.000	0.000	⁻8.66E⁻1	5.00E⁻1	0.000	1.43E⁻2	0.717	0.717
0.000	0.000	0.000	⁻5.00E⁻1	⁻8.66E⁻1	0.000	1.45E⁻5	0.001	0.001
21.667	21.667	21.667	⁻1.00E0	0.00E0	⁻21.667	7.17E⁻3	0.358	⁻21.308

SMOOTHING CONSTANTS

column. The values of these smoothing constants can be computed from (*a*) the value of the discount rate chosen and (*b*) the fitting functions in the model. They do not depend on absolute time or on the data. Hence it is possible to compute tables of program constants and store the results.

In this example the error between the forecast and actual for the next month was specified to be 50 (in the heading of the table). The correction is the product of this error and the smoothing vector. The adjusted coefficients in the last column on the right are the sums of the rolled forward coefficients and the correction.

In Exhibit 6.2, the original coefficients are used to compute the forecasts for the next 12 months—a nice square wave with alternating triplets of 60s and then 190s. Exhibit 6.3 shows the forecasts as computed from the rolled forward coefficients. It is still the square wave pattern, but now it starts with two 60s before the 190s, and slaps another 60 out at the twelfth month. The changes in values of the coefficients have simply changed the origin in time relative to the phasing of the forecast.

Exhibit 6.4 shows the forecasts that result from the smoothing effect of a fairly large error. There is a slight trend now, and the pattern isn't exactly square any more because some of the coefficients that previously were zero now have small values.

Exhibit 6.5 gives the results of a simulation of the smoothing process for 21 periods. The data are precisely described by a six-term model (level, trend, and two seasonal frequencies). Note how the level increases each period but the trend remains constant. Note also how the four seasonal coefficients go their complete cycles in 12 or 6 periods.

6.3 SMOOTHING CONSTANTS

The derivations for this method of smoothing were first published in my book *Smoothing, Forecasting and Prediction of Discrete Time Series*, especially Chapter 12. Later in another book *Decision Rules for Inventory Management* in TM-11, I showed a closed form for computing values of the smoothing vector. Unfortunately there are several conventions in mathematical notations, and compositors have been known to make mistakes in setting such material, so that some users have had a problem in applying the material as presented there. This is an instance which for me highlights the utility of an executable realization of the formal definition of a system (Exhibit 6.6). There is no ambiguity (however much obscurity there is) in Iverson's APL notation, and we know that the statement is correct, because it can be shown to produce the right answers.

The function PROGCONST produces as an explicit result the smoothing vector. The right argument X has four elements: (*a*) the number of observa-

Exhibit 6.2

```
FCSTCALC
COEFFICIENTS = 125  0  0  0  43.333  -75.056  0  0  0  0  0  21.667
```

COEFS						FITTING FUNCTIONS						
	1	2	3	4	5	6	7	8	9	10	11	12
125.000	1.000	1.000	1.000	1.000	1.000	1.000	1.000	1.000	1.000	1.000	1.000	1.000
0.000	1.000	2.000	3.000	4.000	5.000	6.000	7.000	8.000	9.000	10.000	11.000	12.000
0.000	0.866	0.500	0.000	-0.500	-0.866	-1.000	-0.866	-0.500	0.000	0.500	0.866	1.000
0.000	0.500	0.866	1.000	0.866	0.500	0.000	-0.500	-0.866	-1.000	-0.866	-0.500	0.000
43.333	0.500	-0.500	-1.000	-0.500	0.500	1.000	0.500	-0.500	-1.000	-0.500	0.500	1.000
-75.056	0.866	0.866	0.000	-0.866	-0.866	0.000	0.866	0.866	0.000	-0.866	-0.866	0.000
0.000	0.000	-1.000	0.000	1.000	0.000	-1.000	0.000	1.000	0.000	-1.000	0.000	1.000
0.000	-1.000	0.000	1.000	0.000	-1.000	0.000	1.000	0.000	-1.000	0.000	1.000	0.000
0.000	-0.500	-0.500	1.000	-0.500	-0.500	1.000	-0.500	-0.500	1.000	-0.500	-0.500	1.000
0.000	-0.866	0.866	0.000	-0.866	0.866	0.000	-0.866	0.866	0.000	-0.866	0.866	0.000
0.000	0.500	0.500	0.000	-0.500	-0.500	0.000	0.500	0.500	0.000	-0.500	-0.500	0.000
21.667	-1.000	1.000	-1.000	1.000	-1.000	1.000	-1.000	1.000	-1.000	1.000	-1.000	1.000

MULTIPLICATION

```
 125.00  125.00  125.00  125.00  125.00  125.00  125.00  125.00  125.00  125.00  125.00  125.00  125.00
   0.00    0.00    0.00    0.00    0.00    0.00    0.00    0.00    0.00    0.00    0.00    0.00    0.00
   0.00    0.00    0.00    0.00    0.00    0.00    0.00    0.00    0.00    0.00    0.00    0.00    0.00
   0.00    0.00    0.00    0.00    0.00    0.00    0.00    0.00    0.00    0.00    0.00    0.00    0.00
 -21.67  -21.67  -43.33  -21.67   21.67   43.33   21.67  -21.67  -21.67    0.00  -21.67    0.00   43.33
 -65.00  -65.00    0.00   65.00   65.00    0.00  -65.00  -65.00  -65.00   65.00   65.00    0.00    0.00
   0.00    0.00    0.00    0.00    0.00    0.00    0.00    0.00    0.00    0.00    0.00    0.00    0.00
   0.00    0.00    0.00    0.00    0.00    0.00    0.00    0.00    0.00    0.00    0.00    0.00    0.00
   0.00    0.00    0.00    0.00    0.00    0.00    0.00    0.00    0.00    0.00    0.00    0.00    0.00
   0.00    0.00    0.00    0.00    0.00    0.00    0.00    0.00    0.00    0.00    0.00    0.00    0.00
   0.00    0.00    0.00    0.00    0.00    0.00    0.00    0.00    0.00    0.00    0.00    0.00    0.00
  21.67   21.67  -21.67   21.67  -21.67   21.67   21.67   21.67   21.67   21.67  -21.67   21.67   21.67
```

TOTALS

```
  60.00   60.00   60.00  190.00  190.00  190.00   60.00   60.00   60.00  190.00  190.00  190.00  190.00
```

Exhibit 6.3

```
            FCSTCALC
COEFFICIENTS = 125  0  0  0  -43.333  -75.0555  0  0  0  0  0  -21.66666
```

COEFS FITTING FUNCTIONS

COEFS	1	2	3	4	5	6	7	8	9	10	11	12
125.000	1.000	1.000	1.000	1.000	1.000	1.000	1.000	1.000	1.000	1.000	1.000	1.000
0.000	1.000	2.000	3.000	4.000	5.000	6.000	7.000	8.000	9.000	10.000	11.000	12.000
0.000	0.866	0.500	0.000	-0.500	-0.866	-1.000	-0.866	-0.500	0.000	0.500	0.866	1.000
0.000	0.500	0.866	1.000	0.866	0.500	0.000	-0.500	-0.866	-1.000	-0.866	-0.500	0.000
-43.333	0.500	-0.500	-1.000	-0.500	0.500	1.000	0.500	-0.500	-1.000	-0.500	0.500	1.000
-75.055	0.866	0.866	0.000	-0.866	-0.866	0.000	0.866	0.866	0.000	-0.866	-0.866	0.000
0.000	0.000	-1.000	0.000	1.000	0.000	-1.000	0.000	1.000	0.000	-1.000	0.000	1.000
0.000	1.000	0.000	-1.000	0.000	1.000	0.000	-1.000	0.000	1.000	0.000	-1.000	0.000
0.000	-0.500	-0.500	1.000	-0.500	-0.500	1.000	-0.500	-0.500	1.000	-0.500	-0.500	1.000
0.000	0.866	-0.866	0.000	0.866	-0.866	0.000	0.866	-0.866	0.000	0.866	-0.866	0.000
0.000	-0.866	0.866	0.000	-0.866	0.866	0.000	-0.866	0.866	0.000	-0.866	0.866	0.000
0.000	0.500	0.500	-1.000	0.500	0.500	-1.000	0.500	0.500	-1.000	0.500	0.500	-1.000
-21.667	-1.000	1.000	-1.000	1.000	-1.000	1.000	-1.000	1.000	-1.000	1.000	-1.000	1.000

MULTIPLICATION

125.00	125.00	125.00	125.00	125.00	125.00	125.00	125.00	125.00	125.00	125.00	125.00	125.00
0.00	0.00	0.00	0.00	0.00	0.00	0.00	0.00	0.00	0.00	0.00	0.00	0.00
0.00	0.00	0.00	0.00	0.00	0.00	0.00	0.00	0.00	0.00	0.00	0.00	0.00
-21.67	21.67	43.33	21.67	-21.67	-21.67	21.67	-21.67	43.33	21.67	-21.67	0.00	0.00
-65.00	-65.00	0.00	65.00	65.00	-65.00	-65.00	0.00	0.00	65.00	65.00	0.00	-43.33
0.00	0.00	0.00	0.00	0.00	0.00	0.00	0.00	0.00	0.00	0.00	0.00	0.00
0.00	0.00	0.00	0.00	0.00	0.00	0.00	0.00	0.00	0.00	0.00	0.00	0.00
0.00	0.00	0.00	0.00	0.00	0.00	0.00	0.00	0.00	0.00	0.00	0.00	0.00
0.00	0.00	0.00	0.00	0.00	0.00	0.00	0.00	0.00	0.00	0.00	0.00	0.00
0.00	0.00	0.00	0.00	0.00	0.00	0.00	0.00	0.00	0.00	0.00	0.00	0.00
21.67	-21.67	21.67	-21.67	21.67	21.67	-21.67	-21.67	21.67	-21.67	21.67	21.67	-21.67

TOTALS

60.00	60.00	190.00	190.00	190.00	60.00	60.00	190.00	190.00	190.00	190.00	190.00	60.00

115

Exhibit 6.4

```
FCSTCALC
COEFFICIENTS = 125.717 .003 .717 .01 -42.616 -75.051 .717 .003 .717 .002 .717 .001 -21.308
```

COEFS	FITTING FUNCTIONS											
	1	2	3	4	5	6	7	8	9	10	11	12
125.717	1.000	1.000	1.000	1.000	1.000	1.000	1.000	1.000	1.000	1.000	1.000	1.000
0.003	1.000	2.000	3.000	4.000	5.000	6.000	7.000	8.000	9.000	10.000	11.000	12.000
0.717	0.866	0.500	0.000	-0.500	-0.866	-1.000	-0.866	-0.500	0.000	0.500	0.866	1.000
0.010	0.500	0.866	1.000	0.866	0.500	0.000	-0.500	-0.866	-1.000	-0.866	-0.500	0.000
-42.616	0.500	-0.500	-1.000	-0.500	0.500	1.000	0.500	-0.500	-1.000	-0.500	0.500	1.000
-75.051	0.866	0.866	0.000	-0.866	-0.866	0.000	0.866	0.866	0.000	-0.866	-0.866	0.000
0.717	0.000	1.000	0.000	-1.000	0.000	1.000	0.000	-1.000	0.000	1.000	0.000	-1.000
0.003	-1.000	0.000	1.000	0.000	-1.000	0.000	1.000	0.000	-1.000	0.000	1.000	0.000
0.717	-0.500	-0.500	1.000	-0.500	-0.500	1.000	-0.500	-0.500	1.000	-0.500	-0.500	1.000
0.002	-0.866	0.500	0.000	-0.500	0.866	-1.000	0.866	-0.500	0.000	0.500	-0.866	1.000
0.717	-0.866	-0.866	0.000	0.866	0.866	0.000	-0.866	-0.866	0.000	0.866	0.866	0.000
0.001	-0.500	0.500	-1.000	0.500	-0.500	1.000	-0.500	0.500	-1.000	0.500	-0.500	1.000
-21.308	-1.000	1.000	-1.000	1.000	-1.000	1.000	-1.000	1.000	-1.000	1.000	-1.000	1.000

MULTIPLICATION

125.72	125.72	125.72	125.72	125.72	125.72	125.72	125.72	125.72	125.72	125.72	125.72
0.00	0.01	0.01	0.01	0.01	0.02	0.02	0.02	0.03	0.03	0.03	0.04
0.62	0.36	0.00	0.36	-0.62	-0.72	-0.62	-0.36	0.00	0.36	0.62	0.72
0.00	0.01	0.01	0.01	0.01	0.00	0.00	-0.01	-0.01	-0.01	-0.01	0.00
-21.31	-21.31	42.62	21.31	-21.31	-42.62	-21.31	21.31	42.62	21.31	-21.31	-42.62
-65.00	-65.00	0.00	65.00	65.00	0.00	-65.00	-65.00	0.00	65.00	65.00	0.00
0.00	-0.72	0.00	0.72	0.00	-0.72	0.00	0.72	0.00	-0.72	0.00	0.72
0.00	0.00	0.00	0.00	0.00	0.00	0.00	0.00	0.00	0.00	0.00	0.00
-0.36	-0.36	0.72	0.36	-0.36	0.00	-0.36	-0.36	0.72	0.36	-0.36	0.72
0.00	0.00	0.00	0.00	0.00	0.00	0.00	-0.00	0.00	0.00	0.00	0.00
-0.62	0.36	0.00	-0.36	0.62	-0.72	0.00	-0.36	0.00	0.36	-0.62	0.00
0.00	0.00	0.00	0.00	0.00	0.00	0.00	0.00	0.00	0.00	0.00	0.00
21.31	-21.31	21.31	-21.31	21.31	-21.31	21.31	-21.31	21.31	-21.31	21.31	-21.31

TOTALS

60.38	60.37	190.37	190.38	190.38	60.38	60.38	60.38	190.38	190.38	190.38	64.70

Exhibit 6.5

TIME	LEVEL	TREND	SIGMA	SEASONALS			
4	982.000	1.000	0.000	196.410	⁻459.808	⁻769.615	133.013
5	983.000	1.000	0.000	⁻59.808	⁻496.410	⁻269.615	733.013
6	984.000	1.000	0.000	⁻300.000	⁻400.000	500.000	600.000
7	985.000	1.000	0.000	⁻459.808	⁻196.410	769.615	⁻133.013
8	986.000	1.000	0.000	⁻496.410	59.808	269.615	⁻733.013
9	987.000	1.000	0.000	⁻400.000	300.000	⁻500.000	⁻600.000
10	988.000	1.000	0.000	⁻196.410	459.808	⁻769.615	133.013
11	989.000	1.000	0.000	59.808	496.410	⁻269.615	733.013
12	990.000	1.000	0.000	300.000	400.000	500.000	600.000
13	991.000	1.000	0.000	459.808	196.410	769.615	⁻133.013
14	992.000	1.000	0.000	496.410	⁻59.808	269.615	⁻733.013
15	993.000	1.000	0.000	400.000	⁻300.000	⁻500.000	⁻600.000
16	994.000	1.000	0.000	196.410	⁻459.808	⁻769.615	133.013
17	995.000	1.000	0.000	⁻59.808	⁻496.410	⁻269.615	733.013
18	996.000	1.000	0.000	⁻300.000	⁻400.000	500.000	600.000
19	997.000	1.000	0.000	⁻459.808	⁻196.410	769.615	⁻133.013
20	998.000	1.000	0.000	⁻496.410	59.808	269.615	⁻733.013
21	999.000	1.000	0.000	⁻400.000	300.000	⁻500.000	⁻600.000
22	1000.000	1.000	0.000	⁻196.410	459.808	⁻769.615	133.013
23	1001.000	1.000	0.000	59.808	496.410	⁻269.615	733.013
24	1002.000	1.000	0.000	300.000	400.000	500.000	600.000

tions per cycle, such as 12 months or 52 weeks in a year; (*b*) the number of terms in a model, starting with level, trend, and then pairs of terms for sine waves of increasing frequency up to the Nyquist frequency; (*c*) the number of periods of history used, not relevant to this function, but used elsewhere in initial fitting; and (*d*) the discount rate. PROGCONST uses a matrix generated by IFPO based on the expression in *Decision Rules* on p. 146. This function in turn uses four trigonometric functions of the sums of series involving the sine waves and the discount rate.

PROGCONST also produces three global variables. $F1$ is the vector of values of the fitting functions for time $T = 1$. $H0$ is the smoothing constant used in revising the mean square error. LT is the transition matrix. Examples are shown in Exhibit 6.7.

Thus it is quite simple to set up tables for any period of forecast revision and for any values of the discount rate. Note that PROGCONST will also work for a three-term model, which is the equivalent of "triple smoothing" using a parabolic model. This option is provided so that those who have mistakenly used an inappropriate mathematical possibility can run tests to see why it should not be used for demand forecasting.

6.4 FORECASTING PROCESS

The process of forecast revision is carried out using the program illustrated in Exhibit 3.7. The flow chart of the major options considered is shown in Exhibit 6.8.

FORECASTING PROCESS

Exhibit 6.6

```
    ∇ X←COX P
[1]   X←(1-B×2OPxW)÷1+(B*2)-2×B×2OPxW
    ∇

    ∇ M←IFPO X;AM;AP;A1;A2;B;N;V;W
[1]   ⍝ X:OBS/CYCLE,TERMS,HISTORY,DISCOUNT RATE
[2]   B←X[4]*÷X[2]  ⍝ DISCOUNT RATE
[3]   A1←(÷1-B),(-B÷(1-B)*2),B÷(1-B)*3
[4]   A1←A1,(-B÷(1-B)*2),(B×(1+B)÷(1-B)*3),-B×(1+2×B)÷(1-B)*4
[5]   A1← 3 3 ρA1,(B÷(1-B)*3),(-B×(1+2×B)÷(1-B)*4),B×(1+B×4+B)÷(1-B)*5
[6]   →(3<X[2])/L1 × M←(2ρX[2])↑A1 × →0
[7]   L1:A1←(2 2)↑A1 × N←(⌊X[1]÷2)⌊⌊0.5×X[2]-1 × M←O2÷X[1]
[8]   M←⌽((SOX AP)+SOX AM),-(COX AP←(⍳N)∘.+⍳N)-COX AM←(⍳N)∘.-⍳N
[9]   M←(⌽((COX AP)+COX AM),((SOX AP)-SOX AM)),M
[10]  M←0.5×M[V;V←,(⌽(2,N)ρ⍳N)+(N,2)ρ0,N]
[11]  A2←((2,2×N)ρ(COX⍳N),(SOX⍳N),(TCOX⍳N),TSOX⍳N)[;V]
[12]  M←(⌽A1,A2),⌽(⌽A2),M
[13]  M←(V,V←(X[1]+1)⌊(ρM)[1])↑M
    ∇

    ∇ H←PROGCONST X;I;P
[1]   ⍝ H IS SMOOTHING VECTOR.  ALSO PRODUCES GLOBAL VARIABLES
[2]   ⍝ F1 IS FITTING FUNCTION FOR FIRST PERIOD
[3]   ⍝ HO IS SMOOTHING CONSTANT FOR MEAN SQUARE ERROR
[4]   ⍝ LT IS TRANSPOSE OF TRANSITION MATRIX
[5]   H0←X[4] × LT←(P∘.=P)∨P∘.=¯1+P←⍳X[2] × →(X[2]≤3)/L2 × I←3
[6]   L1:LT[¯1+I;I]←0 × LT[I;I]←2OO(I-1)÷X[1] × →(I=1ρρLT)/L2
[7]   LT[I+1;I]←-LT[I;I+1]←1OO(I-1)÷X[1] × LT[I+1;I+1]←LT[I;I]
[8]   →(X[2]≥I←I+2)/L1
[9]   L2:H←(X[2]ρ 1 0)+,×⌽IFPO X × F1←(⌽LT)+.×X[2]ρ 1 0
    ∇

    ∇ X←SOX P
[1]   X←-(B×1OPxW)÷1+(B*2)-2×B×2OPxW
    ∇

    ∇ X←TCOX P
[1]   X←-((B×(1+B*2)×2OPxW)-2×B*2)÷(1+(B*2)-2×B×2OPxW)*2
    ∇

    ∇ X←TSOX P
[1]   X←(B×(1-B*2)×1OPxW)÷(1+(B*2)-2×B×2OPxW)*2
    ∇
```

The program loops through all items in the file until it gets to the end. For items that have assembly usage only, with no terms in the forecast model, the program increments a counter and proceeds to the next item. Next it checks for the release date. If there is one in the item master record, it is checked against today's date. If the release date has passed, it is reset to zero to resume normal processing. If the release date is still in the future, the smoothing rate is checked. If that is zero, as expected, the counter is incremented, the forecast coefficients are rolled forward in time, but there is

Exhibit 6.7

```
     X←12 6 36 .9
     PROGCONST X
0.03341690809  0.0002929672684  0.03332987511  0.001893186401  0.0332532168  0.002566085902
     )VARS
F1       H0       LT       X
         F1
1 1 0.8660254038 0.5 0.5 0.8660254038
         H0
0.9
         LT
    1          1          0          0          0          0
    0          1          0          0          0          0
    0          0         ‾0.866025    0.5       0          0
    0          0          0.5        0.866025   0          0
    0          0          0          0          0.5       0.866025
    0          0          0          0        ‾0.866025    0.5
```

no smoothing for forecast errors. The initial forecasts out to the release dates are plugged with zeros, and control passes to the end of the loop to post the files.

If there is a future release date the smoothing rate is not zero, but if there is no history the smoothing rate is set to zero, because we don't want to revise the coefficients for any error signals. It is possible that an abnormal situation will occur when there are a future release date, nonzero smoothing rates, and some history in the record. In that case the date is set to zero, a counter is incremented to record the abnormality, and we go to normal processing. The user will probably want to retrieve these items from the file, examine them, and perhaps make other changes to the processing.

In the normal processing stream, when there is no release date, the next step is to check whether there is a nonzero smoothing rate code (1 for normal smoothing, 2 for fast smoothing). There may be released items that for one reason or another are not to have the forecast coefficients revised for errors, but they are rolled forward in time.

Normal processing essentially goes through the following steps:

1. Compute the forecast error as the difference between current demand and the forecast previously recorded for this month.
2. Check that the error is less than some number of standard deviations. If there is a potential outlier, invoke the demand filter process (see Chapter 8).
3. Revise the smoothed error and check for a tracking signal trip (also see Chapter 8).
4. Revise the coefficients by rolling them forward in time and adding a correction for the forecast error.

Exhibit 6.8

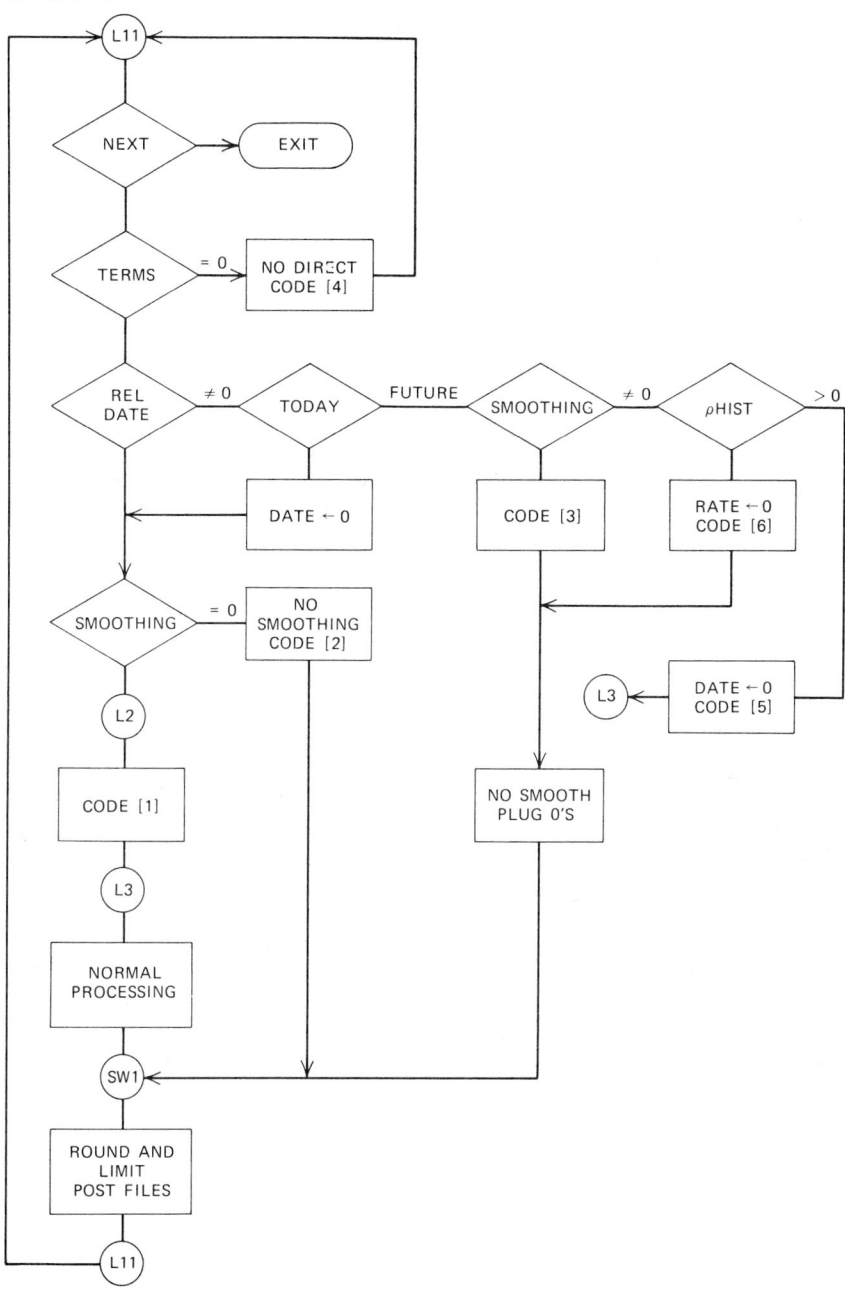

5. If there was marketing intelligence recorded for the period just past, post the record for a report (see Chapter 7).
6. Finally, based on the setting of switch SW1, the forecasts may be rounded to integers or not, limited to nonnegative or not, and posted to the files. The forecasts are stored out to the planning horizon, which is controlled at the item level by the contents of the item master record, and limited by a discontinue date. The forecast coefficients are also stored, so that longer forecasts can be computed, as for the example in Exhibit 3.3.

6.5 EXCEPTION REPORT

A report of the exception codes is printed at the end of processing, to account for all items on the file, so that the user can tell how many items used each of the major paths through the process.

The processing also posts the demand to the history record, so that it is available for reports and analyses. There is no limit to the maximum amount of history that may be stored in the files, but file space does cost something. It is recommended that no more than three or four years of history be stored in live files as a rule. Once a year, when another year of history has been built up, the live files should be transferred to a cheaper storage medium, such as tape. Some people in an excess of zeal have simply erased old data. Even though markets and product lines have changed drastically, there still are occasions when you might want to study ancient data. For example, if you were to develop a system for generating profiles of the response of the market to a promotion, promotions even a long time ago might very well reveal what the response characteristics are.

Therefore it is important to make some provision for saving old demand data in a machine-readable form. The amount of money I have seen spent on keypunching from microfiche for major studies would have paid for a very large number of reels of tape. But old data should be dropped from live files once a year.

CHAPTER 7

Marketing Intelligence

Once upon a time I presented to the Aeronautical Engineering Department faculty at the University of Michigan a proposal for a course in operations research. The faculty listened attentively. At the end a very senior professor behind my right shoulder said, "Mr Brown, ... if I understand what you are proposing ...," (here it comes) "you are suggesting a course ... in how to think." After a brief reflection I agreed that that was one way of looking at it. "Good," he replied, "this university is big enough for one course like that."

For those of you who prefer a materials management system to be automatic and impersonal, I should warn you that this chapter has to do with thinking about the forecast, rather than any nice mathematical technique for getting a forecast so accurate and complete that all planning problems disappear. The chapter is not even about *how* to think, but just, "You *should* think."

"Marketing intelligence" implies neither any superior intellect among the sales staff nor covert espionage. It means simply the gathering, evaluation, organization, and interpretation of all sorts of information that can help identify in advance what the demand is likely to be. There can be no cookbook way of providing a list of what will work and what won't. The effective application of marketing intelligence can materially improve the usefulness of a forecast not only for materials management, but also for marketing and financial management. It takes a reasonable period of time for a group of people to learn how to use their information effectively, and some parts of the system will help to reinforce productive contributions.

There are three major sections to this chapter: (*a*) the people that make up a marketing intelligence group, (*b*) the kinds of information they may consider, and (*c*) the formal feedback mechanisms that encourage continual improvement of the inputs.

7.1 A MARKETING INTELLIGENCE GROUP

Marketing intelligence information often comes from the marketplace that generates the demand, so the marketing organization should normally have a strong role in organizing the intelligence information. In companies that have product managers or brand managers, these people usually convene and chair the meetings.

There are, however, other valid inputs. A corporate, or consulting, economist can indicate the general tenor of the economy and predict what will affect demand, at least in aggregate terms. The General Electric Company has described publicly a process that has some good points. The manager of each operating business in the corporation prepares his own forecasts from the bottom up, based on the information he has about sales, backlogs, new products, pricing plans, and the like. At the same time an economic model works from the top down to project changes in the gross volume of sales by industry, and to identify competitive factors that may change GE's share of the market. The bottom-up and the top-down forecasts meet at Group level, and of course they don't agree. But the company has evolved a process of discussion that permits each of the forecasters to show the information that led him to his conclusions, so that by the end of the dialogue all parties have learned something they hadn't appreciated before. The resulting forecast is in no sense a compromise or an average of the inputs—it is the consensus resulting from sharing information.

A few of the largest corporations have developed and maintain economic models for their segment of the industry, and many other corporations can subscribe to services like those of Chase Manhattan Bank and the Wharton School.

Another sort of forecasting staff service comes from the market research group, who may have information as a result of test markets and surveys.

Purchasing and production people often have significant inputs, too. One of the pharmaceutical manufacturers has a very popular product that is made from a natural bark. They have access to all the world's supply of that commodity—there isn't any more. The material available supports about half the normal demand. But one day the marketing department had the lovely idea of running a promotion, because it was a popular product with a large markup. When production and purchasing people are included in the group, the forecast may be tempered with what it is possible to produce, as well as what the customers might order.

Black and Decker, IBM, and Campbell Soup all have excellent ways of marketing the forecast, instead of forecasting the market. That is, they set a marketing goal, estimate the problems of reaching it, make production commitments, and then tailor sales practices to ensure that the orders received very nearly match that goal. It is commonly accepted that for most companies sales below forecast are very bad, because that means lost income. It is not so commonly recognized, but equally true, that sales above forecast are also bad, because of the extraordinary expense of changing production to meet that demand.

A MARKETING INTELLIGENCE GROUP

The means for ensuring that the market meets the forecast differ from industry to industry and from company to company. But when it is possible, this strategy is often a powerful way to get a forecast that is profitable for the whole corporation.

7.11 Aggregate Forecast Summary

The purpose of the marketing intelligence group is to review all relevant information, together with the current forecasts being used for production planning, and to make changes as necessary so that the production forecasts are consistent with the marketing plans. The aggregate forecasts can be reported, as in Exhibit 3.3, at any level of detail, such as by product line, marketing territory, ABC classification, or any other relevant characteristic. The reports can show forecasts with only the statistical model, with only previous marketing intelligence, or with both of these with the scheduled back orders. They can be produced regionally or nationally.

One of the procedures each group has to evolve for itself is the way of specifying the report grouping that is most useful. It may change from time to time as different aspects of the business become more important.

It is likely that for large numbers of items, the total forecast will appear reasonable, and not require any change at all. In other product lines, or regions, there may be transient or permanent changes in the forecast.

7.12 Temporary Changes

A temporary change would be for something like the effects of a promotion, with a slight decline prior to the promotion while the trade waits for the deal, heavy sales at the beginning of the promotion, and perhaps another peak at the end when the distributors fill their warehouses. If demand is pulled ahead by the promotion, there will be a drop below normal demand afterward. (We deal more with promotions later in this chapter.)

Another sort of temporary change in demand is when there is an announced price rise with an opportunity to order at the old price.

These and other changes in demand can be anticipated, but in the long run demand is expected to return to normal levels. The changes can be specified either in detail, by product or SKU, or in aggregate. At the detailed level the change can be an amount to be added to the forecast (a negative value will reduce the total), or the net result, for the computer to calculate the necessary difference. For changes to the aggregate, the new total can be specified in such a way that the computer will generate additions to the demand for each product in the group in the same ratio.

7.13 Permanent Changes

More permanent changes in the pattern can be reflected by overriding the values assigned to the coefficients in the forecast model. For example, as in Exhibit 5.18, it is possible not only to display the values of the coefficients but also to supply new values. A "vertical" change could increase the level for every item on a list by 10%, or change the trend back to zero.

These changes would be used to reflect a consensus about a turning point in the economy. If a recession has lasted long enough individual item trends will be mostly negative. It might be agreed to leave the level where it is but to change the trends from negative values to zero, or even to positive values. Then if the economy had indeed affected demand in the anticipated way, the actual demand will follow the forecast resulting from the new coefficients, and gradually adapt to small differences, item by item, between actual demand and the gross plan. A similar approach could be taken, for example, when an engineering change reduces the expected usage of a service part to half its previous rate. If the level is set to half what it had been, the resulting forecast should be near to the new usage pattern.

Another procedure the group has to learn for itself is how to set up an agenda and circulate advance information so that the meeting itself can be short, informative, and productive. U.S. Rubber and Honeywell in some of their divisions have permanent "executive secretaries" for these groups, who circulate a short list of problems, discuss the information needed with each party before the meeting, and thus can concentrate the meeting on a real sharing of pertinent information.

7.2 SOURCES OF INFORMATION

Let us consider three instances as examples of the kinds of information that can be discussed by a marketing intelligence group—each company has to learn for itself what is really pertinent.

7.21 Pipeline Fill

As new products are released to the market, every stocking echelon will need an inventory; this creates demand on production, but not continuing demand. For small, cheap service parts there may be a policy to give every technical representative two pieces, and every branch five. Then by a simple count of the branches and technical representatives (perhaps phased in over several months) one can accumulate a reasonable aggregate picture of the amount needed for pipeline fill. For more expensive parts, it is often possible to use the decision rules for safety stocks and lot sizes (see Section III) to build a model of the number of pieces needed by each stocking location, based on the preliminary demand forecasts.

In either case, it is important that when stock is issued to fill the pipeline, usage is distinguished from normal demand for consumption. In one's own distribution network the problem of recording different sorts of issues is straightforward (although often not done). It is harder to get independent dealers and distributors to distinguish stock orders from replenishment orders. However, there may be ingenious ways to get the information.

A major reason for warranty cards for small appliances is not so much to register the owner for warranty as it is to notify the manufacturer that the unit has finally passed out of the pipeline to a consumer.

An excellent example of estimating real consumption in spite of orders received was that of a pulp mill supplying newsprint to several newspaper publishers. It appears that when stocks get low at the newspaper plant, the pressmen urge the purchasing agent to get more, a lot more. When the inventory gets too high the accountants urge him to cut back on orders. The problem was solved when the mill subscribed to the papers published by each of its customers. From the Audit Bureau of Circulation they could get a measure of the number of copies printed, and by counting pages per issue they could determine the true consumption, as a basis for forecasting mill requirements in spite of the erratic behavior of purchasing agents.

7.22 New Product Introduction

Especially in consumer products, the real need is for an assortment of merchandise. The total sales of the assortment are stable and can be forecast. When new products are introduced, they tend to displace older products, but the total for the assortment may remain fairly stable. There is an exception in the case of heavy promotional advertising for a new kind of product, aimed at a totally different consumer need. General Foods is reported to have developed a very elegant model of the market to estimate the response to the initial introduction of the breakfast drink Tang. Unfortunately, details have not been made public.

The point is that if one has an estimate of the probable sales volume initially for a new product, and the total sales for the assortment will remain stable, then there should be some sort of adjustment to reflect the amount of demand that will be taken away from older products. Amateur camera film, apparel, and toys seem to exhibit this phenomenon. The model of the market differs from industry to industry, but the general concepts seem to be quite universal.

7.23 Promotions

There are three quite separate reasons for forecasting the effects of a promotion, with corresponding differences in the way that one forecasts. First, the logistic reason is to get the right goods at the right place at the right time, in the right amount. Especially when promotions are scheduled at regular cycles, a purely descriptive statistical forecast based on the past patterns of total consumption can be quite adequate. There are many consumer products where this appears to be true, especially in food and cosmetics.

Second, the evaluation of the net plus business as a result of a promotion requires a forecast of what the level of demand would have been without the promotion. This issue gets clouded by impressions of what a competitor's promotion would have done. The purpose here is somewhat different from the logistic forecast. Production planning needs to know in advance how much to produce and when. The evaluation can take place after the promotion is over, to weigh the costs against the benefits.

Still a third reason is to plan promotions. These forecasts predict what results would be achieved from different forms of promotion, to set up a strategy that in some sense maximizes the returns on the efforts. This latter type of forecast requires a continuing experimental program. First there must be some sort of a model of the market, such as a brand loyalty percentage, and a Markov migration over time. Then there must be some conjecture as to the effects of particular types of promotions on those probabilities, and a way of observing actual results. The hypothesis must then be put in jeopardy by an experiment that will, if the model is correct, produce very different results from those if the model is wrong. From the results of the experiment, the model is modified and the process repeated.

The experiments don't need to be huge—about 1% of the advertising budget can produce very effective results if applied under strict design conditions. Experiments designed to prove that something is right may be comforting, but they don't lead to much learning. One learns from experiments carefully designed to expose fallacies in one's reasoning. If those fail, the reasoning might be right, and then one can start to plan strategies. But this latter type of promotional forecasting is well outside the scope of this book.

The profile is one approach to forecasting the marginal effect of a promotion over normal sales. Although there are many types of promotions, the response to a promotion is a characteristic of the market rather than the promotion itself. The promotion is a stimulus. The way that a car's suspension settles down after a bump is a property of the springs and shock absorber, not whether the car hit a brick, a curb, or a pothole.

SOURCES OF INFORMATION

There are theoretical reasons for believing that certain types of markets respond in a particular way to a promotion. For example, a price reduction (or anything that looks like a price reduction) might encourage consumers to buy ahead, and purchase a larger quantity now than they normally would, to anticipate future consumption. One model predicts that the amount of future demand pulled ahead is proportional primarily to the percentage price reduction. (See 11.05.)

There are, of course, many other results of a promotion, such as more shelf space, which reduces the space for competitive products, and an increase in the probability that an impulse buyer will see your product. There is also the phenomenon that when one brand and size of mayonnaise, for example, is on sale, the sales of all sizes and all brands apparently go up.

The approach to developing a forecast of these effects is first to set up a classification of markets into characteristic shapes of the profile of response. The duration of the promotion is one key parameter, and a measure of intensity is typically the other. A price reduction of 10% has twice the intensity of one of 5%. Even promotions that are only remotely connected with price reductions can often be put onto a scale of relative intensities. Then for a particular forthcoming promotion the planner can identify the response as "Type II curve, duration 3 weeks, and intensity 6." The relevant profile can then be scaled for duration and intensity to multiply normal demand forecasts by factors (which may be less than 1 before and after the promotion) to get the net effect.

7.24 Changes in Demand

The foregoing examples only indicate the kinds of phenomena that the marketing intelligence group should consider in deciding whether to modify the plans that are used in production.

The principal concern should be with changes—what will be different from the forecasts now on the data base? There may be changes in the product line as new products are released and old ones discontinued, or engineering changes that make service parts last longer. (The razor industry got caught badly when they first started using stainless steel blades, which last very much longer than carbon steel.)

There may be changes in marketing, such as price changes, promotions, or advertising. Department stores used to start Christmas merchandising at Thanksgiving. A few years ago they changed to the first of November. It is not clear that total season sales went up much, but November sales were certainly higher as a result.

There may be changes in the marketplace as a result of the general economy, government regulation, or competitive actions. There was an interesting run on yellow carpets one year when two different ladies' magazines happened to have four or five ads, from different manufacturers, that all featured yellow rugs in the illustrations. As I recall, several of these were furniture ads, which weren't advertising carpets at all.

There may be changes in consumption caused by changes in the number of warehouses, the level of customer service, or the range of products stocked. Simply the fact that your product is more available may increase its sales.

The important thing is to think about all these changes, try to estimate their impact on demand, record that estimate, and then measure what actually happened after the fact. Gradually the group will learn to give more weight to considerations that work, and reject some of the mythology of marketing.

7.3 POSTING RECORDS

The marketing intelligence group may want to post changes to a whole block of items, based on the current aggregate forecast (Exhibit 3.3).

For example, Exhibit 7.1 shows how the revised totals may be specified for a selected group of items, for the seven-month period from September through next March. The computer reports the factors (which could have been supplied directly by the user). The marketing intelligence for each of the 41 Class A items is adjusted so that, for example, the statistical model plus the new marketing intelligence plus the scheduled backlog increases by 7.7% for Indianapolis in September and drops 5.1% for Atlanta in March.

Of course, sometimes the changes are to be posted directly to the record for individual SKUs. Exhibit 7.2 was constructed to illustrate the variety of types of changes that can be made:

1. For the master warehouse, 50 is added for each month.
2. For Indianapolis, enough is added to bring the net forecast up to 75.
3. For Atlanta the forecasts are made 10% larger. For example, in September the present net is 325 − 31 = 294. A 10% increase would bring that up to 323.4, which makes the new marketing intelligence only −2.
4. Sometimes one doesn't want to change the records, as for Denver.

In all cases the right arguments (50, 75, and 1.1, respectively) could have been strings of seven different values corresponding to the different months.

For large volumes of data, the additions or net changes can be posted from file data rather than via a terminal.

EVALUATION

Exhibit 7.1

```
    PRORATE

FRIDAY, AUGUST 20, 1976
EASTERN DAYLIGHT TIME 10:08:16


FORECASTS REVISED AS OF    7/31/76

WHICH ITEMS = L
LIST OF INDEX NUMBERS
[]:
       GET'DIRECTORY'
COMPONENT = CLASS A
41 ITEMS WILL BE USED.
LOCATIONS TO BE INCLUDED = ALL
6 LOCATIONS WILL BE USED.
BEGINNING AND ENDING MONTH FROM NOW = 2 8
PROVIDE THE ADJUSTMENT FACTORS THEMSELVES? NO
WEIGHT FORECASTS BY MASTER FIELD = 5
                       FORECASTS WEIGHTED BY TOTAL COST
                  9/30/76   10/31/76  11/30/76  12/31/76   1/31/77   2/28/77   3/31/77
MASTER             398404    409412    375831    156349    173492    145812    191882
INDIANAPOLIS, IN    27858     28952     24372     24751     37737     33191     41949
NEW YORK, NY        33234     38546     37381     30954     32902     28202     35024
ATLANTA, GA         44227     58657     56505     44649     52436     44425     52684
DENVER, CO          60671     73396     71786     59195     62842     58490     70210
LOS ANGELES, CA     24862     27729     27019     23540     24854     22350     25797

ENTER THE ADJUSTED TOTALS:
MASTER           = 400000 410000 380000 160000 175000 150000 200000
INDIANAPOLIS, IN = 30000 30000 25000 25000 38000 35000 45000
NEW YORK, NY     = 35000 40000 40000 32000 33000 30000 35000
ATLANTA, GA      = 40000 50000 55000 40000 50000 40000 50000
DENVER, CO       = 60000 75000 75000 60000 65000 60000 75000
LOS ANGELES, CA  = 25000 30000 30000 25000 25000 25000 25000
                                       v
THE RATIOS ARE:

                   9/30/76   10/31/76  11/30/76  12/31/76   1/31/77   2/28/77   3/31/77
MASTER              1.004     1.001     1.011     1.023     1.009     1.029     1.042
INDIANAPOLIS, IN    1.077     1.036     1.026     1.010     1.007     1.055     1.073
NEW YORK, NY        1.053     1.038     1.070     1.034     1.003     1.064     0.999
ATLANTA, GA         0.904     0.852     0.973     0.896     0.954     0.900     0.949
DENVER, CO          0.989     1.022     1.045     1.014     1.034     1.026     1.068
LOS ANGELES, CA     1.006     1.082     1.110     1.062     1.006     1.119     0.969

ADJUST FORECASTS BY THESE RATIOS? YES

ELAPSED TIME       4M 15.073S
CPU TIME              2.239S
```

7.4 EVALUATION

There are two sides to the evaluation of marketing intelligence. One has to do with the report (Exhibit 3.8) that is issued at the end of a period in which there was marketing intelligence recorded. There are usually some instances where the change was in the wrong direction, or too far in the right direc-

Exhibit 7.2

```
     EDITINTELL

FRIDAY, AUGUST 20, 1976
EASTERN DAYLIGHT TIME 10:13:03


FORECASTS REVISED AS OF    7/31/76

WHICH ITEMS = L
LIST OF INDEX NUMBERS
☐:
       39 40
2 ITEMS WILL BE USED.
LOCATIONS TO BE INCLUDED = ALL
6 LOCATIONS WILL BE USED.
CLEAR OUT PRESENT MARKETING INTELLIGENCE? NO
BEGINNING AND ENDING PERIODS FROM NOW = 2 8

                9/30/76  10/31/76  11/30/76  12/31/76   1/31/77   2/28/77   3/31/77
32-007-035         IGNITION  | FILE INDEX = 39

MASTER
STAT MODEL         1771      3219      2316      1060      1631      1753      2912
MKT INTELL            7         5        26        25        14        50       123
SCHED DEM

NEW MARKETING INTELLIGENCE.
☐:
    ☐← ADD 50
57 55 76 75 64 100 173

INDIANAPOLIS, IN
STAT MODEL                     56        44
MKT INTELL                      2         1
SCHED DEM

NEW MARKETING INTELLIGENCE.
☐:
     ☐←NET 75
75 19 31 75 75 75 75

ATLANTA, GA
STAT MODEL          325       769       493       311       398       404       546
MKT INTELL          ⁻31      ⁻113       ⁻13       ⁻32       ⁻18       ⁻40       ⁻28
SCHED DEM

NEW MARKETING INTELLIGENCE.
☐:
       ☐←FACTOR 1.1
⁻2  ⁻47  35  ⁻4  20  ⁻4  24

DENVER, CO
STAT MODEL         1896      2384      1772      1168      1606      1587      2412
MKT INTELL         ⁻21        52        79        16        55        41       165
SCHED DEM

NEW MARKETING INTELLIGENCE.
☐:
       ☐←SAME
⁻21 52 79 16 55 41 165
FILE REVISIONS? YES
```

EVALUATION

tion. If the group keeps minutes of the meetings where changes are recorded, then they can go back and review the factors that were taken into consideration at that time, to try to learn how to do a better job next time.

A prime example of this sort of learning from feedback was the Mariner Woolen Mills, in Lowell, Massachusetts. Kenneth Mariner founded the company, owned it, and ran it. He was physically impressive, well over six feet tall, and had been in the wool business in America and Australia all his life. The way that a wool topp company makes money is by hedging the price of wool, by buying and selling futures contracts. It is essential to forecast whether the spot price will go up or down in the next 13 weeks.

It had been the practice in that company for several executives to meet for lunch on Fridays in the president's office, and arrive at a consensus of the direction wool prices would go.

The procedure that improved the process wasn't very technical, but relied on feedback. Before the general discussion each person wrote his own opinion on a slip of paper, dated it, and signed it. These slips were collected and filed. At the end of the meeting, slips from 6 and 13 weeks earlier were retrieved, and the various prices compared with the current spot price. The person who was closest got a score of 5 points, the second closest 3 points, and the third 1 point. The rest got no score that week.

A chart of the cumulative score for each person was posted prominently on the wall of the office. It didn't take long to find that one person, very quiet by nature, was consistently much closer than anyone else. His opinions hadn't carried much weight in general discussion. The large, experienced, influential president's record wasn't anywhere near as good—and the group learned how to reassess the weight paid to various opinions.

7.41 Tracking Signals

The other aspect of the evaluation of marketing intelligence is change in demand patterns in ways not reflected by the forecast. In Chapter 8 we develop the notion of a tracking signal by which the computer can monitor every forecast to see whether any consistent bias is being detected. Too many positive errors in a row is a sign that demand is consistently above forecast. That fact should be reviewed by the marketing intelligence group to figure out why, and therefore what changes to make.

There are several types of action that can be taken. The most common one is to ignore the whole thing and hope it will go away. A slightly more responsive action is to put the item onto fast smoothing to try to get the model to catch up with the new pattern of usage. One step beyond that would be to go through the initial process of selecting and fitting a forecast model for recent data. The Trigg/Leach approach to adaptively revising the smoothing constant tries to make continual changes so that the forecasts will follow the market more closely.

I have little faith in any of these mechanistic actions. Tracking signals should put the product onto the agenda for the marketing intelligence group, for them to find the assignable cause of the change. When there is agreement, from their combined experience and diverse sources of information, then it is likely that they will know more clearly what the change is likely to mean in the future, if only by broad product line or region. If the change is temporary, the forecasts can be left alone. If there is a reversal in the direction of the market, the trends can be set accordingly. If it is a step change to a new level of demand, levels can be changed in the forecast models for the items affected.

In the 1958 recession a company economist had been telling the board about the coming downturn, but they had high hopes that he would be wrong. But when the tracking signals for the parts forecasting system came out with an abnormal number of reports, there was conclusive evidence for a significant downturn in the business. The result was not only a change in the parts forecasts as such, but some major changes to production plans for prime products, along the lines the economist had been recommending. The president of the company said afterward that he thought they had taken action about six months earlier in the cycle, as a result of the abnormal volume of tracking signal reports, then they had in any previous recession— although the economist had been right then, too.

7.5 SCHEDULED BACKLOG

Although it is not really a matter of marketing intelligence, the open order book should be considered in setting up forecasts as well as the statistical forecasts. In some companies with largely OEM demand, the whole purpose of marketing intelligence seems to be to add increments in the distant months to anticipate the probable level of the backlog before the orders are booked.

Specific customer orders for future delivery can be recorded as booked, with customer identification, part number, quantity, and date promised. For each part number the quantities can be summarized by period as in Exhibit 3.1. For each customer, the open orders can be summarized by part number, date, or purchase order number (Exhibit 3.2).

In the production planning system, the requirements for filling these scheduled orders can be posted to planning periods that are not necessarily the same length of time as the forecast periods.

SCHEDULED BACKLOG

Scheduled orders may come from customers, as for boilers, airplanes, and computers. Even in the service parts and consumer products companies, there may be some significant requirement to supply products or semifinished materials to affiliates and overseas plants. The mechanism for recording scheduled demand from customers can also be used to record the planned requirements from these other divisions of the corporation as well.

The orders in the backlog can be changed any time up until they are shipped. But when the material is available, one generally assumes that the orders in the backlog are filled as recorded; there is no forecast error to be measured or used in setting safety stocks.

When the near-term backlog is extended by marketing intelligence, however, then one wants to measure the error in those forecasts and to have a reasonable provision for minimum stock levels that can be used to meet backlogged orders that were not anticipated in sufficient time to allow for a complete purchasing and manufacturing cycle.

CHAPTER **8**

Forecast Errors

Of all the advances in the state of the art in materials management in the past 30 years the single area that has contributed the most dramatic improvements has been in the measurement of forecast errors. Many companies have traditionally based safety stocks on a certain number of weeks of supply. That number of weeks is a rough compromise between getting good enough service to be competitive and keeping the investment within reasonable bounds. When safety stocks are based on measurements of forecast errors the investment may be reduced by at least 10% (and not uncommonly 30%) while cutting the number of shortages in half.

The reason for this dramatic improvement is that not all items are equally hard to forecast. The ones that give a problem have a high degree of uncertainty. Because management cannot increase weeks of supply across the board, these items do have occasional surges in demand that can't be filled on time, and that hurts service. However, these items do exert a continual pressure to increase the safety stocks. In the meantime, other items that can be forecast relatively accurately have more than enough inventory.

The measurement of forecast errors makes it practical to take investment away from the latter items, without hurting service, and give some of it back to the first class of items. Even when the service is brought up to standard on the difficult items, there is still some inventory savings left for management.

Chapter 10 deals with the decision rules for computing safety stocks. In this chapter we treat the measurements of the forecast errors. There are three major subjects to be tackled: (*a*) the form of the probability distribution that represents the forecast errors, with the key parameters, including the effect of lead time on those measures; (*b*) the variance law as a basis for getting reasonable initial conditions for items where there isn't enough history to compute the standard deviation from the data; and (*c*) tracking signals and demand filters to monitor the average error in the forecasts.

8.1 FORM OF THE DISTRIBUTION

The forecast as discussed in Chapters 5 and 6 states the amount of demand we expect in each future period. The word "expect" has very specific

FORM OF THE DISTRIBUTION

technical meaning in mathematical statistics—it means that in the long run, over a large series of events of the same type, the average result is the expected value. In one specific trial or event, the observation may be much higher or much lower than the expected value.

A complete forecast would give not only the expected value but also probabilities attached to a whole range of values above and below that average. It is important to distinguish a plan from the forecast in this sense. A plan is one specific level at which management aims. There are costs and benefits associated with having demand above, or below, the planned level during the period. In various ways we want to minimize those costs in the long run.

Exhibit 8.1 is a rough sketch of the probability that the demand during a particular future period will exceed any level X. If X itself is a large value, there is a small probability that actual demand will exceed X. Hence we don't have to worry much about the costs when demand is above plan—that is not very likely to happen. But we can be relatively sure of incurring the costs that result when demand is below plan—there is a good chance of that happening. The sales department, for example, might set sales quotas, or goals, at the high end of the range, since there aren't many costs to them of having demand below quota. When the quota is low there are costs of not getting all the sales that would be possible.

The financial planners might set a relatively low value of X for their plan, to ensure that the odds are heavily in favor of getting more income than planned, which is easy to finance. Production plans usually are on the high side, but not quite so high as sales plans, since with overtime, subcontracting, and substitution, production has some options for coping with demand above plan, but demand below plan results in inventory.

The sketch in Exhibit 8.1 is somewhat S-shaped, which would be true for

Exhibit 8.1

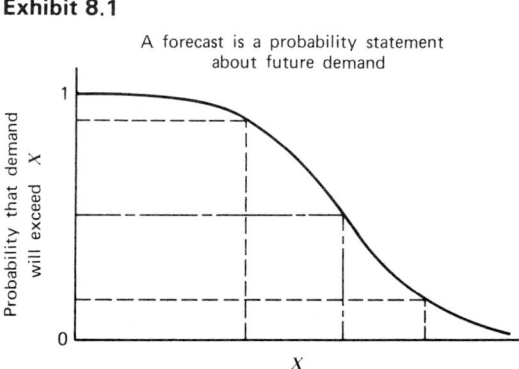

A forecast is a probability statement about future demand

Exhibit 8.2

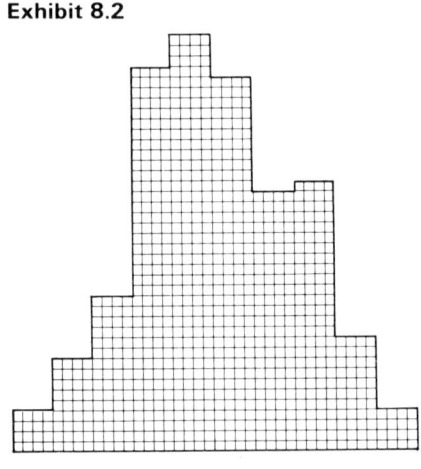

(a)

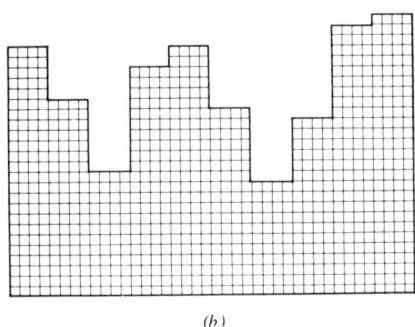

(b)

some probability distributions. But the forecast errors are not always distributed that way.

Exhibit 8.2a represents a histogram with 10 class intervals between the smallest and largest forecast errors in a particular series where we observed these errors 200 times. Each vertical square represents one event where the error fell into that class interval. It is clear that most of the errors occur in the middle of the range, with very few occurrences at either extreme. If the forecast errors looked more or less like that, one could represent the distribution by a normal probability distribution.

Another set of 200 observations is shown in Exhibit 8.2b. There appear to be three peaks, one at each end and one in the middle. It may seem supris-

FORM OF THE DISTRIBUTION

ing, but those peaks and valleys could easily have resulted from a process where it was equally likely that a particular error would fall into any class interval. Another run of 200 observations for the same process might well show a similar range from the largest to smallest values in each class interval, but the intervals with the large tallies might be those that in this sample were the ones with small tallies. The uniform distribution is one model of this sort of process (which hardly ever is found in practice).

Exhibit 8.3a shows a very definite tendency for most of the errors to be in the leftmost class interval, with a steady decline in occurrences, until there

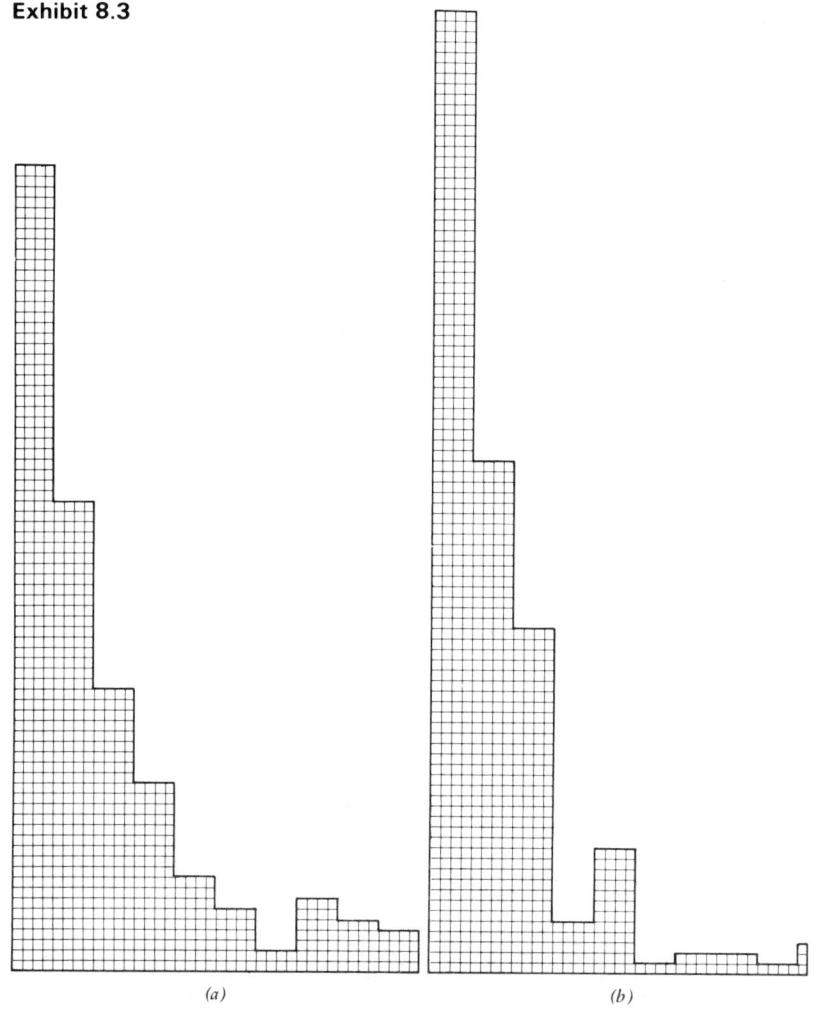

Exhibit 8.3

(a) (b)

are very few in the rightmost interval. This sort of distribution could be represented by the exponential distribution.

Exhibit 8.3b is another example of a heavily skewed distribution, with a great many small errors, and very few large errors to the right. This distribution could be modeled by the log-normal distribution.

8.11 Functions of the Distribution

There are three functions of the probability distribution in which we shall be interested when deriving various decision rules in later chapters. The density function is like a smooth curve drawn through either of the histograms in Exhibit 8.2. The probability that the next observation will fall into a class interval defined by any two values of X is the area under the density curve between those values.

Exhibit 8.1 represents the probability function itself. It is obtained by integrating the density curve backwards from the upper limit. At any given value of the planning level X the height of the curve $F(X)$ is the probability that the next observation will exceed X, that it will fall into the class interval from X to infinity (Exhibit 8.4).

We shall also be interested in the partial expectation function $E(X)$, which is the area under the probability curve to the right of X. That area is proportional to the expected amount of demand back ordered when demand exceeds the planning level X.

Appendix D contains a table that gives the density, probability, and expectation functions for values of X, for both the exponential and the normal distributions. We use these tables in Chapter 10. In this chapter we are more concerned with determining which of the distributions to use.

8.111 Normal Distribution. The 200 observations from the normal distribution are analyzed in Exhibit 8.5. In addition to the mean and standard

Exhibit 8.4

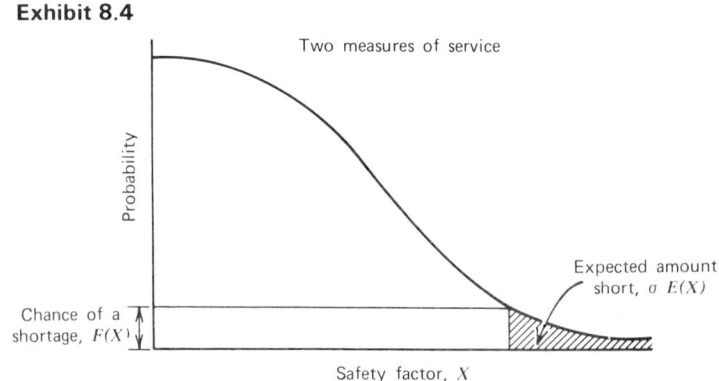

FORM OF THE DISTRIBUTION

Exhibit 8.5

```
COMPONENT = NORMAL
200 OBSERVATIONS HAVE RANGE 120, MEAN 103.1 AND SIGMA 23.83
MEDIAN = 104, M.A.D. = 19.34
COEFFICIENT OF VARIATION = 0.2313
DISTRIBUTION FUNCTION = 1

NORMAL

     o      *
     oooooooo    *
     oooooooooooo   *
     ooooooooooooo   *
     ooooooooooooooo   *
  P  oooooooooooooooooo*
  R  ooooooooooooooooooo*
  O  ooooooooooooooooooooo*
  B  oooooooooooooooooooooo*
  A  ooooooooooooooooooooooo⊛
  B  oooooooooooooooooooooooo⊛
  I  ooooooooooooooooooooooooo*
  L  oooooooooooooooooooooooooo*
  I  ooooooooooooooooooooooooooo*
  T  ooooooooooooooooooooooooooooo  *
  Y  oooooooooooooooooooooooooooooo*
     oooooooooooooooooooooooooooooooo  *
     ooooooooooooooooooooooooooooooooo  *
     oooooooooooooooooooooooooooooooooo    *
     ooooooooooooooooooooooooooooooooooooooo
                      DATA
```

		EMPIRICAL		THEORETICAL	
SAFETY	ORDER	SHORTAGE	PARTIAL	SHORTAGE	PARTIAL
FACTOR	POINT	PROBY	EXPECT	PROBY	EXPECT
0.00	103.06	0.51500	0.40430	0.50000	0.39894
0.25	109.02	0.40500	0.28612	0.40224	0.28611
0.50	114.97	0.34000	0.19424	0.30988	0.19713
0.75	120.93	0.24500	0.12534	0.22769	0.13037
1.00	126.89	0.15000	0.07938	0.15912	0.08285
1.25	132.85	0.11000	0.04939	0.10561	0.05063
1.50	138.80	0.07000	0.02764	0.06657	0.02966
1.75	144.76	0.04500	0.01409	0.03987	0.01651
2.00	150.72	0.02500	0.00701	0.02267	0.00864
2.25	156.68	0.01500	0.00293	0.01223	0.00423
2.50	162.63	0.00500	0.00029	0.00623	0.00194
2.75	168.59			0.00299	0.00086
3.00	174.55			0.00135	0.00038

deviation (sigma), the analysis reports the median value, the mean absolute deviation (MAD), and the coefficient of variation, which is the ratio of the standard deviation to the mean.

The graph plots a cumulative histogram of the data, with small circles in proportion to the number of observations that exceed any particular value. The asterisks plot the theoretical form of a normal distribution with the same mean and standard deviation.

The real test of whether the normal probability distribution is a good representation of this set of data is given in the table under the graph. Both the probability function $F(X)$ and the partial expectation function $E(X)$ are computed empirically for the data, and theoretically for the normal distribution that was chosen.

The expected amount back ordered depends on the partial expectation function. Therefore, to make good decisions about safety stocks, we should be reasonably sure that the theoretical values predicted by the model are close to the actual values observed. The agreement shown in Exhibit 8.5 is reasonably close.

8.112 Uniform Distribution. The second example (Exhibit 8.6) is the data that didn't look like a very uniform distribution when the histogram was plotted in Exhibit 8.2b, but where the tests of the probability and expectation confirm the choice of that model.

8.113 Exponential Distribution. The third example (Exhibit 8.7) is the data from Exhibit 8.3a, which show reasonably good agreement with the exponential distribution.

8.114 Log-Normal Distribution. The last example, for the log-normal distribution, is shown in Exhibit 8.8. Although to the naked eye the shapes of the exponential and log-normal distributions are very similar, there is a significant difference between the partial expectation functions for large values of the safety factor. For a safety factor $k = 2.75$, the exponential distribution predicts a partial expectation of 0.024, whereas this particular log-normal distribution predicts 0.037, a value about 50% larger. That is a significant difference in the expected level of service to be given, and it is well worth the effort to be sure the correct distribution is used.

8.12 Choice among Models

In the cases where extensive studies have been done along these lines for large numbers of forecasts, in several companies, it has been found that the

Exhibit 8.6

```
COMPONENT = UNIFORM
200 OBSERVATIONS HAVE RANGE 49, MEAN 124.8 AND SIGMA 15.22
MEDIAN = 126, M.A.D. = 13.25
COEFFICIENT OF VARIATION = 0.122
DISTRIBUTION FUNCTION = 2
```

UNIFORM

```
     ⊛
     ○ *
     ○○○ *
     ○○○○○ *
     ○○○○○○   *
P  ○○○○○○○○    *
R  ○○○○○○○○○○     *
O  ○○○○○○○○○○○○○ *
B  ○○○○○○○○○○○○○○○ *
A  ○○○○○○○○○○○○○○○○○*
B  ○○○○○○○○○○○○○○○○○○*
I  ○○○○○○○○○○○○○○○○○○○○  *
L  ○○○○○○○○○○○○○○○○○○○○○○  *
I  ○○○○○○○○○○○○○○○○○○○○○○○○  *
T  ○○○○○○○○○○○○○○○○○○○○○○○○○○  *
Y  ○○○○○○○○○○○○○○○○○○○○○○○○○○○○  *
   ○○○○○○○○○○○○○○○○○○○○○○○○○○○○○○  *
   ○○○○○○○○○○○○○○○○○○○○○○○○○○○○○○○○ *
   ○○○○○○○○○○○○○○○○○○○○○○○○○○○○○○○○○○ *
   ○○○○○○○○○○○○○○○○○○○○○○○○○○○○○○○○○○○○
              DATA
```

		EMPIRICAL		THEORETICAL	
SAFETY FACTOR	ORDER POINT	SHORTAGE PROBY	PARTIAL EXPECT	SHORTAGE PROBY	PARTIAL EXPECT
0.00	124.75	0.53500	0.43415	0.50000	0.43301
0.25	128.55	0.44000	0.31372	0.42783	0.31703
0.50	132.36	0.36500	0.21500	0.35566	0.21910
0.75	136.16	0.25000	0.13678	0.28349	0.13920
1.00	139.96	0.21500	0.07912	0.21132	0.07735
1.25	143.76	0.14500	0.03381	0.13916	0.03354
1.50	147.57	0.06500	0.00646	0.06699	0.00777
1.75	151.37				
2.00	155.17				
2.25	158.97				
2.50	162.78				
2.75	166.58				
3.00	170.38				

Exhibit 8.7

```
COMPONENT = EXPONENTIAL
200 OBSERVATIONS HAVE RANGE 115, MEAN 183.8 AND SIGMA 26.7
MEDIAN = 175, M.A.D. = 18.74
COEFFICIENT OF VARIATION = 0.1453
DISTRIBUTION FUNCTION = 3

EXPONENTIAL

         ⊛
         O*
         O*
         OO*
         OOO*
    P  OOO  *
    R  OOOOO*
    O  OOOOO*
    B  OOOOOO  *
    A  OOOOOOO  *
    B  OOOOOOOO  *
    I  OOOOOOOOO*
    L  OOOOOOOOOO  *
    I  OOOOOOOOOOO  *
    T  OOOOOOOOOOOO  *
    Y  OOOOOOOOOOOOO  *
       OOOOOOOOOOOOOOOO  *
       OOOOOOOOOOOOOOOOOO    *
       OOOOOOOOOOOOOOOOOOOOOOO      *
       OOOOOOOOOOOOOOOOOOOOOOOOOOOOOOOOOOO
                  DATA
```

		EMPIRICAL		THEORETICAL	
SAFETY	ORDER	SHORTAGE	PARTIAL	SHORTAGE	PARTIAL
FACTOR	POINT	PROBY	EXPECT	PROBY	EXPECT
0.00	183.78	0.35000	0.37595	0.36788	0.36788
0.25	190.46	0.28000	0.29920	0.28650	0.28650
0.50	197.13	0.23500	0.23617	0.22313	0.22313
0.75	203.80	0.16500	0.18571	0.17377	0.17377
1.00	210.48	0.14000	0.14922	0.13534	0.13534
1.25	217.15	0.11000	0.11813	0.10540	0.10540
1.50	223.82	0.09500	0.09222	0.08208	0.08208
1.75	230.50	0.08500	0.06997	0.06393	0.06393
2.00	237.17	0.08000	0.04950	0.04979	0.04979
2.25	243.84	0.05500	0.03404	0.03877	0.03877
2.50	250.52	0.04500	0.02198	0.03020	0.03020
2.75	257.19	0.02000	0.01184	0.02352	0.02352
3.00	263.86	0.02000	0.00684	0.01832	0.01832

Exhibit 8.8

COMPONENT = LOG1
200 OBSERVATIONS HAVE RANGE 108, MEAN 19.05 AND SIGMA 19.57
MEDIAN = 12, M.A.D. = 12.36
COEFFICIENT OF VARIATION = 1.028
DISTRIBUTION FUNCTION = 4

LOGNORMAL

```
      O*
      OO*
      OOO*
      OOOO*
      OOOO*
P     OOOOO*
R     OOOOOO*
O     OOOOOOO*
B     OOOOOOO  *
A     OOOOOOOO  *
B     OOOOOOOOO  *
I     OOOOOOOOOO  *
L     OOOOOOOOOOOO *
I     OOOOOOOOOOOO  *
T     OOOOOOOOOOOOOOO*
Y     OOOOOOOOOOOOOOOOOO*
      OOOOOOOOOOOOOOOOOOOOO    *
      OOOOOOOOOOOOOOOOOOOOOOOO      *
      OOOOOOOOOOOOOOOOOOOOOOOOOOOOOOO        *
      OOOOOOOOOOOOOOOOOOOOOOOOOOOOOOOOOOOOOO
                    DATA
```

		EMPIRICAL		THEORETICAL	
SAFETY FACTOR	ORDER POINT	SHORTAGE PROBY	PARTIAL EXPECT	SHORTAGE PROBY	PARTIAL EXPECT
0.00	19.04	0.32500	0.34709	0.33694	0.31747
0.25	23.94	0.28000	0.27106	0.24511	0.24622
0.50	28.83	0.19500	0.21436	0.18137	0.19492
0.75	33.72	0.13000	0.17515	0.13647	0.15687
1.00	38.61	0.11500	0.14491	0.10433	0.12784
1.25	43.50	0.10500	0.11744	0.08094	0.10519
1.50	48.39	0.07500	0.09357	0.06363	0.08720
1.75	53.28	0.06000	0.07734	0.05064	0.07276
2.00	58.17	0.04500	0.06554	0.04074	0.06105
2.25	63.06	0.04500	0.05429	0.03309	0.05150
2.50	67.95	0.03500	0.04429	0.02712	0.04366
2.75	72.85	0.03000	0.03576	0.02241	0.03719
3.00	77.74	0.03000	0.02826	0.01865	0.03183

form of the distribution tends to be similar for most of the items in the inventory—bearing in mind that a single company may have several different inventories, such as service parts versus prime products. If that is true, then one can examine a reasonable sample of a few dozen sets of forecast errors, and see what sort of a distribution function applies, with reasonable assurance that the form chosen will be appropriate as well for the items not analyzed in the sample. However, the consequences of basing safety stock theory on the wrong assumption about the form of the distribution function can be serious.

If you have access to a trained statistician, he can carry out chi-square tests to determine which form of the distribution is the best model of the actual experience in your inventory. If you don't have a statistician there are some simple tests which are quite adequate.

The two forms of the distribution one is most likely to encounter are the normal (which has a symmetrical distribution) and the exponential (as a simple skewed distribution). In a normal distribution about 2% of the observations exceed a level two standard deviations above the mean. In an exponential distribution the probability of exceeding the mean by more than 2.75 standard deviations is about 2%. Therefore if the number of standard deviations it takes to account for all but about 2% of the observations is near 2, a normal distribution should be used. If it is above 2.7, the exponential distribution should be used.

It should be kept in mind that primary manufacturing, which sees demand filtered through many levels of distribution, is quite likely to see normal distributions. On the other hand, retailers, dealing with the ultimate consumer, are more likely to see exponential distributions.

Note that the form of the distribution should be decided on the forecast errors, not the distribution of the demand itself. For example, in Exhibit 5.14 the standard deviation of the demand was 258, but when a proper forecast model is selected, the standard deviation of the forecast errors is only 48. Furthermore, the decisions made for safety stocks (Chapter 10) will use the probability model of the distribution of errors in forecasting demand over a lead time, not just for one forecast period. One reason that manufacturing companies often find the normal distribution to be a good model is that the lead times cover several forecast review periods. Hence the errors of concern are the sums of several samples of the errors in forecasting one period ahead. By the central limit theorem, even if the errors period by period have some very peculiar distribution, sums of samples from these distributions tend to be normally distributed. Retailers, on the other hand, with very short replenishment lead times, may find very skewed distributions.

FORM OF THE DISTRIBUTION

8.13 Formulas

Exhibit 8.9 gives a summary of the mathematical formulas for the probability distribution and partial expectations for all four distributions illustrated. Note that the log-normal distribution (which we meet again in Chapter 9) reverts to a simple normal distribution of the logarithms of the values observed.

The essential probability concepts that we expect to use in later chapters are probability density, probability functions, partial expectation, the mean, the standard deviation, and the variance. To follow all the development of the safety stock strategies in Chapter 10 you should be able to look up any of the probability functions in the table given the safety factor, or conversely, if you are given a value for one of the functions, you should be able to look up the corresponding safety factor.

Exhibit 8.9

If the order point, or planning level, is expressed as OP = mean + k standard deviations, then the relations among the probability of a shortage $F(k)$, the partial expectation $E(k)$, and these functions of the order point are as follows.

Distribution		Probability	Partial Expectation
Normal		$F(OP) = F(k)$ $F(k) = \int_k^\infty p(t)\,dt$	$E(OP) = \sigma E(k)$ $E(k) = \int_k^\infty (t-k)p(t)\,dt$
	Density	$p(t) = \dfrac{1}{\sqrt{2\pi}} e^{-t^2/2}$	
Exponential		$F(OP) = F(k)$ $F(k) = e^{-(1+k)}$	$E(OP) = E(k)$ $E(k) = e^{-(1+k)}$
Uniform from A to B		$F(OP) = \dfrac{B - OP}{B - A}$ $F(k) = 0.5 - k/\sqrt{12}$	$E(OP) = \sqrt{3}\left(\dfrac{B - OP}{B - A}\right)^2$ $E(k) = \sqrt{3}(0.5 - k/\sqrt{12})^2$
Log normal		Let the demand, in pieces, be $X = \sigma_X + k\mu_X$ Let $Y = \ln X = \sigma_Y + T\mu_Y$ Covariance $\;\text{cov} = \sigma_X/\mu_X$ Parameter $\;\sigma_Y^2 = \ln(1 + \text{cov}^2)$ Parameter $\;T = (1/\sigma)\ln e^{\sigma^2/2}(1 + k\,\text{cov})$ Use the normal distribution for $F(T)$ and $E(T)$	

8.2 MEASURES OF DISPERSION

The mean and standard deviation are the essential parameters to describe a distribution (once the form has been chosen), and the planning level X is the mean plus the safety factor times the standard deviation. The variance is the square of the standard deviation. The probability for any safety factor is purely a matter of consulting the right table. The numerical values of the mean and the standard deviation pertain to a particular item in the inventory.

In the forecasting system, the forecast itself is the mean of the distribution for any item for any future time period. The measure of error computed is the mean square error (MSE), which is the variance of the distribution of errors.

8.21 Standard Deviation and Mean Absolute Deviation

In earlier systems, going back to the early 1950s when I first set up statistical forecasting on an IBM Type 602A multiplying punch, there was no practical way to compute a variance or to take the square root to get the standard deviation. The internal buffers were too small to hold large numbers, and the procedure for extracting square roots was too cumbersome to contemplate. Hence the notion of the mean absolute deviation (MAD) was born. See my 1959 book, *Statistical Forecasting for Inventory Control*, p. 93, footnote.

Then as successive generations of computers were developed, the notion stuck and has been thoroughly embedded in all of IBM's program products ever since. In the early 1400 series computers the allowance for core was so small that they could still not hold large numbers or take square roots. And so it went.

A neurosis has been defined as a response that is no longer appropriate to the real environment, no matter how appropriate it was when the response was first learned. In that sense the mean absolute deviation is neurotic.

MAD is no longer appropriate to the real world of computers. It never was the correct measure of dispersion. (It is correct when one is fitting a median line, not a least-squares line, and happens to work reasonably well with normally distributed noise.) But with today's computers the space and the speed are both entirely adequate and there is no longer any excuse, except habit and a large investment in training manuals, for continuing to use the MAD.

There is even some potential degradation of the accuracy with which the system will compute safety stocks if the standard deviation has to be

MEASURES OF DISPERSION

inferred by multiplying the mean absolute deviation by 1.25, the theoretical factor for the normal distribution. In the set of data in Exhibit 8.5 the actual ratio is 1.23, which is fairly close. Actual checks on several thousand real time series over a number of years have found factors ranging from 1 to 1.5. That range of uncertainty might be acceptable, but then don't bother to erect a large edifice of safety stock theory on it. Admit that you want a crude system and use crude methods throughout. The range in actual values of the factors is large enough to be taken seriously if you really want a good inventory management system. In Exhibits 8.7 and 8.8 the ratios are 1.42 and 1.58, respectively.

8.22 Effect of Lead Time

If the lead time is known in advance, then the standard deviation that we shall want to use in safety stock theory is not just the square root of the mean square error, which measures the forecast accuracy for only the next period. We need the standard deviation of the distribution of forecast errors over the lead time. The dispersion will be larger for forecasting the total demand during a lead time than for forecasting demand in the next month.

The effect of lead time is plotted in Exhibit 8.10 for four different time series (in this case actual measurements in the real world, not synthetically constructed series) where I happen to have at least 100 observations. A simulation of the forecasting process captured the errors not only for just one period ahead, but for all lead times from 1 to 12 months. At the end of the simulation the standard deviation of the actual errors was computed for

Exhibit 8.10

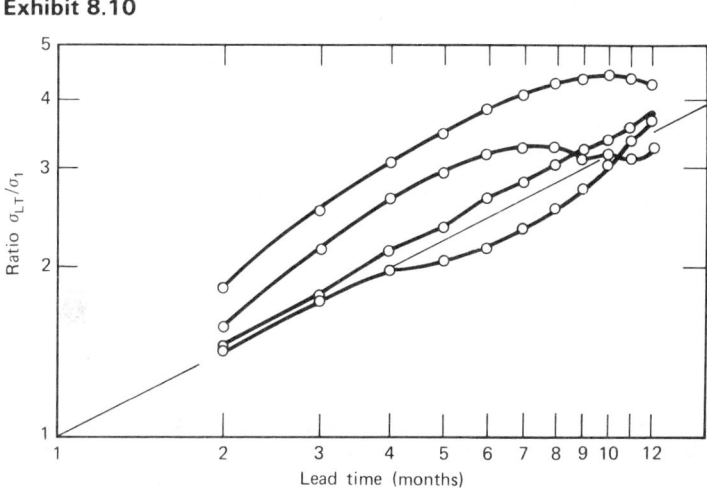

total accumulated demand for each lead time. The ratios of the standard deviation for a given lead time are normalized by dividing by the standard deviation of errors in one-ahead forecasts.

The solid line represents ratios that are proportional to the square root of the lead time, which would be expected if the noise in the process is strictly uncorrelated. In actual practice there is sometimes some serial correlation which makes errors in periods near each other more likely to be on the same side of the average error. That is reflected by the series of points in Exhibit 8.10 that is somewhat higher than the typical square-root line.

As a practical matter, the standard deviation for longer lead times (or for shorter ones) is estimated as proportional to the square root of the lead time. That means that the standard deviation for any lead time is the square root of (lead time × mean square error) which saves one square-root computation.

(In IBM's IMPACT system and a host of descendants supplied by many different computer vendors, it is stated that the standard deviation is proportional to the 0.7 power of the lead time, which was based on one such study for one such pilot account, and apparently never repeated. It is easy to get the 0.7 power, or even higher values, if the forecast model is incorrectly selected (like using a horizontal model on data with some trend) so that the necessary serial correlation is introduced.)

8.221 Variable Lead Times. Lead times may vary in the sense that they are sometimes long and sometimes short. If the lead time is known reasonably well for the next order, then it can be treated as a known lead time. It is just that the value changes from order to order.

There are situations in which experience shows that the lead times have varied and there is no way of predicting in advance how long the next lead time will be. There are three approaches to the problem.

1. Set up a theoretical model of the distributions of the lengths of the lead time, and of the distribution of forecast errors. In my book *Smoothing, Forecasting and Prediction of Discrete Time Series*, p. 367, there are two derivations of the effective resultant standard deviation. One assumes that the process takes a random number of periods and adds the errors for that number of samples. The other assumes that it takes a random length of a lead time and multiplies the randomly selected demand rate by that length of time. The derivations lead to significantly different models of the standard deviation, and both are likely to be wrong in fact.

    In these mathematical models, a key assumption is that the variation in the length of the lead time is uncorrelated with the variation in the

MEASURES OF DISPERSION 151

demand. That is likely not to be true and to have a major bearing on the result. An absolutely precise and rigorous mathematical derivation of the answer to a problem you don't have isn't much help in running a business. Therefore I strongly advise steering clear of mathematical models of the standard deviation over randomly varying lead times.

2. Manage the lead time. In 13.3 we treat in some detail methods of establishing a specific freeze period, which may be of about the same length as a typical lead time, but it is agreed by both the supplier and the user to be the relevant period of time in changing requirements. Although actual lead times may vary, the relevant period of time for computing safety stocks is known and fixed by agreement, so one can extrapolate standard deviations to that lead time.

   The same approach can often be used with outside vendors to stipulate the delivery date, which makes the effective lead time known in advance.

3. If you really do have lead times that vary unpredictably, and which cannot be managed through agreement with the source (as with imported materials), then the following procedure will work precisely and simply. Don't forecast demand per period. Forecast demand per lead time. A lead time starts when you trigger a replenishment order. As part of the open order file, record the demand year to date at that time. Later, whenever material is received is by definition the end of the lead time. Examine the demand year to date then. The difference between the current demand year to date, and the value when the order was released is precisely, by definition, the demand during a lead time. The values of this variable can be forecast (usually with very simple forecast models) and the mean square error can be measured. But this mean square error is the variance of demand during a lead time, precisely the value being sought. We return to this notion in Chapter 12 when we consider methods of managing inventories of items with "lumpy" demand.

8.23 Measuring the Mean Square Error

Initially the mean square error can be computed at the time when the forecast model is fitted to the data. The chosen model is evaluated at each historical point in time. The differences between actual history and that model are squared and summed. The total sum of squares is divided by the number of degrees of freedom to get the initial value of the mean square error. The number of degrees of freedom is the number of observations of history, less the number of terms in the forecast model. Each additional term in the forecast model takes away degrees of freedom and therefore increases the estimate of the standard deviation.

For an example, look back at Exhibits 5.15 and 5.16. Note that even though a small season amplitude would "explain" some of the variation in the raw data, the decrease in the number of degrees of freedom makes the standard deviation actually increase.

As each new observation of demand is processed to revise the forecast, the square of the current forecast error is averaged, by simple exponential smoothing, to revise the previous value of the mean square error.

The variance of the distribution is a measure of the second moment (square) around the mean. But because the mean of the forecast errors had jolly well better be zero, the variance about the origin should give the same value. Hence we can use the simple mean square error and not worry about correcting for the mean.

8.24 Variance Law

It is very common to find that there is a strong relationship between the standard deviation of forecast errors and the level of the forecast.

Eighteen different time series that I have collected for some time were processed to get the results shown in Exhibit 8.11. Some of these series are Friday closing prices of shares traded on the New York Stock Exchange. Some represent natural phenomena like the height of the spring floods of the Nile River, sunspots, and rainfall in Concord, Massachusetts. Other series represent retail sales of apparel and furniture. The only unusual property of these series is that they are all much longer than is normal in common industrial files. But they do represent a wise mix of types of time series, including some demand on inventories.

For each series a model was fitted to the most recent 72 observations. The standard deviations of the residual differences between the model and the raw data were computed, allowing for 2 to 13 degrees of freedom as the process selected different kinds of seasonal profiles.

For each series there is one point. The vertical coordinate is the value of the standard deviation, and the horizontal coordinate is the level of the forecast. Because of the very wide spread in values, logarithmic scales are used on both axes. Even with the wide variety in sources of data, there is a clear line of central tendency, and the equation of that line is called the variance law.

For actual inventories, the scatter is likely to be somewhat more closely bunched around the line of central tendency. At Phillips Lamp, in Holland, several years ago, a plot like this revealed two quite distinct scatter diagrams. Further investigation uncovered two radically different markets in which they sold, and that discovery led to some reorganization of the marketing departments to serve these markets effectively.

MEASURES OF DISPERSION

Exhibit 8.11

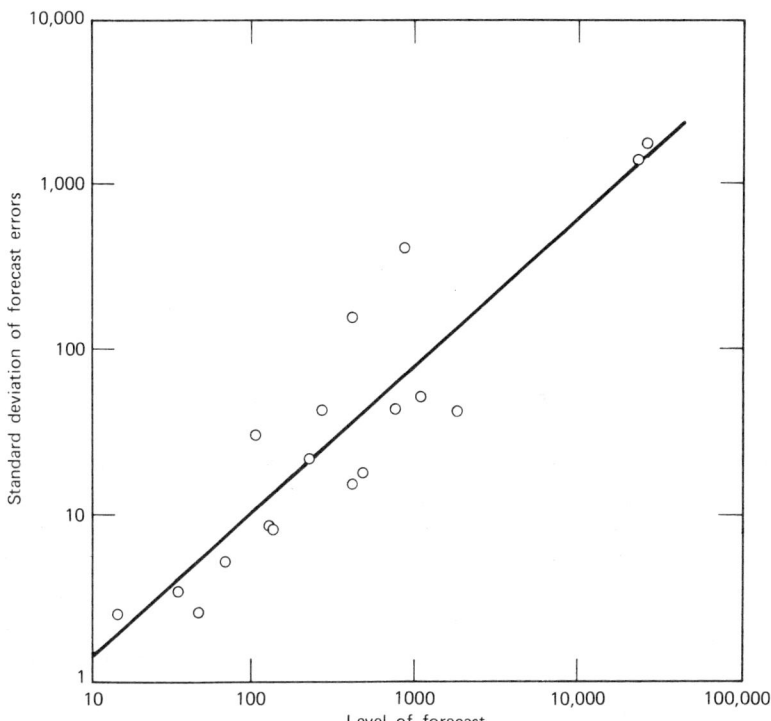

When forecast models have been fitted to a large number of items in the inventory that have adequate history, then the line of central tendency can be measured and stored in the data base. See Exhibit 3.6.

Then as items are introduced which have no history, the variance law can be used to get reasonable initial values. Suppose the responsible brand manager who was introducing a new product had plugged in a level of 200 units per month. In Exhibit 8.11, items that have a level of usage of 200 a month have a standard deviation of about 20, so that value could be used as the initial condition.

8.3 EXCEPTION REPORTS

Tracking signals were reported in Exhibit 3.7. See 7.31 for a discussion of what to do about them.

So far we have been primarily concerned with the mean square error and the standard deviation, as a measure of the dispersion of forecast errors. It is assumed that the average forecast error is zero. But it isn't safe to assume anything in the real world, so we want some checks that the average forecast error is reasonably close to zero.

8.31 Tracking Signal

The tracking signal is a means for monitoring the average forecast error and for printing an exception report when the average departs significantly from zero. Some of the forecast errors are positive and some are negative, as the demand is above or below the forecast. In the long run these values should cancel each other out. The least-squares process of fitting the model initially does ensure that the average error starts at zero.

Obviously if in the first month the demand is above the forecast, the average error at that point is not exactly zero, but positive. We want to set up some reasonable limits around zero and, when the average forecast error exceeds those limits, call the attention of the marketing intelligence group to the fact that demand is moving in one direction faster than the forecast can adapt.

There are three possible schemes for tracking signals. Two use a cumulative sum of the forecast error, and one uses an exponentially smoothed average error.

1. With the method of simple cumulative sums, initially the cumulative sum of the errors is zero. Each month the value of the forecast error is added, with sign, to the previous value of the sum. If positive and negative values are reasonably scattered together, the cumulative sum wiggles up and down, but it won't get very large in either direction. However, when the demand starts growing faster than the forecast can adapt, there will be a long string of positive forecast errors, and the cumulative sum will grow.

   In my 1959 book *Statistical Forecasting for Inventory Control*, I worked out some confidence limits on this sum in terms of the standard deviation of forecast errors. Various tests indicated it would work, but when it was implemented in practice two phenomena came to light—that is the value of having an executable realization of the formal definition of the system, to allow Murphy's Law to help identify the real needs of the environment.

   The first strange consequence is that the cumulative sum always starts, for the remainder of the series, from where it is today. It is like the say-

EXCEPTION REPORTS 155

ing, "Today is the first day of the rest of your life." If the cumulative sum starts from zero, then the theoretical model of the variation does correctly predict confidence limits. But let us suppose there is one isolated large error, not large enough to trip the tracking signal limits but enough to move the sum definitely away from zero. From then on the system may be in control and the cumulative sum wiggles back and forth around that level. Perhaps much later a second error in the same direction finally trips the tracking signal. Thus one needs a system that forgets isolated errors.

The other peculiarity was that a perfect forecast can trip the tracking signal. A perfect forecast generates zero forecast error, so the cumulative sum doesn't change. But a zero error reduces the estimate of the standard deviation, and may bring the confidence limits below what was an acceptable (barely) sum last month.

2. The second method that uses the same sort of cumulative sum was published in *Decision Sciences* "Detecting Turning Points in a Time Series." The technique is an extension of Wald's sequential analysis, through Barnard's V-masks, to develop a parabolic mask based on the Type I and Type II errors of detection. The computations are far too elaborate for use in monitoring the thousands of forecasts revised every period for an inventory, but they have proved extremely powerful in detecting turning points in the movements of prices of shares traded on the stock exchange. I use this method every weekend to track the Friday closing prices and usually can find a bottom early enough after a turn to leave room for a considerable period of growth in price, and similarly can find that the prices have moved past a peak and are now started downward.

The concepts might be worth implementing for monitoring the major sales series for a corporation, but not at the detailed level of individual products.

3. The formal definition uses a smoothed error tracking signal (SETS), which each month uses simple exponential smoothing to revise the estimate of the average error, which started at zero when the forecast was initially set up.

Decision Rules for Inventory Management, p. 164, derives the expression that the variance of the smoothed error is proportional to the variance of the forecast errors, and the constant of proportionality depends on the value of the smoothing constant being used. The formulas are given in Exhibit 8.12.

Exhibit 8.12

Smoothed error tracking signal (SETS)
Revision

$$\text{SETS} = \beta\, \text{SETS} + (1 - \beta)\, \text{error}$$

Standard deviation

$$\sigma_{\text{SETS}} = \sqrt{\text{MSE}\,(1 - \beta)/(1 + \beta)}$$

Hence the limits will be some multiple of the standard deviation of the smoothed error, which in turn is proportional to the standard deviation of the forecast errors themselves.

Some items are quite critical to the performance of the inventory, and it may be worthwhile to set the limits rather tight at the risk of getting some exception reports when nothing really has happened. Other items are cheap, so inventory investment is insignificant and may not be essential to the customer; therefore an occasional shortage doesn't matter very much either. For such items we would set the limits quite wide, so that if an exception report is triggered, there is a very high likelihood that something has really happened to change the demand pattern. It is a matter of the relative importance of the Type I and Type II errors. If you will tolerate a few false reports but want to be sure to catch real changes early, set the limits tight, at about twice the standard deviation of the smoothed error. If you want no false reports, and can accept the risk of missing significant changes for a while, set the limits wide, perhaps at something like four times the standard deviation of the smoothed error. In practice you may want to provide for three classes of limits, tight, normal, and loose, and assign different segments of the inventory to different classes.

8.32 Demand Filters

Demand filters are another way of ensuring that the forecasts are believable. Occasionally there are keypunch errors in recording data, or demand that was really a dependent demand or was to fill a large scheduled backlog type of order gets recorded to be used in forecasting. Some of these errors slip through and are processed in revising the forecasts, but we want to catch the big ones. At one time during World War II Captain Emory Stanley, Jr., in the Bureau of Supplies and Accounts, inadvertently wrote

EXCEPTION REPORTS

down a figure one column over from where he intended to, so that his order was 10 times as large as he planned. He had a corner on the country's supply of canned peaches for about a month, until the problem was detected. It is that sort of error that one wants to avoid, unless you're especially fond of peaches and have a lot of money and a big warehouse.

A very simple check on the reasonableness of incoming demand data is the standard deviation of forecast errors. Exhibit 3.7 showed an example of how the opportunity for on-line correction is presented. Any demand that is more than four standard deviations away from the forecast is highly suspect, and should be reviewed before it is processed. The review may show that the demand is reasonable, and it should be processed to increase the standard deviation. However, a quick check in advance can save some problems.

Here too, one wants perhaps three levels of sensitivity depending on the risks involved with letting a real error slip through versus the risks of having to review reports for large, but perfectly reasonable, variations. Something in the range of 3.5 standard deviations for a tight control, 4 for normal control, and 5 for loose control suggests itself.

Summary: The Best Forecast

The forecasting system is a major element of an overall materials management system. The total requirements to be satisfied come from both descriptive and explanatory forecasts of demand, plus a scheduled backlog of firm orders, and as we shall see later, dependent demand exploded from the master schedules for higher level kits and assemblies.

The modular nature of the system permits a user to employ only the forecasting routines and supply the other information from other sources, or to bypass the proffered forecasting techniques in favor of alternatives, so long as the necessary requirements are posted to the data base where other applications can utilize them.

The systems are rife with feedback for control, ranging from the smoothing processes which use forecast errors at a detailed level to modify the forecast coefficients, right up to the marketing intelligence and tracking signals which involve the descriptive part of the forecasting process with the subjective judgment and experience of the managers who have other information and are prepared to take certain kinds of risks.

There is also considerable variety in the choices that can be made, to increase the likelihood that some combination of features will match sufficiently the real needs of any particular operating environment. One can choose the period at which forecasts are revised, the rate of smoothing, the number of terms in the model, the mix of backlog, statistics and judgment, and the sensitivity to exception reports that monitor the whole process.

The primary intent of the materials management systems library is to afford a rich variety from which users can select options that appeal, and still have the architectural unity that permits the whole system to help management run the business effectively. Because the system is modular, other techniques not now in the library could easily be provided to implement, or simply demonstrate and test, the Box/Jenkins, Harrison/Stevens, Winters, Theil, or any other sound forecasting method. A reasonably wide experience in industry, however, has taught me that so long as any technique is properly applied, the resulting forecasts are going to be good. The absolutely best technique might well give a more accurate forecast than the third best technique. But even the third best technique is likely to be good, when measured in terms of the inventory investment required to support a given level of customer service.

If one has readily available a technique that is seen to be good, consider what it takes to be sure that it is the best. First, it takes time to conduct a study of several techniques. During the period of the study one is not getting the benefit even from the good technique. Is the potential improvement going to be large enough to warrant delaying the start of any implementation?

Second, the study takes talent. The study of the merits of alternative techniques of forecasting requires some very able people with highly specialized training in a particular branch of mathematical statistics. A study done by amateurs will produce results that can't be trusted. And if you can't trust the conclusions, why make the study?

Third, the study takes some money that might be better spent elsewhere. It is necessary to ask, "Is there a high enough likelihood that a better method will be found to earn a return on the effort expended to find it?"

Like the Deacon's One Hoss Shay, if all parts of a system are equally good, the system will work satisfactorily. If too much effort is expended to make one piece of the system perfect, time, talent, and money are taken away from other parts of the system, and the overall performance may suffer.

By way of closing this section, let me comment a little on the use of simulations to explore alternative techniques of forecasting. In my 1959 book I put in a paragraph to admit that I didn't really know what value to use for the smoothing constant. But one could run some simulations to look for the best value. I even displayed some rather convincing graphs from simulations I had run. Unfortunately, I inadvertently picked a series where there is an unusually clear dependence of forecast accuracy on the smoothing constant.

For most series, the variation caused by the particular sample selected is quite a bit larger than the effect of the smoothing constant. Honeywell for a time advertised a simulation program, attributed to me, to find the best smoothing constant. I had to kick up quite a ruckus to get them at least to take my name out of the ad—I don't recall whether they dropped the program as well.

You can verify this problem yourself by the following experiment. Construct a very long series using a Monte Carlo random number process. Don't use live data because (*a*) live series are usually much too short, and (*b*) live series generally include some unknown extraneous effects of strikes, promotions, competition, and so on. If you construct the series you can guarantee that it is all one homogeneous stationary series. Divide the long series into samples that are of the length normally used in the simulations. Run the simulation of each segment. There will be a distribution of values of the best smoothing constant found on each segment—remember these are all samples from the same total population, constructed to be uniform throughout.

Now recall that if we were to simulate, the value found at the end of one segment would have to be the value used in forecasting the next segment. We won't know what value is best until that segment becomes history, but if we conduct the measurements properly we would probably find that using the smoothing constant that was optimum for the last small segment, each part in turn, gives somewhat worse results in total than just picking any reasonable value (0.9, for example) and using it throughout.

There is a reason why 0.1 was originally chosen in exponential smoothing, which corresponds to the 0.9 discount factor. On the old IBM Type 602A multiplying punch, one didn't really want to multiply two numbers if possible. It was too slow. But it is easy to multiply by 0.1, move the wires over one hold in the plug board, and add. That's where the magic smoothing constant of 0.1 really came from.

If you really want to justify a foregone conclusion, use percentages in the following way. Consider the Red Method versus the Blue Method.

		Forecast Errors			
		Red Method		Blue Method	
Item	Average Sales	Standard deviation	Percent	Standard deviation	Percent
A	10,000	100	1	1000	10
B	1,000	100	10	100	10
C	100	100	100	10	10
D	1	100	1000	1	10
Total	400	1111	1111	40	
Average	100	278	278	10	

"Clearly" the Blue Method is superior, because the average error is 10%, far below the average error of 278% for the Red Method. However, some managers might really prefer to carry 400 pieces of safety stock from the Red Method, rather than 1111 pieces required by the Blue Method. One must be careful in arguing from average percentages.

SECTION

Inventory Management

To a warehouseman, inventory is bins and pallets full of material. Generally speaking, the bigger the piles, the happier he is, until the stock starts to overflow the normal storage areas and accumulate in the aisles. To him inventory control seems to be summed up in housekeeping: if the building is neat and clean, and the proper chits are prepared and presented, he is happy.

Senior management of a company seems to take quite a different view of inventory, primarily as a figure that shows up on the balance sheet as a lump sum. If business conditions look good, and especially if costs are likely to rise, the inventory investment can inch up without causing too much distress. When times are tight there may be pressure to reduce the inventory investment. Management also doesn't like stock overflowing into the aisles because that means poorer service in filling customer orders, and pressure from the operating people to spend money on expansion of facilities.

During the recession in the mid-1970s the financial papers and magazines watched total inventory figures in relation to sales to try to infer the mood of the economy, when it was bottoming out and when it was starting to rise. There is a puzzling gap between *Fortune's* view of inventories and that of the manager of distribution. *Fortune* talks about inventory going up or down in relation to sales as though it were a deliberate act on the part of rational management. From a microscopic view from within any company, it seems that management "feels inventory is too high" and requests the operating people to "bring it into line."

A third view of business inventories, trying to bridge that gap, is that of the management scientist who sees replenishment decisions according to programmable decision rules that result in predictable inventory levels, and predictable levels of customer service. These rules do contain management policy variables that the senior management of the firm can control as their perception of the economic climate changes.

This section has to do with those decision rules, the management policy variables, and the exchanges between operating expense and capital investment that are possible in a modern materials management system. The decision rules are part of the second-level system, which is gradually becoming understood in industry. The use of the controls in any formal way is part of the third-level system, and only a very few pioneering companies fully understand the power that these controls give to senior management.

CHAPTER **9**

Stratification

Although the inventory investment shows up as a lump sum on the balance sheet, some of the controls probably should be exercised separately on individual classes of inventory. No company lacks controls entirely, but in many cases, the control has been fragmented right down to the product, or SKU (stockkeeping unit, a product in a location) level, and left to the stock clerk to exercise. This puts decisions that have important consequences in the hands of people who do not fully appreciate the corporate goals and especially the way that capital can be invested in support of those goals.

Modern data processing systems can be designed to permit the user to define his own classification at the time he wants a report or to do an analysis. Older conventional systems may allow for inventory classification, but that is considered some fixed element of the records, always to be retrieved and used that way. An extreme case of the permanent classification is the "significant part number" system, in which the unique identifier of any product has an internal structure so that "anyone" can immediately see the products in which it is used, the year it was released, the commodity class it belongs to, the shape of the object, and other attributes that can be very convenient for special studies. For example, when the engineers design a new product, they can easily find existing part numbers that are similar in function, and thus reduce the likelihood of proliferating product variety by introducing new part numbers that have about the same function. When there is a shortage, one can immediately retrieve all the parts affected by that commodity code, and see what the situation is.

The major problem with significant part numbers—aside from the fact that only people who have the key to the code can ever read them—is that the next study to be undertaken always seems to need some attribute that wasn't coded into the system. There is also the problem that the fields in the part number reserved for various attributes have a way of running out of space. Pharmaceutical manufacturers, for example, are now using 17-digit product codes to distinguish among perhaps 700 different products, including package size and language.

An alternative approach is to use nonsignificant part numbers (which are shorter and easier for people to remember and use correctly, and which never run out of room) and to design the information system to be able to retrieve all items that fall into a class that is defined at the time the information is retrieved. Then studies of function can retrieve on use. Studies of shortages can retrieve on commodity. Studies of warehouse space can retrieve on cubic size and annual movement.

The formal definition of the Materials Management Systems library allows three broad classes of retrieval for every program.

1. For some reports and analyses, one wants to retrieve all the items on the file, and they might as well be processed in the same sequence as they are filed.
2. In other cases, one wants a specific list of items. Typical lists would include a set of part numbers, the parents of subordinate items, the subordinates of assemblies, or all items at some particular level code. Lists that are used frequently can be generated and stored in a directory, so that the particular list is called out when one wants a particular report or when some subset of the inventory is processed. These lists are similar to the traditional classifications, except that a given part could be a member of several different classes. For example, a part might be classed by manufacturing plant, by marketing manager, and by type of economic market.
3. The principal use of the data base for management studies, including strategic controls, is applied to sets of items where the characteristics of the set can be defined, but it is up to the computer to find all members of that set. Some tests that are used frequently and are provided for in standard retrieval programs are as follows: (a) items where the available stock is below order point; (b) items where one or more periods of history lie greater than four standard deviations away from the forecast model; (c) items where the absolute value of the trend is more than a specified fraction of the level; and (d) items by specified classes, such as A, B, and C.

Although these standard tests are available, the user can at any time define his own test of any logical combination of attributes that have been recorded in the data base. An example of such a test might be all items that have a unit cost of at least $50, that have no subordinates in the bill of materials, that are stocked in four or more warehouses, and that have some scheduled backlog orders. The test to select those items isn't standard, but it can be written quickly, by the user, at the time he finds he wants that

DISTRIBUTION BY VALUE

peculiar set of items. Furthermore he can retrieve the set, analyze it, and get an answer before he has forgotten what his question was.

9.1 DISTRIBUTION BY VALUE

Exhibit 4.1 showed a typical report that summarizes how many items, and how much value, fall into each of several classes. The classes are automatically defined at semidecade intervals (powers of the square root of 10) to span the values encountered. The list of items processed can be defined by the user according to the purpose of the report. The value is based on the current forecast of annual usage multiplied by any field of the item master record, such as standard cost, selling price, material cost, cubic feet, weight, or anything else that has been recorded. At the same time the summary tabulation is accumulated, a list of specific items at the high end of the value is also built up, so that one can print the details of the few items that contribute the major portion of the value.

9.11 Log-Normal Model

Throughout all industries in all countries, the fractions of items falling into each class and the fraction of total value contributed by that class follow a very standard pattern, which can be represented by a log-normal distribution. That is, the distribution of the logarithms of the values is an ordinary normal distribution. In Chapter 8 we considered the log-normal distribution as a possible model of the errors in forecasting any one product in successive time periods. Here we consider the log-normal distribution as the most probable model of the distribution of annual sales (or usage) values across all the items in an inventory.

There are two purposes to this model. (*a*) It sometimes helps to show that the total inventory is really built up of separate types of inventory, which helps to establish better classification for management control. (*b*) Within any stratum of the inventory, studies done on a sample of the items can be projected in terms of the consequences for the total population. Thus one can examine many more cases, since the cost of analysis on small samples is small, and be surer of implementing the proper management strategy for the whole inventory.

First let's look at how to represent the distribution by value as a lognormal distribution. Exhibit 9.1 is plotted on special graph paper on which both axes are laid out on a probability scale. (One source of this paper is Keuffel and Esser, Form 47 8062.) The horizontal axis is the fraction of active items, ranked in descending sequence by value. The vertical axis is

Exhibit 9.1

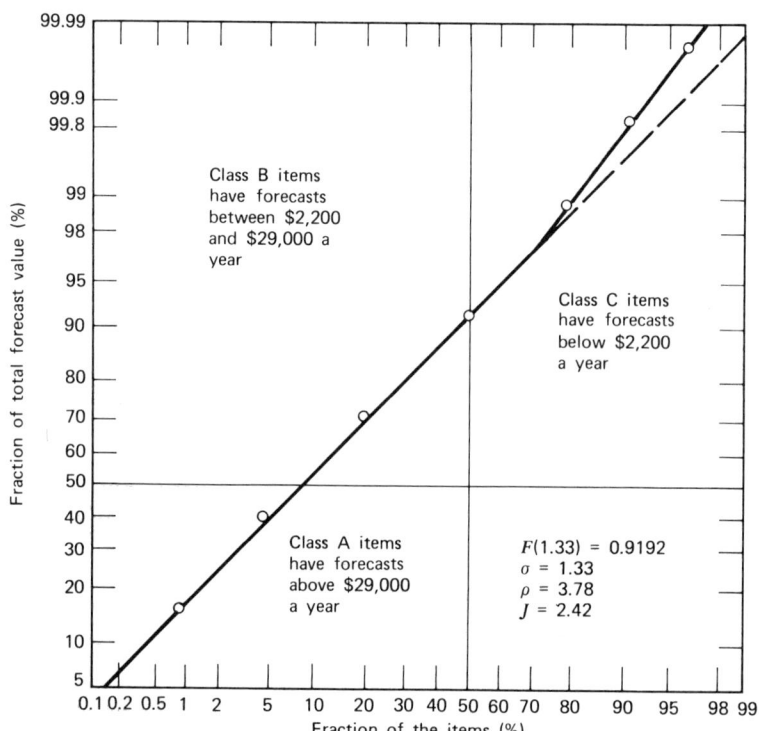

the fraction of the total annual value, contributed by these items. Points can be read from Exhibit 4.1 for each class interval. If the grid were an ordinary rectangular grid, the points would fall along a Pareto curve. On this special graph paper, the points fall along a straight line, with a slope of 45 degrees.

The fraction of total cost represented by the top 50% of the items indicates the parameter sigma of the log-normal distribution. The normal probability function $F(s)$ is the point where the line through the points crosses the line for 50% of the items. In this case $F(s) = 0.91929$, so the parameter $s = 1.40$ (which can be looked up in the tables of the normal distribution in Appendix D.) The "standard ratio" of the distribution is $r = \exp s = 4.055$ in this example. A correction factor $J = \exp 0.5s*2 = 2.664$ is also required to project results from samples up to the whole population.

Exhibit 9.2 is another way of plotting the same information. In this case (Codex form 31,376), the horizontal axis is a logarithmic scale on which we plot the ends of the class intervals. The vertical scale is the same normal probability scale. Here we plot two sets of points. One is the fraction of the

DISTRIBUTION BY VALUE

active items plotted against class interval. The other is the fraction of total value of the forecast plotted against the same class intervals. Each set of points falls nearly along a straight line; furthermore, the two lines are parallel, with a predictable distance apart.

The average sales per item is computed by dividing the total sales (or other measure of usage rate) by the number of active items. In the example that is $8039 per part per annum. The median m_1 is the value of usage corresponding to half the items. It is equal to the average divided by the factor J, in the example $3,017.6 per item per annum. The other median m_2 represents the annual usage that corresponds to half the total value. It is equal to the average times the factor J, in the example $21,416 per part per annum.

These two medians locate a point on the theoretical line, along the line for 50% of the population, vertically in the center of the graph. The common slope of the lines is defined by the standard ratio. Notice the point marked in the right margin for -1, which is one standard deviation below the mean. The value of sales corresponding to that percentage of the items is the standard ratio times m_1, or $8039 \times 2.66 = 21,384$. With a point and a

Exhibit 9.2

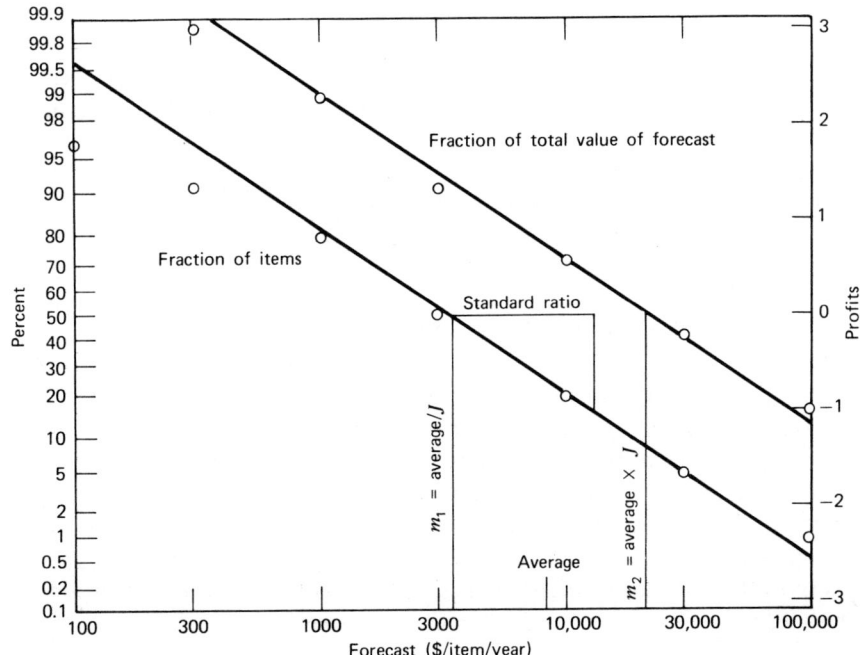

slope for each line, the lines can be drawn, and they will pass nearly through the plotted points. Unless . . .

9.12 Two Populations

Sometimes the set of parts or products selected for the analysis constitutes two (or more) separate populations with significantly different populations of usage. Carborundum, for example, found that some of their grinding wheels are sold primarily through hardware distributors for small shops and hobbyists. Other wheels, which at one time may have been defined (from the inside out) as part of the same product line, are for industrial use, bought by U.S. Steel and the Ford Motor Company. The fact that there were quite different markets came to light by the fact that in Figure 9.1 there was a definite break in the line for the last 20% of the items. In Figure 9.2 the parallel lines fitted by the methods described above did not pass through the points to the right of $1000 per item per year.

Whenever there is a definite break in the pattern, possible ways of separating the inventory into separate populations should be sought; this may require separate management policies.

Breaks in these plots have led to the discovery that hotel suites are not just larger rooms; they appeal to a completely different segment of the traveling public. In another case, such a break led to the discovery of a new phenomenon in the formation of droplets from a spray nozzle. This latter was important in the design of the process for making freeze-dried coffee and detergents (in separate factories), because one does not want too many fine particles that are dusty or too many large particles that don't dry properly.

This model is used in 10.4 to extrapolate service and inventment results from the analysis of a sample to the whole inventory.

9.2 ABC CLASSIFICATION

There is no hard and fast rule about separating inventories into three classes; there might well be half a dozen classes if they served some purpose. Nor is there any standard way of deciding where to define the demarcation between adjacent classes. Throughout this book, Class A items are considered as the few items at the top of a list sorted in descending sequence by annual value that contribute 50% of the total usage. Class C items are those in the last half of the same list, and Class B items are the ones in the middle.

ABC CLASSIFICATION

The number of Class A items differs from industry to industry and can be predicted by the standard ratio. (The percentage of total value for Class C items is obviously the same as the percentage of items that are Class A.)

In the consumer industries, standard ratios seem to be about 3, which means that the Class A items represent about 15% of the items in the inventory. In manufacturing industries, the standard ratio frequently tends to be about 10, which means that about 1% of the items fall into Class A. In highly technological industries, like aircraft and computer, the standard ratio may be as high as 25, so that it takes only 0.05% of the items to contribute 50% of the value of usage. It would be an instructive exercise to locate the 80–20 point on Figure 9.1 (where 20% of the items contribute 80% of the total value), draw a straight line through that point with a 45 degree slope, and figure out the corresponding parameter sigma and the standard ratio.

The ABC classification for inventory management dates to before there were computable decision rules and accessible data bases. H. Ford Dickie, of General Electric, wrote the classic article "ABC Inventory Analysis Shoots for Dollars, Not Pennies." W. Evert Welch, then of Honeywell, and more recently retired from ITT, had a technique he used in talks to get the point across. He would get the whole inventory listed on continuous form paper, which he would throw down the center aisle of the room so that it would unroll to the back wall. After he had talked about that inventory for a while, he would "find" in his brief case the first page—which had half the value of the whole inventory on it.

Thus allocation of management effort to get the best return is the goal. Class A items represent a lot of money and therefore deserve careful management. There are few enough items that the cost of management per item is not important in total, but on such a large base the results of good management are.

At the other end of the list, the Class C items should not get any attention at all. There are so many items that any effort spent per item adds up to a lot of effort. Since the value of Class C is only from 1 to 5% of the total value, and the result of the effort can only be a percentage reduction of cost, there is no return to be realized.

Class B items represent enough money that they deserve good controls, but there are so many of them that they require formal programmable methods, not personal attention. In fact the Class A items should be controlled by the same system developed for Class B. Then, as a base, they get at least as good control as the Class B items. The difference is that in Class A one can afford to review the routine decisions and refine them for special circumstances not taken into account in the formal system.

The ABC classification creeps in from time to time for a variety of other purposes. For example, you might set up special blanket orders with Class A vendors, the small fraction of vendors with whom you place 50% of your total business. Warehouses may be laid out to have Class A items near the packaging area, but in this case Class A represents the few items that generate 50% of the bin trips, not dollars, per year. Class A customers, who buy 50% of your total output, might get special consideration when there are shortages.

9.3 RATE OF RESPONSE TO CHANGE

When there is a change in the flow of material, it takes time for the system to settle down to the new level. The change may be the implementation of a new control system. It may be a change in management policy. It may be a change in the economic climate that affects the general rate of consumption of your products.

Although a formal model of the inventory management system can predict what the new level of investment, operating expense, and service will be for the new conditions, it will take some time for the actual inventory to reach that predicted point.

In fact, there may be a movement in the reverse direction temporarily. Exhibit 2.6 showed a typical report of the way that inventory would migrate from present levels to planned levels over time. If the rate of migration is not acceptable, management may want to take special steps to move more quickly. For example, many years ago when the Paints Department of du Pont was setting up an inventory control system for trade paints in warehouses, such a projection was worked out. The director concluded that he couldn't afford to wait that long to verify that the recommended new control system would actually provide the desired service with so much less stock. So he ordered that all excess stock in the Boston warehouse be removed immediately, to bring at least one location to the planned level, as a test of whether the replenishment routines really did work. If that test hadn't worked, there would have been no point to including the anecdote here.

The reason for the long time taken to react to change is the distribution of usage rates of the items in the whole inventory. The few fast-moving items, with the bulk of the value, are replenished frequently, and hence are very soon at the new levels appropriate for the new conditions. But the very large number of slower-moving items tend to be purchased or manufactured in lot quantities (see Chapter 11) that last a long time. If a new lot was just received under the old conditions it may be a year or more before the next lot is to be ordered under the new conditions. So for a long period of time, the inventories will still reflect the old control system.

The average inventory turnover is related to the characteristic response time for change. In food retailing, the inventory may turn several hundred times a year, so that inventory levels can be adjusted to almost any change within the week. At another extreme, the Ships Parts Control Center of the U.S. Navy has a characteristic time constant of about three years. If an officer makes a policy decision when he first assumes command of the system, by the time his normal tour of duty is over, about two-thirds of the eventual effect will have shown up, to be credited to the fitness report of his successor.

This difference in characteristic response rates, by the way, is one potential stumbling block in mergers. Executives who have developed a good instinct for the way one business responds to change may get quite frustrated when they take on another company with a very different response. There was a time when I was stationed in the Philippines and spent most of a week driving large semi-tractors with trailer trucks in a convoy. When I returned to base and got into my Jeep, at the first corner where I wanted to turn right I managed to turn completely around and head back the way I had come.

9.4 CULLING THE INVENTORY

Inevitably there are a great many odds and ends at the tail end of any inventory. They were once put into the product line for some good purpose, and can't possibly be discontinued on grounds of customer support. If all the marketing mythology were believed, that many large customers also buy these minor items, then one should expect to find their usage much, much higher.

One good effect of the shortages in the early 1970s was that one could always start a rumor that such items were in short supply, and thus transfer them to someone else's inventory.

It is worthwhile to review the Class C items systematically. The problem arises in that the benefit of eliminating them from the product line is a reduction in production expense, whereas the penalty is a reduction in marketing availability. Hence the review usually has to be stimulated from rather elevated executive ranks, where they can't be bothered with the grubby details of the thousands of items in the product line.

There are two useful approaches to culling out the poorest products. One is to start at the bottom of the list of Class C items and ask, "If this item were not available, what would the customers buy instead?" If there is a good chance that the customer could be persuaded to switch to some other nearly equivalent item higher up the list, discontinue the item. The savings in inventory management will accumulate, and the higher demand for the surviving substitute will make it more profitable. That approach works for service parts where it is necessary to support the function, for essential parts, if not the actual part number.

An alternative approach that has worked in the area of retail consumer goods is to line up all the existing products on the counter, for some department. Then get the buyer to play a game, with a willing temporary suspension of disbelief, in which if he could offer only one item, which is the one that he would carry in stock? Move that item to the next counter. Now, having that in the line, allow a second item. Obviously the second item will be as different in appeal as possible from the first. Customers who like the first item, or something near it, will often take the first item. A second one much like it would not enlarge the market very much. But a second one that appealed to a whole new class of customers would also satisfy some other customers who were in a sense "near" those.

Proceed this way through a few items, and it rapidly becomes apparent that the buyer has selected a small set that "spans" the needs of his customers. Additional items in the assortment may actually reduce income, because customers get bewildered by an array of alternatives that are too similar.

For production planning, safety stocks, and economic lot sizes, the formal definition of the Materials Management Systems library offers an assortment of half a dozen options each. Is this too wide an assortment, which confuses the user?

CHAPTER **10**

Safety Stock Strategies

Finished goods stocks in the field play an important role in ensuring customer service in spite of errors in the forecast. The national safety stock, held at the master warehouse for redistribution as needed, ensures that the satellites can get more material when they begin to run short, in spite of errors in the national forecast. In one sense the national safety stock protects the production schedule over the freeze period, so that replenishment orders do not have to be expedited even when total demand on the system exceeds forecast. There may be planned safety stocks of intermediate and raw materials to allow the freeze period for reaction to changed requirements to be shorter than the actual replenishment lead time. Increases in requirements can be filled from this safety stock, even though it takes longer to get the material to restore the planned stock level.

This chapter is concerned with the decision rules for computing the safety factors for individual items in the inventory for a variety of different management strategies. In each case the safety stock is the product of that safety factor and the standard deviation of the distribution of errors in forecasting demand over the lead time (or freeze period); see Chapter 8. The relevant standard deviation may be based on the mean square error for one-ahead forecasts and the (known) length of the lead time, or it may be measured directly from the errors in forecasting demand-during-a-lead-time. Safety stocks enter into materials planning either in various forms of the order-point replenishment systems (see Chapter 12) or in time-phased, net-requirements planning (Chapter 13). Safety stocks are also important in allocating stock among field warehouses (Chapter 17).

There are two sorts of choices that face the managers of a materials planning system with regard to safety stocks. One is the strategic choice of a particular decision rule for computing the safety factors for a given kind of safety stock. We shall consider six alternative decision rules, of which three can be generally recommended, and two are included because they are commonly used.

The other choice is tactical, to balance the investment in inventory against the appropriate measure of customer service. For every decision rule there is an exchange curve. Capital investment shows up on the balance sheet and is of concern to the financial management. Customer service is more likely to affect revenue and profit, and to be of direct concern to marketing management.

The strategic choices tend to be made initially when a system is designed, with the same decision rule being used for broad classes of items. The reasons for preferring one decision rule over another don't change very much with time, so the decision rules may become deeply embedded in the system. The tactical choice of a management policy variable, however, should be reviewed at least once a year as part of the corporate budgeting exercise, to decide whether to invest more or less in safety stocks, with the predicted consequences in customer service. It may also prove advisable to stratify the inventory and to choose different values for the management policy variable for different classes, even though all classes use the same strategic choice of a decision rule.

Some of the distinctions that might indicate a different relative propensity to invest include the following:

> Functional parts versus trim.
>
> Parts used to outfit new products, versus replacement parts.
>
> Sole source products, versus products available from many suppliers.
>
> Current parts also used to assemble products, versus noncurrent parts for service only.
>
> Manufactured products, versus products bought from an outside vendor who gets part of the manufacturing profit.
>
> High markup products, versus loss leaders.
>
> Products that uniquely satisfy a need, versus products that are part of an assortment, with more or less free substitution.
>
> New products with growing demand, versus older products on the way out.

If the retrieval system permits ready access to groups of products according to such attributes, it may be productive to study the tactical choice of an investment level for one inventory class at a time. When Ed Jackson was vice-president for parts and service of the Caterpillar Tractor Company, he was once able to get approval for an increased inventory investment during a period of general budget cuts, because he could show that for one group of parts the improved service would earn a good return on the increased investment.

SAFETY STOCK STRATEGIES

The general image of the inventory status over time is shown in Exhibit 10.1. The stock on hand is diminished with each demand transaction. It is increased from time to time as material is received from the source in some sort of a lot quantity. The total available stock is the sum of the stock on hand and all outstanding replenishment orders. The lead time starts when a new replenishment order is triggered and ends when the material is on hand, available to satisfy demand. There may be instances of a longer lead time, or heavier demand, or both, when the stock on hand is used up, and a net back order is accumulated. In the specific models to be discussed, it is assumed that demand that can't be filled from stock on hand is back ordered and is satisfied from the next receipt.

There are some slight changes in the models if demand is lost and not back ordered. However, note that even in some instances (like retail trade) where it would appear that the store does not record back orders, the customers may accumulate their own back orders, and in effect create extra demand when the store is back in stock, which has the same effect. It is consistent with the general mathematical models to consider back-ordered demand as a "negative" stock on hand.

Exhibit 10.1

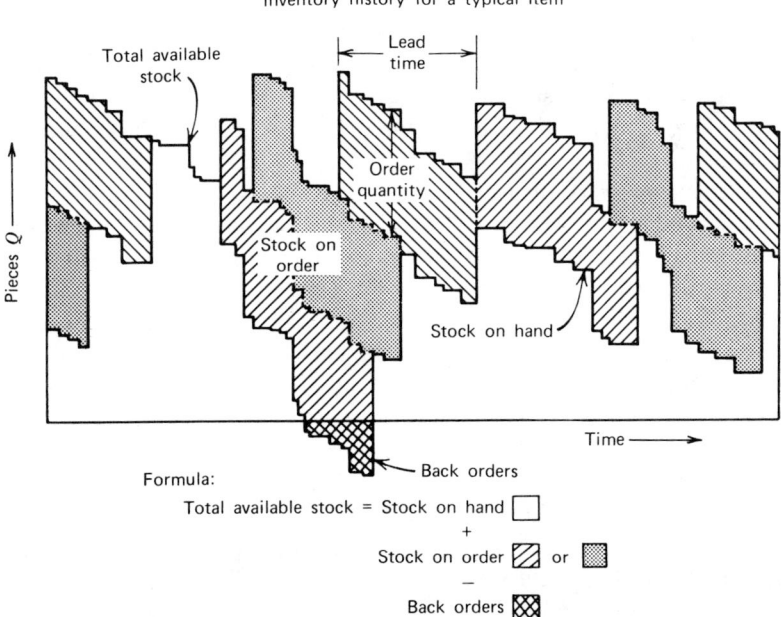

Inventory history for a typical item

10.1 MEASURES OF SERVICE

There are two primary measures of service (Exhibit 8.4). One is the expected amount of demand that will be back ordered $\sigma E(k)$ where σ is the standard deviation of the errors in forecasting demand over the lead time, and it comes from the forecasting process. $E(k)$ is the partial expectation function, where we assume that the item record identifies which form of the probability distribution is to be used.

When back orders become very large, so that the incoming receipts are not large enough to clear all back orders, then the expression of expected amount back ordered on the average must be elaborated. However, in the materials management systems library there are two limitations on this situation on a planned basis. First, the safety factors are limited to be nonnegative, regardless of what the particular strategic decision rule would say. That is, if zero safety stock gives better service than management has requested, the safety stock is not driven negative to bring it down to management objectives. (There are some industries where negative safety stocks are the rule; consider them in 10.5, under end-of-season balance out.) The other limitation, to be covered in Chapter 11, is that the replenishment lot quantities must be at least as large as the standard deviation, so that lot quantities do not become small.

In general the total amount of demand that can be expected to be back ordered in a year's time can be compared with the total forecast of demand during the year, to get a percentage service. However, note that the percentage is an end result of computing back orders in total dollars, and then dividing by demand. It is not the primary control to be implemented for each item.

The second primary measure of service is the expected number of times when a shortage, of any size, will exist at the end of the lead time when the replenishment order is received into stock. Particularly for national safety stock, when replenishment is managed by a materials requirements planning (MRP) system, there are various practical ways of ensuring that a small number of jobs get delivered to stock earlier than the standard freeze period. In any manufacturing process it is practical to expedite one order and get it delivered sooner than normal. It is practical to expedite two orders. It is not practical to expedite half the open orders—nothing gets done then. At some point between one order and half the orders, there is a practical limit. So long as the number of schedule changes is kept below that threshold, it is possible to get material delivered to stock early, and thus give effectively perfect service.

Part of the service comes from stocks normally on the shelf delivered in normal lead time, or even longer if demand materializes below forecast. The

MEASURES OF SERVICE

rest of the service comes from an orderly way of moving the few items needed ahead in the schedule.

The relevance of this concept goes back to Kenneth F. Simpson's paper, "In-Process Inventories." There he showed that to give the best possible service to ultimate customers in a multi-echelon distribution system, with a given total investment in inventory, every stage but the last should give "perfect" service. That is not to say that there is sufficient stock at all intermediate echelons to meet requirements, but there is sufficient stock to meet a large share of the variations, with an information and control system that makes it possible to get what else is needed.

The linear programming model Simpson developed shows that if some intermediate investment is reduced to give more stock at the end of the pipeline next to the customer, service will of course go up in terms of the ability of the warehouse to cope with unforecast demands. But when they have exhausted their safety stocks, the fact that they can't get what they need from the next echelon back results in a longer period of being out of stock, and on the average the total service will be worse.

Therefore we want to consider the possibility of controlling the number of instances when stock will be needed short of the normal freeze period.

There are also two derived measures of service. One is the expected time a shortage will last. This expected time, until the end of the normal lead time, is a fraction of the length of the lead time. The ratio of the time short to the time in stock is the same as the ratio of the expected amount short to the total demand over the lead time, which is the order point. It is an estimate of the average time until normal supplies will clear up back orders. The mean value can be estimated fairly from the diagram in Exhibit 10.2,

Exhibit 10.2

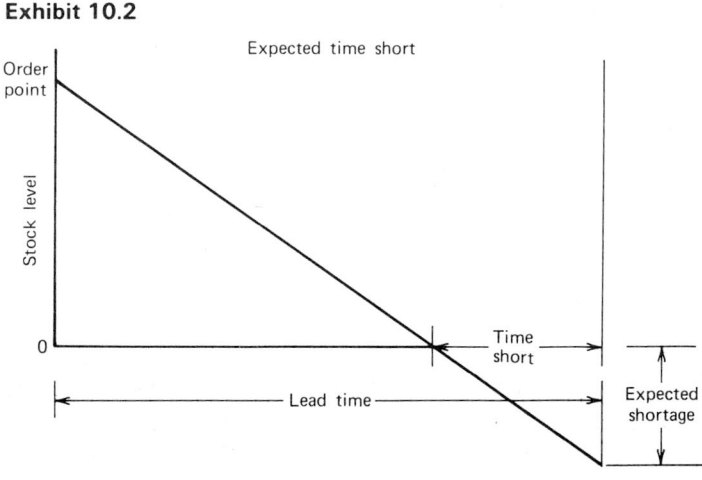

but the variation in the distribution of these times requires empirical simulations—so far as I know, no one has been able to find a closed analytical model of the form and variance of that distribution.

The other measure of service is the number of transactions filled. If $\sigma E(k)$ is the expected number of pieces short on a given replenishment cycle, and there are on the average T pieces on each customer demand transaction (bin trip, line item), then the average number of transactions that have a shortage is $\sigma E(k)/T$.

10.2 DECISION RULES

There are six decision rules routinely provided in the materials management systems library. Any of these rules can be selected for any SKU. It is not only practical but recommended, for example, to choose one decision rule for safety stocks in field warehouses and a different decision rule for the same product for national safety stock. For each of these rules we shall take up (a) a brief discussion of what the rule is intended to accomplish; (b) an example of the computation of the safety factors and three measures of effectiveness on a small sample of seven items; and (c) a computer-generated analysis of investment and four measures of service on a sample of 200 items, for six different values of the relevant management policy variable. In each of these cases, the management policy variables are chosen to give a range from $36,000 to $54,000 in safety stock for the given sample. At the end of the discussion of individual rules, we shall take a look at the strategic selection among rules.

10.12 Specify the Service for All Items

This rule argues that if management wants a given level of service, say, 94%, find values of the safety factor for each individual item that achieve 6% of the demand back ordered. It is based on a model that I developed in may 1959 book *Statistical Forecasting for Inventory Control,* which was implemented by IBM in their IMPACT package and its later derivatives.

Given a management policy of P as the fraction of demand to be filled from stock, for an item that is replenished in lot quantities Q and with standard deviation s, first evaluate the partial expectation function $E(k) = (1 - P)Q/\sigma$.

Exhibit 10.3 introduces a simple example that can be evaluated by hand. There are seven items, and the value of the standard deviation and the order quantity are given. For $P = 0.94$, one can first compute the values for $E(k)$ for each item according to the decision rule. Next go to the tables of the

Exhibit 10.3

AIMS Rule 1 $E(k_i) = (1 - P) Q_i / \sigma_i$
Management policy $(1 - P) = 0.06$ (e.g., 94% of demand filled from stock)
Total sales = $41,280.08 per year

Item i	Standard Deviation σ_i	Unit Cost v_i	Order Frequency N_i	②* Safety Factor k_i	① Expectation $E(k_i)$	③ Probability $F(k_i)$	Order Quantity Q_i	Safety Stock $k_i \sigma_i v_i$	Back Orders $N v \sigma E(k)$	Shortage Occurrences $N_i F(k_i)$
1	875	$2.50	11.17	1.15	0.06137	0.125	895	2575.63	1499.54	1.396
2	515	3.75	7.50	1.29	0.04660	0.0985	400	2491.31	674.97	0.739
3	210	4.26	4.60	1.15	0.06200	0.125	217	1028.79	255.14	0.575
4	65	1.97	1.71	0.63	0.16154	0.264	175	80.67	35.37	0.451
5	26	1.50	0.87	0.30	0.26538	0.382	115	11.70	9.00	0.332
6	18	3.10	0.68	0.68	0.14667	0.248	44	37.94	5.57	0.169
7	8	2.05	0.50	0.67	0.15000	0.251	20	10.99	1.23	0.126
Total			27.03					6177.03	2480.82	3.788
								1.79 mos	0.06	14% of orders

* Circled numbers indicate the sequence in which columns are filled in.

probability distribution in Appendix D and look up the safety factor k. While you are at it, look up the probability $F(k)$ that there will be a shortage.

The three measures of effectiveness to be computed are as follows:

1. Safety stock in pieces is the product of the safety factor, which we have just computed, and the given standard deviation. To get the safety stock in dollars of investment, multiply that by the unit standard cost v. The total safety stock in this case is $6,177.03, or 1.79 months of supply.
2. The number of pieces back ordered per cycle is $\sigma E(k)$, and there are N replenishment cycles per year. The value of the demand back ordered is therefore $Nv\sigma E(k)$ on an annual basis. The total value of back orders comes to $2,480.88, which is (surprised?) 6% of the value of annual demand.
3. The probability that there will be a shortage on any cycle is $F(k)$, and there are N such cycles a year. The expected number of lots that will arrive at the end of the lead time to find a back order condition is 3.8 orders a year, or 14% of all orders generated. (That is probably fairly high for effective expediting.)

Exhibit 10.4 tabulates the safety stocks for a sample of 200 items when

Exhibit 10.4

```
THE CODES FOR THE SAFETY STOCK STRATEGIES ARE:
    1 = FILL THE SPECIFIED FRACTIONS OF DEMAND FROM STOCK.
    2 = MAXIMIZE DOLLAR DEMAND FILLED FROM A GIVEN INVENTORY.
    3 = SET SAFETY STOCK AS SPECIFIED NUMBERS OF SIGMAS.
    4 = SET SAFETY STOCK AS SPECIFIED TIME SUPPLIES.
    5 = MINIMIZE SHORTAGE OCCURENCES FOR A GIVEN INVENTORY.
    6 = MINIMIZE TRANSACTION SHORTAGES FOR A GIVEN INVENTORY.

CODE FOR DECISION RULE = 1
POLICY VARIABLE IS THE FRACTION OF DEMAND TO BE FILLED FROM STOCK.
EXTREME VALUES = .995 .986
```

POLICY VARIABLE	SAFETY STOCK DOLLARS	SHORTAGE OCCUR. ITEMS/YR	BACKORDER DEMAND DOL/YR	SHORTAGE DURATION DA/SHORT	TRANSACT SHORTS NO/YR
0.995	53609	91.4	8638	2.16	2736
0.994	50349	109.1	10762	2.26	3389
0.992	46945	129.3	13358	2.39	4178
0.991	43407	152.2	16511	2.54	5123
0.989	39746	177.7	20319	2.71	6235
0.986	35972	205.6	24901	2.90	7507
CURRENT	46588	48.8	21724	5.13	1701

DECISION RULES

computed by this rule, with values of the desired service ranging from 98.6 to 99.5%. These values were chosen to make the safety stocks range from nearly $36,000 to nearly $54,000 so that all six decision rules can be compared. The number of shortage occurrences and the back-ordered demand are computed for all 200 items for each of the six values of the desired service, in precisely the way that the simple example was worked out in Exhibit 10.3. The shortage duration is based on the model in Exhibit 10.2, and the number of transactions short is accumulated based on the expected pieces short for each SKU and the average number of pieces per demand transaction.

10.22 Minimize Back Orders for a Given Investment

It would appear that the real meaning of a stipulated percentage service is not so much the same service for every item as it is that the total value of back orders shall be no more than a stipulated fraction of the total demand. If that is the real meaning of "percentage service" then some items might get less than the average service and some more, if that will reduce the total inventory investment. In the paper "Decision Rules for Equal Shortage Policies," George Gerson and I showed that the safety factors satisfy the relationship $F(k) = P/N$, where $F(k)$ is the probability distribution (for whatever function represents the distribution of forecast errors), N is the number of replenishment cycles in a year, and P is a management policy variable that has the dimensions of the number of shortages per item per year, corresponding to the expected time between shortages.

In Exhibit 10.5 for the same list of seven items, to apply this rule first compute the probability values $F(k)$ from the given order frequency N and the specified management policy $P = 0.5$. Then look up the corresponding safety factor k in the tables in Appendix D, and the values of the partial expectation $E(k)$. Note that for the last three items in the list, the probability of a shortage would be greater than 0.5, which would mean (for the normal distribution) a negative safety factor. However, the rule is that safety factors are limited to be nonnegative.

Now that we have k, $F(k)$, and $E(k)$, we can proceed as before to compute the safety stock, the value of back ordered demand, and the number of shortage occurrences. Although the planned number of shortages per item per year is 0.5 (one shortage every two years), the nonnegative safety factor says that for the last three items we give better service than that with no safety stock at all. Since the lot size is larger than a year's supply, the working stock gives perfect service for much of the time. In half the replenishment cycles, the demand during the lead time will be less than the forecast, so there is no shortage. In the other half there will be some shortage, but less than planned.

Exhibit 10.5

AIMS Rule 2 $F(k_i) = P/N_i$
Management policy $P = 0.5$ shortages/item/year
Total sales = \$41,280.80 per year

Item i	Standard Deviation σ_i	Unit Cost v_i	Order Frequency N_i	②* Safety Factor k_i	Expectation $E(k_i)$	① Probability $F(k_i)$	Safety Stock $k_i\sigma_i v_i$	Back Orders $N v\sigma E(k)$	Shortage Occurrences $N_i F(k_i)$
1	875	\$2.50	11.17	1.70	0.01829	0.04476	3718.75	446.91	0.5
2	515	3.75	7.50	1.50	0.0293	0.06667	2896.88	424.39	0.5
3	210	4.26	4.60	1.24	0.0516	0.10870	1109.30	212.39	0.5
4	65	1.97	1.71	0.59	0.1857	0.2924	69.15	40.66	0.5
5	26	1.50	0.87	0	0.3989	0.5747 (0.5)	0	13.53	0.435
6	18	3.10	0.68	0	0.3989	0.7353 (0.5)	0	15.14	0.340
7	8	2.05	0.50	0	0.3989	1.0000 (0.5)	0	3.99	0.250
Total			27.03				7794.08	1156.96	3.025
							2.26 mos	2.8%	11.2%

*Circled numbers indicate the sequence in which columns are filled in.

DECISION RULES

In total the 2.26 months of supply for safety stock fill 97.2% of the demand, and create a need for expediting on 11.2% of the replenishment orders.

Exhibit 10.6 shows the effect of applying this rule to the sample of 200 items, with a management policy of between 0.21 and 0.55 shortages per item per year (from 2 to 5 years between shortages). These values were chosen to get the safety stocks in total to range between $36,000 and $54,000.

10.23 Specify Safety Stocks by the Safety Factor Itself

A third possible rule is really quite simple. Safety stock is always expressed as the safety factor times the standard deviation. Management might use the safety factor itself directly as a management policy variable.

In Exhibit 10.7, the sample is worked out for a choice of $k = 0.84$ for all seven items. We can look up the one corresponding value for the probability $F(0.84)$ and the partial expectation $E(0.84)$ in the table, and use those values for all items to compute the safety stock, value of back orders, and the number of shortage occurrences. In this case 1.28 months of safety stock give 88% of demand filled from stock, and 20% of the replenishment orders requiring to be expedited.

When the third strategic decision rule is applied to the sample of 200 items (Exhibit 10.8), values of $k = 1.1$ to 1.65 give safety stocks in the same range of values as for the previous cases.

Exhibit 10.6

```
TRY ANOTHER STRATEGY? Y

CODE FOR DECISION RULE = 2
POLICY VARIABLE IS THE NUMBER OF SHORTAGES PER ITEM PER YEAR.
EXTREME VALUES = .21 .55
```

POLICY VARIABLE	SAFETY STOCK DOLLARS	SHORTAGE OCCUR. ITEMS/YR	BACKORDER DEMAND DOL/YR	SHORTAGE DURATION DA/SHORT	TRANSACT SHORTS NO/YR
0.210	54981	41.7	3056	13.17	586
0.255	51515	50.7	3857	13.87	735
0.309	47961	61.3	4856	14.33	921
0.374	44379	73.8	6082	14.08	1155
0.454	40723	88.6	7603	13.84	1448
0.550	36959	105.9	9504	13.51	1812
CURRENT	46588	48.8	21724	5.13	1701

Exhibit 10.7

AIMS Rule 3 Safety factor = 0.84 for every item
Total sales = $41,280.80 per year

Item i	Standard Deviation σ_i	Unit Cost v_i	Order Frequency N_i	① * Safety Factor k_i	② Expectation $E(k_i)$	③ Probability $F(k_i)$	Safety Stock $k_i \sigma_i v_i$	Back Orders $N v \sigma E(k)$	Shortage Occurrences $N_i F(k_i)$
1	875	$2.50	11.17	0.84	0.11196	0.200454	1837.50	2735.67	2.239
2	515	3.75	7.50	→	→	→	1622.25	1621.67	1.503
3	210	4.26	4.60				751.46	460.73	0.922
4	65	1.97	1.71				107.56	24.52	0.343
5	26	1.50	0.87				32.76	3.80	0.174
6	18	3.10	0.68				46.87	4.25	0.136
7	8	2.05	0.50				13.78	0.92	0.100
Total			27.03				4412.18	4851.56	5.417
							1.28 mos	12% back ordered	20% short

* Circled numbers indicate the sequence in which columns are filled in.

DECISION RULES

Exhibit 10.8

```
TRY ANOTHER STRATEGY? Y

CODE FOR DECISION RULE = 3
POLICY VARIABLE IS THE SAFETY FACTOR.
EXTREME VALUES = 1.1  1.65
```

POLICY VARIABLE	SAFETY STOCK DOLLARS	SHORTAGE OCCUR. ITEMS/YR	BACKORDER DEMAND DOL/YR	SHORTAGE DURATION DA/SHORT	TRANSACT SHORTS NO/YR
1.100	37405	111.8	13396	4.37	2607
1.193	40564	95.9	11142	4.18	2168
1.294	43991	80.5	9066	4.00	1764
1.403	47707	65.9	7192	3.81	1400
1.521	51737	52.5	5538	3.62	1078
1.650	56107	40.5	4117	3.43	801
CURRENT	46588	48.8	21724	5.13	1701

10.24 Specify Weeks of Supply

Quite often people talk about safety stocks in terms of months of supply or weeks of supply, and in fact issue guidelines to the inventory clerks and purchasing agents to work toward a "90-day supply" or some such rule of thumb.

In Exhibit 10.9 we use a 60-day supply, or two months, for safety stock. In this case we know the safety stock, based on annual sales and unit costs, to begin with. Since the safety stock is always the product of the safety factor and the standard deviation, the first step in the analysis is to compute the safety factor by dividing the safety stock by the standard deviation. Then we can look up the probability and partial expectation in the tables of the appropriate probability distribution, and so compute the safety stock, the value of back orders, and the number of replenishment orders that might need expediting. The two months of supply will fill 94.93% of demand, and require expediting on about 13.4% of the replenishment orders.

Exhibit 10.10 applies this sort of a rule to the 200-item sample, with between 1.05 weeks of supply ($35,000 in total) and 1.65 weeks of supply ($56,000 in total).

10.25 Minimize the Number of Shortage Occurrences

In the Gerson and Brown paper referred to above, we showed that it is possible to distribute safety stocks among items in an inventory to minimize

Exhibit 10.9

AIMS Rule 4 Safety stock = 2 months supply for each item

$$k_i = \left(\frac{S_i}{12} \times 2\right) \div \sigma_i$$

Total sales = $41,280.80 per year

				①*	②	③				
Item i	Standard Deviation σ_i	Unit Cost v_i	Order Frequency N_i	Safety Factor k_i	Expectation $E(k_i)$	Probability $F(k_i)$	Annual Sales S_i	Safety Stock $k_i\sigma_i v_i$	Back Orders $Nv\sigma E(k)$	Shortage Occurrences $N_i F(k_i)$
1	875	$2.50	11.17	1.90	0.01105	0.02872	10,000	4166.67	270.00	0.321
2	515	3.75	7.50	0.97	0.08819	0.16602	3,000	1875.00	1277.38	1.245
3	210	4.26	4.60	0.79	0.12234	0.21476	1,000	710.00	503.45	0.988
4	65	1.97	1.71	0.77	0.12669	0.22065	300	98.50	27.74	0.377
5	26	1.50	0.87	0.64	0.15797	0.26109	100	25.00	5.36	0.227
6	18	3.10	0.68	0.28	0.27448	0.38974	30	15.50	10.41	0.265
7	8	2.05	0.50	0.21	0.30271	0.41683	10	3.42	2.48	0.208
Total			27.03					6894.09	2096.82	3.631
								2 mos	5.07%	13.4%

*Circled numbers indicate the sequence in which columns are filled in.

DECISION RULES

TRY ANOTHER STRATEGY? Y

CODE FOR DECISION RULE = 4
POLICY VARIABLE IS THE WEEKS OF SUPPLY FOR SAFETY STOCK.
EXTREME VALUES = 1.05 1.65

POLICY VARIABLE	SAFETY STOCK DOLLARS	SHORTAGE OCCUR. ITEMS/YR	BACKORDER DEMAND DOL/YR	SHORTAGE DURATION DA/SHORT	TRANSACT SHORTS NO/YR
1.050	35331	140.4	21745	15.82	2119
1.149	38673	131.6	20466	16.40	1918
1.258	42332	123.0	19233	17.02	1730
1.377	46337	114.7	18046	17.69	1555
1.507	50721	106.7	16901	18.39	1393
1.650	55520	99.0	15794	19.14	1245
CURRENT	46588	48.8	21724	5.13	1701

the total number of replenishment orders that require expediting. The decision rule results in an expression involving the probability density function $p(k)$, which is to be equal to $Pv\sigma/N$, where P is a management policy variable (which actually appears in the derivation as a Lagrange multiplier), v is the unit cost, σ is the standard deviation of forecast errors, and N is the number of replenishment cycles per year.

Exhibit 10.11 walks through the evaluation of this rule for the example of the standard seven items. First form the expression using a policy variable $P = 0.001$. Go to the table of the probability distribution and look under the column for the probability density to find a value for the safety factor that makes the expression balance both sides of the expression. From that value of the safety factor, note the probability and partial expectations. Then you can compute the safety stock, the value of back orders, and the number of shortage occurrences. In this example, a 1.72 month supply provides 95.62% service and requires expediting 12.1% of the replenishment orders.

Contrast this rule with Rule 2. Both rules have safety factors generally between 1 and 2 for the first few items, which are replenished at between quarterly and monthly intervals. But the items at the lower end of the sample, which are replenished in much longer intervals, have quite different safety factors under the two rules.

Rule 2, which seeks to maximize dollar demand filled from stock, doesn't give any safety stock at all to the slow-moving items, where the working stock alone already gives better service than intended on the average.

In contrast, Rule 5, which doesn't want to expedite unless it is worthwhile, tends to give quite large safety factors to the slow-moving items. The risk of having to expedite is concentrated in the Class A items, where there

Exhibit 10.11

AIMS Rule 5 $p(k_i) = Pv_i\sigma_i/N_i$
Management policy $P = 0.001$ (year/$)
Total sales = $41,280.80 per year

				② *	③	④	①			
Item i	Standard Deviation σ_i	Unit Cost v_i	Order Frequency N_i	Safety Factor k_i	Expectation $E(k_i)$	Probability $F(k_i)$	Density $p(k_i)$	Safety Stock $k_i\sigma_i v_i$	Back Orders $Nv\sigma E(k)$	Shortage Occurrences $N_i F(k_i)$
1	875	$2.50	11.17	1.19	0.5726	0.11702	0.1958	2603.13	1399.11	1.307
2	515	3.75	7.50	0.93	0.9503	0.17619	0.2575	1796.06	1376.45	1.321
3	210	4.26	4.60	1.20	0.0561	0.11507	0.1945	1073.52	230.86	0.529
4	65	1.97	1.71	1.83	0.01323	0.03363	0.07488	234.33	2.90	0.058
5	26	1.50	0.87	2.09	0.00665	0.01831	0.04483	81.51	0.23	0.016
6	18	3.10	0.68	1.77	0.1539	0.03836	0.08206	98.77	0.58	0.026
7	8	2.05	0.50	2.24	0.00436	0.01255	0.328	36.74	0.04	0.006
Total			27.03					5924.06	1810.17	3.263
								1.72 mos	4.38%	12.1%

* Circled numbers indicate the sequence in which columns are filled in.

DECISION RULES

is a lot of money to be saved by reducing the safety stock, and few enough items to be controlled. These items are replenished frequently enough that there is a good chance that there is an order in the pipeline to be expedited when demand is above forecast.

When applied to the sample of 200 items (Exhibit 10.12), a range of values for the policy variable between 80 and 220 results in inventory investment in the standard range for comparison among strategic alternatives.

Exhibit 10.12
TRY ANOTHER STRATEGY? Y

CODE FOR DECISION RULE = 5
POLICY VARIABLE IS THE COST OF A SHORTAGE.
EXTREME VALUES = 80 220

POLICY VARIABLE	SAFETY STOCK DOLLARS	SHORTAGE OCCUR. ITEMS/YR	BACKORDER DEMAND DOL/YR	SHORTAGE DURATION DA/SHORT	TRANSACT SHORTS NO/YR
80.000	36122	57.8	22728	16.55	1116
97.939	39861	47.6	20951	16.25	948
119.901	44112	38.3	15597	17.64	707
146.788	48871	29.7	11448	17.73	499
179.703	53032	23.5	9071	17.50	377
220.000	57041	18.7	7361	17.73	288
CURRENT	46588	48.8	21724	5.13	1701

TRY ANOTHER STRATEGY? Y

CODE FOR DECISION RULE = 6
POLICY VARIABLE IS SHORTAGES/$/YEAR.
EXTREME VALUES = .2 .06

POLICY VARIABLE	SAFETY STOCK DOLLARS	SHORTAGE OCCUR. ITEMS/YR	BACKORDER DEMAND DOL/YR	SHORTAGE DURATION DA/SHORT	TRANSACT SHORTS NO/YR
0.060	56832	24.1	5909	21.25	213
0.076	52728	30.2	7674	21.42	280
0.097	48927	37.5	8978	21.56	359
0.124	44980	46.3	10648	21.72	463
0.157	40818	57.2	12908	22.09	602
0.200	36703	69.7	15742	21.61	777
CURRENT	46588	48.8	21724	5.13	1701

TRY ANOTHER STRATEGY? N

ELAPSED TIME   7M 48.710S
CPU TIME   6.636S

Between 80 and 220 whats? Percent service has a physical meaning. So do the safety factor, weeks of supply, and mean time between shortages. In this decision rule the arbitrary nature of the management policy variable becomes apparent. In the derivation it arises as a Lagrange multiplier, introduced to minimize an expression subject to constraints. The expression is the number of shortage occurrences. The constraint is the budgeted level for safety stocks. The management policy variable doesn't really "mean" anything. Dimensionally its reciprocal is the imputed marginal cost of a shortage, based on the cost of investing in safety stock to avert it. However, it is not a value that can be measured objectively by any accounting or industrial engineering study. The way that a value is assigned is as in Exhibit 10.12—try a range of values, look at the investment and various measures of service that result, and choose a value that generates the results you want for the company.

10.26 Minimize Number of Transactions Short

One possible measure of the effectiveness of safety stocks is the expected number of demand transactions (bin trips, line entries) from customers that will not be filled, based on the expected quantity short, divided by the average number of pieces per demand transaction. I published the derivation in "Improved Customer Service at the HAL Division," which also displays the formal definition of the computations in APL programs. The decision rule derived is $F(k) = PvT/N$, where P is a management policy variable, v is the standard cost of the item for inventory valuation, T is the average number of pieces per demand transaction, and N is the number of replenishment orders per year.

The lower part of Exhibit 10.12 shows these computations for the 200-item sample, for values of the management policy variable P ranging from 0.06 to 0.2, to make the investment in safety stocks come out between $36,000 and $57,000. By now it should be clear how to go through the computations. Form the expression on the right side of the equation, look up the safety factor that satisfies the equation, and the corresponding value of the partial expectation. Then you have all the information required to evaluate the inventory investment, value of back orders, and the number of shortages.

This last decision rule is not generally recommended. It has the effect of giving rather high safety stocks to items that have a low extended invoice value of a demand transaction, and running the risk of shortages on the items with a high extended value. That is, by this rule, to maximize the number of transactions satisfied the supplier makes sure there is adequate stock for items of which the customer wants 10¢ worth at a time, but may

Exhibit 10.13

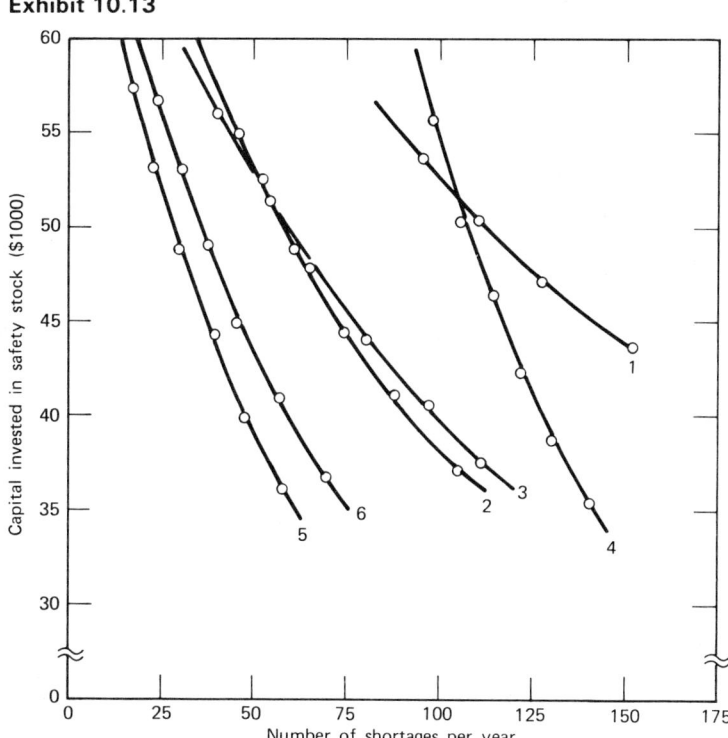

say, "Well, when you want to order $15,000 worth of a single item, that is only one transaction, and that's where I'll be short." This is not generally considered the best merchandising policy.

10.3 EXCHANGE CURVES

Exhibit 10.13 plots an exchange curve for each of the six decision rules. The vertical axis is the capital investment in safety stocks, ranging in all cases approximately from $35,000 to $56,000. The horizontal axis is the number of shortage occurrences per year, or the expected number of times that one would have to expedite to avert a potential shortage. Clearly at all levels of investment Rule 5 is significantly better than all the other rules tried, as it should be because it was derived to minimize the shortage occurrences for any level of investment. Thus it is not surprising, if one has faith in mathematics, to find that it lies to the left of the other curves. The interesting thing for this example is that it lies so far to the left.

10.31 Strategic Choices

Rules 2 and 3 give about the same service, but with about twice as many orders that would need expediting as with Rule 5. Rules 1 and 4 generate another significant increase in the number of orders that would run short.

The results shown in Exhibit 10.13 are for this particular sample only, and should not be taken as a general conclusion for all inventories. The exchange curve for Rule 5 will always be farthest to the left, but in some inventories it may not be very much farther to the left than the next best rule.

Exhibit 10.14 also plots exchange curves for each of the six strategic rules, with inventory plotted along the vertical axis. In this case, the horizontal axis is the value of back orders on an annual basis.

Rule 2 is the best of the six rules, as it should be because it was derived to minimize the back orders for a given investment. But two other rules, 3 and 6, are about equally good and almost as good as Rule 2. In the middle of the range, for a $45,000 investment in safety stocks, these rules generate

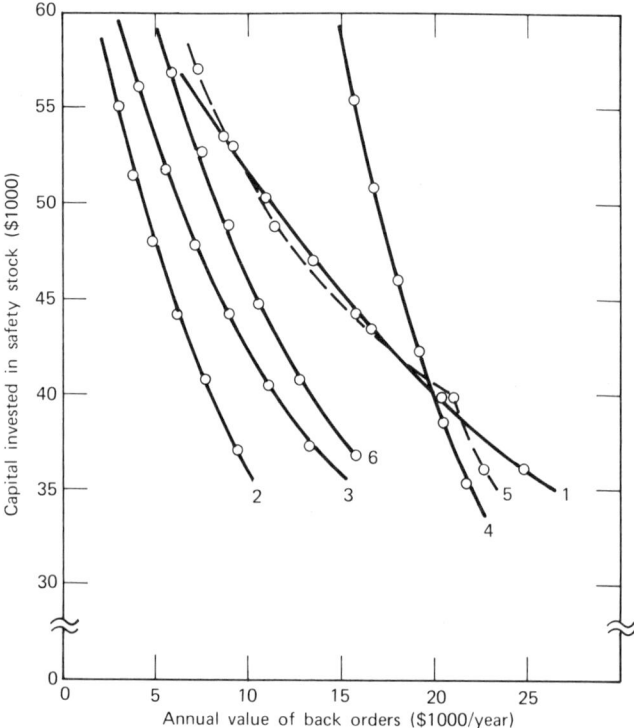

Exhibit 10.14

EXCHANGE CURVES

about $10,000 in back orders as compared with $6000 for the best possible rule. Clearly Rules 1, 4, and 5 are completely out of the running.

In Exhibit 10.13, where service is measured by the number of orders to be expedited, Rule 5 is the best, and Rule 2 is about in the middle. In Exhibit 10.14, where service is measured by back orders, the results are reversed: Rule 2 is the best and Rule 5 is among the worst. How does one choose between them?

This is the essence of the strategic choice to be made by marketing management on the basis of the way safety stock supports marketing policy. As a general guideline I would recommend Rule 2 for safety stocks in satellite field warehouses. These stocks protect customer service. Expediting is not usually practical at field distribution centers.

Customer demand may be referred to another location that has stock but will take longer to supply the customer, and this will reduce his satisfaction.

In the Federal Supply Service, however, service is measured in terms of the time taken to ship an order to fill demand from some federal establishment. The system is not a free market, so the time required for the merchandise to reach the customer is not of major consideration. In that system still another decision rule was derived. It takes account of both the fixed cost of the transaction to refer customer demand, and the marginal cost per pound to ship from a more remote stocking location.

The effect of that decision rule is to bias safety stocks in an interesting way. Safety stocks will he higher on a heavy item, like a bathtub, than on a light one like a Leroy Lettering Set. The idea is that one doesn't want the cost of shipping heavy products around the country, but light ones can cheerfully be sent parcel post. An item that tends to have a single order for many pieces, like bulk orders of knives and forks, will have a lower safety stock than an item like a jackknife, which might have the same total volume but several individual requests for one at a time. The idea here is that referring a single order is all right, but one doesn't want the expense of processing a great many individual demand transactions.

For national safety stocks, especially for manufactured products managed under a good time-phased system, where expediting is easy to accomplish in a routine way, I would recommend Rule 5, which minimizes the number of times an order has to be pulled ahead in the production schedule to meet extraordinary demand. Thus it is effective to have safety stocks to meet most of the unusual demand, and restrict the rescheduling to a reasonable few items.

10.32 Tactical Choices

If one were to choose Rule 5 to minimize rescheduling actions at the master warehouse, and Rule 2 to maximize service in the satellites, then management has the second chore, the tactical choice of a value for the management policy variable in those rules. The values might well be different for different strata of the inventory.

Consider first Exhibit 10.13 for Rule 5. In general the manufacturing source can form some judgment, for example, that 5 to 10% of the replenishment orders can be rescheduled, without creating chaos in the shop. Locate that number of shortage occurrences on the horizontal axis, read up until you get to the curve for Rule 5, and read the investment required on the left. Going back to the table of values from which the exchange curve was plotted, you can infer the value of the management policy variable that will achieve those results.

For Rule 2 at the satellite warehouses, pick a level of back orders, based on an acceptable level of service, along the horizontal scale in Exhibit 10.14. Read up to the exchange curve for Rule 2, then to the left to see the inventory investment required. The table behind the exchange curve gives the corresponding value for the management policy variable.

The values used for the management policy variable may well be different for different classes of items in the inventory, and will almost certainly change from year to year as the balance between investment and marketing objectives changes. The skillful managers have learned how to use these controls to shift investment from one class of items to another.

For example, Upjohn markets two forms of an anticoagulant. One is used generally for hemophiliacs, and the other is used primarily in open-heart surgery. The safety stocks of the latter product are biased so that when there is a shortage of the product in the country—a very relative thing—the stock that is available is concentrated in the regions that have a great many hospitals that do heart surgery. The other product can be substituted in other parts of the country for other applications.

10.33 Service Comparison for Same Investment

Exhibit 10.15 is based on a cross-plot from the information in Exhibits 10.13 and 10.14. There are two points plotted for each of the six decision rules. One point is based on a safety stock investment of $45,000, and the other on an investment of $55,000.

The vertical axis is the number (out of 801 replenishment orders per year) that would need expediting. The horizontal axis is the value (out of $1,750,000 in sales) that could be filled from stock without expediting. Note that Rule 2 does give the maximum service in minimizing back orders, but it generates an appreciable number of shortage occurrences. The way the rule works is to ensure good protection on Class A items, which represent a big value of demand. The risks of shortage are concentrated in the Class C

EXCHANGE CURVES

Exhibit 10.15

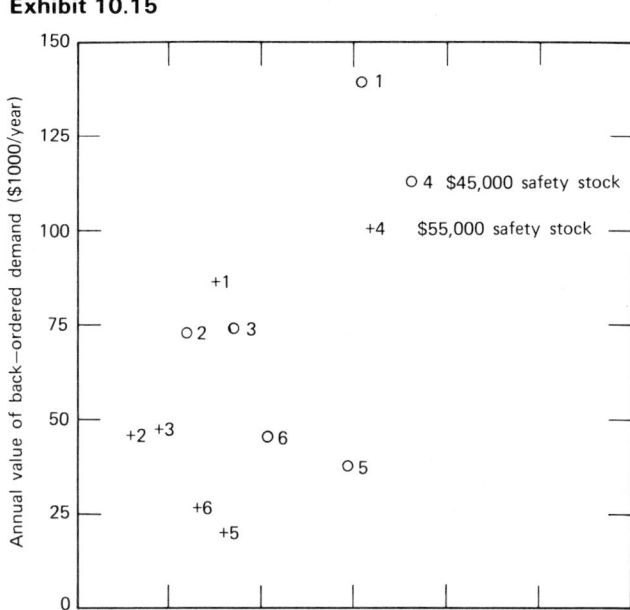

items, where there are lots of shortage occurrences, but none is very serious. Retail stores usually try to carry a good stock of size 16 by 33 broadcloth shirts, but the customer who wants a size 18 by 31 has learned to buy the entire stock in the few instances he finds any in the store, even if they have purple polka dots.

At the other extreme Rule 5 minimizes the number of times when expediting would be required, but at a significant cost in back orders if the expediting isn't effective. All the nuts, bolts, washers, and grommets are amply protected, but it may be necessary on occasion to expedite a lot of five-horsepower motors. It is hard to justify the effort to stunt through a $3 supply of lock washers—have plenty in stock to keep the line running. But if management can reduce the investment in diesel motors at the expense of a little stunting, that repays the effort taken. The stunting had better be effective, however, because the shortages will be large ones if they do occur.

Service is best on both measures in the lower left corner of Exhibit 10.15. When the value of safety stock is increased by a quarter, the service improves for all the rules.

Rules 2, 5, and 6 are all much better than the other three candidates. Rule 3 is nearly as good as Rule 2.

10.4 EXTRAPOLATING RESULTS FROM A SAMPLE TO THE POPULATION

Studies can be done very rapidly for samples of perhaps 200 items at a time. It takes about eight minutes to explore all six strategic rules, iterating through the ranges of values for the management policy variables, to get the results shown with a common range of investment values. But you would not want to do all that trial and error experimenting on the whole inventory data base. At first you may want to take two or three independent samples from each inventory class and work out the estimates of the exchange of service for investment. As you come to see that the same results apply for all samples, then you may rely more on a single sample from time to time.

After one of the strategies has been selected and the chosen value implemented for the items in a sample, you can extrapolate those consequences from the sample to the entire population. The first report (Exhibit 10.16) is a standard appraisal of the service and investment for the particular sample. The first three measures of service are given both in absolute measurable terms and as percentages of the relevant attribute.

Now we rely on (*a*) the usage rates of all items in the whole inventory being represented by the log-normal distribution, and (*b*) both the safety stock and the working stock tending to be proportional to some power of the value of usage.

It is possible to find a line of central tendency in the sample between the dollar value of safety stock and the dollar value of sales. In this example safety stock is proportional to the 0.725 power of the dollar value of sales.

The working stock, as we will come to expect in Chapter 11, is proportional to the 0.48 power of the value of sales.

From the standard ratio of the log-normal distribution of usage rates in the whole inventory we can get the conversion factor J which was used to find the two medians of the distribution from the average value. It is well-known that if a variable x is log-normally distributed, then the mean of any power p of that variable is proportional to the pth power of the mean of x. The constant of proportionality is J raised to the power $p(1 - p)$.

$$\overline{x^p} = \overline{x}^p J^{(1-p)p}$$

Therefore when we have a good line of central tendency that models investment as a power (0.725 for safety stocks and 0.475 for working stocks) of the dollar value of usage rates, we can readily use that relationship to estimate the total value of each component of stocks for the entire population.

EXTRAPOLATING FROM SAMPLE TO POPULATION

Exhibit 10.16

```
        DISVALUE

WEDNESDAY, AUGUST 4, 1976
EASTERN DAYLIGHT TIME 14:09:04

ENTER THE INVENTORY RECORD.
☐:
        GET'STATUS'
COMPONENT = MANAGER
1-NORMAL/2-EXPONENTIAL DISTRIBUTION = 1
THE RECORD HAS 200 ITEMS.
FOR THIS SAMPLE, THE ACTUAL STOCK STATUS IS:

        THE 200 ITEMS IN THIS RECORD:
                    AMOUNT          VALUE
SALES               540,220      $1,749,705.86
LOTS ORDERED            801         $19,395.70

                        CUSTOMER SERVICE
                    SHORTAGES       PERCENT SERVICE
DEMAND TRANSACTIONS   908.74      99.83°/° OF TRANSACTIONS
SHORTAGE OCCURRENCES   58.96      92.64°/° OF RECEIPTS
VALUE BACKORDERED   4,682.59      99.73°/° OF SALES
AVERAGE DURATION              12.79 DAYS PER SHORTAGE.

    INVENTORY INVESTMENT (DOLLARS)
SAFETY STOCK
        $48,572.82
WORKING STOCK           112,416.22
THEORETICAL ON HAND     160,989.04
STD. DEV. OF ON HAND     10,023.50
ACTUAL ON HAND          299,558.91
THEORETICAL ON ORDER    972,635.91
ACTUAL ON ORDER       1,595,983.36


THE AVERAGE SALES ARE $8,750.00 PER ITEM PER YEAR.


FRACTION OF SALES FROM TOP HALF OF ITEMS = .9192
THE STANDARD RATIO IS 3.98
THE "J-FACTOR" FOR ESTIMATING AVERAGES OF POWERS IS 2.6

 17 CLASS A ITEMS, REPRESENTING HALF THE REVENUE, HAVE SALES ABOVE $22,700.00
100 CLASS C ITEMS, THE SLOWEST-MOVING HALF OF THE INVENTORY, HAVE SALES BELOW $3,380.00
```

Two estimates are actually given in Exhibit 10.17. One assumes that the average usage for the sample is the same as the average for the population, and merely scales up the sample in terms of the number of items in the population from which the sample was taken. The second estimate uses the total value of sales for the population to estimate the average, which might be different for the sample, and bases the extrapolation on that figure.

When one implements the chosen strategy and the chosen policy variable for the whole inventory, then there is a report that verifies how close the projection came, with alternatives for higher and lower values of the management policy variable, to indicate sensitivity. See Exhibit 4.3.

Exhibit 10.17

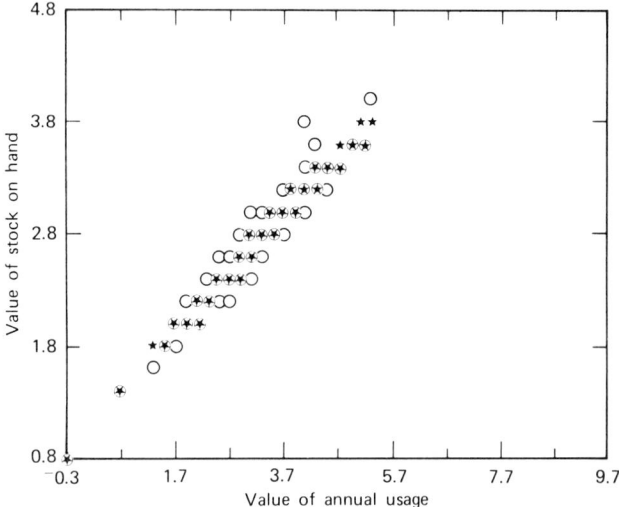

The line of best fit is $INV \sim 9.27 \times \$SALES*0.527$:
      Safety stock $\sim 0.37 \times \$SALES*0.725$
      Working stock $\sim 10.7 \times \$SALES*0.475$

Items in the whole population = 713.
Based on average sales of $8,748.53 per item per year, the theoretical on hand for the population should be:

Working stock	$442,000.00
Safety stock	$149,000.00
Total	$618,000.00

Total dollar sales of the population = 5265476.66
Based on average sales of $7,384.96 per item per year, the theoretical on hand for the population should be:

Working stock	$408,000.00
Safety stock	$132,000.00
Total	$566,000.00

10.5 BALANCE-OUT AT THE END OF A SEASON

The developments discussed above generally apply to repetitive replenishment of an inventory. There are times, however, when one wants to balance out stocks at the end of a selling season or a model year. The essence of the problem is a classic "newsboy" problem based on the discussion by George Kimball and Philip Morse in their *Principles of Operations Research*, based on wartime experiences in the Operations Evaluation Group of the U.S. Navy. If one knows the costs of having extra stock left over at the end of the season and the costs, in terms of lost profits, of running short (with no opportunity to get more), then there is a perfectly explicit level of safety stock to plan on to minimize the total of both kinds of costs.

In the real world of merchandising, however, the cost of carrying stock over is a moot question. The value of lost markup on lost sales, in the presence of a good deal of substitution, and consumer attitudes at the end of the year, is even more moot. Hence the factors that go into the model are highly subjective.

The following procedure has been used effectively to establish the correct safety stocks as well as can be expected when the explicit values are not available. Draw a line segment on a blackboard or a flip chart. Label the left end "absolutely no chance of any stock being left over at the end of the season." Label the right end "absolutely no chance of any customer going away empty-handed."

Wouldn't it be nice if we could manage the inventory to achieve both goals simultaneously? However, because of the uncertainty in the forecast through the end of the season, we have to take one sort of risk or the other.

Now take any specific item in the inventory. In discussion with production, purchasing, marketing, and financial people—all at a fairly responsible level—get a consensus of where that item should be on the line segment. Should it be near the left, or near the right, or perhaps in the middle. When there is a choice, go to the next item. Should it be farther to the left or farther to the right than the first one?

Experienced managers have a pretty good intuitive feel, as will become apparent from the discussions, of the factors to be considered. If there are lots of substitutes for the item, it may not be so serious to run short. If it is very expensive, or a high-fashion item, the costs of having any left over are ruinous. Novelty items can be sold out, but a standard line item will have good sales next season. Functional parts must be available, but trim might be discontinued. And so on.

When there is clearly a consensus of where various items fall on the line—and the first two or three may get modified as the session wears on—

then see if whole classes of items can be placed on the line segment. What are the characteristics of all items that go far to the left? Far to the right?

Ultimately (in an hour or so usually) the whole inventory will be dealt with. Now the safety factors for terminal safety stock can be computed directly. Mark off the line segment as 1 at the left and 0 on the right. The location of any point on the line can be directly interpolated, on a uniform scale, between the two extremes. That number, between 0 and 1, is a probability of running short. Look up the value of a safety factor that achieves that probability, and you have your safety stock.

This is one instance where you should allow negative safety factors. For example, the chance of selling all chocolate Easter rabbits should be virtual certainty, with none left on Monday, even if the stock levels run the risk of having some customers who can't get the particular model at the last moment.

10.6 OPTIONS AND ACCESSORIES

Some capital products are sold with a variety of options and accessories that are specified by the customer. The build schedule for the products, let us say, is established well in advance, so that we know the total number of forklifts, tractors, computers, tension testers, or what have you, to be built

Exhibit 10.18

If M is the number of units scheduled to be built of a product during a particular period, and p_i is the probability that the ith option will be required for the next customer order, then

Expected number of units of the option $= Mp_i$

Standard deviation $\sigma_i = \sqrt{Mp_i(1 - p_i)}$

Choose a safety factor k_i that satisfies

$$p(k_i) = \lambda v_i \sigma_i$$

where λ is a management policy variable, with dimension 1/$, v_i is standard cost of the ith option, and $p(\cdot)$ is the probability density for a binomial distribution. For large values of M the binomial can be approximated by the normal distribution.

Hence the total coverage required for the ith option is

$$Mp_i + k_i\sqrt{Mp_i(1 - p_i)}$$

OPTIONS AND ACCESSORIES

during a given planning period. However, because we don't know the particular configuration of the options and accessories the customers will want, we have to plan to cover a stock of the possible components that will be required.

An option is something like the mast on a forklift, or the starting engine on a tractor—the product must have one, but there are a few different types that can be specified. An accessory is also something that may have a list of variations that can be used, but in some cases none of them will be ordered by the customer. Thus an accessory can be considered as a special option, in which one member of the list is "none," which costs nothing to carry in stock.

Let us further assume that from previous history of orders we know the probabilities $p(i)$ that the ith option will be called for on any particular customer order, such as the average fraction of products calling for option i.

In this case there is important special information—the total number of products to be built. Therefore, rather than measuring the standard deviation of the errors in forecasting each option, we can infer the standard deviation from the multinomial distribution of configurations. Both the mean or expected number, and the standard deviation of the requirements of the ith option can be inferred from the number M of products to be built and the probability $p_i F$ that the ith option will be required (Exhibit 10.18).

If the objective is to carry a stock of options that minimizes the expected number of customer orders that will require expediting more of a particular option, for a given total investment in safety stock, the safety factor satisfies the first equation in Exhibit 10.18 in terms of the option's unit cost, the standard deviation, and a management policy variable that controls the exchange of capital investment for number of orders requiring expediting. The total coverage for the option is the sum of the expected requirement and this safety stock.

CHAPTER **11**

Lot Quantity Decision Rules

The concept of purchasing or manufacturing products in economical lot sizes has quite a long history. Roy Mennell has traced the literature back to George D. Babcock's paper in *Iron Age* in 1914. The literature is still rich in extensions of the basic concepts into more and more elaborate problems, balanced with an equal number of papers debunking the whole notion as inappropriate.

There is not, of course, a single "economical order quantity" formula. Every formula is based on five types of assumptions, and the variety comes from the selection of the alternative assumptions in each type. The primary purpose of this chapter is to display the structure of the variety of economic lot size formulas (*a*) to indicate how to find the quantity in each case and (*b*) to give some rules of thumb to determine whether a particular alternative will make any real difference in operations. There are no derivations here; references are given to the places where the derivations can be found. We display the formulas that define the computations that one must carry out to get each kind of answer.

The organization of the material in this chapter is roughly as follows:

1. Structure of the design assumptions.
2. The basic EOQ formula.
3. Common extensions.

11.1 DESIGN ASSUMPTIONS

There are five areas in which some assumption must be made about the environment in which lot quantities are to be used. In each area there are several optional cases. In most instances the choice of any one kind of an assumption is fairly independent of choices in the other four areas. Therefore there could be more than 100 different combinations, but we need discuss only about a dozen options. The areas are covered in no particular

DESIGN ASSUMPTIONS

order, since some choice must be made in each of the five before getting the economical lot.

11.11 Setup Costs

It costs something to process a replenishment order. There are setup costs in manufacturing, sometimes explicitly allowed in the engineering standards. The obvious cost is the time that it takes a mechanic to set up the machines to start making the next product. There is probably also a fixed cost of all the paper work associated with each manufacturing order as well. If there is a learning curve before the process is working at standard efficiency, the scrap loss on the initial pieces is part of the cost associated with each new lot.

Recently one of the GTE plant managers described a case in which it was assumed that the setup cost was about $50, based on the direct accountable time used. However, when the losses in starting up the process were taken into account, it turned out that the setup cost was more than $9,000, which makes some difference in the length of the production run.

There is some question as to whether the productive time lost during a setup is part of the cost or not. Certainly the wages and fringe benefits paid to direct labor during that period, if they are not assigned to some other operation, would be part of the setup cost. If demand is high enough to require all the plant capacity, then time lost for setups means loss of product that could have been sold if it had not been for the changeover; this is clearly a setup cost attributable to each change. But if there is adequate plant capacity to fill all the demand, then there is no loss of gross profit during the changeover. The setup cost thus might change with the season of the year—more expensive in the peak season than in slack seasons.

For purchase orders there are costs associated with paper work in placing the order, following up on progress, and receiving. If there is a standard sample, such as one piece, tested to destruction from each lot, that is part of the cost associated with each order. However, if 10% of every lot is inspected, then 10% of a year's supply will be inspected every year, whether ordered in 12 monthly lots or one annual lot.

Not all the operating costs of the purchasing, production scheduling, and receiving departments are properly part of the ordering cost. Rather one wants the marginal increase in cost with an increase in the number of lots processed. Suppose, for example, that the total department costs were $150,000 a year while processing about 10,000 purchase orders. That looks like an average of $15 per order. But when the workload goes up to 15,000 orders a year, the total department operating costs might go up to $175,000 a year. Hence an increase of 5000 orders a year corresponds to an increased operating cost of $25,000, or an average of only $5 per order. The latter figure would be a more appropriate one to use.

The purpose of buying or manufacturing in lot quantities in advance of current need is to spread these setup and ordering costs over more items, and reduce the total annual cost of operations.

There are two primary types of assumptions that can be made about the setup cost, represented by the symbol A, $/lot.

1. The base case assumption is that for the next lot, the cost A will be incurred for each product produced (a portmanteau word meaning manufactured or purchased). The value of A may be different from item to item, but when a given item is scheduled to be produced, the amount A will be incurred.
2. The alternative is in the case of joint orders for a family of items. For example, in weaving carpet there is a major cost of loading a warp beam onto a loom, but very minor costs associated with changing the fill to make different colors. In a punch press there may be a major cost of changing all the guides for a different gage, width, and material of coil stock, but minor costs of changing from one die to another to make different items out of the same stock. In packaging operations there is frequently a major changeover cost for changing the size of the bottle, but minor costs for cleanout between products in the same type of bottle, and even smaller costs of changing language labels for the same product. In wholesaling there is a header cost of preparing an order for a vendor, but a smaller line cost of adding one more item to the order. This latter case will be considered as one of the common extensions of basic lot-size decision rules, to generate joint and coordinated orders. (11.07)

11.12 Usage Rates

The rate at which the product is used after it is produced has an effect on the average amount of working stock in the inventory investment. That is the other essential aspect of the whole concept of economical lots. The reason one doesn't acquire a lifetime supply of everything the first time it is needed (which would clearly reduce the average unit cost to a minimum) is that such a plan would generate a great deal of inventory, tying up capital investment.

The common base assumption in computing lot sizes is that usage is known at an annual rate S pieces per year, which will continue indefinitely, so that when stock is used up another lot of the same size will be produced, and the investment can be based on the average amount in stock. There are

DESIGN ASSUMPTIONS

at least four alternative images of the reality of the operating environment:

1. Demand is forecast but there is an inherent uncertainty represented by the distribution of forecast errors. Although there are optimum joint determinations of the replenishment lot size and the safety stock, we can show that the effect of that optimum procedure can be realized by a much simpler rounding technique. Recall that in all the expressions for safety stock, one of the considerations was the number of replenishment orders per year, which affects the number of times that stock is low, with an exposure to running out of stock.

   The greater the number of lots, the smaller the working stock (Exhibit 11.1) but the larger the safety stock required to achieve an overall objective of service, because of the more frequent exposure to shortage. The total costs of replenishment and carrying both safety and working stock can be minimized, but the computations require iteration and that becomes expensive to implement and more difficult to check manually. (11.04)

2. Demand is known, and varies significantly by time period. The reason for the variation may be a trend seasonal forecast, or the results of exploding lot-size withdrawals to build higher-level assemblies. This case has excited the most attention from the theoretical community, because it is a difficult problem to solve. Tom Whiten and Harvey Wagner published the correct solution in 1958 in an excellent paper. The problem

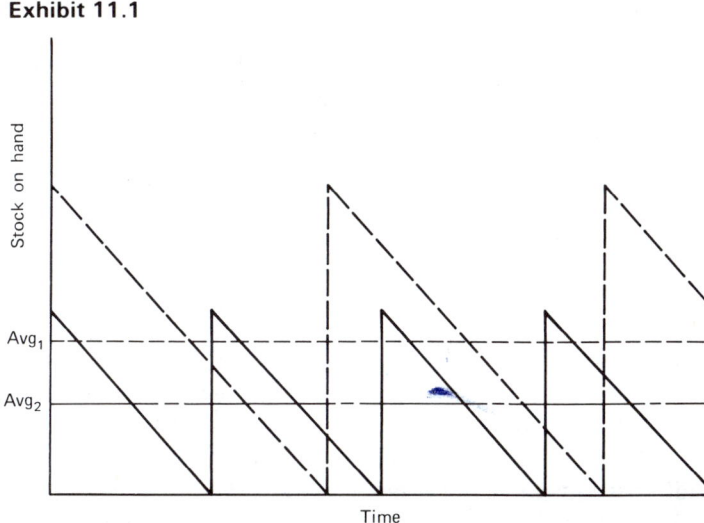

Exhibit 11.1

is correctly solved, and the authors have credit for first publication. However, the solution is so obscure that all the other authorities who dutifully refer to the paper obviously don't grasp what it is trying to do, and thus continue to offer other solutions, many of them inherently wrong.

We go briefly into the essential concepts behind the correct dynamic programming solution, but then show a practical procedure which gets very nearly the correct results in all but extreme cases. We also mention a couple of the more widely publicized approximations and comment on the practical aspects of their use. (11.10)

3. Demand may be forecast to continue, but a sudden government decree or engineering change for safety reasons leaves one with an unexpected obsolete stock to be written off. If the probability of such an event can be estimated, then the carrying charge can be increased to take account of that risk. (11.11)

4. Last buy. At the end of the life of a product, the last lot will be one that should cover all remaining requirements. We cover briefly the concepts in determining when that last lot is required, and how to estimate the total remaining supply to be covered. It turns out that although the problem presents certain aspects of theoretical interest, practical implementation is really quite simple. (12.7)

11.13 Unit Costs

The working stock left in the inventory when a lot is made for more than current requirements represents an investment of working capital. That investment is usually valued at the standard cost of the product. The costs used should be the same as the accountants use in preparing the balance sheet. It matters not whether this is the "real" cost of the inventory—it is the value that management and the investors will see in the annual report.

The standard unit cost will be expressed throughout the discussion as v \$/piece. The simplest image of reality is that any reasonable quantity can be produced at any time for the same unit cost. There are two alternatives:

1. There may be quantity discounts, so that the unit cost for a larger order is smaller than the unit cost for a minimal order. We discuss evaluation of the economics of ordering enough more to qualify for a quantity discount, and also a simple rule of thumb useful in purchasing situations to tell whether a salesman's offer is at all reasonable. (11.06)

2. The unit cost will increase when the next lot is produced. There are several ways in which this can occur. Especially in consumer products,

DESIGN ASSUMPTIONS 207

during a trade promotion the effective price is low, and the wholesaler can stock up at the end of the promotion, to defer the time when he'll have to get more at standard price. (In some products, the promotions are so closely spaced that a reasonably big wholesaler need never buy at list. He can always afford to buy enough at each promotion to last until the next one.)

It may be trade practice to announce a price rise, with one last opportunity to buy at the old price. In manufacturing automobiles, during the model year the tooling for various parts will be based on assembly volumes. At the end of the model year the production process may be retooled for much smaller volumes anticipated for service spares. For lower volumes the unit cost of manufacture may rise. Hence there is a typical bridging run at the end of the model year to buy ahead in anticipation of the increase in costs of getting more when the part has become noncurrent. The bridging run also builds a stock so that the factory has time to shut down and retool. We show that the briding run quantity can be simply expressed as some number of weeks of supply in addition to the normal lot quantity. (11.05)

11.14 Delivery into Stock

1. If an entire lot of Q pieces is produced at one time, the maximum stock will be Q pieces. The usage rate diminishes the stock until it reaches zero, then the stock goes back up to Q. On the average in this case the working stock is an investment of $0.5Q$ pieces. There are a couple of alternatives that may be more realistic in some environments.
2. When the lot goes into production, it is delivered into stock at an annualized rate of P pieces per year. Exhibit 11.2 shows that during the time the lot is in production, the usage consumes stock at the annualized rate of S pieces per year. Hence the maximum working stock is only $Q(1 - S/P)$ pieces, and the average contribution to working stock is $0.5Q(1 - S/P)$. In this case, since the investment in working stock is lower, the lot sizes can afford to be larger, to spread the setup costs over more items per lot. This extension is a simple factor in the basic formula that becomes 1 and so has no effect if the production rate becomes much larger than the usage rate. In fact, if the production rate is much more than twice the usage rate, the correction factor becomes unimportant. But it is easy to incorporate all the time, since it automatically disappears when it is unimportant. (11.03)
3. Coordinated deliveries: in a proper time-phased materials planning system (MRP, or materials requirements planning is the term currently

Exhibit 11.2

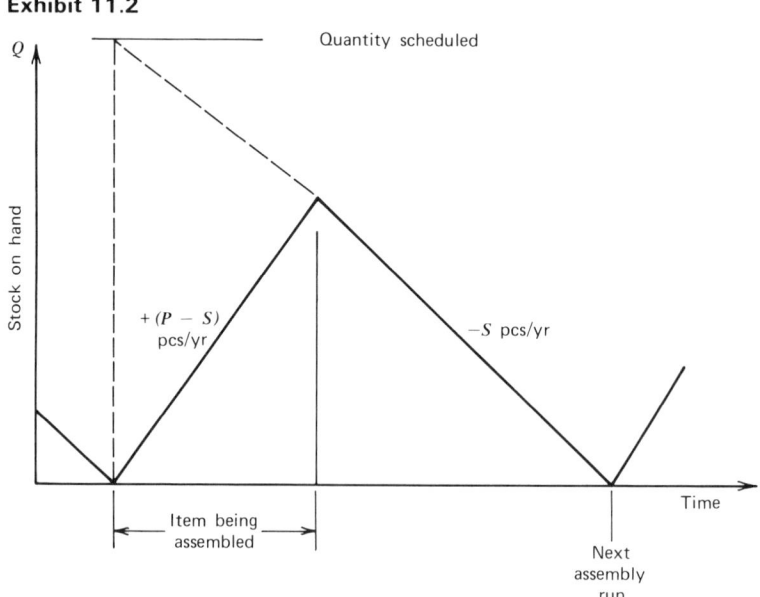

popular), the arrival of the subordinate materials can be coordinated with the usage in higher levels of assembly. The assembly lot size is an integral multiple of the machining lot for the subordinate parts. (11.09)

11.15 Premium on the Investment

The classical premium charged on inventory investment is the "carrying charge" represented by r \$/\$/year. The carrying charge does not appear at all in the chart of accounts, and has therefore stimulated a great deal of controversy over what value to use. If you believe in the du Pont formula for return on investment and want to maximize corporate return on assets employed, there is a very simple value for the carrying charge on inventories. The carrying charge should be the same as corporate return on net worth. That result can be obtained quite simply by setting up the complete equation for return on investment. The only two effects of the choice of a lot size are the annual costs of setups and the investment in working stock. All other expenses, revenues, and investments of the corporation do not depend on the decision about lot sizes, and hence may be considered fixed. If you differentiate the expression with respect to the carrying charge used, you will find that to maximize total return, you must charge inventories at the current actual corporate return.

DESIGN ASSUMPTIONS 209

Another way of thinking about the carrying charge is the rate at which future incomes and expenses are discounted to present value. If your company has a standard value to be used in that sort of an exercise, the same value should be used in computing lot quantities.

There are, however, some extenuating circumstances, such as risk and liquidity. The investment in working stock is not particularly liquid. True, you do sell the stock and realize the money from it, but the environment is usually that you have to reinvest that money immediately in more inventory. Inventory investments are more liquid than plant and equipment. (The president of a Texas company wanted an airplane, but the banks wouldn't lend him any money for it. So he raised the carrying charge, which reduced the inventory investment, and used the difference between revenue and replenishment cost to buy his airplane. The effective rate of interest was about 25%, but that was in Texas.) Inventory investments are not as liquid as working capital. If inventories are less liquid than the average investment of capital, then the carrying charge should be correspondingly higher than the average return on assets.

Inventories also represent a risk. Cash has the minimum risk, and research and development usually have the highest risk of investment. If inventories are more risky than the average investment of the corporation, then the carrying charge should be increased above average return to reflect that risk.

The du Pont corporation is knowledgable about financial management. In at least one department they have decided that raw materials are relatively safe, because there are many products that can be made from a given material. Finished goods at the plant are more risky, because the materials and labor are now committed to one specific product. Finished goods out in the field are still more risky because they depend on a regional market. Therefore the carrying charge that applies to inventory decisions increases progressively from raw materials to final field stocks.

The carrying charge on capital invested in the inventory may not always be the only, or even the prime, consideration of the premium charged on the working stocks. Space occupied can also be an important consideration, especially for bulky products. The basic lot size formulas can be extended to allow for another term that places a carrying charge on cubic feet used. For example, in the automotive parts business, gaskets, sparkplugs, and miscellaneous bin hardware can store a lot of dollars in a few cubic feet. But exhaust systems, sheet metal, and windshields take up a great deal of space per dollar. The effect of the premium on space occupied is to make the normal replenishment lots for the bulky items smaller than they would be without the correction. (11.12)

In both cases, the premium, as a carrying charge on cost and space, can be viewed as a management policy variable, with an exchange curve that shows the change in capital invested in working stocks versus the annual operating expense of processing replenishment orders. Within reason management can change the value of the carrying charge to get the operating results they want.

There are two warnings about using the carrying charge as a management policy variable.

1. If you change it at all, make big changes. Let's say the normal carrying charge in some class of the inventory is 20% a year. You might investigate 10 and 40% as alternatives that will have some detectable effect on the investment and operating expense. The range from 18 to 22% will not produce enough results to make it worthwhile for the management to review the proposal to make the change.
2. (b) There is a limit to the amount by which the investment can be reduced by increasing the carrying charge. A higher carrying charge makes the inventory look more expensive, so the decision rules in general will get less of it. But as lot sizes decrease, the frequency of replenishment increases, and so does the exposure to a shortage. Therefore the safety stocks have to increase to maintain a desired level of service. There is usually some upper limit where the decrease in working stocks is offset by the increase in safety stocks, and further changes in the carrying charge have no detectable effect except to increase ordering expense.

11.2 BASE CASE

The various forms of the economical lot quantity (EOQ) formula have to make some assumptions under each of those five headings. For a base case, to be used in comparison with alternatives, let's make the following simple assumptions:

1. Setup cost is A dollars for each lot, with no effect of other items in the same family.
2. Usage will continue indefinitely at the known constant rate of S pieces per year.
3. The unit cost is v dollars per piece, for any reasonably sized lot at any time.
4. The entire lot of Q pieces is delivered to stock at one time, so the average working stock is $0.5Q$ pieces.
5. The carrying charge is r \$/\$/year, and space is not a consideration.

In that case, the model of annual costs looks like Exhibit 11.3 As the lot quantity Q is increased, the costs of carrying the working stock increase in

BASE CASE

direct proportion. The annual costs to order decrease in proportion to the reciprocal of Q. The total costs have a minimum. The economical lot quantity Q is the lot size that corresponds to that minimum total annual cost. The expression is given by equation 1 in Exhibit 11.9 and may be expressed as a lot of Q pieces, or of T weeks of supply.

The carrying charge r is of course common to all items, like the factors 12 and 2. If the setup cost A is common to a whole class of inventory items, then the economical weeks of supply is inversely proportional to the square root of the annual value of usage. A cheap fast-moving item, and a more expensive slow mover both have the same economical time supply if the annual value of the forecast, extended at standard cost, is the same.

11.21 Sensitivity

The results are quite insensitive to changes in the factors that go into the expression. Because of the square-root effect, if any factor in the expression

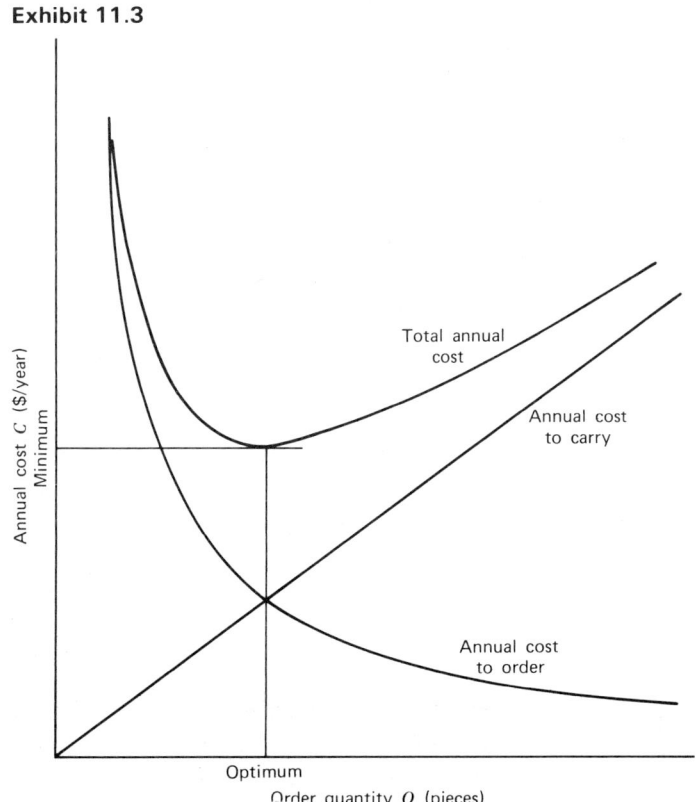

Exhibit 11.3

were to double, the lot size would change only by a factor of about 1.4. Now look at Exhibit 11.3 and visualize lots that are up to 40% larger than the most economical lot, or down to 70% of the optimum quantity. The total annual cost curve rises in both directions from the minimum, but if the lots are within the range 70 to 140% of the true optimum, the total annual costs rise less than 6% above the true minimum.

Therefore in all applications of the theory of economical lot quantities, it is quite safe and practical to round off the quantities to reasonable values. In the materials management systems library, for example, lot sizes are expressed only to two significant digits: 73,000, 680, or 15, but not 73,124 or 676. A possible refinement would be to make the number of digits depend on the unit cost—the higher the unit cost, the more digits saved.

Another result of the robustness of the costs is that the results should be rounded to practical quantities. So long as the rounding doesn't take one outside the limits of 70 to 140%, round to pallet loads, layers, cases, and cartons. In manufacturing, round to whole shifts of production.

If the process is one that has a yield factor of less than 1, then divide the computed lot by the yield factor to get the scheduled lot. For example, if the process usually yields 90% of the scheduled quantity, schedule 111% of what you want. The analysis was based on the finished stock that will be delivered, after the effects of yield loss.

Finally, there may be maximum and minimum limits on the lot quantity, expressed either as a time supply or a number of pieces. A maximum limit of one, two, or three years' supply can be imposed to guard against gross obsolescence, engineering changes, and major changes in usage patterns. The minimum time supply is imposed by the interval between opportunities to order. If the vendor will accept only 12 stock orders a year, the minimum time supply is obviously a month. If the production is scheduled in weekly planning periods, you may find it necessary to ensure that each lot is at least a week's supply. You might also schedule several discrete lots in the same planning period.

The minimum lot quantity is obviously one unit, and may be higher if the vendor has a minimum lot he will accept. For example, it is not generally possible in the United States to buy 13 cigarettes at one time.

The maximum lot quantity may be dictated by space availability. Especially in warehouses there may be a certain amount of space allotted to a given product, and the lot size should be restricted to a quantity that will fit. If the maximum limit is too small compared with an economic lot then the space available might be increased. At Anheuser Busch's St. Louis brewery the warehouse was, several years ago, only large enough to hold about eight hours of production, so that their inventory turnover rate was three times a day. That was much too rapid, and they could economically justify having

BASE CASE

twice as much inventory or 16 hours' supply, in order to get longer packaging runs. During the period until a new warehouse could be built, the carrying charge was much higher than most people would think reasonable, just to get the inventory small enough to fit into the existing building, in a balanced stock.

11.22 Calculations

The first 10 items in a file of 200 in a sample are listed in Exhibit 11.4, with the sales rates S, unit costs v, ordering cost A = $15, and the resulting simple EOQ lots, based on a nominal carrying charge of r = 0.24 $/$/year. The annual expense is computed at $15 per lot times the average number of replenishment lots per year. The working stock is an average of half the lot quantity, expressed at standard cost.

The top 25 items, in descending sequence by annual value of usage, are listed in Exhibit 11.5 for the same case. Note that the number of lots per year decreases as the value of usage decreases. There are some items that would be ordered more often than every other week.

Now consider introducing some of the limits (Exhibit 11.6). The maximum lot quantity is limited to a two-year supply, and the minimum lot quantity is limited to 20 working days, or a month's supply. No maximum limit is imposed on the number of pieces. (We shall return to the business of limiting lot sizes to be larger than the standard deviation.) Compare the resulting lot sizes with Exhibit 11.4

Exhibit 11.4

FOR A NOMINAL CARRYING CHARGE OF 24 PERCENT A YEAR, THE ECONOMICAL ORDER QUANTITIES ARE:

ITEM NUMBER	ANNUAL SALES UNITS/YR	UNIT COST DOLS/UNIT	FIXED COST DOL/ORD	ECONOMIC ORDER UNITS	ANNUAL EXPENSE DOLS/YR	WORKING STOCK DOLS
3001	54280	0.14	15.00	7020	115.98	484.38
3006	1408	0.64	15.00	523	40.38	168.67
3018	10300	0.06	15.00	4800	32.19	134.64
3028	10430	0.04	15.00	5790	27.02	112.62
3030	2613	0.07	15.00	2170	18.06	75.95
3035	2671	0.04	15.00	2970	13.49	56.43
3038	15380	0.01	15.00	14900	15.48	65.34
3047	884	0.02	15.00	2170	6.11	25.50
3049	1409	14.70	15.00	110	192.14	808.50
3062	860	0.02	15.00	2190	5.89	24.75
(THERE ARE MORE ITEMS IN THE FILE.)						
	3771992	0.19	15.00	4645500	9353.71	39130.67

Exhibit 11.7 lists the same 25 items from the top of the ABC list, where the number of orders has been reduced to about 12 (for monthly orders) at the top of the list. Safety factors have not been changed. Compare with Exhibit 11.5 the effect on service of reducing the number of chances for a shortage.

Exhibit 11.8 shows two exchange curves, both for the same sample of 200 items. The vertical axis is the capital investment in working stocks and the horizontal axis is the annual cost of setups, based on the $15 per lot assumed in this analysis. The lower curve is for the simple EOQ case, and the upper curve shows what happens when lots are limited by both a minimum and a maximum time supply. The points on the curve were generated for carrying charges ranging from 10 to 50% a year, a somewhat larger range than many managers would ordinarily contemplate.

In the typical range of about 20 to 24% a year, the effect of rounding is to increase the capital investment by perhaps 10% for the same annual cost of changeovers. To get the same number of lots, with rounding, one has to use a considerably higher value for the carrying charge.

Exhibit 11.5

ITEM	ANNUAL $ SALES	INVENTORY $ VALUE	ORDERS PER YR	SHORTAGE NO/YR	BACKORDER $/YR
3464	130,857.20	4,301.99	32.90	3.82	3,609.48
3072	80,848.00	4,364.75	25.92	4.05	5,832.06
3830	57,792.00	2,447.02	21.84	3.53	2,090.41
3683	44,276.60	2,488.36	19.16	3.47	2,714.96
3880	35,262.00	2,154.23	17.09	3.45	2,558.99
3583	28,714.35	1,591.81	15.44	2.96	1,225.09
3713	24,114.35	1,361.83	14.17	2.84	953.01
3049	20,712.30	1,256.95	13.05	2.87	972.14
3289	17,889.50	987.06	12.21	2.54	441.54
3530	15,741.00	954.16	11.43	2.65	551.45
3876	13,987.22	781.27	10.78	2.42	240.05
3488	12,555.62	613.16	10.33	5.14	3,966.52
3545	11,346.48	826.39	9.69	3.04	955.36
3147	10,381.35	577.50	8.99	4.49	4,140.08
3083	9,459.20	639.45	8.83	2.49	273.66
3268	8,718.15	643.07	8.50	2.69	465.23
3414	8,052.72	572.45	8.15	2.41	218.80
3001	7,490.64	528.50	7.89	2.33	144.25
3980	6,958.24	526.97	7.59	2.45	234.23
3747	6,531.12	539.01	7.38	2.55	405.41
3315	6,095.96	496.40	7.09	2.82	511.08
3658	5,740.78	449.32	6.90	2.31	117.13
3276	5,405.96	447.79	6.70	2.82	448.78
3248	5,105.08	432.56	6.51	2.72	383.43
3458	4,818.18	418.80	6.33	2.55	277.82
	(THERE ARE MORE ITEMS IN THE FILE.)				
	701,340.53	50,439.79	636.16	238.60	40,905.37

EFFECT OF FINITE DELIVERY RATE

Exhibit 11.6

```
LIMIT ORDER QUANTITIES? Y
MAXIMUM TIME SUPPLY, YEARS = 2
WORKING DAYS BETWEEN ORDER OPPORTUNITIES = 20
MAXIMUM ORDER QUANTITY = 1E10
MAKE QUANTITY LARGER THAN A STANDARD DEVIATION? Y
```

THE RESULTING QUANTITIES ARE:

ITEM NUMBER	ORDER QUANTITY UNITS	ANNUAL EXPENSE DOLS/YR	WORKING STOCK DOLS
3001	8688	93.72	599.47
3006	564	37.45	181.89
3018	4944	31.25	138.68
3028	5840	26.79	113.59
3030	2090	18.75	73.15
3035	2994	13.38	56.89
3038	14800	15.59	64.90
3047	1776	7.47	20.87
3049	114	185.39	837.90
3062	1722	7.49	19.46

(THERE ARE MORE ITEMS IN THE FILE.)

	349 09 69	8668.32	46222.00

11.23 Yield

If the production process suffers some predictable yield loss, the scheduled lot quantity should be increased. For example, if one expects to accept 90% of the pieces started, the scheduled lot quantity should be $1/0.9 = 1.111$ times as large as the theoretical lot. The analyses in this chapter are based on the average quantity actually produced. See also 14.11.

11.3 EFFECT OF FINITE DELIVERY RATE

When material is delivered to stock at a finite rate, annualized to P pieces per year, as in Exhibit 11.2, the effective investment in working stock is reduced by the factor $(1 - S/P)$, so that it is economical to make larger lots. Equation 4 in Exhibit 11.9 shows how the factor appears in the denominator of the expression. Clearly the total production rate must be at least as large as the usage rate. If the product is made on several machines, the effective production rate per machine may be less than the total usage rate. In that case, one or more machines should be set up to run continuously. Their contribution to the production is subtracted from the total usage rate. In addition, there may be one machine that is cycled, sometimes producing this product and sometimes being used for other jobs

Exhibit 11.7

ITEM	ANNUAL $ SALES	INVENTORY $ VALUE	ORDERS PER YR	SHORTAGE NO/YR	BACKORDER $/YR
3464	130,857.20	7,193.38	13.41	1.56	1,470.86
3072	80,848.00	6,029.45	12.54	1.96	2,820.70
3830	57,792.00	3,644.02	11.47	1.85	1,097.47
3683	44,276.60	3,103.61	12.50	2.26	1,771.70
3880	35,262.00	2,548.43	12.37	2.50	1,851.39
3583	28,714.35	1,810.88	12.50	2.40	991.47
3713	24,114.35	1,475.45	12.50	2.51	840.72
3049	20,712.30	1,301.05	12.36	2.72	920.97
3289	17,889.50	975.96	12.40	2.58	448.33
3530	15,741.00	895.30	12.50	2.90	603.00
3876	13,987.22	692.17	12.49	2.80	278.26
3488	12,555.62	1,047.16	6.03	3.00	2,313.80
3545	11,346.48	695.57	12.48	3.91	1,230.39
3147	10,381.35	577.50	8.99	4.49	4,140.08
3083	9,459.20	480.56	12.55	3.54	389.02
3268	8,718.15	469.50	12.85	4.06	703.32
3414	8,052.72	723.25	6.25	1.85	167.62
3001	7,490.64	653.25	6.25	1.84	114.23
3980	6,958.24	625.25	6.25	2.02	192.88
3747	6,531.12	660.27	5.79	2.00	318.24
3315	6,095.96	553.21	6.26	2.49	451.41
3658	5,740.78	493.06	6.25	2.09	105.98
3276	5,405.96	477.89	6.24	2.62	417.62
3248	5,105.08	448.67	6.25	2.62	368.29
3458	4,818.18	421.80	6.28	2.53	275.65
(THERE ARE MORE ITEMS IN THE FILE.)					
	701,340.53	57,931.26	584.05	231.64	31,541.61

or completely idle. The cycled runs on that machine would be computed from equation 4, in which the usage rate S is the net usage, after the contribution from the continuously running machines has been taken into account.

This correction is routine to make. If the whole lot quantity is delivered at one time, P can be set equal to a very large number, and the effect of the correction factor is negligible. The correction becomes important only when the production rate into stock is less than about twice the usage rate. Exhibit 11.10 is based on a case where for all items the delivery rate is 1.3 times the usage rate.

One has to be a little careful in applying this correction. In the pharmaceutical industry, for example, products are clearly packaged at a finite rate, which in some cases is not much larger than the sales rate. But because of quality control, the entire lot must be accumulated before it can be released to finished goods stock, so there is no effect of reducing the stock on hand by shipments during the packaging run.

11.4 INTERACTION BETWEEN LOT SIZES AND SAFETY STOCK

The expressions for computing the service that results from a given safety stock in Chapter 10 all involve N, the number of times the stock is replenished in a year. The more replenishments there are, the more exposures to the risk of a shortage, and thus the greater the safety stock has to be to maintain a given desired level of service.

Exhibit 11.11 shows a simple case of an item with fixed characteristics where we want to maintain a total level of service equivalent to filling 95% of the demand from the shelf. Consider half a dozen different possible

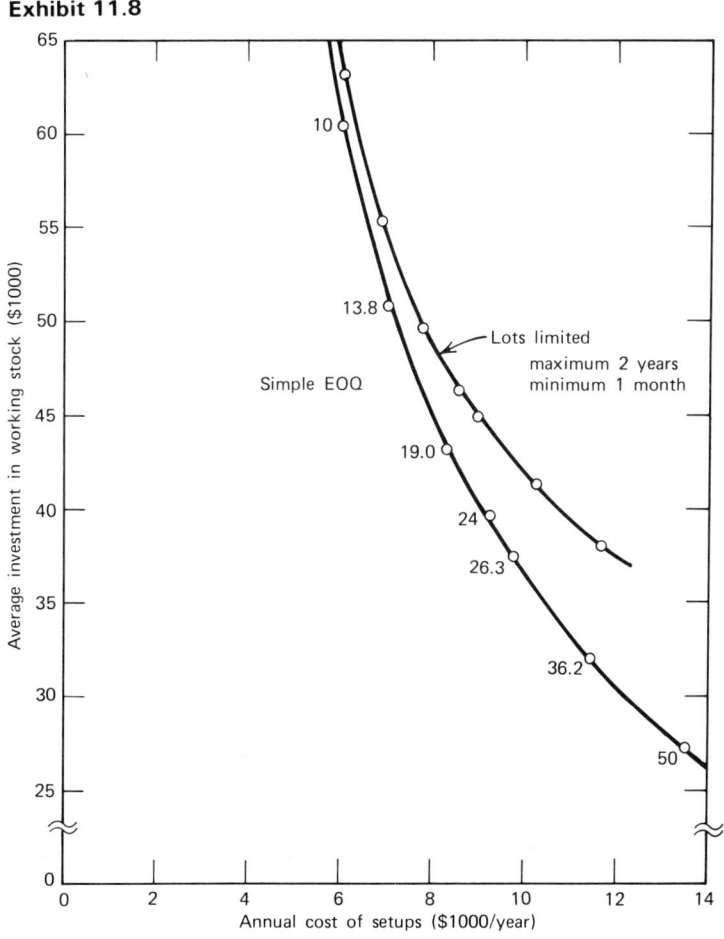

Exhibit 11.8

Exhibit 11.9

A = Setup cost, \$/lot
S = Annualized usage, pieces/year
v = Standard unit cost, \$/piece
r = Carrying charge, \$/\$/year

(1) $Q = \sqrt{2AS/rv}$ pieces; $T = 12\sqrt{2A/rSv}$ months

(2) $C(Q) = (AS/Q) + \tfrac{1}{2}rvQ$

(3) $C(Q^*) = \sqrt{2ASrv}$

P = annualized delivery rate, pieces/year

(4) $Q = \sqrt{2AS/rv(1 - S/P)}$
$C = (AS/Q) + \tfrac{1}{2}rvQ(1 - S/P)$

(5) Present value

$$W(Q) = A + QV + e^{-rQ/S}W(Q)$$
$$W(Q) = \frac{A + Qv}{1 - e^{-rQ/S}}$$

(6) Price change: v_1 now, v_2 later.

$$W(Q_1) = A + Q_1 v_1 + e^{-rQ_1}W(Q_2)$$

(7) $\dfrac{Q_1 v_1 - Q_2 v_2}{Sv_1} = \dfrac{v_2 - v_1}{rv_1}$

Exhibit 11.10

STILL FOR A NOMINAL 24 PERCENT CARRYING CHARGE, THE ECONOMICAL ORDER QUANTITIES, TAKING ACCOUNT OF PRODUCTION RATES ARE:

ITEM NUMBER	MACHINES REQ'D NO.	ANNUAL SALES UNITS/YR	ECONOMIC QUANTITY UNITS	ANNUAL EXPENSE DOLS/YR	WORKING STOCK DOLS
3001	1	54280	14600	55.77	232.48
3006	1	1408	1090	19.38	81.12
3018	1	10300	9980	15.48	64.60
3028	1	10430	12100	12.93	54.31
3030	1	2613	4500	8.71	36.35
3035	1	2671	6180	6.48	27.10
3038	1	15380	30900	7.47	31.27
3047	1	884	4520	2.94	12.26
3049	1	1409	228	92.70	386.72
3062	1	860	4540	2.84	11.84
(THERE ARE MORE ITEMS IN THE FILE.)					
200	200	3771992	9690253	4491.78	18804.49

INTERACTION BETWEEN LOT SIZES AND SAFETY STOCK

```
ANNUAL USAGE RATE = 1000
STANDARD DEVIATION OF LEAD-TIME FORECAST ERRORS = 250

1 = NORMAL/2 = EXPONENTIAL DISTRIBUTION = 1
SERVICE MEASURE: 1 SHORTAGES/2 BACKORDERS = 2

FRACTION OF DEMAND TO BE FILLED FROM STOCK = .95
```

LOT QUANTITY	PARTIAL EXPECT.	SAFETY FACTOR	SAFETY STOCK	WORKING STOCK	TOTAL STOCK
42	0.008	2.044	511	21	532
84	0.017	1.796	449	42	491
167	0.033	1.477	369	84	453
500	0.100	0.879	220	250	470
1000	0.200	0.476	119	500	619
2000	0.400	0.000	0	1000	1000

replenishment lot quantities, ranging from a six-week supply to a two-year supply. In each case the results are fed into a safety stock decision rule (Rule 1, in fact) to compute the partial expectation, and hence the safety factor and the safety stock. The working stock is half the replenishment lot quantity. The total stock is the sum of the working stock and the safety stock, and is a minimum when the lot quantity represents about a three-month supply.

The Gerson and Brown paper in the *Naval Research Logistics Quarterly* dug into the question of the optimum joint determination of lot sizes and safety stocks under several different service strategies. In each case one gets a pair of simultaneous equations involving the safety factor and the lot quantity (equations 5 and 6 in Exhibit 12.4). Since the safety factor is a function of a nonlinear (and even nonanalytic) probability function, it is impractical to seek a closed form for the solution. One has to assume a lot quantity (say, the simple EOQ), solve for the safety factor, and then substitute that value and recompute the lot quantity. The iteration converges rapidly, but it is fairly taxing on computer resources. That would be no problem if the results were worthwhile, but there's no point in burning up the meter simply for the sake of academic truth and beauty.

11.41 Evaluation of Effect

Exhibit 11.12 shows the case of one "item" where the usage rate S is increased from 1 to more than 1,000,000 pieces/year. In each case the standard deviation of forecast errors is based on the variance law characteristic of the whole inventory. In the left set of three columns, the lot sizes are computed as ordinary EOQ quantities, and the safety stock is computed

Exhibit 11.12

SALES RATE PCS/YR	STANDARD DEVIATION PCS	INDEPENDENT QUANTITY PCS	INDEPENDENT SAFETY PCS	INDEPENDENT STOCK $	JOINT QUANTITY PCS	JOINT SAFETY PCS	JOINT STOCK $	ANNUAL SAVINGS $/YR
1	1	7		18	7		18	
2	1	9		23	10		25	
4	2	13		33	14		35	
8	4	18		45	20		50	
16	7	26		65	29		73	
32	14	36		90	45		113	⁻1
64	25	51	7	161	72		180	4
128	47	72	27	317	116	6	318	17
256	88	102	74	623	176	36	619	27
512	165	144	174	1231	275	102	1195	51
1024	307	203	389	2450	445	238	2303	105
2048	573	287	837	4902	744	514	4431	227
4096	1070	405	1765	9836	1277	1064	8514	503
8192	1996	573	3651	19690	2240	2147	16336	1104
16384	3725	810	7438	39213	3994	4263	31299	2382
32768	6951	1145	14931	77519	7200	8378	59891	5009
65536	12971	1620	29596	152030	13072	16360	114478	10274
131072	24205	2290	58080	296125	23831	31809	218620	20670
262144	45169	3239	113128	573736	43530	61672	417185	41010
524288	84288	4580	219339	1108144	79575	119328	795579	80838
1048576	157286	6477	424369	2138037	145456	230533	1516303	159300

to achieve a certain desired level of service. The resulting stock is shown in dollars as the sum of the safety stock and the working stock.

In the right set of three columns the joint optimum lot quantity and safety factor are found by iteration, taking account of the effect of lot quantities on annual setup costs.

The rightmost column in Exhibit 11.12 shows the annual savings by using the optimum joint strategy, based on the reduction in carrying costs for both elements of the inventory, and the effect on longer intervals between setup costs.

The savings begin to look interesting perhaps when usage rates are on the order of about 500 pieces/year, and get more and more interesting for larger and larger usage rates. I have run this analysis several hundred times for a wide range of cases, and have drawn a general conclusion. For slow-moving items, where the simple EOQ is larger than the standard deviation of forecast errors, there isn't any appreciable saving in using the optimum algorithm for joint determination of lot sizes and safety factors. For fast-moving items, where the lot size would be smaller than a standard deviation, there are apparent savings.

11.42 Practical Approach

Therefore the recommended strategy is first to compute the lot size taking account of all other factors. Then simply limit it to be at least as large as

INTERACTION BETWEEN LOT SIZES AND SAFETY STOCK

the standard deviation. This does not produce the same lot size and safety factor as would be obtained by the optimum joint strategy. But it does produce lot sizes that are large enough that there isn't much improvement from going through the more extensive calculations. If we can get the practical effect of the best strategy (which can be large) without the effort (which can also be large), that is like eating one's cake and also having it for the next day.

11.43 Effect of Policy Variables

There are various analytical programs by which one can experiment with samples of up to 200 items at a time to see the effects of this optimum joint strategy, compare with the pragmatric effect of simply limiting the lot size, and then compute the safety factor from the resulting replenishment frequency.

Exhibit 11.13 illustrates a serious game that was designed primarily to make managers comfortable with the notion of using the carrying charge and service policy as management policy variables.

The display starts out with four measures of effectiveness based on the factors now in the file for the sample items: replenishment order setup cost, standard deviation of forecast errors, safety factor, and unit cost. The replenishment expense is based on the number of lots per year for each item

Exhibit 11.13

POLICY VARIABLES	REPLENISHMENT EXPENSE DOLS/YR	SHORTAGE OCCURRENCES ITEMS/YR	BACKORDERED DEMAND DOL/YR	INVENTORY INVESTMENT DOLLARS
PV = .25 1	10943	286	36632	47150
PV = .5 1	8452	141	10486	68371
PV = .7 1	10741	187	12394	59992
PV = .7 4	12882	165	9790	58403
PV = .7 2	12604	349	47760	41150
PV = 1 2.5	12647	260	23073	49716
PV = 1 3	14313	315	29795	44746
PV = .7 3	14331	342	36350	42356
PV = .7 2.5	12783	302	34238	44906
PV =	12643	290	29965	46680

times the setup cost per lot. The shortage occurrences are computed from the safety factor as was illustrated in Chapter 10, and for the dollar value of back-ordered demand. The inventory investment is the sum of the values for the working stock and the safety stock, at standard cost, over all items in the sample.

This is an interactive gam in which the computer prints a prompt "$PV = $" and then unlocks the keyboard for the user to enter a value for the carrying charge (as a decimal) and the number of shortages per item per year as the management policy variable to control service. The computer then evaluates all the lot quantities and safety factors and prints out the four measures of effectiveness that result. With the Amdahl 470 computer I have been using recently, the computations are so fast that the results start printing as soon as the user presses the carriage return to indicate that he has entered the values. Then the prompt is repeated.

This game has some very useful properties. On the one hand it engages top managers actively in manipulating the policy variables, with a chance to see the effects immediately. Some people take a very cautious approach and need quite a push to even contemplate the use of carrying charges like 1 or 150%. But "it's only a game," and usually they can be encouraged to try bolder strategies, which sets a background against which to recommend actual values for use.

The other use of this game emerged only after top managers began using it in earnest. There are four measures of effectiveness, and in a conversation most managers would say something like, "Keep the inventory investment to six turns, but keep the setup costs low. Service of course has to be 98%." But as they begin to explore the consequences of changing the management policy variables, it becomes very obvious what their real priority of interest is among investment, costs, and the two measures of service. Quite often this experience has led to a much more productive discussion of the strategic choice among decision rules, because of the appreciation of what is meant by the two different measures of service, and how they tend to move in opposite directions.

Exhibit 11.14 shows an exchange surface in three dimensions. The capital investment in the vertical direction is the sum of the safety stocks and working stocks. The axis pointing out to the left is the annual operating expense of processing replenishment orders, so that any slice through the surface by a plane perpendicular to the paper and parallel to the vertical axis would produce an exchange curve as in Exhibit 11.8.

The horizontal axis is a measure of service (which could be either back-ordered value or number of lots that require expediting). Any section through the surface by a plane parallel to the paper would produce an

BRIDGING RUNS   223

Exhibit 11.14

A three—dimensional exchange surface

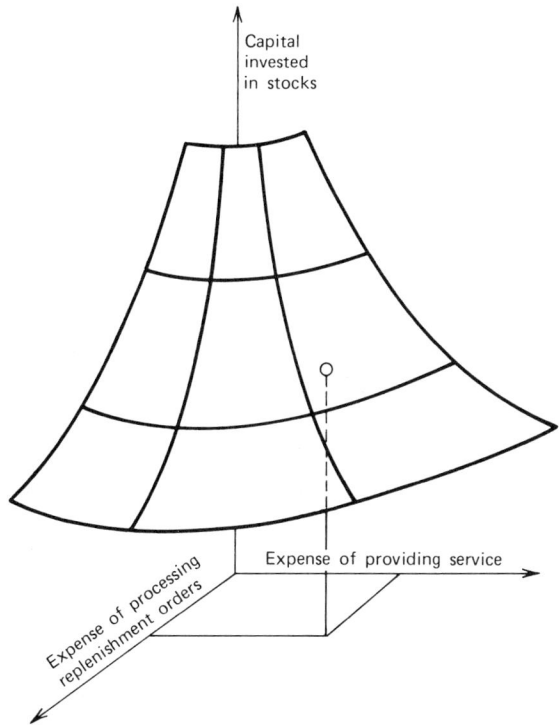

exchange curve like the ones in Chapter 10. What would a section perpendicular to the vertical axis represent?

Management's tactical job is to find some point on this surface that represents a practical balance among the competing interests of marketing, finance, production, and purchasing.

Exhibit 11.15 shows the listing of the top 25 items after the lot sizes and safety stocks were computed as of the last line in Exhibit 11.13.

11.5 BRIDGING RUNS

There can be several instances where the unit cost in the lot being produced now is lower than the unit cost is expected to be in future lots. Change in tooling at the end of the model year, end of a promotion, and announced

Exhibit 11.15

ITEM	ANNUAL $ SALES	INVENTORY $ VALUE	ORDERS PER YR	SHORTAGE NO/YR	BACKORDER $/YR
3464	130,857.20	4,956.79	26.81	2.59	2,372.10
3072	80,848.00	5,129.14	21.73	2.59	3,529.04
3830	57,792.00	2,525.89	28.67	2.59	1,372.53
3683	44,276.60	2,767.19	18.98	2.59	1,898.44
3880	35,262.00	2,419.07	17.01	2.58	1,779.32
3583	28,714.35	1,601.59	18.21	2.58	9 3.97
3713	24,114.35	1,328.44	17.34	2.58	802.89
3049	20,712.30	1,246.79	15.66	2.57	804.94
3289	17,889.50	842.39	17.27	2.58	412.66
3530	15,741.00	866.04	15.13	2.57	489.57
3876	13,987.22	605.14	16.24	2.57	233.02
3488	12,555.62	1,253.59	6.03	2.50	1,746.11
3545	11,346.48	883.71	10.84	2.53	717.15
3147	10,381.35	1,077.47	5.49	2.50	2,182.53
3083	9,459.20	526.16	12.55	2.54	251.66
3268	8,718.15	598.32	10.92	2.53	392.85
3414	8,052.72	455.03	11.87	2.54	207.12
3001	7,490.64	392.57	11.97	2.54	141.14
3980	6,958.24	428.17	10.89	2.53	215.22
3747	6,531.12	510.47	8.68	2.51	372.26
3315	6,095.96	492.35	8.81	2.51	395.23
3658	5,740.78	327.00	10.56	2.52	113.65
3276	5,405.96	432.44	8.80	2.51	338.94
3248	5,105.08	406.87	8.44	2.51	304.72
3458	4,818.18	362.46	8.74	2.51	237.57
(THERE ARE MORE ITEMS IN THE FILE.)					
	701,340.53	46,679.76	842.84	290.08	29,965.43

price rise are some of the cases where this change occurs. Equation 5 in Exhibit 11.9 is taken from my 1963 book, *Decision Rules for Inventory Management*, as the present value of buying (or making) an item in lot quantities Q, at a unit cost v, with an ordering or setup cost A per lot. Note that the "carrying charge" r appears as the rate at which future expenses are discounted to present value, which is more of a risk determination than any bank rate on the cost of borrowing capital.

When the unit cost now is v_1 but on all later lots the cost will rise to v_2, equation 6 gives the expression for the present value of the strategy of acquiring a lot of Q_1 units now. With a little judicious algebra one can work through to equation 7, which has a very simple implication. The left side of the equation is the difference, in dollars, between the lot quantity to be bought now and the future lot, divided by the annual usage rate in dollars, so it has the effect of representing the extra quantity as a time supply. The right side of the equation is the percentage increase in unit cost, divided by the discount rate or carrying charge.

QUANTITY DISCOUNTS

Suppose that the price increase is going to be 10%. If the carrying charge is 20% a year, then equation 7 says that the lot to be acquired now can exceed the normal EOQ lot by half a year's supply.

However, when the implications of this rule are tested in actual buying situations, it appears that the effective discount rate is usually much higher than the normal carrying charge used in simple EOQ analyses. An experienced buyer will buy ahead at the end of a deal. Choose a record of several purchases in which you can determine the extra amount bought, over the normal EOQ quantity, and the price rise. Plot the extra quantity, in weeks of supply, versus the price rise, in percent. The points will scatter about a straight line, but the effective slope of that line is often equivalent to 50, 80, or even 100% a year discounting of future savings by increasing stock now. This may be because of a perceived risk of obsolescence when the demand rate changes, pressure on warehouse space, or simple caution.

An implication of this phenomenon for manufacturers of consumer goods is that they may expect their customers (the wholesalers and distributers) to buy this way at the end of the promotion, and it can be used to infer the profile of the pattern of response of the trade to a deal (see 7.23).

11.6 QUANTITY DISCOUNTS

Another type of change in unit cost that may be considered in computing the quantity to buy is the quantity discount. Consider, as an example, a case where one can buy an item with a list price of $v = \$25$. But if you order at least 2000 at a time, the price drops to \$24.50. There may be other "breakpoints" such as \$22 at 5000, \$20 at 10,000, and \$15 for lots of more than 50,000 each.

The first step in the computation is to compute simple EOQ lots for all five unit prices. Only one of these lots will fall in a range of quantities that is consistent with the unit price assumed. For example, if the ordering cost is $A = \$35$, the usage rate is $S = 10{,}000$ a year, and the carrying charge is $r = 0.24$, then the five EOQ quantities will be 342, 345, 364, 382, and 441. Of these, only the 342 units for a unit cost of $v = \$25$ falls in the range for which that assumed price applies. Thus one candidate for the lot size is 342 units, with no price breaks.

Now apply equation 5 in Exhibit 11.9 to compute the present value of strategies of ordering 342 every time, and 2000, 5000, 10,000 and 50,000 at a time. It is necessary to analyze only a finite list of quantities which are all at breakpoints and which are all larger than the first consistent EOQ. The present value of ordering 342 each lot is \$1,050,229. The lowest present value is associated with ordering lots of 10,000 at a time: \$937,493, about a

10% savings in present value. Hence in this case the best strategy is to go up to the 10,000 quantity which happens to have a very favorable discount.

The cost curves are illustrated in Exhibit 11.16. The annual cost of ordering is independent of unit cost and decreases as lot sizes are increased. The cost of the inventory does, of course, depend on the unit cost, and there may be different costs for different ranges of values. The total cost curve is the heavy line, which is the sum of the cost to order and the pertinent segment of th cost to hold inventory.

There can be a minimum in the total cost curve either at (*a*) the "consistent" EOQ lot, or (*b*) one the of the breakpoints to the right, for larger quantities. Hence we need look at only a finite number of cases, and pick the best one.

There is a simple rule of thumb, very approximate, which can be used to estimate the payout from different discounts to find the best one. The rule is "2% per month," which means this. First figure the normal quantity you would buy anyhow. It may be the minimum, or an EOQ, or what you bought last time. Now consider any larger quantity at which you get a reduction in unit cost. Express the extra amount you would have to buy to qualify for the discount in months of supply. Suppose it is a two-month supply. If the discount is more than 4% (2% for each extra month of supply) it

Exhibit 11.16

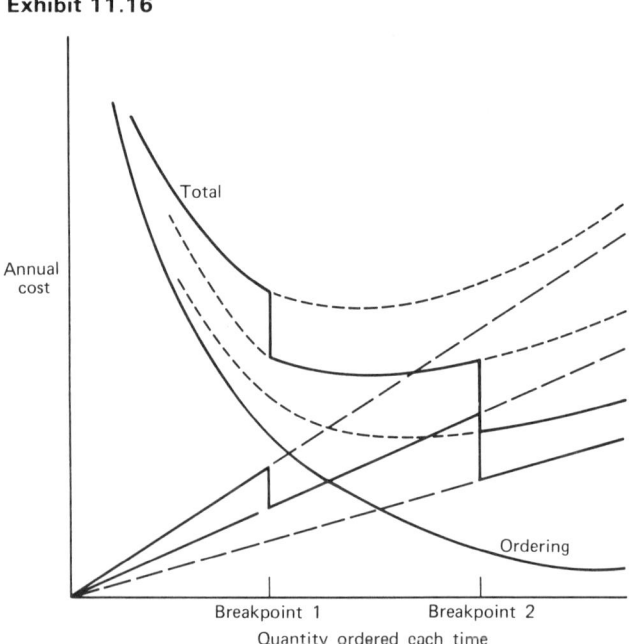

JOINT ORDERS

will pay to order the larger quantity. But it would not pay to order an extra two-month supply to get only a 3% discount.

This rule has some limitations and won't work for very large discounts or very many months of supply. But it may have more value than just deciding whether to take it or leave it. Some astute buyers who know this rule may use it in negotiating with a salesman. "Give me 5% for going to 4000 cases, and I'll take it." The effect of getting the better discounts may do more for corporate profits than any amount of economic theory and computer analysis.

11.7 JOINT ORDERS

When there is a family of related items that share in part of the setup or ordering cost, then one may use the following procedure to determine the proper lot quantity for each item in the family. The situation arises, for example, when there is a major changeover cost on a bottling line for a change in bottle size, but smaller cleanout costs between different products that may go into the same size bottle. In wholesaling there is a header cost of preparing an order to a vendor, but a much smaller line cost of adding additional items to the order.

Represent the major cost for setting up the whole family as A dollars per lot, and the minor costs of changing from one item to another within the family by a dollars per changeover. The minor changeover costs may depend on the sequence of products, such as the progression from light to dark flavors of cake mix, or paint. Sometimes the progression is obvious. If there is a general matrix of changeover costs, the best sequence can be found using the "branch and bound" technique to solve the traveling salesman problem. Or the foreman who makes the product can be asked; chances are he knows by bitter experience what the preferred sequence is, close enough that the precise mathematical solution won't improve by as much as the probable error in the engineer's estimates of what the changeover costs are. In any case, the minor changeover costs a are the costs in the best sequence of making the items in the family.

The family can be planned to be set up and run every T weeks, where T is given by equation 2 in Exhibit 11.17. Each item within the family may be run every time the major setup is made, or some of the slower-moving items may be run every k cycles, in a large enough supply to last for Tk more weeks. The values for the multiples k are given by equation 1. Since the values of the multiples appear on both sides of the equation, one must use an iterative approach. Assume all $k = 1$, and evaluate the square-root expressions to get the left side of the equation. Round the results to integers.

Exhibit 11.17

Major setup cost A dollars/lot for the family
Minor changeover costs a_i for ith item

The ith item is made once every k_i cycles

(1) $\quad k_i = \sqrt{\dfrac{a_i}{S_i v_i}} \sqrt{\dfrac{\Sigma\, k_i S_i v_i}{A + \Sigma\, a_i/k_i}}$

Assume all $k_i = 1$, evaluate the right side of (1), and round. Repeat until all left sides equal values assumed on right.

Weeks supply per setup of the family

(2) $\quad T = 52 \sqrt{\dfrac{2(A + \Sigma\, a_i k_i)}{r \Sigma\, k_i S_i v_i}}$

If the jth item has less than T weeks of supply, make quantity $Q_j = k_j T S_j/52$ pieces, less stock available now.

Repeat the process until the values assumed on the right produce the same values on the left.

A family of seven items, where one has 61% of total sales and another has only 1%, are considered in Exhibit 11.18. The items that represent smaller fractions of the total sales of the family will have the cycle multiples greater than 1.

The effects of ignoring the refinement in cycle multiples are not very important. The total cost would rise only 5% if all items were made every time the family were set up. However, if items were made independently, so that each one incurred the major setup cost of $75, then the total annual cost would be 66% larger than the optimum joint strategy. That is a big enough difference to be considered.

Note that the cycle multiples do not involve the carrying charge—if the cycles are short or long, the multiple applicable to a given member of the family is the same. The carrying charge does affect the length of the cycle. The higher the carrying charge, the more expensive the working stock, so the shorter the cycle. For carrying charges ranging from 10 to 50%, the cycle varies from once a quarter to once every six weeks.

11.8 CYCLED PRODUCTION

When products in a family are cycled with finite rates of production, there is an interesting procedure for determining when to stop producing one

Exhibit 11.18

THE RECORD HAS 7 ITEMS.
COMMON COST INCURRED TO ORDER THE FAMILY = 75

INDIVIDUAL ITEMS SHOULD BE ORDERED IN MULTIPLES
OF THE BASIC ORDER CYCLE.

ITEM IDENT	FRACTION OF SALES	MULTIPLE
3033	0.010	3
3347	0.611	1
3371	0.003	5
3424	0.213	1
3442	0.095	1
3460	0.022	2
3564	0.046	1

ORDER STRATEGY	COST RATIO
OPTIMUM JOINT	1.000
EQUAL FREQUENCY	1.048
INDEPENDENT EOQ	1.660

EXTREME VALUES FOR THE CARRYING CHARGE = .1 .5

CARRYING CHARGE	WEEKS PER ORDER	WORKING STOCK	ORDERING COST
0.10	13.55	4811.15	481.12
0.14	11.53	4095.93	565.13
0.19	9.82	3487.03	663.81
0.26	8.36	2968.65	779.72
0.36	7.12	2527.33	915.88
0.50	6.06	2151.61	1075.81

CARRYING CHARGE TO BE USED = .25

THE INVENTORY RECORD HAS NOW BEEN BROUGHT UP TO DATE.
LIST THE CURRENT RECORD CONTENTS? Y

LINE	IDENT	SALES	COST	M.A.D	LTIME	SETUP	SFACT
1	3033	1022	0.331	19	3.00	10.00	1.00
2	3347	6996	3.060	114	3.00	10.00	1.00
3	3371	5866	0.020	64	3.00	10.00	1.00
4	3424	1872	3.990	29	3.00	10.00	1.00
5	3442	8896	0.376	119	3.00	10.00	1.00
6	3460	14460	0.052	115	3.00	10.00	1.00
7	3564	13100	0.122	108	3.00	10.00	1.00

LINE	POINT	QUANT	OHAND	ORDER	PRATE	PACKQ	TRANS
1	296	168	434	508		200	204
2	1997	1153	621	1311		12	33
3	1606	966	1293	4932		6	4
4	531	308	309	198		6	5
5	2482	1466	1612	1405		48	89
6	3864	2382	4055	4801		10	24
7	3510	2158	2238	2992		48	153

product and go to the next. If there is only one product, the only reason to stop making it is that requirements are covered. If there are two products, the procedure is simple. Produce one until the other runs out, then change over. When there are three products the situation gets a little more complicated.

Exhibit 11.19 uses barycentric coordinates to illustrate the stock status. The position of a point within the triangle represents the mix of the stocks of the three products. When the point moves to the line AB that means we are out of C so the natural thing to do is to start making C. Meanwhile we use stocks of A and B, and the mix of inventory moves until we are out of, say, B. When we make B, we use up A and C until we are out of A. And so the long day wears on.

This procedure works very well until we get into a corner, where we are out of two products simultaneously and we can't make them both at once. Therefore we want to set up a barrier that causes a changeover before we are out of anything, if the inventory mix is headed for a corner.

In my 1973 book, *Management Decisions for Production Operations*, I derived the expression shown at the bottom of Exhibit 11.19, on the basis of first working forward to the inventory that would result from the best economical lots for a family of items. Then, given an existing inventory, we limit the amount for any one product to the share that would be represented

Exhibit 11.19

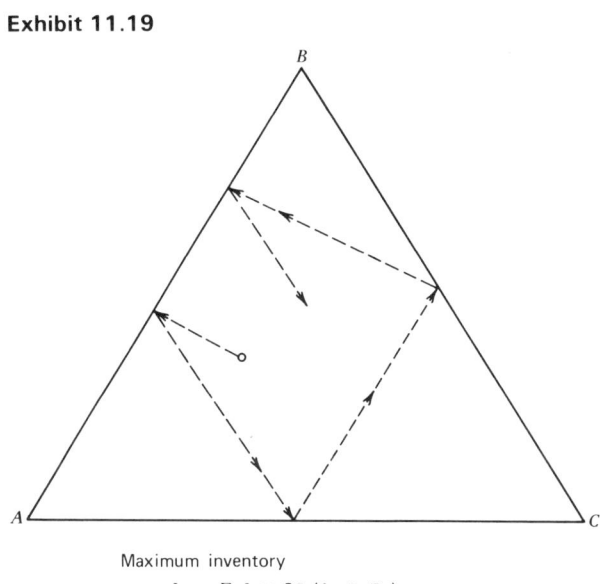

Maximum inventory
$$I_i = \frac{\sum I_j \times 2S_i(1-S_i/P_i)}{\sum S_i(1-S_i/P_i)}$$

by the economic lot if the carrying charge had produced the inventory we've got. In Chapter 13 we consider the master scheduling procedures that keep the total inventory in balance, and that may require the process to run at a slower rate, or be shut down entirely, to keep the inventory from growing too large.

11.9 COORDINATED DELIVERIES

In a time-phased planning system it is possible to plan to receive a lot of material just at the time a substantial part of that lot is consumed into the assembly of a parent item. In that case the lot quantity for the subordinate material should be an integral multiple of the lot size for the parent. (This assumes that the material has only one use, such as a forging that is machined into parts. It also depends heavily on the assumption that a portion of the castings is machined immediately upon receipt, and that there is a period of time when no castings would be required in stock.) The concept of the situation is illustrated in Exhibit 11.20. Note how the parent stock goes through the typical sawtooth pattern, but the stock of the subordinate castings is more like a staircase.

Equation 1 in Exhibit 11.21 shows the total annual cost expression for the lots of the two items. If we substitute the lot quantity for the subordinate as a multiple of the lot quantity for the parent, we can get an expression for the economic parent lot quantity, in equation 2. Note that the effective setup cost is the parent setup plus a fraction of the setup for the subordinate. Similarly the effective unit cost is the sum of the costs of the two items.

The ratio between the lots is given by equation 3. The procedure is first to use equation 3 to find the multiple k. Round it to an integer (at least 1). Substitute into equation 2 to find the parent lot quantity. Finally, set the subordinate lot quantity as k times the parent lot quantity.

11.10 LOT QUANTITIES WITH TIME-VARYING DEMAND

The general discussion to this point has considered usage at the annualized rate of S pieces per year. For products with a trend or seasonal pattern, the forecast may be anything but a nice uniform rate of usage. In manufacturing companies, the consumption of purchased parts and raw materials may be very "lumpy" because of the sporadic withdrawal for assembly into a lot of a parent item. Chapter 13 deals with the procedures by which we can

Exhibit 11.20

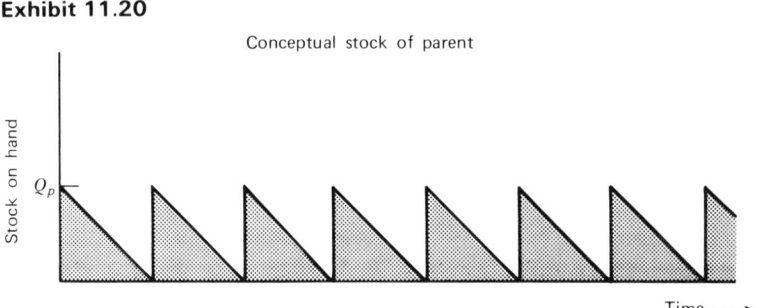

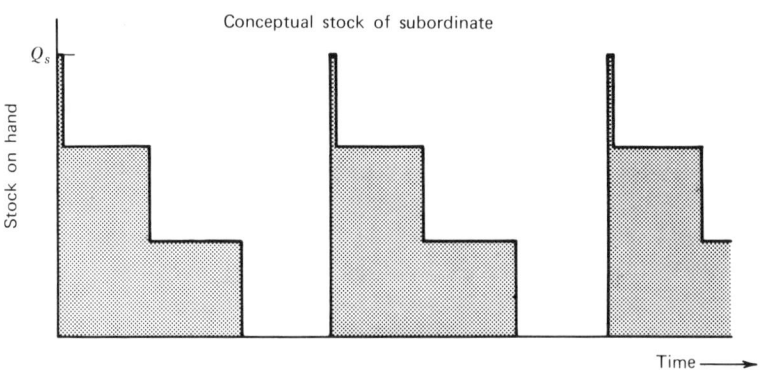

maintain a reasonable record of the demand by planning period. The theoretical economical lot for this case has been of considerable academic interest. The earliest solution was published by Wagner and Whiten in 1958, and they got the correct answer to the problem as stated. The "rules" of the game are that the long-term costs of setups and of carrying inventory are to be minimized, and the lots are to cover discrete demand in integral numbers of planning periods. This is balderdash on the shop floor, of course, but it does produce PhDs.

The difficulty with the right answer is that it requires dynamic programming which not many people comprehend readily, and even those who do find it hard to convert into working computer code. The literature is full of proposed solutions (a few years ago I counted 158 technical papers on the subject), many of which are dead wrong.

One common fallacy argues from Exhibit 11.3 that the minimum total cost must be where the cost to acquire is equal to the cost to hold. This

LOT QUANTITIES WITH TIME-VARYING DEMAND

coincidence, which is true for the assumptions of the simple EOQ, is not true in general, especially when usage is not uniform, so that the average inventory is not half the lot size.

11.101 Exact Solution

Let's look first at the concept behind the correct answer, and then at a practical way of getting a good working answer. Then we'll consider a couple of the popular techniques that have had fairly wide publicity through IBM's applications.

Exhibit 11.22 is a diagram with time represented by the horizontal axis, and cumulative requirements by the vertical axis. The forecast of requirements (from whatever source) is represented as the cumulative number of units required between now and the end of any planning period, out to the horizon. The forecast is represented by the wavy line that moves up to the right. It has waves or wiggles in it because the demand is not constant from period to period.

In this particular case we have determined that we are going to cover the total requirements in precisely three lots. (We'll return to that assumption

Exhibit 11.21

S = Annual usage, pieces/year
A = Setup cost, \$/lot
v = Unit cost, \$/piece
r = Carrying charge, \$/\$/year
Q = Lot size, pieces per lot

Subscripts: p = parent item
s = subordinate item

Total annual cost

(1) $\quad C = (A_s S/Q_s) + \tfrac{1}{2} Q_s v_s r + (A_p S/Qp) + \tfrac{1}{2} Q_p v_p r$
Let $\quad Q_s = kQ_p$

(2) $\quad Q_p = \sqrt{\dfrac{2(A_p + A_s/k)S}{r(v_p + kv_s)}}$

(3) $\quad k = \sqrt{A_s v_p / A_p v_s}$

(a) Find multiple k, round to an integer
(b) Solve (2) for parent lot Q_p
(c) Subordinate lot $Q_s = kQ_p$

Exhibit 11.22

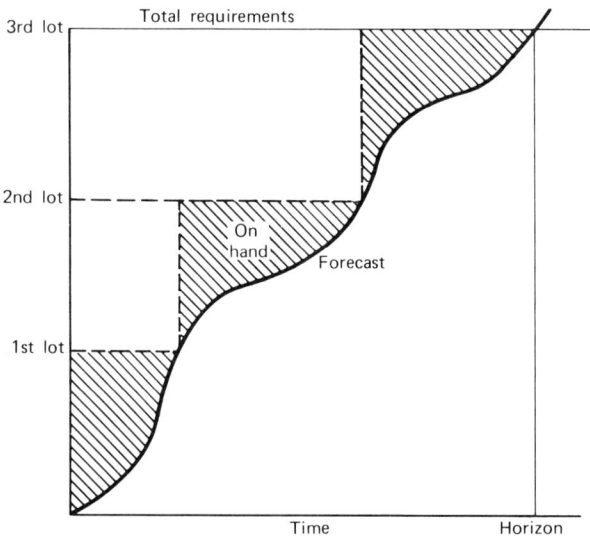

of three in a moment.) The first lot covers requirements to the end of a particular period. The next lot covers the requirements to a later period, and the third lot covers the remainder of the requirements.

Because the plot is cumulative, it is easy to represent the inventory at any time. The forecast represents the cumulative withdrawals, and the lots represent the cumulative deliveries to stock. Hence the shaded areas represent the stock expected to be on hand at any time.

If we are to cover total requirements in three lots, there are only two choices to make: the periods through which the first and the second lots cover. As these points move back and forth along the forecast line, they affect the size of the shaded area and hence the average amount of inventory. There is always a pair of values for the coverage of the first and the second lots which will minimize the total area shaded to represent inventory.

If we were to make the total requirements in one lot, the entire upper triangular area would be shaded—more inventory, but only one setup. If we cover the total requirements in two lots, there would be two setups, but the minimum inventory would be less than the inventory from one lot. As we increase the number of lots, for each one we can find the optimum coverage in terms of the smallest inventory for that number of lots. The inventory carrying charge keeps decreasing and the cost of additional setups keeps increasing. At some point we can't save enough inventory to make one more setup worthwhile. Then we go back down to the number of lots that

LOT QUANTITIES WITH TIME-VARYING DEMAND 235

gave the most economical total and look at the period covered by the first lot of the optimum sequence, to find the best strategy.

Exhibit 11.23 displays the results of a program that carries out this analysis for a stipulated schedule of requirements, examining from one to six lots to cover the total requirements provided. The first table shows the stock in "piece months," which is a measure proportional to the shaded area in Exhibit 11.22. The total cost reflects the cost to carry that inventory and the cost of the number of setups for the number of lots considered. The minimum total cost is $1449.84, for three lots to cover a total of 3770 pieces of requirements.

Two other strategies are shown for comparison. The equal-quantity strategy divides 3770 pieces by the number of lots, and then finds as nearly as possible a sequence that covers discrete planning periods with that number of pieces per lot. That is, the vertical axis in Exhibit 11.22 is divided into equal increments, and lots cover to the nearest planning period.

The equal-frequency strategy divides the 25 periods by the number of lots, and makes each lot cover (as nearly as possible) the same number of periods. In effect it divides the horizontal axis in Exhibit 11.22 into equal increments, and the lots cover to the nearest planning period.

Once the values of the strategies have been computed, then you can look at the details of the individual lots in all three strategies, for three lots and for four lots. Since all three strategies cover 3770 pieces in 25 periods within the same number of lots, the comparison is strictly between the average stock resulting from each.

11.12 Practical Approach

After performing a great many of these analyses, I have come to the following recommendations.

1. Compute an effective annualized rate of usage S from the total requirements scheduled out to the planning horizon.
2. Use that rate to compute the economical lot quantity that takes account of any finite rates, quantity discounts, interaction with safety stocks, or joint orders that are appropriate to the operating environment.
3. Convert the resulting lot quantity Q into a time supply as $T = Q/S$, using the average usage rate that went into the calculation of Q.
4. Schedule as an actual lot the requirements planned for the next T planning periods.

This procedure is admittedly an approximation. A great many trials have shown that it produces results close to the best possible. It does build on the experience of lot size theory for steady consumption. It is easy to apply.

Exhibit 11.23

```
ORDER PROCESSING COST = 200
UNIT COST = 3
CARRYING CHARGE PER PERIOD = .02
THE TOTAL DEMAND OF 3770 UNITS COULD BE COVERED WITH
BETWEEN 3 AND 4 EOQ LOTS BASED ON AVERAGE DEMAND.

CHANGE ANY ECONOMIC FACTORS? N

THREE STRATEGIES FOR COVERAGE YIELD THESE RESULTS:
```

STRATEGY:	MINIMUM-STOCK		EQUAL-QUANTITY		EQUAL-FREQUENCY	
NO. OF	STOCK	COST	STOCK	COST	STOCK	COST
LOTS	PC-MO	DOLS	PC-MO	DOLS	PC-MO	DOLS
1	47746	3064.76	47746	3064.76	47746	3064.76
2	21310	1678.60	23274	1796.44	22097	1725.82
3	14164	1449.84	14709	1482.54	16049	1562.94
4	10964	1457.84	12884	1573.04	12257	1535.42
5	8455	1507.30	10470	1628.20	9111	1546.66
6	6866	1611.96	7925	1675.50	7737	1664.22

```
YOU MAY NOW DISPLAY THE SEQUENCE OF LOTS THAT GENERATED THE
RESULTS FOR ANY LINE OF THIS SUMMARY TABLE.

NUMBER OF LOTS = 3
```

LOT	MINIMUM-STOCK		EQUAL-QUANTITY		EQUAL-FREQUENCY	
NUMBER	END TIME	LOT QTY	END TIME	LOT QTY	END TIME	LOT QTY
1	9	1130	10	1279	8	1114
2	15	1003	17	1330	17	1495
3	25	1637	25	1161	25	1161
AVERAGE STOCK		567		588		642

```
DISPLAY DETAILS OF ANOTHER COVERAGE? Y

NUMBER OF LOTS = 4
```

LOT	MINIMUM-STOCK		EQUAL-QUANTITY		EQUAL-FREQUENCY	
NUMBER	END TIME	LOT QTY	END TIME	LOT QTY	END TIME	LOT QTY
1	9	1130	6	957	6	957
2	15	1003	14	1065	13	840
3	19	837	19	948	19	1173
4	25	800	25	800	25	800
AVERAGE STOCK		439		515		490

```
DISPLAY DETAILS OF ANOTHER COVERAGE? N

COMPARE THESE RESULTS WITH THE FIRST LOT COMPUTED BY THE TWO
STRATEGIES IN "PICS".
```

	L.U.C.	P.P.A.
ENDS AT	7	7
PIECES	1036	1036

LOT QUANTITIES WITH TIME-VARYING DEMAND

There are some circumstances under which none of the approximations really work, and one should use the full dynamic programming analysis. These seem to be where the requirements are very concave: that is, all the high requirements are at one end and the low requirements at the other end of the planning horizon, so that the forecast in Exhibit 11.22 is definitely bow-shaped. But those cases are rare in practice. Chapter 13 covers techniques of implementing this strategy in a time-phased system.

11.103 Other Approximations

There are a couple of other approximations that have been widely publicized by IBM as part of their PICS application. One is the part-period balancing algorithm developed by deMatteis and Mendoza in Yorktown. The other is the least unit cost technique, originally from Kraus in Stuttgart.

Although they are not usually presented this way, Exhibit 11.24 shows the effect of these procedures. The setup cost is A dollars per lot. The carrying charge is r dollars per dollar per year. The unit cost of the item is v dollars per piece.

The schedule of requirements is represented cumulatively in Exhibit 11.24. The part-period balancing algorithm considers successively larger and larger quantities until the triangular area above the forecast is equal to A/rv.

Exhibit 11.24

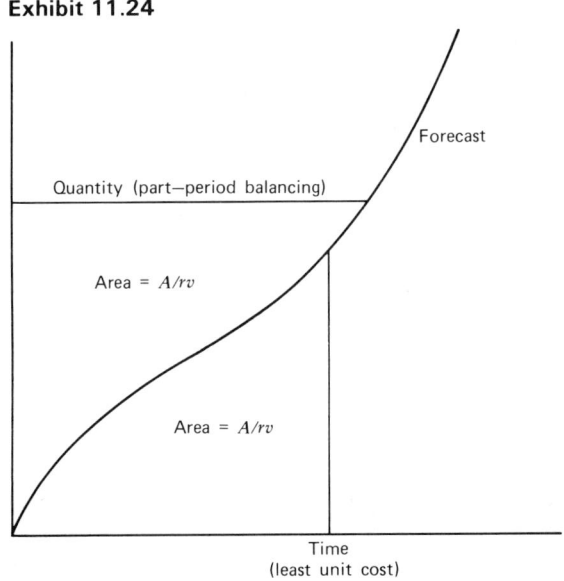

The least unit cost algorithm considers a lot that covers successively more and more periods, until the area below the curve is equal to A/rv.

Note that when requirements are uniform, the cumulative forecast is a straight line, and the two methods arrive at the same answer, which is the EOQ. When requirements vary, one lot will be bigger than the other, so they can't both be "right." The procedures recommended above strike a balance between the extremes. The difficulty with both techniques is that they don't consider the pattern of demand in future periods.

There is a "look ahead" feature which makes some adjustment. If the requirements in the last planning period covered by the first lot are above the average annualized rate S, then the coverage is reduced one period. Then the large requirement will be the first withdrawal from the next lot, instead of the last from the first lot. The effect is to reduce inventory.

11.11 SUDDEN OBSOLESCENCE

For some kinds of electronic, aviation, and pharmaceutical products there is a chance that something will happen which makes it mandatory to scrap any stock now on hand, and these events occur unexpectedly. In Chapter 13 we deal with effectivity dates, where the time when a part of material is to be discontinued can be determined in advance. Here we are concerned with some defect that affects the safety of the user, or a government regulation, which does not allow time to work off existing stocks.

In a note in *Production and Inventory Management* I showed that the effect on the economic order quantity formula is to increase the effective carrying charge, as in equation 7 in Exhibit 11.25. It does require that an engineer or product planner be able to specify the expected time, in years, until such an event will occur. "I don't know when it will come, but on the average over many such products, I would expect that this product will get discontinued suddenly in about two years" is the sort of statement one wants. In that case the parameter p is $\frac{1}{2} = 0.5$, and the effect is to increase the present carrying charge by adding 0.5 to it. That makes the stock look more expensive, because of the possible write-off, so that lot sizes are smaller than they would otherwise be.

11.12 SPACE OCCUPIED

In an inventory of all bulky items, like insulation or empty cans, the carrying charge can be increased, as a management policy variable, in order to shrink the inventory to fit within the space available. In an inventory where

Exhibit 11.25

Sudden obsolescence [see *Production and Inventory Management* Vol. 12, No. 2 (1971), pp. 89–91]

(7) $Q = \sqrt{\dfrac{2AS}{v(r+p)}}$

where p is the reciprocal of the expected time until demand ceases (1/years)

Space occupied

(8) $Q = \sqrt{2AS/(rv + r'c)}$

where r' = management policy variable to control exchange of space for setup expense, \$/cubic feet/year
c = cubic feet per piece (storage)

---

some items can be stored densely and others are bulky, it is necessary to differentiate among items and reduce the lot size only for the bulky ones. A good case in point is automotive parts, which range from bin items like breaker points, sparkplugs, and piston rings, to very bulky items like exhaust systems and windshields.

In this case the denominator in the formula for a lot quantity in pieces is increased by an additional term $rv + r'c$, where r is the financial carrying charge and r' is a space carrying charge. The factor v is the unit cost of the item, representing the capital investment, and c is the size, in cubic feet per piece.

In the case like equation 8 in Exhibit 11.25, management now has to explore two management policy variables, much in the way Exhibit 11.14 does, to balance the capital and space investments against the annual cost of setting up new replenishment lots.

11.13 SUMMARY

Although each of the variations on the basic EOQ formula has been shown separately, most of these variations can be combined into one, rather cumbersome calculation in which various bits and pieces become ineffective with the following default values:

P the annualized rate of production (large)
a the minor changeover among members of a family (0)

k the number of cycles between making slow moving members of a family (0)

c the cubic feet per piece (0)

p the probability that stock will suddenly become obsolete this year (0)

In the materials management systems library the computations are in fact set up this way in the formal definition. Default values are initially posted to the item master record that make that aspect of the lot quantity decision rule inoperative. Furthermore, in order to allow the production planning operations to use either a lot quantity in pieces or a coverage interval in planning periods, the item record posts both values. Planning, for example, may be done in economical periods of coverage, but for management summary reports of the target for comparison with actual, the analysis can be done in terms of average numbers of pieces (see Chapter 13).

CHAPTER **12**

Inventory Control

Now that we have gone through the box of parts in the materials management Erector set and looked at lots of different ways of forecasting, setting safety stocks, and computing replenishment order quantities, we can start to build some simple control systems. This chapter is concerned mainly with various techniques of signaling the answers to two questions:

1. WHEN to order more stock.
2. HOW MUCH to order.

It is assumed that we have a record that keeps track of how much stock is on hand, how much is due on open replenishment orders, and how much we owe customers on back orders that are past due. The signal that it is now time to order more stock is based on the comparison of the available stock with some sort of an order point. The available stock is the sum of stock on hand and on order, less any unfilled back orders. The cases considered here are intended for filling customer demand immediately from stock on the shelf—that is, there are no forward scheduled orders to be filled at a specified date in the future. Furthermore, we can order more stock from the source of supply whenever we need it, rather like buying bread and eggs at the supermarket.

In Section IV several chapters are devoted to the materials requirements planning systems by which we can keep track of time-phased requirements, do some rescheduling of open orders within the freeze period as requirements change, and take advantage of long-term notional orders to give the source of supply advance warning of probable needs. Here we are concerned more with the basic inventory replenishment situation.

The first part of the chapter deals with the sequence of operations that take place, more or less on a first-level basis, to generate replenishment orders at the right time for the right amounts of stock. Then we consider two special cases, for "lumpy" demand and a "two-bin" system for Class C items. The latter part of the chapter deals with exceptional situations, such as identifying excess stock, the initial buy for new material, and terminal service at the end of the life of a product.

12.1 TYPES OF CONTROL SYSTEM

12.11 When to Order

There seem to be three basic ways in which systems can be designed to trigger replenishment orders at about the right time.

12.111 Order Point, or Minimum Levels. After posting each demand transaction, check the resulting available stock against an order point quantity. If the available stock is at or below order point it is time to order more of that item. Note that a receipt transaction cannot reduce the available stock, so it is not necessary to check for ordering at that time.

12.112 Fixed Intervals. The supply boat on Lake Maracaibo in Venezuela visits the drilling rigs on a regular schedule. In that case the whole inventory of supplies is reviewed and everything for which there is not enough in stock to wait until the next visit of the supply boat is ordered. This situation is very common for joint orders of merchandise from a vendor who will only allow 26 stock orders a year. If the parts department has to order material from a manufacturing plant that schedules its production only once a month, then all parts orders can be grouped and submitted just prior to the next planning cycle.

12.113 Joint Orders. Orders for a family of related items can be triggered when the total stock status of the group reaches a point where it is not advisable to wait any longer. There are two variants on this. In IBM's Wholesale IMPACT package, the stock status for a vendor's list of products is reviewed each day to accumulate the total expected amount likely to be short at the end of a lead time if an order is triggered today. When the total value reaches some threshold, the order is triggered for the whole product line. Thus an order can be triggered by low stock on a single important item or on a whole raft of minor items.

The other variation has been suggested by Ed Silver, as a "can-order" point. If any member of a family of items reaches the order point, all other items are reviewed and those that have available stock below the can-order point are included on the order. Since this procedure may trigger replenishment of some items earlier than they themselves are needed, the average stock will be somewhat higher, and hence the order points themselves would

TYPES OF CONTROL SYSTEM 243

be lower than for independent ordering. See also Chapter 17 on fair shares allocation and priority lists for making up loads to go to each satellite warehouse.

12.12 How Much to Order

When an order is triggered, there are likewise three basic ways in which the quantity for each can be determined.

12.121 Fixed Order Quantity. The quantity is computed by the appropriate decision rule at reasonable intervals and stored in the item master file. When the need for an order is triggered, the quantity is the standard order quantity in the file. This is particularly true when there are quantity discounts or vendor minimums, or when the product is made in a process that tends to fix the quantity. For example, many pharmaceutical products and paint are made in such a way that one wants to use all the capacity of the equipment, but not make more than the equipment will hold. There are both financial and quality reasons for making these sorts of products in fixed lots. The sizes of the equipment can be chosen at reasonable intervals to conform more or less to overall economic lot theory, but the actual quantities are forced to be equal to the tank size.

12.122 Maximum Operating Level. If there is no restriction on the order quantity, then it is generally preferable to order a quantity that is equal to the difference between a predetermined maximum level and the current operating stock. Note that if the demand transactions are posted one unit at a time, the available stock will exactly equal the order point or minimum level at some stage, so that there is no practical difference between ordering a fixed order quantity and ordering the difference between the available stock and a fixed maximum. Especially when we discuss lumpy demand, however, there may be single demand transactions that take the available stock from just above the order point to considerably below it. In these cases better service from a given inventory investment is obtained in the long run by ordering up to a maximum, which restores the deficit by which available stock is below order point.

12.123 Allocation. If there is a truckload capacity, or a discount on a total order, for a list of related items ordered from the same source, then one may want to order each item on the list in a quantity that is a fair share of the total quantity to be ordered. We defer discussion of this case to Chapter 17.

Note that in any case, it is prudent to round the order quantities to reasonable increments, like full pallet quantities, pallet layers, or cases. Rounding should be done as the last step before posting the new replenishment order.

The replenishment order is then added to the balance on order when the administrative action is taken to issue the order to the source, so that the next review will see that it is in the stock due in and will not reorder for the same need. When the stock is received, the actual quantity received is added to stock on hand, but the original quantity ordered is subtracted from stock on order if the order is closed short or more material is delivered than was ordered.

12.13 The Order Point

The order point or minimum is established in the second-level system of decision rules and revised, the new forecast and standard deviation of forecast errors can be used to revise the order point. The order point is the sum of the forecast of demand during the lead time and the safety stock. The safety stock is the product of the safety factor and the standard deviation of errors in forecasting the demand over the lead time. The forecast and the standard deviation come from the second-level forecasting system, and the safety factor comes from a second-level decision rule. The resulting order point is stored in the item master record in the data base and is available to the first-level system to use in reviewing stock status after each transaction is posted. Note that if the stock status is posted at regular (long) intervals, the effective lead time must include the time between postings. The same effect is true if the inventory can be reviewed for ordering only at intervals—the length of the review period between opportunities to order must be included as part of the overall lead time.

12.14 Order Quantity

The order quantities would also be computed as a second-level decision rule, probably at the same time the order points are recomputed, unless of course the order quantities are fixed by external considerations. In an order-point, order-quantity system, both the order point and the order quantity would be recorded in the item's record. In a max–min, or (s,S), system the minimum (order point) and maximum (order point plus order quantity) would be recorded.

Note that any system of forecasting can be combined with any decision rule for safety factors and with any decision rule for lot quantities, to produce a sufficient variety of second-level decisions, which can be used in several combinations of first-level control. Somewhere in all that variety there should certainly be a combination to meet any real operating situation that replenishes stock in a basic inventory control system.

12.2 BASE STOCK SYSTEM

Since earlier echelons in the supply chain typically get their information about requirements from the orders placed by later echelons, it would make the entire system most stable if these orders always represented true consumption. George Kimball years ago proposed a "base stock" system of replenishment, which operates with a maximum stocking objective level for each item at each echelon. The value of that level would be set as maximum reasonable demand over the replenishment lead time, normally one piece larger than a conventional order point. Whenever demand reduces the available stock below that level, enough should be ordered to restore the level. Thus each order will be precisely for the quantity used.

The level itself is changed from time to time, as the forecast, the standard deviation, the lead time, or the desired service change. In that case, a "stock order" is placed with the source to increase or decrease the stock level. Normal "replenishment" orders represent demand; stock orders (which may be for positive or negative quantities) adjust stock levels. Thus the source can distinguish true demand from adjustments in stock level.

This concept can be especially important for customers who are outside the corporate materials management system, but who are themselves intermediate distributors.

12.3 LUMPY DEMAND

Especially in inventories of service parts to support mechanical and electronic equipment, perhaps as many as two-thirds of the items in the inventory have "lumpy" demand. These items require some special extensions to the basic notions of inventory control.

What is a "lumpy" item? Fast-moving popular items tend to have demand where there is a recognizable pattern with trends and possibly seasonal variation. It is true that there is some random variation, but not so much as to obscure the basic pattern. The demand for a "lumpy" item has so much noise, or random variation, that no such pattern can be discerned. Slow-moving items are not necessarily lumpy, nor are all lumpy items necessarily slow moving.

I prefer to define a lumpy item as the result of the following procedure. Try to fit a forecast model by the standard procedures (Chapter 5).

Measure the standard deviation of the residual differences between the historical data and the best model you can find. If that standard deviation is greater than the level in the forecast model, classify the item as "lumpy." When the item is so classified, set the forecast model as a simple average of the history, with only one term, and measure the initial mean square error from the history (if there is enough of it) or from the variance law for short histories. The process of forecast revision each period can modify the level by simple exponential smoothing and revise the observed mean square error. Since any one period's demand does not yield much information, the forecast model should not react to current demand very fast. Either normal smoothing could be used or the model could be locked so that it doesn't react to current demand but just rolls the forecast forward each period. In the latter case the model should be unlocked and refitted to recent history perhaps once a year.

12.31 Replenishment Procedure

The replenishment control for lumpy items should definitely be a max–min system. When available stock fails to the order point, order a quantity sufficient to bring available stock up to the maximum. Round that quantity to a reasonable multiple of the package quantity before releasing the order.

Exhibit 12.1 is a diagram of the way stock on hand might look during a replenishment cycle. Stock on hand was above the minimum, and then a single large transaction brought the demand below the minimum, triggering a replenishment order. After a lead time has elapsed, the material comes in from the source.

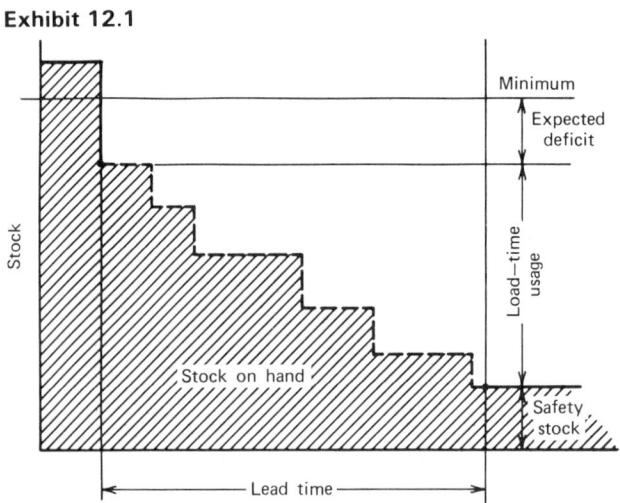

Exhibit 12.1

LUMPY DEMAND

Exhibit 12.2

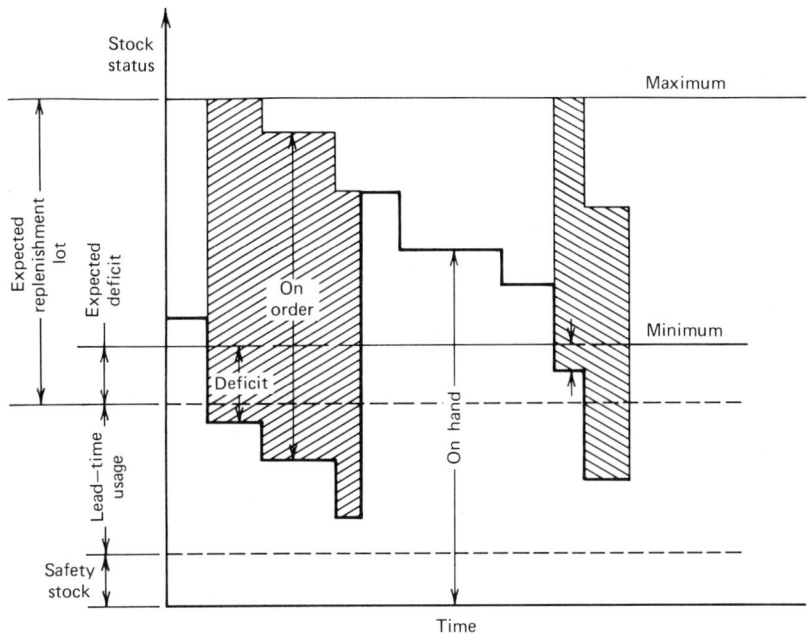

In normal cases, the order point is the sum of the expected demand during a lead time and the safety stock. In the case of lumpy items it is necessary to add a third term to the expression for the order point, to allow for the expected deficit, the average amount by which available stock is below order point at the times when replenishment orders are triggered.

Exhibit 12.2 shows the stock on order, which starts as a quantity large enough to bring available stock up to the maximum. Since we expect the stock status at the time for a new order to be below the minimum by the expected deficit, the maximum is equal to the minimum plus the standard order quantity minus the expected deficit.

12.32 Revising Max and Min Levels

The process of revising the statistics for computing the minimum and the maximum is as follows. We want to measure the average lead time usage and the standard deviation of lead time usage. As was noted in 8.221, the lead time starts when we trigger a replenishment order, and ends when the resulting material is received. By keeping track of the demand year-to-date we can measure the demand during a lead time directly. At the time of each receipt transaction, we revise two statistics for the demand during a lead time X as shown in equations 1 and 2 in Exhibit 12.3. Note that exponential smoothing is used simply as a way of conveniently keeping track of these two statistics without a long history.

We also need the mean and variance of the sizes of demand transactions, so that after each disbursement, we use equations 3 and 4 to modify the mean and mean square value of the number of pieces D on that transaction.

The computations are pointless except at long intervals. There is no information about demand in the results for a normal forecast period—we can expect several periods with zero, or occasional periods with very high demand. The fact that either occurred is not surprising, and affords no new information. Perhaps once a year, or after at least 30 demand transactions if that occurs earlier, is an appropriate interval for revising the second-level planning factors. When it is time to apply the decision rules to recompute the minimum and maximum levels, we can use these statistics as follows.

The standard replenishment lot quantity can be computed by any of the appropriate formulas from Chapter 11, but be sure to round it upward to be at least as large as the standard deviation. As an alternative you might like to use equations 5 and 6 in Exhibit 12.4 as the exact iterative approach for computing the joint optimum lot size and safety factor. First assume that the lot quantity is a standard EOQ, rounded to be as large as the standard deviation. Use that lot size to compute N, the number of replenishment orders a year. Substitute that value into equation 5 to compute the required safety factor. Now use that value in equation 6 to recompute the lot size.

Note that the total effective setup cost includes not only the cost incurred when the replenishment lot is triggered, but also an effective "cost" associated with the expected amount short at the end of the replenishment cycle. (It might be advisable to test these more elaborate computations

Exhibit 12.3

At each receipt, revise statistics of lead-time demand

(1) Average $\quad AL = \beta AL + (1 - \beta)X$
where X is the actual demand during the lead time just ended, and β is smoothing constant, approximately 0.9
(2) Mean square $\quad MSL = \beta MSL + (1 - \beta)X^2$

At each disbursement, revise statistics of transactions

(3) Average $\quad AD = \beta AD + (1 - \beta)D$
where D is the quantity on the demand transaction
(4) Mean square $\quad MSD = \beta MSF + (1 - \beta)D^2$

LUMPY DEMAND

Exhibit 12.4

Safety factor

(5) Probability $F(k) = P_1/N$

where P_1 is a management policy variable (shortages per item per year)

N is number of replenishment cycles per year $N = S/Q$

Lot size

(6) $Q = \sqrt{2[A + (r/P_1)v\sigma E(k)]S/rv}$

A = cost of processing replenishment order $(r/P_1)v\sigma E(k)$ is "cost" associated with expected amount short

---

against the simpler procedures recommended above, to see if the extra precision in the theory pays sufficiently in practice to warrant programming and maintaining the more complex methods.)

The standard deviation of lead time demand can be computed by equation 7 in Exhibit 12.5, so that the safety stock is given by equation 8. The expression for the expected deficit, first published by Ed Silver, is given by equation 9, so the order point or minimum is given by equation 10. The maximum stocking objective is then given by equation 11. These procedures may be justified in cases where there are fairly expensive items that have

Exhibit 12.5

Safety stock
(7) Standard deviation $\sigma = \sqrt{MSL - AL^2}$
(8) Safety stock $= k\sigma$

Expected deficit

(9) $ED = MSD/2AD$

Order point, or minimum

(10) $OP = AL + ED + k\sigma$

Maximum stocking objective

(11) $MAX = Q + AL + k\sigma$

lumpy demand. For the ordinary Class C items that are lumpy, simple order quantities rounded to a standard deviation, with ordinary decision rules for safety stocks, will be quite adequate.

12.33 Not All History with Spikes is Lumpy

Some items that may at first appear to have a lumpy history need not be treated this way. If, for example, the lumps occur because of occasional extraordinary requirements from customers, it may be possible to negotiate terms for advance notice, so that their requirements can be included as scheduled demand, rather than having to be forecast. In the U.S. Navy, for example, there was a classic O ring used in the boiler tubes on a particular class of carrier. The demand history went something like 0 0 1 3 2 0 0 1 307 0 1 0 0 4 3 5 307 0 3 1 0 0 3 307.... That looks lumpy. But digging deeper, we discovered that the "demand" was in the single digits, and the occasional 307 pieces was for an overhaul that could be carried out only in a shipyard. Those overhauls were scheduled up to two years in advance. (See Chapter 14.)

The issues of various raw materials may appear very lumpy, but it is all dependent demand explored from the master schedules for the products on which they are used (Exhibit 14.1). In that case the normal time-phased net-requirements planning system will deal with the situation nicely with no special provisions required to deal with the lumpiness. There are, however, genuine lumpy demand patterns for many service parts for which there is no way of anticipating the requirements. The procedures outlined in this section have proved to be satisfactory for control of replenishment orders.

12.4 TWO-BIN CONTROL FOR CLASS C ITEMS

The Class C items in an inventory together represent about half of the line items (Chapter 9) but only 1 to 3% of the total value of usage. There are so many items that it is not wise to use very elaborate methods of inventory control—the expense of processing becomes rather large. At the same time the risk of using simpler controls is minimal: suppose 3% of the total inventory were 10% larger than it really needs to be. Surely management has better areas in which to concentrate efforts.

There may be special items for which good control is justified, even though the item is cheap and relatively slow moving. But those ought to be exceptions to the general Class C control system.

TWO-BIN CONTROL FOR CLASS C ITEMS

12.41 Issues

The basic form of the two-bin control system has two bins for each item (Exhibit 12.6). One is the working bin which is open for anyone to help himself as needed, without requisitions, unnecessary paper work, expense, or delay. The other is a reserve bin, which is usually physically sealed, as in a bag or a carton. Some of the stock will get lost, or stolen, or misappropriated, but is it worth $25 worth of control system to prevent $3 worth of stock getting lost? If a little better control is wanted, the two bins can be put in the stockroom, where there is limited access. But there still should be no paper work for each withdrawal.

12.42 Ordering

Sooner or later it is necessary to open the reserve bin. Inside there is a traveling requisition like Exhibit 12.7. Some discipline is required at this point to ensure that the traveling requisition is returned to the office as a signal to reorder the item. The fact that the reserve bin is open but the traveling requisition is not there should be trusted as a signal that more is being ordered.

Exhibit 12.7 shows that the reserve bin was opened on 2/26/74. The last replenishment lot was received on 10/4/73, about five months ago. Five months is posted in column 6. The stock on hand when that lot was received was 74 pieces, in the working and reserve bins combined. The reserve quantity was 40. Hence in the past five months 34 pieces were used. The average rate of usage is about seven pieces a month.

Exhibit 12.6

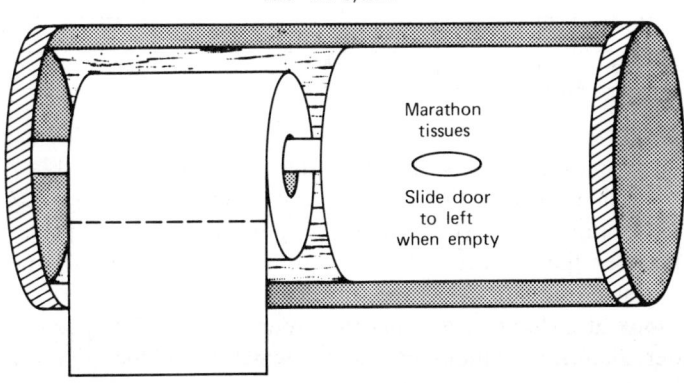

Two—bin system

Exhibit 12.7

Part No **137452** Description **PAD**							
Vendor **J. B. BIGLEY** **930 THIRD AVE** **NEW YORK NY 10020**				Unit Cost **25¢** Lead Time **2 MOS**			
--- Post at Receipt ----				--- Post When Ordering ------			
Date Rec'd	Prior On Hand	Reserve Stock	Initial On Hand	Date Ordr	Months Elapsed	Usage Rate	Order Quantity
(1)	(2)	(3)	(4)	(5)	(6)	(7)	(8)
	count	table	(2)+(8)		(5)−(1)	$\frac{(4)-(3)}{(6)}$	table
8-10-72	7	40	79	1-2-73	5	8	66
3-6-73	15	32	81	7-30-73	5	10	70
10-4-73	4	40	74	2-26-74			

The ordering clerk looks at a planning table like Exhibit 12.8. The lead time for getting more of this pad is two months. For a usage rate of seven pieces a month, the reserve stock level ought to be about 30 pieces, interpolating between the rows for five and eight pieces a month. The new reserve stock is posted to column 3 of the traveling requisition.

Now look at Exhibit 12.9 to get the order quantity. The pad costs 25¢, so the order quantity is about 66 pieces, which could be rounded to some figure like 60, and posted to column 8.

TWO-BIN CONTROL FOR CLASS C ITEMS

Now the traveling requisition looks like Exhibit 12.10. The clerk orders another 60 No. 137452 pads, and files the traveling requisition, waiting for the material to arrive in about two months.

12.43 Receipts

On 4/24/74 the material arrives. The order clerk retrieves the traveling requisition and sends it with the material to the storeroom.

At that time the storekeeper counts the stock on hand that is still left in the open reserve bin, and posts it to column 2 of the traveling requisition. The advantages of doing it this way are as follows:

1. Someone had to be at the bin anyhow to put the material away.
2. The traveling requisition was there so there is neither travel expense nor posting expense to do the cycle count.
3. It is well-known that people can count small quantities accurately, but rapidly lose accuracy when counting more than seven objects in a set. The quantity to be counted is as small as it ever will be.
4. The more active the item, the more frequently it will be counted, so that effort is allocated automatically in proportion to the value of the item.

Finally the storekeeper posts the date in column 1 and the total quantity now on hand in column 4, sets up the reserve quantity with the traveling requisition, seals the bin, and puts the balance into the working bin. Now we are back at the beginning of the cycle.

Exhibit 12.8

RESERVE STOCK LEVELS

LEAD TIME = USAGE	1	2	3	4	5	6
1	3	5	7	9	10	12
2	6	10	13	16	19	22
3	8	14	18	23	27	31
5	13	21	29	36	43	50
8	19	32	44	55	66	76
12	27	46	63	79	95	110
18	39	66	90	114	137	159
27	55	94	130	165	199	232
41	80	137	190	242	292	341
62	115	199	278	354	429	502
93	165	288	403	516	626	734
140	238	418	589	755	918	1079

Exhibit 12.9

REPLENISHMENT ORDER QUANTITIES

UNIT COST =	0.01	0.02	0.03	0.04	0.06	0.10
USAGE						
1	120	92	73	58	46	37
2	170	130	110	82	66	52
3	200	160	130	110	80	64
5	260	210	170	130	110	82
8	330	260	210	170	140	110
12	400	320	260	210	160	130
18	490	390	310	250	200	160
27	600	480	380	310	240	190
41	740	590	470	380	300	240
62	910	730	580	460	370	290
93	1200	890	710	560	450	360
140	1400	1100	870	690	550	440

DO YOU WANT TO USE ANOTHER RANGE OF UNIT COSTS? YES
RANGE OF UNIT COSTS = .1 1
ALIGN PAPER

REPLENISHMENT ORDER QUANTITIES

UNIT COST =	0.10	0.16	0.25	0.40	0.63	1.00
USAGE						
1	37	30	24	19	15	12
2	52	42	33	26	21	17
3	64	51	40	32	26	20
5	82	65	52	41	33	26
8	110	83	66	52	42	33
12	130	110	80	64	51	40
18	160	130	98	78	62	
27	190	160	120	96		
41	240	190	150			
62	290	230	190			
93	360	280				
140	440					

Note that Exhibit 12.9 cuts off for larger usage rates and higher unit costs, because now the lot sizes are beginning to represent time supplies that are less than a lead time. This scheme works only for items that never have more than one replenishment order outstanding at a time.

The materials management system library provides routines for setting up the planning factor tables for any range of values of usage, lead time, variance laws, and economic factors in the lot size decisions. Once a set of tables has been generated, that is the end of the data processing expense for controlling these Class C items.

EXCESS STOCK

12.5 EXCESS STOCK

Periodically the inventory record should be reviewed to find the items that have too much stock on hand or on order. If there is too much stock on order for any reason, cancel the orders. If you can't cancel them, defer delivery. If you can't defer delivery cut the quantity. In any event, cancellation charges now are preferable (from the corporate viewpoint) to having to write off surplus stock later. Of course, to minor managers with tight departmental budgets, it might appear better from a parochial view to let

Exhibit 12.10

Part No. **137452** Description **PAD**
Vendor **J. B. BIGLEY**
930 THIRD AVE.
NEW YORK NY 10020
Unit Cost **25¢**
Lead Time **2 MOS**

Post at Receipt				Post When Ordering			
Date Rec'd	Prior On Hand	Reserve Stock	Initial On Hand	Date Ordr	Months Elapsed	Usage Rate	Order Quantity
(1)	(2)	(3)	(4)	(5)	(6)	(7)	(8)
	count	table	(2)+(8)		(5)−(1)	$\frac{(4)-(3)}{(6)}$	table
8-10-72	7	40	79	1-2-73	5	8	66
3-6-73	15	32	81	7-30-73	5	10	70
10-4-73	4	40	74	2-26-74	5	7	60
		30					

the material come in—someone else will have the job later when it is necessary to write off the excess.

The only real inventory control is control over the input. Inventory cannot be controlled any more than the water in a bathtub. You can control the tap that affects the rate at which water comes into the tub, and the plug that controls the outflow. But the level of water is the net balance between the rates of inflow and outflow, and all you can control are those rates, not the level itself.

Why the stock is excess, I view as irrelevant. What has been done has been done, and management controls the future. Nor can I make any useful suggestions about how to get rid of excess stock on hand—that is bound up in questions of salvage and rework, with tax considerations. Aside from starting a rumour that the product is in short supply, one has to figure out how to get rid of the material in the best way for himself. But we can set up formal procedures for reviewing the file to find the excesses.

1. Stock on Hand. Prior to the receipt of new material, we expect to have the safety stock on hand. The safety stock level is set high enough so that reasonable variations in demand during the lead time will result in zero stock actually on hand when demand is high. By the same token it ought to be equally reasonable for a new lot to arrive when the stock on hand is twice the safety stock. Hence the maximum reasonable stock on hand at any time would be a whole lot, plus twice the safety stock, or effectively twice the planned average stock for that item.
2. Available Stock. The available stock is the stock on hand plus stock on order. If we were to look at the record for an item just after it triggered a new replenishment order, the total available stock could be the sum of the order point and the order quantity, or the maximum operating level if that is the sort of control system used.

Any stock on hand larger than the order quantity plus twice the safety stock is potential excess. Any available stock larger than the order point plus an order quantity is also potential excess. But there is no point in being concerned about small excesses for trivial amounts. Set two limits, such as six months and $5000. Only if the value of the excess stock is more than $5000 and if the excess will last at present forecast rates more than six months should the item be reported. I prefer to list the excess items in descending sequence by the value of excess, so that the most significant ones are at the top of the list, to be looked at first. Show the excess amount both in dollars and in months of supply, as an indication of how serious the problem is.

Exhibit 12.11 shows a sample of such a report. The first six items are

Exhibit 12.11

PART NO	FILE INDEX	ON HAND PIECES	ON ORDER PIECES	EXCESS DOLLARS	EXCESS ON HAND MONTHS	EXCESS AVAILABLE DOLLARS	MONTHS
39-758-253	668	3,719		205,306	240		
49-797-748	694	2,553		200,581	3385		
36-181-015	667	3,505		119,697	44		
35-789-193	685	2,416		96,926	275		
34-752-354	666	2,193		82,346	2167		
44-796-500	693	3,202		75,198	71		
32-793-708	689	4,337	375	51,924	104	3,645	7
33-766-221	646	3,203	1,243	51,582	71	20,790	29
37-707-683	677	3,980	983	44,065	41	10,833	10
45-188-707	686	3,000	436	39,560	25	5,032	3
48-274-577	669	3,316	1,425	37,969	42	17,489	19
32-280-241	678	2,688	992	33,957	23	13,447	9
50-785-190	680	4,876	1,325	30,561	26	8,464	9
36-094-909	670	3,503	1,148	26,463	25	7,736	7
46-792-777	688	2,401	896	26,284	64	9,825	24
43-782-291	676	2,949	415	23,547	44	2,870	5
36-775-375	659	4,176	908	21,926	13	4,610	3
39-279-455	696	2,915	805	21,168	33	5,972	9
39-777-766	661	4,072	801	20,718	19	3,441	3
50-776-745	660	3,402	665	19,757	18	3,858	3
36-774-998	658	3,890	1,139	17,780	25	5,670	8
48-786-765	681	3,156	1,450	17,354	20	9,188	11
32-784-830	679	2,626	1,238	12,681	113	6,043	54
42-258-018	692	3,180	1,147	12,546	24	4,345	8
40-778-642	662	4,615	1,613	12,543	63	4,430	22
41-787-033	682	3,033	470	11,179	30	1,277	3

STORE INDEX NUMBERS IN FILE = DIRECTORY
COMPONENT = EXCESS
REPLACE IT? Y

ELAPSED TIME   3M 37.377S
CPU TIME   8.782S

quite significant. The first two items have more than $200,000 in excess, all of it on hand, and the excess will last several years at current rate. Here is an excellent chance for the marketing department to promote, but one should be careful not to reflect the resulting special demand in the history used for forecasting, which might order more of that stock.

12.6 INITIAL BUYS

When a new product is to be released to the market, it is usually necessary to place some stock on order to fill the pipeline and to cover initial consumption.

Figure 12.12 illustrates the essential concepts in determining how much to have on order initially. We show two forecasts, the minimum and maximum reasonable requirements (including pipeline fill) in cumulative units from the time of introduction to the planning horizon. The lines are shown curved but in many cases there isn't enough information to draw more than straight lines. At any rate, it is necessary to get a range of esti-

Exhibit 12.12

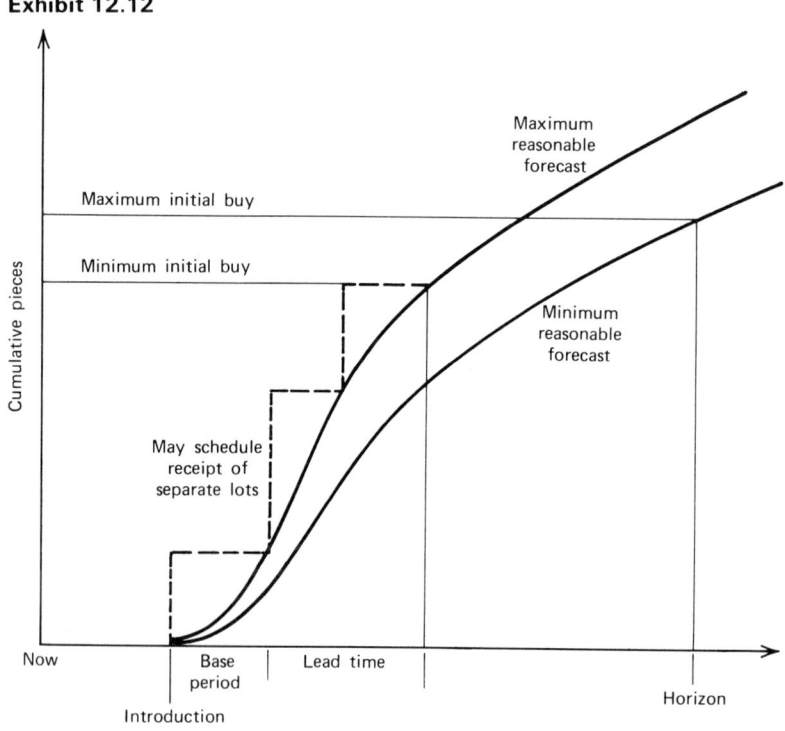

mates, if only by applying positive and negative safety factors to the standard deviation based on a variance law (10.5).

After the product is on the market there will be some base period (a week for consumer goods at retail, to three to six months for service parts for machinery) before the actual demand record will furnish any basis whatsoever for revising one's estimate of the real requirements.

Beyond that there is some lead time for getting more material from the source, or for modifying the sequence of notional orders already issued.

Hence the minimum initial buy is equal to the maximum reasonable demand forecast through the base period and the lead time. That coverage can, of course, be scheduled in several discrete lots to arrive at various times during the period, as shown by the dotted lines.

The maximum initial buy is the minimum forecast through the end of the planning horizon. More than that may lead to buying initially more than an all-time supply, like the six drive shafts for 2200-ton destroyers in the Navy's warehouse in Mechanicsburg, Pa. These monstrous chunks of metal were ordered during World War II. One was used, and the destroyers are now all out of commission. But the United States taxpayers own some hefty paperweights.

This diagram can also display potential conflicts. If the maximum amount that can safely be bought is less than the minimum amount to satisfy the forecast, the problem ought to be sent back to the product manager to review whether it is worth introducing the product at all.

12.7 TERMINAL SERVICE

At the end of the life of a product, the demand is declining and will sooner or later reach zero, or a small enough level that it can be discontinued. Before that period comes the time to place the last buy for a quantity that is intended to satisfy all remaining demand. For nonessential service parts and most consumer products it is possible to stipulate that if stocks are exhausted the item will be discontinued as of a certain date, and plan replenishment to satisfy the requirements through that date. (See 10.5 for a discussion of safety factors to balance out stocks at the end of the model year.)

For essential service parts there are usually both trade practices and government regulations that stipulate a period of time during which requirements must be filled. However, beyond that period the item need be kept in stock only if there is significant demand.

There are two models one could use to project the total remaining requirements. For items that are being forecast by models that include a

Exhibit 12.13

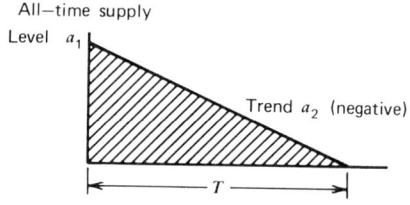
All-time supply

(12) Time to end of demand $T = a_1/-a_2$ months
(13) Total remaining usage $= -\frac{1}{2} a_1^2/a_2$

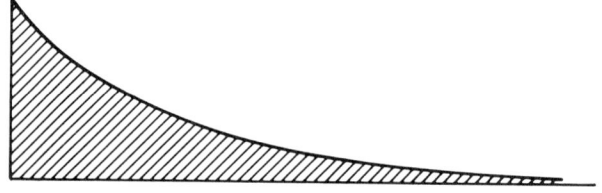

If annual demand in at least the last three years has been less than the year before, let $X_1, X_2, X_3, \ldots, X_n$ be the natural logarithms of annual demand starting with the year (1) through the current year (n). Fit a least-squares line

$$X = A - BT$$

Total remaining usage e^A/B

linear trend, when that trend is a negative value, the demand is projected to decline. By simple geometry one can estimate the time until demand reaches zero, and the total demand during that period of time, as shown by equations 12 and 13 in Exhibit 12.13. Note that in the general requirements planning system to be discussed in the next section, there is an automatic

Exhibit 12.14

LAMBDA = .3
CARRYING CHARGE = .1

IDENT	CURRENT LOT	EOQ LOT	EXPONENTIAL QUANTITY	LOTS NUMBER
3623	3875	6002.2	6103.9	13
3472	2326	3601.9	3728.7	7
3637	5763	8927.9	8208.7	5
3025	16682	25843.6	24582.5	3
3387	4396	6809.0	6024.1	2
3251	2348	3637.1	3410.0	1
3551	19734	30571.2	16926.7	1

way of accumulating all remaining demand, and for controlling excesses that might cover requirements beyond the end of the planning horizon.

Especially in service parts for machinery it is generally found that the population of equipment tends to decline at a constant percentage from year to year, thus diminishing the requirements for parts at an exponential rate.

If the total annual demand has been less in at least each of the three past years than in the preceding year, one can conclude that demand is declining. Go back to the peak year at which the decline started, and fit a least-squares line to the logarithms of the annual demands. (If demand was zero or negative in some years, assign those years zero weight and fit a weighted least-squares line, with weights 1 for years with positive demand.)

The total remaining demand can be estimated from the current level divided by the time constant, as shown in equation 13 in Exhibit 12.13. The level is the antilog of the intercept.

If stock on hand is larger than that amount, the excess can be scrapped when the accountants find it convenient for tax purposes. If available stock reaches an order point, one can order up to that level, but no more.

There is a dynamic programming model of the economic sequence of lots for the case when demand is projected to decline exponentially based on an argument like Exhibit 11.22. When the formulas are calculated for various cases, however, it appears that the following simple rule will work just as well. Order the normal order quantities, from any of the procedures discussed so far, but always check (when the trend in the forecast is negative) against the total remaining demand. Do not order more than will satisfy the remaining demand. There seems to be no significant advantage to worrying about the theoretically economical sequence of lots prior to the last one—they tend to be of much the same size as the standard lots, as shown in Exhibit 12.14.

The two parameters requested are the time constant (from the slope of the least-squares line fit to annual demand history) and the carrying charge. Note that when the formula says there are more than one more lot to cover the rest of the demand, the lot size is about the same size as an ordinary EOQ computed for the same carrying charge.

Summary: Why Have Decision Rules?

In this section we have been concerned with (*a*) inventory stratification to set up classes for different strategic and tactical controls, (*b*) safety stocks to protect customer service, (*c*) lot sizes that balance costs to acquire against costs to hold, and (*d*) inventory control procedures that use the results of these decision rules to trigger orders at the right times and in the right amounts to replenish stocks. Why is all this formality necessary?

In the manufacture of Scotch whisky the technology hasn't changed for hundreds of years, the sales forecast is equal to plant capacity and is backed up with scheduled orders for the next 10 years, and one can always drink his mistakes. In such a stable environment there is no need for formal controls. The experience and judgment of people, built up over very long periods of time, are more than ample to control the process.

Just so in some other industries that have a stable product line, stable technology, and a stable market. The informal controls that evolve with experience are probably sufficient.

The need for formal decision rules comes with change. If the environment changes in demand rates, lead times, or costs, it may take people a considerable time to learn how best to react to that change. If the factors are properly taken into account in the decision rules, the response is automatic. Furthermore, management can experiment on a "what if?" basis to get a good intuitive feeling for what to expect the system to do when the environment changes.

Management may have changing needs for controlling the flow of material, too, if *Fortune* and the *Wall Street Journal* are to be believed. With a good second-level system of decision rules and a third-level simulation capability, management can see the trade offs, inventory class by inventory class, among various types of expense, service, and capital investment. When the ultimate effect of the system on the balance sheet and the P&L statement can be seen, and believed, in advance under a number of different operating systems, then management really can have control over

SUMMARY: WHY HAVE DECISION RULES?

the system. They can appreciate the consequences in investiment for a change in service policy, and furthermore know about how long it will take for the results to show up on operating reports.

The effective use of these third-level management controls will take time to learn. It takes time to learn to drive a car, and a lot of time to learn to drive it well. Part of learning to drive well is practice in unusual situations, like taking the car into an empty parking lot on a snowy day to experiment with how the car goes into, and comes out of, skids. By deliberate practice under such situations, when a real emergency arises one's instincts are properly tuned to make the right reaction. Without the practice, the reaction of the driver of a car, or the driver of a materials management system, is quite likely to overcompensate and to go into an uncontrollable series of oscillations. In heavy traffic, or with heavy competition, the results can be serious.

Thus the real virtue in a formal system with good decision rules is to respond to change, generated either by management or by the external environment. It requires practice and training to be able to use such a system effectively, but there are an increasing number of senior executives who have taken the trouble to learn and can use the system to get the results they want quickly and effectively.

SECTION **IV**

Production Planning

The simple inventory control procedures described in Chapter 12 work well for wholesale operations and for the procurement of various types of common, cheap hardware used in manufacturing. However, they lose sight of some important facts about the planned material flow. The stock on order is maintained simply as a total balance quantity. It should be enough to cover the order point or minimum target, or additional orders are placed. When a replenishment order is triggered, it is assumed to be due at the end of a lead time. In an order-point system there is no practical way to keep track whether the stock due to come in on each open order will arive in time to cover the requirements. The order may have been good when it was placed, but requirements can change.

The other kind of information that is potentially available but that is not used in simple order-point inventory control procedures is the present outlook for future orders to be placed beyond the lead time. Vendors who supply a significant portion of their capacity to a given customer could well use that information to see what sort of requirements are likely to occur in the future, for planning labor, machine capacity, and perhaps even some raw materials. With the longer period of visibility, it is possible to get some of the long lead time procurement cycles started in advance of a firm order, which reduces the effective lead time to the customer. Lacking the forward visibility, the supplier has to forecast from his history of orders received, and if the customer uses any sort of lot sizes for replenishment, that demand can appear very lumpy and difficult to forecast.

In this section we deal with methods of time-phased, net-requirements planning which overcome both these difficulties. There are opportunities to move orders ahead in the schedule when requirements increase, and to move them back, or even cancel them, when requirements drop. In particular the notional orders extending to a planning horizon provide a basis for planning what will be required in the future. This is especially important in exploding the dependent demand to subordinate items, but once the mechanisms are in place, the same schedule of notional orders can be used to provide intelligence to outside suppliers for their planning processes.

As an alternative to current expositions on material requirements planning (MRP) systems, the orders to cover requirements are dealt with first in Chapter 13. Then Chapter 14 discusses the explosion of the schedule to generate dependent demand at lower levels. In practice the two steps occur in sequence at each level. The discussion of concepts may be made clearer by separating them.

Exhibit IV.1 is a generalized block diagram of the concepts to be explored in this section. Section II dealt with the requirements system that produces the forecasts of direct demand, as a statistical forecast, marketing intelligence, and scheduled backlog of customer demand. The direct demand is one of four inputs to the master scheduling process to be covered in Chapter 13.

Another input is the safety stock targets and planned replenishment lot quantities, developed from the strategic system considered in Chapters 10 and 11.

The stock status is recorded in the common data base to show stock on hand currently, and firm open replenishment orders. In Section V we

Exhibit IV.1

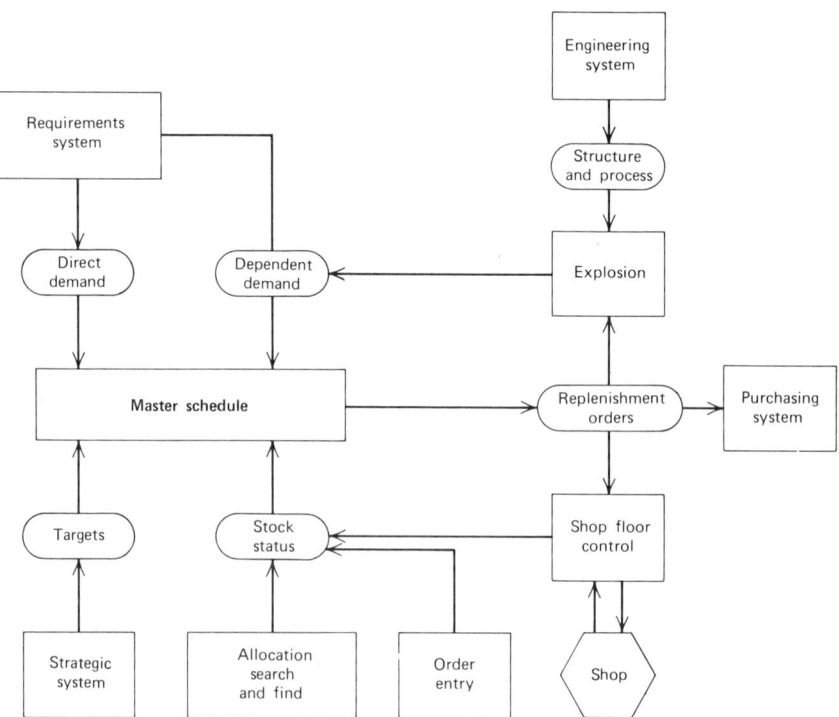

PRODUCTION PLANNING

consider how the allocation system affects the status of finished goods. The environment includes some sort of order entry procedures (not part of the materials management systems library formal definition) that will also affect stock status.

The principal output from the master schedule is a set of replenishment orders. These orders go to purchasing or the shop floor control system (Chapter 15) to generate new material coming into stock, and that affects the stock status.

The replenishment orders are exploded (see Chapter 14) to generate the dependent demand on subordinate items. That is another part of the requirement to be considered in the master schedule for those items. The dependent demand is also posted to the requirements system forecast array to be available to the strategic system as part of the annual demand on which lot sizes and safety stocks are computed.

The process of exploding the master schedule for assemblies (or recipes) into the time-phased net requirements for subordinate items requires both a product structure and a process routing, which are presumed to come from an engineering system. The design of the engineering system that produces these descriptions of how to make the products is outside the scope of the materials management systems library, but the common data base does record what the structures and routings are, with provision for reporting and editing those records to keep up with changes.

The ultimate objective of all this planning is to get detailed instructions to all parts of the manufacturing and purchasing process about what is needed, how much, and when, on a current basis. The plans can be kept current by getting back reports of actual status from the people doing the work so that the revised schedules are credible and relevant. Procedures for accomplishing these objectives are considered in Chapter 15.

Though it may appear convenient to plan to produce something last month to meet a requirement, the unpleasant truth should be faced. The data in the system should reflect reality, if one is to get good schedules that help the plant.

CHAPTER **13**

Master Schedule

The production planning process starts with the end products that one sells to customers, to determine, in view of the current requirements and stock status, how much of each one to produce and when. The programmed decisions and routine data processing make it possible for the computer to give enormous aid to the production planner in rapidly showing him the consequences of any plan that he wants to consider. The production planning process, however, is primarily the responsibility of a person who knows his products, the processes to make them, the production facilities, and the objectives of meeting the requirements of time, budget, and standard quality. Too often a production planner is so bogged down with detailed calculations that he has no hope of seeing the bigger picture. The proper role of the computer is to do those calculations faster, cheaper, and more completely than a person can. The proper role of the person is to see the alternatives to be examined, to take risks, and to apply his skill, judgment, and experience to get a realistic production plan that helps the plant manufacture the right things in the right quantities at the right time.

The primary ingredients of the procedures available in the materials management systems library to aid the planner can be covered under the following topic headings:

1. The time-phased planning array.
2. Due dates.
3. Notional orders to cover requirements.
4. Firm replenishment orders.
5. Budgets for input, output and investment.

13.1 TIME-PHASED PLANNING ARRAY

The planning process can be carried out with information recorded in four columns of an array, with a row for each time period.

Exhibit 13.1 shows portions of such an array for three different products. At this stage only the first column of the array has been filled in, for the direct requirements. The direct requirements represent the current forecast of demand. The elements of that forecast come from essentially three sources: a statistical forecast, marketing intelligence to override that

Exhibit 13.1

```
0203378      GASKET                              FILE INDEX = 2    LEVEL CODE 0
MINIMUM STOCK TARGET = 21.   AS OF  2/28/76 STOCK ON HAND = 85
SCHEDULING RULE: NET REQUIREMENTS BY PERIOD
```

PERIOD ENDING	DIRECT REQUIREMENTS	DEPENDENT REQUIREMENTS	FIRM ORDERS	NOTIONAL ORDERS	PROJECTED AVAILABILITY
3/12/76	16				48
3/26/76	17				31
4/09/76	16				15
4/23/76	17				⁻2
5/07/76	17				⁻19
5/21/76	18				⁻37
6/04/76	18				⁻55
6/18/76	18				⁻73
7/02/76	19				⁻92

```
0203663      LOWER UNIT 50-60HP                  FILE INDEX = 3    LEVEL CODE 1
MINIMUM STOCK TARGET = 1095.  AS OF  2/28/76 STOCK ON HAND = 1350
SCHEDULING RULE: SMOOTHED PRODUCTION RATE
```

PERIOD ENDING	DIRECT REQUIREMENTS	DEPENDENT REQUIREMENTS	FIRM ORDERS	NOTIONAL ORDERS	PROJECTED AVAILABILITY
3/12/76	169				586
3/26/76	182				404
4/09/76	148				256
4/23/76	140				116
5/07/76	128				⁻12
5/21/76	117				⁻129
6/04/76	102				⁻231
6/18/76	80				⁻311
7/02/76	74				⁻385

```
0203909      HOSE                                FILE INDEX = 4    LEVEL CODE 0
MINIMUM STOCK TARGET = 502.  AS OF  2/28/76 STOCK ON HAND = 1300
SCHEDULING RULE: MINIMUM LOT QUANTITY
```

PERIOD ENDING	DIRECT REQUIREMENTS	DEPENDENT REQUIREMENTS	FIRM ORDERS	NOTIONAL ORDERS	PROJECTED AVAILABILITY
3/12/76	156				642
3/26/76	167				475
4/09/76	160				315
4/23/76	159				156
5/07/76	167				⁻11
5/21/76	172				⁻183
6/04/76	169				⁻352
6/18/76	163				⁻515
7/02/76	165				⁻680

TIME-PHASED PLANNING ARRAY

Exhibit 13.2

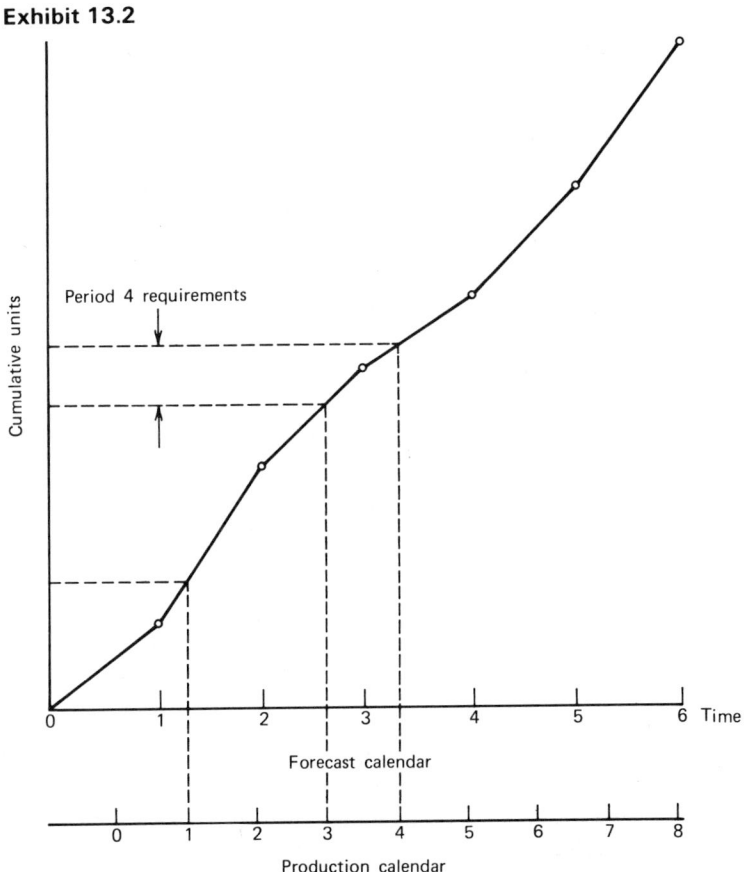

forecast, and scheduled backlog of orders. Each of these elements was covered in Section II, and the totals are recorded in forecast periods as in Exhibit 13.1.

13.11 Interpolation

For production planning we may want to consider intervals that are different from the intervals in which forecasts are recorded. For example, it is common to forecast by months, but to plan production in one- or two-week periods. Exhibit 13.2 illustrates how requirements expressed in one calendar can be interpolated to estimate requirements for any other calendar. The cumulative requirements for forecast periods 1 through 6 are shown, with time along the horizontal axis and cumulative units along the vertical axis.

Underneath the forecast calendar is another calendar, such as for planning periods. Note that the origins can be at different times, and the lengths of the periods can be different for the two calendars. The requirements in the first planning period will be the cumulative requirements, interpolated through that point in time. For the requirements in any other planning interval, say, period 4, the cumulative requirements through the beginning of that period are subtracted from the cumulative requirements through the end of that period.

By the choice of a forecast interval, the "fine structure" of the pattern of demand within the period is not considered to be relevant. We can use linear interpolation. If the fine structure is important, we use a shorter interval between forecast revisions.

Scheduled backlog, of course, is not interpolated from monthly totals. We can slot the backlog into planning periods by the actual date when the requirement is to be filled.

13.12 Planning Periods

The length of the planning period is a matter of compromise. The shorter the period, the more precise the production schedule can be set, but at the cost of extra data processing. Longer periods permit more economical planning computations, but at the loss of some precision. For most manufacturing plants there already exists a reasonable planning period, such as a week or a fortnight. In the St. Louis brewery of Anheuser Busch the volume of orders is so large that the natural scheduling period is a shift of production. Babcock and Wilcox's factory that produces enormous steam boilers for the public utilities might find that a month is a short enough increment of time.

At any rate, we can slot the direct requirements into the first column of the planning array by planning period. The minimum stock target for the product is usually the safety stock computed in Chapter 10. Actual stock on hand is posted periodically.

(For a complete system, including physical distribution, we must also take account of the reorder points for all stocking locations, as part of the total minimum stock target. See Chapter 17.)

The "master schedule" could be simply the list of frozen orders, or the whole set of requirements checked for feasibility of materials and labor. Or the term could refer to the process of generating the coverage. The term is used widely but loosely. In this book the term generally refers to the whole schedule at any time in the planning process together with the projected availability.

Any time that the master schedule is displayed for an item it also shows the projected availability, as a fifth column on the report. The availability

DUE DATES

for the 0203378 gasket starts with 85 on hand, which is 64 more than the planned target of 21 pieces. By the end of the first planning period ending 3/12/76, when we will have used 16 pieces, the availability will drop to 48 pieces. Note that this projected availability is always a net figure—the stock on hand will exceed this availability by the minimum stock target.

Since in this example there are no replenishment orders schedules yet, the projected availability eventually becomes negative.

For some consumer goods industries that rely heavily on promotions as a marketing strategy, the minimum stock target itself may vary with time. That is, the safety stock required during periods of normal sales may be one figure, but during a promotional period the safety stock can be much larger, because of the inherent uncertainty of promotional forecasts. In these cases, it is usually necessary to develop two variance laws (see Chapter 8), one for normal periods and one for promotions. The safety stock decison rules can be used to develop the safety factor for each type of sales period, which in turn generates the safety stock. If the planned safety stock does change by period, it is necessary to include in the direct requirements the net difference in the safety stock from period to period. When safety stocks are to increase, that is an additional net requirement. When safety stocks are to decrease, that is a reduction in direct requirements.

13.2 DUE DATES

In general there is some period during which open replenishment orders are to be considered frozen. This freeze period can be different for different items in the inventory. For many items it will be the same as the lead time normally stipulated for placing new orders, or the same as the manufacturing cycle time. There are instances, however, where the freeze period might be less than a lead time. When the freeze period is shorter than the replenishment lead time, the supplier needs to carry a safety stock to protect against unforeseen changes in requirements during his lead time. A common example is that of the supermarket, which may have a lead time of several days to get more stock from the wholesaler's warehouse, but the customer has an effective freeze period of zero—any requirements can be met, including impulse buys.

There are also instances in which the freeze period should be much longer than a manufacturing cycle. Fermentation processes in pharmaceutical manufacture have a very definite cycle that cannot be expedited or extended. In a company where fermentation capacity is tight, it is very important to schedule batches in a particular sequence that will get the maximum total throughput. To allow the planner to line up such a schedule and stick to it, the freeze period might be several times as long as the fermentation cycle. In that case, the user must carry a safety stock to protect his needs against unforeseen fluctuations in that long freeze period.

Orders may have to be frozen long before any work starts on an assembly, simply to protect the materials schedule for long-lead-time subordinates. For example, computers can be assembled and tested in a short period, but not if the solid-state devices haven't been produced.

Thus the length of the freeze period affects the stock that must be carried by the distribution system for longer periods and by manufacturing for shorter periods. In general, the earlier in the process that stocks are carried, the less value added and the more flexible the uses of the material. Hence safety stock ought to be carried at a stage from which it can be processed and delivered to the customer within an acceptable time. One of the implications of the freeze period is that all new orders to replenish stocks are scheduled to be due after the freeze. Another is that the quantities on frozen orders are not changed—this means that a previous "order" for zero pieces in some period cannot be changed routinely to generate a short-dated order. The planner can, of course, generate, cancel, and modify any orders at any time for any reason. But the system will not routinely modify frozen orders as requirements change.

The date when the next replenishment order is needed can be determined from the date when the projected availability becomes negative.

13.21 Need versus Schedule Date

Exhibit 13.3 shows five different cases to illustrate the way that need dates and schedule dates can be determined. In the first one the initial available stock (above safety stock) of 25 pieces will last part of the first planning period. By interpolation of dates at the beginning and end of that period, one can infer that the need date is 6/12/76. However, because the freeze period extends through 7/13/76, the schedule date for any new order in this case would be 7/13/76.

In the second example, there isn't enough on hand now even to cover the minimum safety stock, so the need date is before 6/01/76—and could be extrapolated to be required about two weeks before then. However, it is impossible to start an operation now to produce something last week, so the need date is shown as the date when stock was posted. Because of the freeze period, the schedule date is still 7/13/76.

In the third example there is already a firm open order due sometime in the second planning period, and that will cover requirements through the end of the freeze period. We might want to slide that open order forward to 6/12/76 to cover a temporary deficiency. The need and schedule dates are

Exhibit 13.3

THE NET REQUIREMENTS ARE:

	POSTED 6/01/76	1 6/15/76	2 6/29/76	3 7/13/76	4 7/27/76	5 8/24/76	6 10/05/76	7 11/30/76
REQTS	50	30	40	50	35	45	55	65
AVAIL	75							
STOCK	25	⁻5	⁻45	⁻95	⁻130	⁻175	⁻230	⁻295

NEXT ORDER NEEDED   6/12/76
SCHEDULED FOR   7/13/76

THE NET REQUIREMENTS ARE:

	POSTED 6/01/76	1 6/15/76	2 6/29/76	3 7/13/76	4 7/27/76	5 8/24/76	6 10/05/76	7 11/30/76
REQTS	75	30	40	50	35	45	55	65
AVAIL	50							
STOCK	⁻25	⁻55	⁻95	⁻145	⁻180	⁻225	⁻280	⁻345

ORDER NEEDED BEFORE   6/01/76
SCHEDULED FOR   7/13/76

THE NET REQUIREMENTS ARE:

	POSTED 6/01/76	1 6/15/76	2 6/29/76	3 7/13/76	4 7/27/76	5 8/24/76	6 10/05/76	7 11/30/76
REQTS	50	30	40	50	35	45	55	65
AVAIL	75		125					
STOCK	25	⁻5	80	30	⁻5	⁻50	⁻105	⁻170

NEXT ORDER NEEDED   7/25/76
SCHEDULED FOR   7/25/76

THE NET REQUIREMENTS ARE:

	POSTED 6/01/76	1 6/15/76	2 6/29/76	3 7/13/76	4 7/27/76	5 8/24/76	6 10/05/76	7 11/30/76
REQTS	50	30	40	50	35	45	55	65
AVAIL	75		150				100	
STOCK	25	⁻5	105	55	20	⁻25	20	⁻45

NEXT ORDER NEEDED   8/08/76
SCHEDULED FOR   8/08/76

THE NET REQUIREMENTS ARE:

	POSTED 6/01/76	1 6/15/76	2 6/29/76	3 7/13/76	4 7/27/76	5 8/24/76	6 10/05/76	7 11/30/76
REQTS	50	30	40	50	35	45	55	65
AVAIL	75	500						
STOCK	25	495	455	405	370	325	270	205

NO FURTHER ORDERS NEEDED.

both 7/25/76 since schedule dates can be set to anything beyond the end of the freeze period. Another replenishment order is required in the first planning period beyond the freeze, but it could arrive as late as 7/25 and still cover the projected requirements, leaving the planned safety stock.

The fourth example shows need and schedule dates at 8/08/76 even though there is an open order scheduled in the sixth planning period. That order, being outside the freeze period, should be moved ahead (and possibly changed in quantity) to cover the earlier requirements. Such changes are permitted beyond the freeze period. In practice the firm order would be moved into the period beyond the freeze, so that this case does not arise.

The last example shows a case where there is more than enough on order to cover planned requirements through the end of the planning horizon. Such an order should be checked against the planner's information about requirements beyond the planning horizon, as a guard against obsolescence. If demand continues, the 500 on order may be all right. But if the item is to be discontinued, or has declining demand, perhaps it should be cut back now to avoid buying or making excess stock.

As new schedules are computed, the date when a frozen order is due can be changed to the need date (but the quantity cannot be changed by the system). The planner can lock the schedule for any item, and then even the schedule dates won't be changed. The planner can still maintain control by manually adding, deleting, or changing order quantities and dates.

13.22 Manufacturing Calendar

To keep track of working days, the system provides for a manufacturing calendar, with an internal representation of dates in total number of days since December 31, 1900. Weekends, holidays, and vacation periods are eliminated from the list. Planned shutdowns of the manufacturing facility for vacation, physical inventory, or even contract negotiations can be taken into account in the schedule merely by eliminating those dates from the manufacturing calendar. As a result, the requirements get interpolated into working periods, so that stock can be built up in a proper way to anticipate periods when there won't be a normal supply.

All dates are represented in ordinary calendar form as MM/DD/YY on output. The user specifies dates as MMDDYY.

13.3 DUAL ACCOUNTING

Another aspect of the freeze period is illustrated by the following procedure for accounting for the stock on hand. The example is based on finished

DUAL ACCOUNTING

goods inventory where the user might be the distribution system and the supplier the factory. The same concepts would apply, however, for raw materials where the purchasing operations supply stock to be used by manufacturing. In one petroleum company something like 47 such interface inventories were defined between pairs of operating departments such as production and refining, refining and transportation, transportation and tank farms, and tank farms and retail distribution.

Normally inventories are accounted for in some single account that tends to obscure the real managerial decisions that create it. Let's call that account for sake of illustration account 4000, and arbitrarily split it into two subaccounts, 4001 as the supplier's inventory and 4002 as the user's inventory (Exhibit 13.4). The using department or organization has the responsibility for determining the net requirements, period by period, based on their forecast and stock status. The supplying organization has the freedom to schedule production in any efficient way, provided they cover these requirements in time.

Inventory accounts are the net results of a string of debit and credit transactions. Actual production is added to the 4001 account as it is completed, whether early or late, over or under quantity. Actual demand, whether filled or not, is subtracted from the 4002 account.

Exhibit 13.4

Account 4000 Finished Goods Inventory	
Account 4001 Supplier's Inventory	Account 4002 User's Inventory

Supplier: plans economical production	User: determines net requirements from forecast and stock status
Actual production added to 4001	Actual demand subtracted from 4002

Each planning period the net requirement as of a freeze period earlier transferred from 4001 to 4002.

Account 4000 is the sum of 4001 and 4002. User may ship any stock physically on hand, regardless of responsibility account.

The net requirements stated a freeze period earlier are transferred from account 4001 into account 4002 once each planning period. That is, in March the net requirements for August were stated as 500. In August, 500 are transferred from 4001 into 4002, even though the user would now like to have 750 for August. In August net requirements are frozen for transfer in January.

If the user can state net requirements that are consistent with actual demand, and if the supplier produces on schedule, then in both accounts the inputs each period match the outputs and the accounts stay in balance.

Supposing the supplier wants to schedule production in economic lots, or to build up stock in anticipation of a promotional peak. The actual production goes into account 4001 as it is completed, but the stock is relieved only as it was stated as required. As a result the working stock and the stabilization stock tend to stay visibly in the supplier's account 4001. There may be excellent justification for this investment in terms of production economics, but the investment should be accountable to the production side of the organization.

If the supplier second-guesses the forecast and falls behind schedule, then stock is withdrawn ineluctably from his account, but nothing is getting added, so the account could show a net back-order condition. If the supplier has yield loss or late delivery problems, he may have to carry a safety stock to ensure that he meets the user's requirements on time.

If the user consistently forecasts too high, then the stock delivered into his account will exceed the actual demand and the account will grow. The opposite effect will happen if he consistently forecasts too low.

The supplier and the user may be so used to working with each other that they compensate for schedule delays and bias in the forecast. If they are good at it, the total 4000 account will remain in balance. But when the gross account is split into its components by accountable organization, it is immediately visible to both parties that something is out of control. Each can take action to manage his own operations, without interference with the scope of freedom of the other.

Note that this accountability has nothing to do with the physical flow of material. Working stock and stabilization stock made in advance of current need may actually be distributed to the field to fill customer orders, even though it stays in the 4001 account. This is a management device, which will have no perceptible effect on the warehousemen and materials handlers.

Many variations can be made on this theme, such as charging the user for public warehousing necessary to store material that results from a biased forecast.

From time to time the user will want to expedite open orders, short-date his requirements, and get something not shown in the net requirements at

NOTIONAL ORDERS TO COVER REQUIREMENTS

least a freeze period in advance. The supplier will of course try to oblige and get the material in time. He may use the opportunity to ask for some other favor, such as moving other products back in the schedule to make capacity and materials available, or for the user to accept into his account the total working stock. People develop marvelous ways of horse-trading to their individual advantage. But the key element of this procedure is that the visibility of the accounting tends to make all the horse-trading also work to the advantage of the corporation.

13.4 NOTIONAL ORDERS TO COVER REQUIREMENTS

The orders to cover the net requirements beyond the freeze period are called "notional" orders to distinguish them from the "firm" orders that are due within the freeze period. Notional orders are computed on each planning cycle to cover all projected requirements to the planning horizon, far past the freeze period. There are six basic ways provided by which the system can generate these notional orders. The selection of the scheduling rule, as well as the length of the planning horizon, is controlled by data stored in the item master record, so they can be different for different types of items.

13.41 Net Requirements by Period

In this case the amount scheduled on the notional order in each planning period is equal to the net requirements in that period.

The mechanism can be illustrated simply by the diagram in Exhibit 13.5 and the table below it. The basic graph is the cumulative gross requirements by planning period. The time axis is plotted horizontally, in increments of planning periods. The vertical axis is the cumulative requirements, starting with the targeted safety stock, and adding the direct requirements, period by period. There is some amount of stock, already frozen, from stock on hand and on order due within the freeze.

Here we are concentrating on the notional orders beyond the freeze period. Details of the time-phased requirements within the freeze are in a sense invisible. We consider expediting and short-dating in 14.6.

In the diagram, current available stock lasts slightly into the planning period beyond the end of the freeze period, so the due date for the next order is indicated by the vertical dashed line. By then the stock available now will have been consumed by the requirements and the target stock.

In scheduling Rule 1, the amount scheduled for each planning period is simply the net requirements for that period: the gross requirements less

Exhibit 13.5

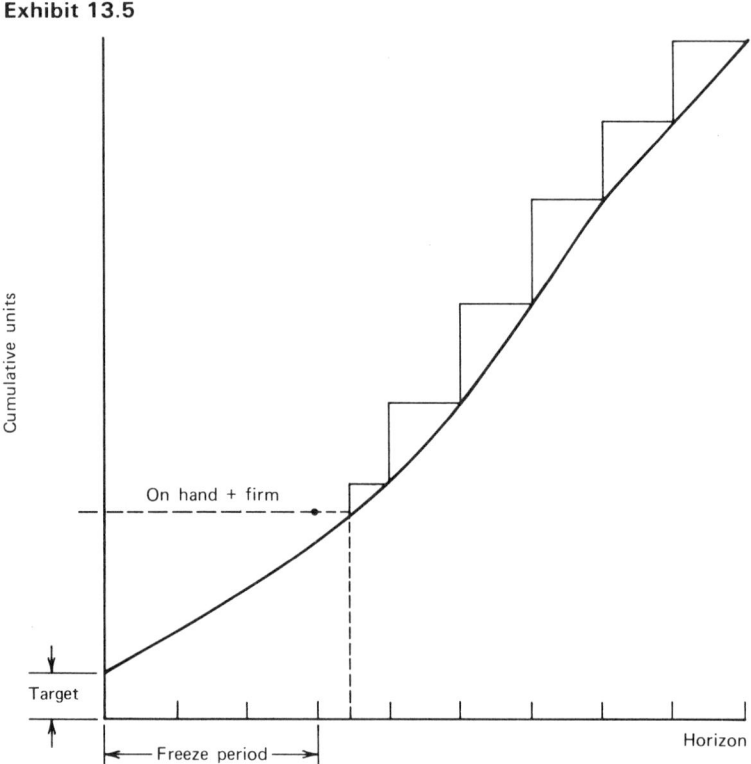

Use Rule 1.
Schedule using net requirements by period

	Posted	1	2	3	4	5	6	7
	6/01/76	6/15/76	6/29/76	7/13/76	7/27/76	8/10/76	8/24/76	9/07/76
Reqts		50	30	40	50	35	45	55	65
Avail		75		125					
Stock		25	⁻5	80	30				
Sched						5	45	55	65

whatever is already available. Note that when available stock lasts beyond the freeze period, the net requirements will be less than the gross requirements in some period, but thereafter net and gross requirements are the same period by period. If present available stock is not enough to cover the freeze period requirements, then the net requirements in the first period beyond will exceed the gross requirements by enough to make up the deficit.

NOTIONAL ORDERS TO COVER REQUIREMENTS

Thereafter, however, the net and gross requirements will be equal in every period.

Net requirements by period would be used, for example, to generate the net requirements at a subsidiary assembly operation which is one customer of a corporate machine shop or foundry. The central manufacturing plant can accumulate these net requirements by period from each of the other plants it supplies, and then work out the economical production lots. An overseas affiliate using semifinished materials from a parent plant would do well to transmit net requirements period by period. If the dual accounting system is used then each user would generate net requirements and let the supplier work out the most economical manufacturing schedule. Satellite warehouses may schedule their replenishment this way (16.3).

13.42 Smoothed Production

When there is significant variation in the rate of requirements, as for promotions or seasonal peaks, it may not be economical to plan to produce requirements in the period when they are needed. The supplier may want to anticipate the peak, produce above current requirements for several periods in advance, and build a stabilization stock. That makes for a more level use of manpower, and for a more even rate of utilization of the equipment. The need date will be much later than the schedule date while stock is being built up, but the schedule is locked to ensure that work is deliberately released early.

Exhibit 13.6 illustrates the way that the schedule is generated in this case. Visualize a line pivoted at point A. Swing that line until it is just tangent to the cumulative gross requirements at point B. The slope of that line is a production rate that could remain constant until time B and cover all the requirements and leave the planned safety stock. In the table below Exhibit 13.6 the necessary rate is computed as 21.25 units per week, or (because of rounding in the printout) about 43 units per two-week planning period. Note that the stabilization stock builds up in periods 4, 5, and 6, but is gone entirely by period 7.

The vertical distance at the left axis of Exhibit 13.6 is number of units in stock, and the schedule line (AB) represents cumulative additions to stock. The solid broken line represents cumulative deductions from stock. Therefore the vertical distance between the two lines at any point in time represents the projected availability. The shaded area is called "stabilization" stock, because it is inventory, properly accountable to the supplier, built up to stabilize the production rates.

This sort of schedule is frequently required in consumer products where

Exhibit 13.6

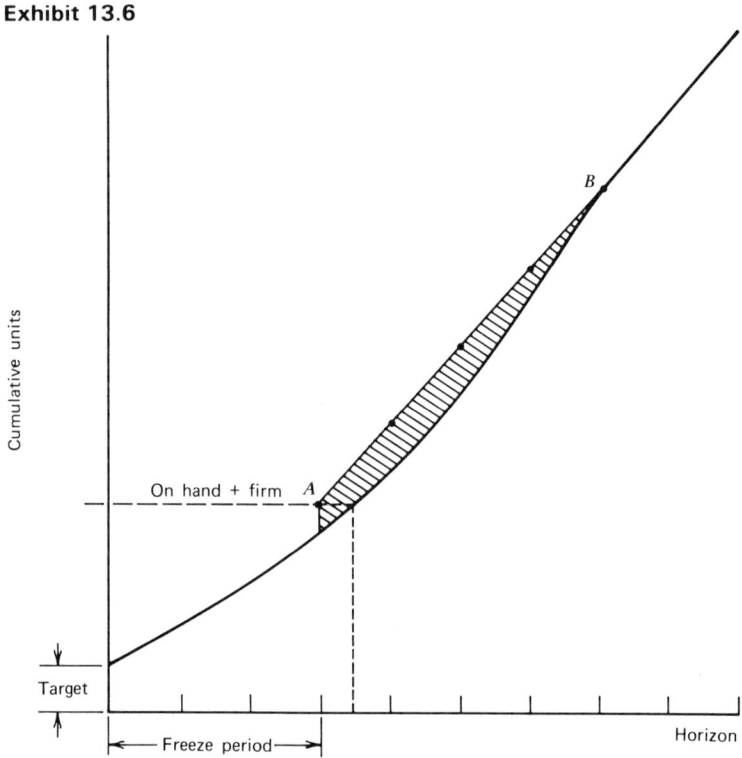

Use Rule 2.
Production rate is 21.25 per week.
Schedule using smoothed production rate:

	Posted 6/01/76	1 6/15/76	2 6/29/76	3 7/13/76	4 7/27/76	5 8/10/76	6 8/24/76	7 9/07/76
Reqts	50	30	40	50	35	45	55	65
Avail	75		125					
Stock	25	⁻5	80	30	38	35	23	
Sched					43	43	43	43

there are large seasonal peaks and promotions and where the manufacturing process runs continually, rather than producing discrete lot quantities. When there are capacity problems this procedure reduces the risk of requiring production greater than capacity.

If the actual production is different from plan, the rates will change to make up the difference, just as they will when stock targets or forecasts change.

NOTIONAL ORDERS TO COVER REQUIREMENTS

13.43 Minimum Lot Quantity

There are some manufacturing processes where the quantity scheduled for any period (if anything is needed) must exceed a certain minimum run quantity. Perhaps the most prevalent example is for purchased materials where the vendor has a minimum delivery quantity.

Exhibit 13.7 shows how the lots are scheduled. The first lot is due at the need date for the first order. That increases the available stock, which will last until time B, when the second lot for the same quantity is due. That in turn will last until C, and so on. In this scheduling rule, the quantity is either the minimum quantity or enough more to last until the end of the period in which it is due. For example, in the table below the figure, in period 6 the requirements are for 55 pieces, which exceeds the minimum lot of only 50 pieces. Hence 55 are scheduled. In the same way 65 are scheduled for period 7.

13.44 Fixed Time Supply

When we discussed lot sizes for time-varying demand in 11.10, the point was made that where there is flexibility in the production lot quantities, a good practical scheme is to compute the economical interval between lots but to schedule an amount sufficient to cover the actual requirements in that many periods.

For the example in Exhibit 13.8 let us assume that the economical production interval is three weeks. The first lot is due on 7/25/76 as before, and covers the remainder of that week and the next two weeks. The second lot is then scheduled as due at the beginning of that period, and the quantity is computed from the scheduled requirements during the following three weeks.

This is the recommended procedure for products where the economics of setups suggests that the product be made in lots, but where there are no physical constraints on the sizes of particular lots. They can vary from lot to lot, to cope with variations in the planned rate of demand.

13.45 Fixed Lot Quantity

There are some manufacturing processes where the lot quantity is really fixed. For example, in making paint, cereals, and many pharmaceuticals, the lot size is figured out roughly as an EOQ, but then the product is made in a tank with a fixed capacity. A tank that is within the roundoff tolerance is selected, and production is scheduled in tank-full quantities to use the equipment efficiently. In some cases the quality control programs require

Exhibit 13.7

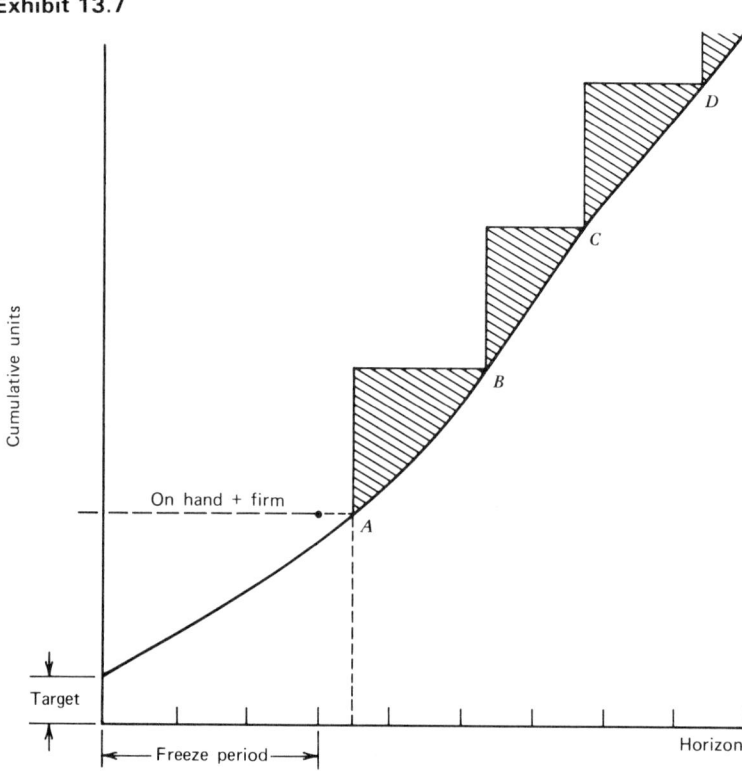

Use Rule 3.
Minimum lot quantity = 50.
Schedule using minimum lot quantity:

	Posted	1	2	3	4	5	6	7
	6/01/76	6/15/76	6/29/76	7/13/76	7/27/76	8/10/76	8/24/76	9/07/76
Reqts	50	30	40	50	35	45	55	65
Avail	75		125					
Stock	25	⁻5	80	30	45			
Sched					50		55	65

that the same quantity be made every time to ensure proper blending of all the ingredients.

In this case, a lot of the specified quantity is scheduled at the first need date. The time when the second lot will be required can then be computed from the cumulative gross requirements, and another lot is scheduled then.

NOTIONAL ORDERS TO COVER REQUIREMENTS

Exhibit 13.8

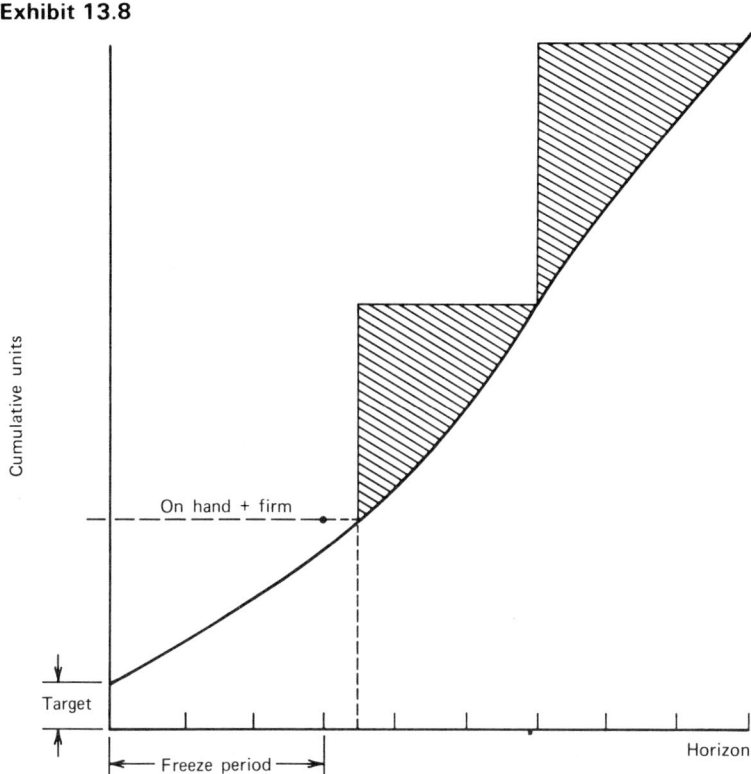

Use Rule 4.
Weeks of supply per lot = 3.
Schedule using time supply:

	Posted	1	2	3	4	5	6	7
	6/01/76	6/15/76	6/29/76	7/13/76	7/27/76	8/10/76	8/24/76	9/07/76
Reqts	50	30	40	50	35	45	55	65
Avail	75		125					
Stock	25	⁻5	80	30	65	20	57	
Sched					70		92	8

The process is repeated to the end of the planning horizon. The diagram would look much like Exhibit 13.7, except that instead of increasing lot quantities to fill out the remainder of a planning period, an extra lot is scheduled, which will probably carry over to fill part of the requirements in subsequent planning periods.

13.46 Maximum Stocking Objective

The sixth alternative rule in the library was developed for the following situation: the finished product, in cases, is stored in a large conveyor from which actual shipments are made. The conveyor has capacity for roughly an economic production run, but sometimes there is a fair amount of stock left on the slide, and at other times it is practically empty. One wants to schedule production that will just about fill the conveyor but not overflow it. This is the technique recommended for controlling the replenishment of items with lumpy demand (12.31).

So a maximum stocking objective is established equal to the capacity of the conveyor. If there is enough stock to last through the next planning period, nothing is scheduled. If the stock won't last through a complete planning period, enough to bring the stock up to the maximum objective is scheduled.

In the table below Exhibit 13.9, at the beginning of period 4 there was a net available stock of 30, which is not sufficient to cover the total of 35 pieces required. So a new production order is scheduled, due 7/25/76. The quantity is the objective of 100 less the 30 as of the beginning of the period. That leaves enough to cover period 5 as well, but another lot is required in period 6.

Three of these options are illustrated in the standard requirements planning array in Exhibits 13.10 and 13.11.

The gasket (Exhibit 13.10) is scheduled as net requirements by period, which makes the projected availability identically zero in all periods beyond the freeze. The hose (Exhibit 13.10) is scheduled in minimum lots of 170 at a time, but in a few of the periods the lot quantity is increased to cover the requirements during the period. Note that no notional order is needed for the period ending 7/02/76. The shear pin (Exhibit 13.11) is scheduled in lots periodically to bring the availability up to a patriotic 1776. In general that lasts about three planning periods, or six weeks.

13.5 FIRM ORDERS

The system generates notional orders as required to cover projected requirements, period by period, out to the planning horizon. The next time the master schedules are computed, the period now beyond the freeze will then be inside the freeze, so any notional requirements due in that period should be frozen.

Every replenishment lot, no matter what scheduling rule was used, is assigned a reference number to identify it when the planner decides that that

FIRM ORDERS

Exhibit 13.9

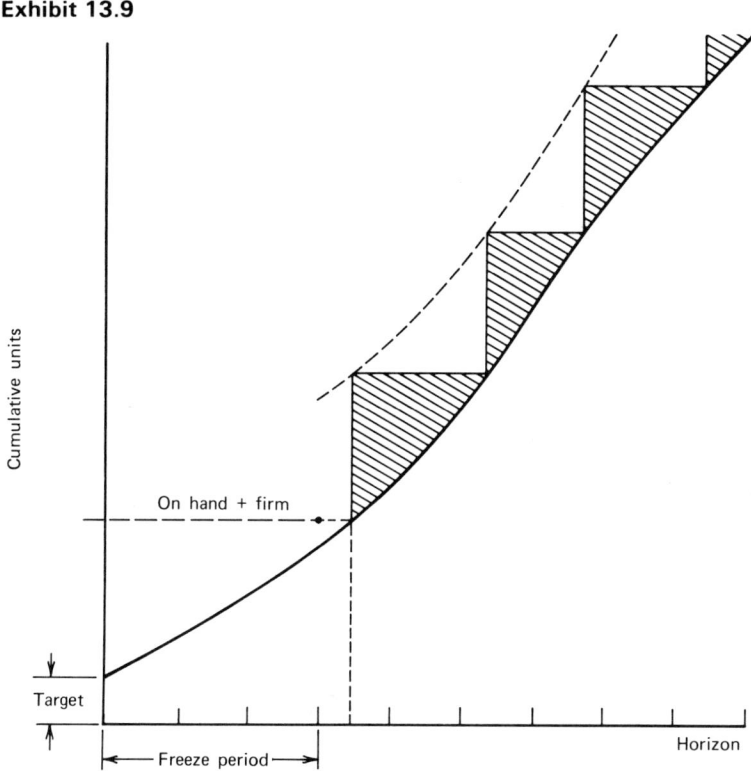

Use Rule 6.
Maximum stocking objective = 100.
Schedule using maximum stocking objective:

	Posted	1	2	3	4	5	6	7
	6/01/76	6/15/76	6/29/76	7/13/76	7/27/76	8/10/76	8/24/76	9/07/76
Reqts		50	30	40	50	35	45	55	65
Avail		75		125					
Stock		25	⁻5	80	30	65	20	45	35
Sched						70		80	55

is the quantity to be scheduled. Reference numbers are assigned in sequence and are used in several places throughout the system to distinguish among different replenishment orders for the same product. In a pharmaceutical company this lot identification is required by federal law, and usually has a standard procedure for assigning the next number in the process. Even in nonregulated companies, it helps considerably in tracking the progress of scheduled orders to be able to distinguish among them.

Exhibit 13.10

```
0203378      GASKET                          FILE INDEX = 2    LEVEL CODE 0
MINIMUM STOCK TARGET = 21.  AS OF  2/28/76 STOCK ON HAND = 85
SCHEDULING RULE: NET REQUIREMENTS BY PERIOD
```

PERIOD ENDING	DIRECT REQUIREMENTS	DEPENDENT REQUIREMENTS	FIRM ORDERS	NOTIONAL ORDERS	PROJECTED AVAILABILITY
3/12/76	16				48
3/26/76	17				31
4/09/76	16				15
4/23/76	17				⁻2
5/07/76	17			19	
5/21/76	18			18	
6/04/76	18			18	
6/18/76	18			18	
7/02/76	19			19	
7/16/76	19			19	
7/30/76	19			19	
8/13/76	20			20	
8/27/76	19			19	
9/10/76	21			21	

```
0203909      HOSE                            FILE INDEX = 4    LEVEL CODE 0
MINIMUM STOCK TARGET = 502.  AS OF  2/28/76 STOCK ON HAND = 1300
SCHEDULING RULE: MINIMUM LOT QUANTITY
```

PERIOD ENDING	DIRECT REQUIREMENTS	DEPENDENT REQUIREMENTS	FIRM ORDERS	NOTIONAL ORDERS	PROJECTED AVAILABILITY
3/12/76	156				642
3/26/76	167				475
4/09/76	160				315
4/23/76	159				156
5/07/76	167			170	159
5/21/76	172			170	157
6/04/76	169			170	158
6/18/76	163			170	165
7/02/76	165				
7/16/76	171			171	
7/30/76	171			171	
8/13/76	168			170	2
8/27/76	168			170	4
9/10/76	179			175	

When a reference number is assigned to a notional order, turning it into a firm order, a record is set up in the file for that particular order.

A short list of such orders is displayed in Exhibit 13.12. The product is identified both by its part number and by an internal file index number, used in the retrieval process, so that the planner can directly access the records for any item he wants to examine. If the schedule were locked (13.21), an asterisk would be printed. Each of the products shown in the listing has several outstanding orders identified by reference number.

The original quantity is the quantity computed by the scheduling

FIRM ORDERS

procedure, when the order was first released. The good quantity may change during the course of production as scrap losses are reported. Both the schedule date and the need date are shown, and in most cases they will be the same.

In general there can be a process routing in the file that tells the sequence of steps required to make the process. We go into more detail about that process routing in Chapter 15. The status of open orders is indicated both by the operations sequence number where the lot is now reported, and by the (working) days remaining until the completion of the last operation. Days allowed for move, queue, setup, and run time are posted as part of the process routing for every step. Hence if we know the schedule completion date and the number of days allowed to complete the remaining operations, we can back schedule to determine the latest start date for the current operation.

There are several ways that the need date can move earlier than the schedule date, indicating a potential need to review the schedule. Exhibit 13.13 illustrates a hot list of items where the need date is more than 10 days earlier than the schedule date. The product is identified by part number, description, and internal file index, and the orders are indicated by reference number. The level code is discussed in 14.1. It indicates whether the item is subordinate to some other assembly and thus may have dependent requirements generated by the schedule of that master item.

The planner may change the schedule date if it is practical, or change the requirements to something that can be met. If that means rescheduling requirements for finished goods, he may have to go back to marketing

Exhibit 13.11

0203230   SHEAR PIN   FILE INDEX = 9   LEVEL CODE 0
MINIMUM STOCK TARGET = 1724.   AS OF   2/28/76 STOCK ON HAND = 4100
SCHEDULING RULE: MAXIMUM STOCKING OBJECTIVE

PERIOD ENDING	DIRECT REQUIREMENTS	DEPENDENT REQUIREMENTS	FIRM ORDERS	NOTIONAL ORDERS	PROJECTED AVAILABILITY
3/12/76	477				1,899
3/26/76	513				1,386
4/09/76	491				895
4/23/76	483				412
5/07/76	505			1,364	1,271
5/21/76	519				752
6/04/76	507				245
6/18/76	490			1,531	1,286
7/02/76	495				791
7/16/76	510				281
7/30/76	509			1,495	1,267
8/13/76	497				770
8/27/76	496				274
9/10/76	526			1,502	1,250

Exhibit 13.12

PART NUMBER	FILE INDEX	LOCK SCHED	REFERENCE NUMBER	ORIGINAL QUANTITY	GOOD QUANTITY	SCHEDULE DATE	NEED DATE	NOW AT OP SEQ	DAYS REMAINING
32-62-4530	4		10115	3,180	3,000	7/08/76	5/11/76	30	7
			10131	1,411	1,411	7/23/76	1/02/76	1	65
			10004	200	200	12/25/76	12/25/76	1	65
			10053	373	373	1/26/77	1/26/77	1	65
			10076	373	373	1/26/77	1/26/77	1	65
30-47-4646	5		10116	4,061	4,061	7/08/76	5/10/76	10	25
			10132	1,490	1,490	7/23/76	1/02/76	1	65
			999	100	100	1/25/77	1/25/77	983	2
			10054	500	500	2/04/77	2/04/77	1	65
			10077	500	500	2/04/77	2/04/77	1	65
37-36-0819	6		10012	240	240	7/22/76	7/22/76	2	16
			10133	862	862	7/23/76	6/27/76	1	65
			10102	444	444	8/23/76	8/13/76	2	16
33-28-2343	7		10118	3,560	3,560	10/13/76	10/13/76	1	50
			10134	2,820	2,820	1/30/77	1/30/77	1	50
36-32-6386	8		10119	3,651	3,651	9/19/76	9/19/76	1	50
			10135	3,072	3,072	12/09/76	12/09/76	1	50
37-56-4105	9		10120	13,028	13,028	6/10/76	5/07/76	10	4
			10035	13,000	13,000	7/22/76	7/22/76	2	9
			10105	2,270	2,270	8/15/76	8/15/76	1	50
			10136	2,200	2,200	10/12/76	10/12/76	1	50

BUDGETS

people to let them change their marketing intelligence, or notify customers that firm backlog has to be rescheduled.

13.6 BUDGETS

Exhibit 2.6 showed an aggregate projection of the combined schedules (expressed usually in dollars at standard cost) for any group of related items, such as a product line. The format is the same as that for the individual master schedule for any product, except that the entries are in dollars rather than in units. The column for projected availability shows the anticipated total stock on hand, and does not deduct the planned target stock as the schedule does.

Once a month the planner should copy the data from this routine report onto a slanted chart. The computer could of course keep this record, or a secretary could post it. The physical act of transferring a few numbers from the computer output to a permanent log, however, enables the planner to think about what the computer is telling him. Exhibit 13.14 shows a sample record for the forecasts of requirements. A new line is posted each month. The total forecast of sales is recorded for each of the next 12 or 13 months, depending on the length of the report. A comparison vertically along any column shows how the forecasts for a particular fixed month are changing with successive revisions. For example, between the April and May projections (made this year), next April and May forecasts changed fairly sharply. This gives the planner almost a year's notice of something happening, and if it is going to affect production schedules, he has time to enquire about the cause and probable future implications.

The same sort of chart can be maintained for the total scheduled production, period by period (Exhibit 13.15). It is worth investigating the process that makes next March jump so much from the schedule produced in one month to the next.

The third chart is a standard set of slanted charts is the projected stock on hand, which serves as a check on the requirements and the production schedule (Exhibit 13.16).

The records are nicknamed "slanted charts" because of their appearance as rows are posted in successive months. About once a year one has to start over on a fresh sheet of paper. It would be possible to save paper by listing forecasts, or production, or inventory, by relative month into the future, but that is not so informative as when the reports line up the facts about a particular calendar month.

Another way of summarizing the consequences of the present master schedule is in a report of where the workload is today and where it will be

Exhibit 13.13

HOTLIST

SATURDAY, JULY 10, 1976
EASTERN DAYLIGHT TIME 9:17:21

WHICH ITEMS = ALL
ALL 29 ITEMS WILL BE USED.
MINIMUM DAYS DIFFERENCE IN DUE DATES = 10

PART NO	DESCRIPT	INDEX	LEVEL	REF NO	GOOD QTY	NEED DATE	SCHEDULE	DAYS REM
33-28-2343	MOTOR 0.5	7	1	10162	34,650	5/23/76	7/13/76	15
39-91-0374	HEAT EXCHA	10	1	10165	30,000	5/22/76	7/13/76	7
33-65-3387	HUMIDIFIER	11	1	10286	2,658	1/02/76	8/25/76	15
32-47-0389	BRACKET	12	2	10219	114,733	6/30/76	7/19/76	10
				10237	215,374	6/25/76	7/20/76	10
				10254	251,246	6/30/76	7/26/76	10
				10271	315,810	6/23/76	7/27/76	13

30-72-6859	FAN	13	2	10220	66,000	7/04/76	7/19/76	2
				10238	66,000	7/06/76	7/20/76	2
				10255	84,674	7/10/76	7/26/76	2
				10272	112,853	7/02/76	7/27/76	5
36-51-5186	TAP	19	2	10224	17,363	6/19/76	7/19/76	13
				10242	9,446	6/21/76	7/20/76	13
				10259	11,780	6/23/76	7/26/76	13
				10276	14,166	6/21/76	7/27/76	16
				10190	16,460	6/05/76	7/05/76	11
				10207	17,273	6/12/76	7/12/76	11
39-82-5503	HOUSING	22	2	10244	116,799	6/13/76	7/20/76	7
				10278	56,717	6/18/76	7/27/76	10
				10192	20,540	6/21/76	7/05/76	7
37-22-6605	BEARING	23	2	10210	11,431	6/26/76	7/12/76	12
				10245	27,936	6/19/76	7/20/76	12
				10279	23,941	6/25/76	7/27/76	15

Exhibit 13.14

FORECASTS OF SALES ($1000 per 4-week period)

	May	Jun	Jul	Aug	Sep	Oct	Nov	Dec	Jan	Feb	Mar	Apr	May	Jun	Jul	Aug	Sep	Oct	Nov	Dec	Jan
Apr	138	107	129	113	102	116	117	114	118	130	131	117	138								
May		122	117	110	109	111	113	117	120	125	126	132	130								
Jun			117	109	108	114	113	118	123	125	127	129	131	131	128						
Jul				107	108	115	114	118	123	125	128	129	132	131	129	124					
Aug					108	115	113	118	123	125	127	129	132	131	129	124	114				
Sep						118	116	119	126	124	128	131	131	131	128	121	115	113			
Oct							116	119	126	124	128	131	131	131	128	122	115	113	121		
Nov								119	127	124	128	130	131	131	128	121	115	113	120	120	
Dec									130	127	128	132	130	130	126	119	115	115	120	121	123

Exhibit 13.15   PROJECTED PRODUCTION ($1000 completed per 4-week period)

	May	Jun	Jul	Aug	Sep	Oct	Nov	Dec	Jan	Feb	Mar	Apr	May	Jun	Jul	Aug	Sep	Oct	Nov	Dec	Jan
Apr	157	181	54	119	118	121	94	115	145	113	119	118									
May		182	47	112	131	114	122	91	117	145	114	119	117	157							
Jun			85	115	128	74	120	117	125	151	115	122	116	123	117						
Jul				161	124	72	125	121	115	120	150	122	154	123	117	124					
Aug					206	79	120	116	117	153	115	121	126	116	125	116					
Sep						79	124	115	152	114	124	116	118	125	155	123	116	121			
Oct							123	155	119	112	118	119	114	122	119	125	121	128			
Nov								162	120	112	121	115	118	124	117	124	157	119	124	122	
Dec									119	119	223	14	116	188	120	93	118	119	122	122	121

Exhibit 13.16 PROJECTED STOCK ON HAND ($1000 as of end of 4-week period)

	Apr	May	Jun	Jul	Aug	Sep	Oct	Nov	Dec	Jan	Feb	Mar	Apr	May	Jun	Jul	Aug	Sep	Oct	Nov	Dec	Jan
Apr	123	143	217	142	147	164	167	170	150	146	162	144	146	127								
May		152	212	142	144	166	168	176	150	147	167	154	147	132	159							
Jun			176	144	150	170	130	137	136	138	164	152	146	130	122	110						
Jul				103	157	174	131	142	145	136	131	154	147	169	160	148	148					
Aug					101	199	163	170	171	164	156	182	168	158	153	140	141	143				
Sep						184	146	153	149	175	165	161	145	133	126	153	155	156	164			
Oct							143	151	186	178	166	155	144	127	118	109	112	152	160	168		
Nov								143	187	181	169	162	146	134	127	116	119	161	167	172	174	
Dec									160	149	142	237	118	104	162	156	130	133	137	139	139	137

BUDGETS

performed. The tabulation shown in Exhibit 2.8 has a column for each department that has work on the schedule due to start there sometime during October. The column totals show the total amount of work the department is scheduled to do, and the row totals show the total amount of work now in some earlier department. This sort of report is one of the signals of the need to find a more practical schedule.

The implications of the master schedules can also be translated into direct labor, based on factors in the process routing, by operation. Exhibit 2.7 tabulated, by planning period, the number of people in each department by labor grade called for in the present schedules, based on a standard planning factor of the number of standard hours produced per person per planning period. The report warns of a major work load next November, for which some work should be released now.

The schedule, before it can be released to the shop, must be checked to ensure that the people, materials, and machinery are all available at the right time to meet the requirements. If capacity can't be found in time by expediting, then requirements will have to change.

CHAPTER **14**

Explosion

The preceding chapter dealt with the question of various ways of deciding how much of a product to make in each planning period, and what consequences such a schedule would have on total production work loads and on the projected inventories. We dealt strictly with the direct requirements to sell the product, or at least ship it, to an outside customer.

Exhibit 14.1 shows (*a*) the stock that would be on hand to meet a series of "lumpy" demands if the procedures of 12.3 were used on the basis of a forecast and safety stock. Contrast that with the stock (*b*) that results when we bring in enough, when needed, to cover the next five periods.

In most manufacturing processes end products are made of components and subassemblies, which in turn are made of parts and materials. Even a pharmaceutical product is made from a recipe of active and inert ingredients, plus a very long list of packaging supplies: bottle, cap, cotton, label, literature, carton, and so on. The plan to produce end products in various quantities each period generates dependent requirements on all the subordinate items that must be covered by the production plan.

14.1 BILL OF MATERIALS

The bill of materials for a product defines its structure. For example, in Exhibit 14.2, the product structure listed for the 37-62-1981 furnace shows a list of half a dozen subordinate parts. Some of the parts are shown with a quantity of one each, meaning that to build one furnace requires one part number 33-65-3387, for example. Others are required in quantities of three each—it takes three pieces of 33-28-2343 to build one furnace.

Therefore the schedule to build 617 furnaces during the period ending 8/31/76 will require 1851 pieces in total of part number 33-28-2343, and 617 pieces of part number 33-65-3387.

A second attribute of the product structure is to specify when these parts are needed. The lot of furnaces is scheduled to be completed in the period

Exhibit 14.1

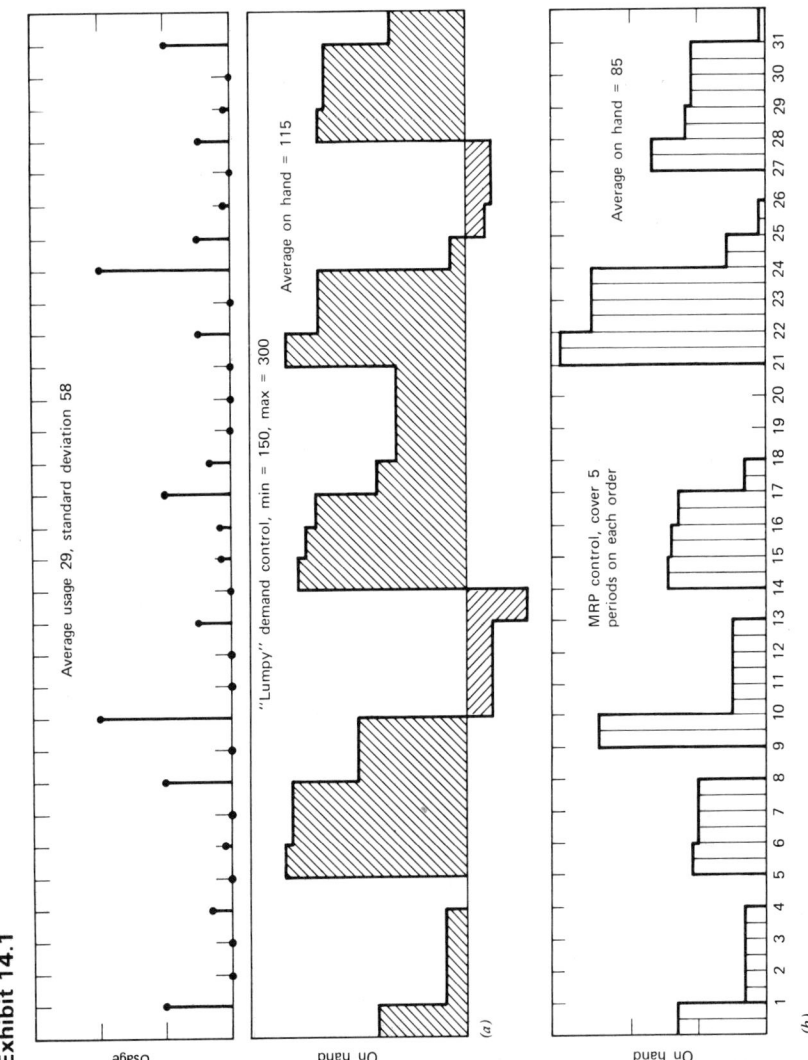

Exhibit 14.2

```
37-62-1981     OIL FIRED FORCED AIR FURNACE           FILE INDEX = 3    LEVEL CODE 0
MINIMUM STOCK TARGET = 247.  AS OF  6/08/76 STOCK ON HAND = 1110 *
SCHEDULING RULE: NET REQUIREMENTS BY PERIOD
```

PERIOD ENDING	DIRECT REQUIREMENTS	DEPENDENT REQUIREMENTS	FIRM ORDERS	NOTIONAL ORDERS	PROJECTED AVAILABILITY
6/22/76	140				723
7/06/76	149				574
7/20/76	165				409
8/03/76	160				249
8/17/76	136				113
8/31/76	137		617		593
9/14/76	136				457
9/28/76	136				321
10/12/76	145				176
10/26/76	147				29
11/09/76	150			121	
11/23/76	154			154	
12/07/76	155			155	
12/21/76	157			157	
1/04/77	150			150	
1/18/77	124			124	
2/01/77	124			124	
2/15/77	155			155	
3/01/77	154			154	

```
              37-62-1981     OIL FIRED FORCED AIR FURNACE
              LEVEL CODE = 0,  FILE INDEX = 3
```

PART NO	QUANTITY	PROC SEQ	A	P	N	D	E	DATE
33-28-2343	3	2						
36-32-6386	3	2						
33-65-3387	1	2	X					
30-72-6859	3					X		12/29/76
37-66-4948	1				X			12/29/76
34-77-7318	1	2						

ending 8/31/76. The detailed record of the order would give the actual due date within that period. For four of the six subordinate parts, the part is required to be available at operations sequence step 2 in the process routing. We can determine from the route sheet how many working days are allowed from all operations from step 2 to the end of the process, for move time, queue time, setup time, and direct running time, in total. Hence the date when these parts are required, to support the furnace schedule, can be determined by offsetting the scheduled completion date for the furnace by the total working days allowed (15.1).

The master schedule for the furnace shown in Exhibit 14.2 will thus generate dependent requirements on each of the subordinate parts. The firm order for 617 furnaces due 8/31 will generate some requirements (provided the assembly process has not yet gone past step 2). The notional orders in successive periods starting 11/09 will also generate dependent requirements.

Consider first the 33-28-2343 motor that is used at operations step 2 in

BILL OF MATERIALS

quantities of three parts per finished assembly (Exhibit 14.3). Note the dependent requirements listed in the appropriate column of the requirements planning table. The total production plan has to cover the sum of the direct requirements and the dependent requirements. This part also has some forecasts of direct requirements, possibly as service parts, and also as scheduled OEM orders. The two firm orders now open are sufficient to cover these requirements. For purposes of these examples, only the requirements from the furnace are shown, so the projected availability might seem a trifle high. However, if all the products that used this motor had their master schedules exploded, the total dependent requirements might well support the stock on hand. Our purpose here is to look at the process of generating dependent demand; the procedures of Chapter 13 will schedule the appropriate orders to cover them. Note that both the firm and the notional order quantities for the furnace have been multiplied by three. Furthermore, the requirement to support furnaces due in the period ending 8/31 is shown in the period ending 7/20. It takes about six weeks for the furnaces to go from operation step 2 to the end of the process. Therefore we need the piece parts that much earlier.

14.11 Yields

When the assembly process has a predictable yield loss, the quantity each on the bill of materials can be increased to generate sufficient requirements

Exhibit 14.3

33-28-2343   MOTOR 0.5 HP   FILE INDEX = 7   LEVEL CODE 1
MINIMUM STOCK TARGET = 893.   AS OF 6/08/76 STOCK ON HAND = ⁻5141
SCHEDULING RULE: SMOOTHED PRODUCTION RATE

PERIOD ENDING	DIRECT REQUIREMENTS	DEPENDENT REQUIREMENTS	FIRM ORDERS	NOTIONAL ORDERS	PROJECTED AVAILABILITY
6/22/76	446				⁻6,480
7/06/76	475				⁻6,955
7/20/76	1,832	1,851	38,947		28,309
8/03/76	507		8,258		36,060
8/17/76	402				35,658
8/31/76	960				34,698
9/14/76	1,483				33,215
9/28/76	49	363			32,353
10/12/76	477	462			31,414
10/26/76	1,838	465			29,111
11/09/76	2,239	471			26,401
11/23/76	546	450			25,405
12/07/76	517	372			24,516
12/21/76	2,541	372			21,603
1/04/77	456	465			20,682
1/18/77	371	462			19,849
2/01/77	1,992	384			17,473
2/15/77	485	381			16,607
3/01/77	485	447			15,675

on subordinate materials. (See 11.023.) For example, suppose it takes 20 glass bottles per 1000 pills to make packages of 50. If 3% of the bottles are rejected on the backing line, the quantity of bottles per 1000 pills should be $1.03 \times 20 = 20.6$. There are other instances where the quantity each will be a fraction, such as the number of kilograms of an active ingredient needed to make a liter of product.

14.2 LEVEL CODES

As a method of organizing the computations neatly, the materials management systems library goes through all the items one level at a time. The first level has level code 0. These products are not used in any other assembly, and have direct requirements only. In some companies all products are level code 0. To build items with level code 0, the subordinates used must have level code at least 1. If we develop the master schedule for all items at level code 0, and explode the dependent requirements, we can guarantee that by the time we begin to develop master schedules for items with level code 1, all the dependent requirements will have been generated, so the schedule can take account of all requirements. Now the items at level code 1 are considered to be master items, and we set up their master schedule, exploding the requirements. The subordinate items required to make items at level code 1 will be at level codes at least 2.

The level codes are automatically maintained by the system as new product structures are posted to the files, or as old product structures are revised to show new bills of material. All subordinates used to build items (whether products, assemblies, components, or parts) at level code LC must have level code at least LC + 1. The level code is an attribute of the item, and is the largest number required for any of the parent items on which it is used. The furnace is at level code 0, and one of its subordinates, the motor, is at level code 1.

It may be useful to know how many subordinate items there are on the file with at least a given number of parents. Exhibit 14.4 shows, by level code and in total, how many items have at least each of a specified list of numbers of parents. Some of the items with more than five or six parents each, for example, might be treated as common materials where the usage could be projected from past issues, without the expense of elaborate time-phased planning systems. That would eliminate 14 of the items on the file (out of 69 items beyond level code 0) from the planning process. These items can still be shown in the product structure, but with a code in the column marked "N" that would indicate that the requirements are not to be exploded. For a cheap enough item, a simple two-bin system can prove

DEPENDENT REQUIREMENTS

Exhibit 14.4

INFRASTRUCTURE

THURSDAY, AUGUST 5, 1976
EASTERN DAYLIGHT TIME 14:52:44

NUMBERS OF PARENTS = 1 2 3 4 5 6 7 8 9 10

PARENTS =	1	2	3	4	5	6	7
SUB LEVEL							
1	60	53	11	9	3	2	
2	8	8	4	4	4	3	
3	1	1	1	1	1	1	
TOTAL	69	62	16	14	8	6	

ELAPSED TIME	17.043S
CPU TIME	0.573S

completely adequate. The part shows in the product structure for the record only.

The idea of generating time-phased net requirements is to have more precise control over the availability of materials, especially as top-level requirements change. But for many consumer products, the production schedules for individual models may be quite steady, and common hardware used on several different models can be projected quite well from past usage. Furthermore, some of these items are so cheap that it is not worthwhile to spend $25 a year on a planning process to ensure against the risk of having to write off $3 worth of stock when the requirements do dry up. Nor is it worth the planner's time to review such items. It is better to provide $10 worth of safety stock—a whole year's supply—to be sure that there is a sufficient supply of nails to avoid losing the horse's shoes. Lumpiness in requirements resulting from explosion of lot-size withdrawals tends to get smoothed out when the part has many parents.

14.3 DEPENDENT REQUIREMENTS

There are two ways available for generating the dependent requirements in the planning array for subordinate items: regeneration and net change.

"Regeneration" means to generate all requirements, level by level, each planning cycle. One starts at the top with level code 0, plans them, explodes the requirements, and then takes the resulting dependent requirements into account in planning level code 1, and so on. The process is quite fast, and with the provisions for retrieving any set of items for scheduling, can be carried out selectively.

The other method of generating requirements is a net change process. Rather than regenerating all the requirements from the top down when one wants to change a schedule, one can first back out all the dependent demand that resulted from the present schedule and replan, starting from any intermediate point to see the consequences.

There has been some discussion in the literature about using a net change process routinely to modify the dependent requirements, and hence the production schedule, every time there is a change to the top-level requirements, as from the posting of a new scheduled backlog order or a change in customer requirements. The process of net change requires much more computer time than a straight top-down explosion. Hence one should be very careful of recommendations emanating from computer vendors about the desirability of net change.

There are enormous advantages in using net change on a selective basis to discover and correct schedules for individual items that cause problems in availability of materials or manufacturing capacity. It is unlikely that immediate conversational rescheduling on line throughout the day will have much practical effect on getting goods delivered from the shop on time, on design, and on cost.

There is provision for both an "official" and a "tentative" schedule. The official schedule is used to generate actual firm orders from the notional orders due in the period beyond the freeze. The tentative schedule is just that. The planner can develop a tentative schedule for any block of items, examine the consequences in terms of machine capacity, material availability, and labor workload. If the schedule looks feasible he can move the tentative schedule into the official record. But if there are problems, which show up as lists of items to be short-dated or expedited, he may want to try a variety of different schedules, with considerable personal intervention, before deciding to release the results.

When the planner is satisfied with the schedule, the dependent requirements from the official schedule are also posted to the forecast array in the data base to be available for reports and to the strategic system for computing lot quantities and safety stocks.

The same interpolation scheme illustrated in Exhibit 13.2 is used to convert the dependent demand by planning period into the forecast array which may have a different calendar.

14.4 SCHEDULE FEASIBILITY

If the schedule generated for any subordinate item poses problems, indicated by a shortage of material or an overload on the manufacturing

SCHEDULE FEASIBILITY

capacity, then the schedule should be changed to something more reasonable. The schedule must of course cover the requirements, which means a change to the requirements. As a result of having the product structures in the file to show the bill of materials required to make any product, we can also work backward and get a listing of the parents on which each subordinate is used.

Materials problems show up as the need to short-date new orders or to expedite frozen orders. The truth is often easy to ignore—just leave the problem up to Joe on the shop floor, and see what happens.

For example, part number 36-31-6348 (Exhibit 14.5) is used on nine different parent items, in various quantities. The parent items are identified by the internal file index number, so that their records can be retrieved quickly, as well as by part number and description. The where-used listing can also be quite handy when it comes to making engineering changes, to be sure that the change will work everywhere the new part of material is substituted for the old one.

14.41 Pegged Requirements

When the planner wants to review the source of the dependent requirements derived from these parents, it is useful to have a report of "pegged" requirements as in Exhibit 14.6. Only seven of the nine parent items have schedules that generate dependent requirements on the copper tubing. The quantity each is listed from the product structure, and the offset time is shown in planning periods, based on the length of the planning period used and the time allowed in the routing from the step where parts are required until the end of the process.

The dependent requirements are shown parent by parent. In each case the schedule for the master item has been multiplied by the quantity each, and

Exhibit 14.5

36-31-6348   0.5 *INCH COPPER TUBING*

INDEX	QUANTITY	PART NO	DESCRIPTION
29	1	87-65-4321	*CABLE ASSEMBLY*
28	1	35-45-5678	*LOWER UNIT*
11	3	33-65-3387	*HUMIDIFIER*
8	2	36-32-6386	*COMPRESSOR*
6	2	37-36-0819	*SPRAY*
5	2	30-47-4646	*MOBILE UNIT*
4	2	32-62-4530	*FREEZER*
2	1	39-10-3209	*FOUNTAIN*
1	1	37-01-1906	*HOME UNIT*

Exhibit 14.6

```
36-31-6349      0.5 INCH COPPER TUBING         FILE INDEX = 14

                                      E X T E N D E D   R E Q U I R E M E N T S   B Y   P E R I O D
PART NO    QUANTITY EACH  OFFSET
                                 5/28/76  6/11/76  6/25/76  7/09/76  7/23/76  8/06/76  8/20/76  9/03/76  9/17/76

33-05-3337        3         2                2235     2235     2235     2235     2235     2235     2235     2235
36-32-6386        2         2                5876     5876     5876     5876     5876     5876     5876     5876
37-36-0819        2         2                                                    658      676      680      734
30-47-4606        2         3                                  410     1640     1640     1674     1674     1674
32-62-4530        2         3                                  224     1300     1300     1296     1298
30-10-3200        1         3                           349    359      394      401      494      495
37-01-1006        1         4                    79      84    106      104       90       91       96

TOTAL DEPENDENT DEMAND              984     9479   15716    8544    9210   12007   12218   12346   12408
DIRECT DEMAND ON THIS ITEM
```

SCHEDULE FEASIBILITY

moved over by the offset time, so that the requirements line up with the periods in which the subordinate items are required.

The total dependent requirements in the period 5/28 are 984, but no detail is shown. Likewise, in the period ending 6/11, details are shown for 8111, but the total is 9479. The difference is the requirements that come from firm orders, already released, which cannot in most cases be changed. The detailed pegged requirements are shown for notional orders only. Since these are outside the freeze period, they can be rescheduled.

When one or two parents are seen to have a large effect on the schedule for the problem subordinate, those requirements may be moved back and forth either by a schedule change or by a change in requirements at still a higher level. Ultimately, if direct requirements must be changed, the problem lands squarely in the lap of the marketing intelligence group, or with order entry to advise customers about delays in filling the scheduled backlog. It may seem difficult to change the requirements, but once the methods are worked out it is very much more comfortable than merely being late with no warning to the customer. If it can be shown that all requirements cannot be made as of the desired date, then the date should be modified. It can be done in an orderly way in advance, with the user having a chance to make choices among options, or it can be done after the fact. When the product is late and the user didn't expect it, that may give him all sorts of other problems. A customer who has problems with a vendor is likely to look elsewhere next time.

The production planner has the tools and the obligation to notice when there is a problem with an infeasible schedule. He has the tools to explore what sorts of changes might alleviate the situation. But the actual decision to change direct requirements—dependent requirements are within the planner's province—should be made by the marketing organization charged with customer service.

Let us take a specific case. The planner displays the master schedule for each of the items that is reported as requiring a short-dated order (need date is within the freeze period). It is immediately clear that the reason is some rather large spikes in the direct demand within the freeze period, which suggests scheduled orders. Then he looks at the current forecast array for the item and sees a large scheduled demand in the first month. That puts him on the track of the scheduled orders, and he looks at the list for all orders on that product. There is one customer with a large order, due shortly. He checks with marketing whether it would be possible to notify the customer to expect delivery in eight weeks, beyond the freeze, instead of in three. The salesman checks with the customer and finds that it is all right. The order is rescheduled for later delivery.

That scenario changes the forecast of direct requirements, which changes the schedule for the top-level item. The effect on subordinate dependent requirements is backed out by a net change to the tentative schedule, and then all affected items are rescheduled. The tentative schedule is checked, and leads to feasible materials availability at all levels, so it is made official.

Just as a check, the planner also looks at the work load by department, and finds that one change in one promise date to a customer for a large order would alleviate several overtime situations in various departments that would have had to stunt through subordinate materials to meet total requirements.

The customer isn't particularly in a hurry—the original promise date had been set by the salesman before checking on availability. It is just possible that next time the salesman might check before quoting delivery.

14.5 SPECIAL CASES

We have already mentioned the special case where some subordinate is coded "don't explode." Three other special cases are illustrated by the subordinates listed in the product structure in Exhibit 14.2.

14.51 Effectivity Date

The first example is part number 37-66-4948, No. 10 wire (Exhibit 14.7). In this particular bill of materials the wire is scheduled to be deleted (as for an

Exhibit 14.7

```
37-66-4948     NO 10 WIRE 2 CONDUCTOR                 FILE INDEX = 20    LEVEL CODE 1
MINIMUM STOCK TARGET = 0.    AS OF  6/08/76 STOCK ON HAND = 11757
SCHEDULING RULE: SMOOTHED PRODUCTION RATE
```

PERIOD ENDING	DIRECT REQUIREMENTS	DEPENDENT REQUIREMENTS	FIRM ORDERS	NOTIONAL ORDERS	PROJECTED AVAILABILITY
6/22/76			5,054		16,811
7/06/76			4,567		21,378
7/20/76		617			20,761
8/03/76					20,761
8/17/76					20,761
8/31/76					20,761
9/14/76					20,761
9/28/76		121			20,640
10/12/76		154			20,486
10/26/76		155			20,331
11/09/76		157			20,174
11/23/76					20,174
12/07/76					20,174
12/21/76					20,174
1/04/77					20,174
1/18/77					20,174
2/01/77					20,174
2/15/77					20,174
3/01/77					20,174

SPECIAL CASES

engineering change) on any furnace made after the end of 1976. Until that time the wire is used in quantities of one each. No process sequence is shown for picking the parts, so the programs use a standard default sequence recorded in the state variables for the implementation of the application. Note that the firm and notional orders for the furnace are duplicated in Exhibit 14.7, but the furnaces scheduled after 12/29 are not shown as dependent requirements on the subordinate part.

There are provisions for computing the date when present stock will be used up to set up a discontinue date for a planned engineering change, or the product structure can be posted directly to record a date that must be coordinated with other changes. The program for computing the date when stocks will be used up can also be used to report the date, without making the change.

Next we consider the 30-72-6859 fan (Exhibit 14.8), which is to become effective on 12/29 and be added to the product structure. (It is possible to delete one subordinate and reinstate the same subordinate with a different quantity, to accommodate changes in strengths of ingredients in pharmaceutical products at different seasons of the year.)

For this item the notional orders for furnaces after the beginning of the new year are exploded and appear as dependent requirements on the fan. But furnaces scheduled before the change in bill of materials do not generate these requirements.

Exhibit 14.8

```
30-72-6859    FAN                              FILE INDEX = 13    LEVEL CODE 2
MINIMUM STOCK TARGET = 0.  AS OF  6/08/76 STOCK ON HAND = 135633
SCHEDULING RULE: MINIMUM LOT QUANTITY
```

PERIOD ENDING	DIRECT REQUIREMENTS	DEPENDENT REQUIREMENTS	FIRM ORDERS	NOTIONAL ORDERS	PROJECTED AVAILABILITY
6/22/76					135,633
7/05/76					135,633
7/20/76	1,578				134,055
8/03/76					134,055
8/17/76					134,055
8/31/76	1,879				132,176
9/14/76	980				131,196
9/28/76					131,196
10/12/76					131,196
10/26/76	1,924				129,272
11/09/76	1,461				127,811
11/23/76		450			127,361
12/07/76		372			126,989
12/21/76	749	372			125,868
1/04/77		465			125,403
1/18/77		462			124,941
2/01/77	679	384			123,878
2/15/77		381			123,497
3/01/77		447			123,050

14.52 Phantom Bill

Now let us consider the 33-65-3387 humidifier (Exhibit 14.9), which has a code for a "phantom bill" in the bill of materials for the furnace. This means that in constructing the furnace we do not build humidifiers as such and then assemble them into the furnace. Rather the term "humidifier" is a convenient term for a related group of parts. They may even be assembled as kits or subassemblies for service parts. But we don't want to create dependent demand for humidifiers and schedule to cover them. We will build the humidifiers right into the furnaces in one process.

The effect of the phantom bill code is to remove the humidifier from the bill of materials of the furnace, at the time schedules are being developed, and substitute the whole parts list for the humidifier. The dependent requirements then are exploded directly to each of the parts that are required to make a humidifier, such as the 39-82-5503 housing shown in Exhibit 14.9.

Exhibit 14.9

```
33-65-3387      HUMIDIFIER
LEVEL CODE = 1,  FILE INDEX = 11

   PART NO      QUANTITY
  39-82-5503        2
  36-51-5186        3
  36-31-6348        3
  34-77-7318        2
```

```
39-82-5503      HOUSING                          FILE INDEX = 22    LEVEL CODE 2
MINIMUM STOCK TARGET = 0.  AS OF  6/08/76  STOCK ON HAND = 41344
SCHEDULING RULE: MINIMUM LOT QUANTITY
```

PERIOD ENDING	DIRECT REQUIREMENTS	DEPENDENT REQUIREMENTS	FIRM ORDERS	NOTIONAL ORDERS	PROJECTED AVAILABILITY
6/22/76					41,344
7/06/76			39,381		80,725
7/20/76		1,234	15,489		94,980
8/03/76			14,704		109,684
8/17/76					109,684
8/31/76					109,684
9/14/76					109,684
9/28/76		242			109,442
10/12/76		308			109,134
10/26/76		310			108,824
11/09/76		314			108,510
11/23/76		300			108,210
12/07/76		248			107,962
12/21/76		248			107,714
1/04/77		310			107,404
1/18/77		308			107,096
2/01/77		256			106,840
2/15/77		254			106,586
3/01/77		298			106,288

SPECIAL CASES

Exhibit 14.10

```
37-62-1981      FURNACE | FILE INDEX = 3, LEVEL CODE = 0, UNIT = EACH

REL LEVEL    QTY EACH      UNIT       ITEM
    1            3         EACH       33-28-2343    MOTOR 0.5 HP
      2          3         EACH       32-47-0389    BRACKET
        3        3         EACH       38-84-7072    STOVE BOLT 1/4 × 3
        3        3         EACH       32-72-7100    NUT 1/4 INCH
        3        3         EACH       34-36-4115    WASHER
        3        3         FEET       32-37-7745    1/4 INCH SQUARE STEEL BAR
        3        3         SQ FT      32-74-9069    NO 11 GALVANIZED SHEET
        3        3         POUNDS     33-59-2650    SOLDER
      2          3         EACH       39-82-5503    HOUSING
        3        3         SQ FT      32-74-9069    NO 11 GALVANIZED SHEET
      2          1         EACH       37-22-6605    BEARING
        3        3         EACH       34-77-7318    COUPLING
        3        3         EACH       34-86-5174    GASKET
      2          3         EACH       38-84-7072    STOVE BOLT 1/4 × 3
      2          1         EACH       32-72-7100    NUT 1/4 INCH
      2          1         EACH       34-36-4115    WASHER
    1            3         EACH       36-32-6386    COMPRESSOR
      2          1         EACH       39-82-5503    HOUSING
        3        3         SQ FT      32-74-9069    NO 11 GALVANIZED SHEET
      2          2         EACH       30-72-6859    FAN
      2          2         FEET       36-31-6348    0.5 INCH COPPER TUBING
      2          1         EACH       34-77-7318    COUPLING
    1            1         EACH       33-65-3387    HUMIDIFIER
      2         48         EACH       39-82-5503    HOUSING
        3        3         SQ FT      32-74-9069    NO 11 GALVANIZED SHEET
      2         72         EACH       36-51-5186    TAP
        3        3         FEET       32-37-7745    1/4 INCH SQUARE STEEL BAR
        3        3         EACH       34-86-5174    GASKET
      2         72         FEET       36-31-6348    0.5 INCH COPPER TUBING
      2         48         EACH       34-77-7318    COUPLING
    1            3         EACH       30-72-6859    FAN
    1            1         FEET       37-66-4948    NO 10 WIRE 2 CONDUCTOR
    1            1         EACH       34-77-7318    COUPLING

DISPLAY ANOTHER BILL OF MATERIALS? NO

ELAPSED TIME       1M 37.580S
CPU TIME              0.605S
```

Exhibit 14.10 shows a complete indented bill of materials, generated from the level-by-level product structures. The direct subordinates of the 37-62-1981 furnace are shown with relative level code 1 in this display. Indented under each of these subordinates is a list of the subordinates with relative level 2 to the furnace. Note that the relative level code can be smaller than the actual level code for a part number, which will be the largest of any of the relative level codes for any product on which it is used.

The phantom bill of materials substitutes, at the time dependent demand is exploded, for some relative level 1 item the whole list of its relative level 2 subordinates.

14.6 AUTOMATIC SEQUENCE

The modular design of the materials management systems library makes it possible to carry out each of the planning operations, one step at a time, for any selected group of parts. This procedure is valuable in helping planners to learn how to use these tools effectively, and even to explore certain problem areas. Exhibit 14.11 illustrates the appearance of the terminal output for an automatic production planning sequence.

(A) The planner can choose whether to develop an official schedule or to work first with a tentative schedule.

(B) Normally one would start by posting the direct requirements from the requirements planning system. The alternative is to start with a planning array (especially a tentative one) already in existence and modify certain parts of it, as when the planner wants to try several different plans for material availability and capacity. If the planner chooses such an option, he can execute a net change to remove the effects of the present schedule for any selected item and all its subordinates.

(C) This is one of the places where the data base records the date when stock status was posted as the beginning date for the production planning arrays. Under a normal process, the computer first picks up all the items at level code 0. The master schedule is developed to cover direct requirements, with notional orders to the end of the planning horizon. These orders, plus any firm orders that have not gone past the step where parts are picked, are exploded to generate the dependent demand on all subordinates. The computer prints a log at the terminal as each level code is processed, so that the user can track progress.

When all items with level code 0 have been processed, we know that the dependent requirements for all level code 1 items have been generated. Hence the program can set up a master schedule for each of those items, taking account of both dependent and direct demand. Those notional orders, and the relevant firm orders, are exploded to generate dependent requirements at level code 2 and beyond. And so the process continues (for nine minutes or so).

(D) When all items have been processed, level by level, the planner may want to review the resulting schedules before acting on them. If he foresees no problems he can ask the computer to assign reference numbers to all notional orders due in the planning period beyond the freeze period, and to set up the records as of the first operation in the process. Note the option to either use the official schedule or interchange the official and tentative schedules first.

Exhibit 14.11

    AUTOMATIC

WEDNESDAY, AUGUST 18, 1976
EASTERN DAYLIGHT TIME 20:56:49

(A) *SCHEDULE: OFFICIAL TENTATIVE = 0*
(B) *START BY POSTING DIRECT REQUIREMENTS? YES*

    FORECASTS REVISED AS OF   7/31/76

(C) *CALENDAR DATE WHEN STOCK STATUS WAS POSTED = 80276*
    PLANNING ARRAY: OFFICIAL ONLY, TENTATIVE INCLUDED = 0
    630 ITEMS AT LEVEL CODE 0
    60 ITEMS AT LEVEL CODE 1
    6 ITEMS AT LEVEL CODE 2
    3 ITEMS AT LEVEL CODE 3
(D) *POST THE NEW NOTIONAL ORDERS IN THE PERIOD BEYOND FREEZE? YES*
    WHICH ITEMS = ALL
    ALL 713 ITEMS WILL BE USED.
    NEW REPLENISHMENT ORDERS WILL BE POSTED FROM THE OFFICIAL SCHEDULE.
    INTERCHANGE TENTATIVE AND OFFICIAL FIRST? N

    STARTING TO ASSIGN REFERENCE NUMBER 17825

    LAST REFERENCE NUMBER POSTED 18214

    SUBMIT PRINT REQUEST YET? YES
    PRINT REQUEST BEING SUBMITTED FOR FILE =   3076822 MWSPT
    DELIVER OUTPUT TO:
    R G BROWN
    PO BOX 403
    VERNON, NJ 07462

    SPECIAL INSTRUCTIONS:

(E) *294 ITEMS HAVE SHORT-DATED ORDERS. FILE = DIRECTORY*
    COMPONENT = SHORT
    REPLACE IT? YES
    234 ITEMS NEED TO EXPEDITE OPEN ORDERS. POST TO DIRECTORY? YES
    COMPONENT = EXPEDITE
    REPLACE IT? YES
    14 ORDERS MAY LEAD TO OBSOLESCENCE. POST TO DIRECTORY? YES
    COMPONENT = OBSOL
    REPLACE IT? YES
(F) *POST DEPENDENT DEMAND TO THE FORECAST ARRAY? YES*
(G) *PRINT THE NEW SCHEDULE? NO*

    ELAPSED TIME   9M 03.434S
    CPU TIME   1M 31.572S

The details of all the orders generated are not only set up in the data base but also posted to a file from which they can be printed for the stockroom, production planning, purchasing, and other parts of the organization that must act on them. The print request can be submitted now, or several print requests can be accumulated to be processed at one time.

(E) There are three sorts of warning messages printed at the end of the process.
  1. Short-dated orders are those for which the current need date for a new order falls within the freeze period. The schedule date is set at the end of the freeze period, but the planner can save a list of the item file index numbers in a directory so that he can retrieve them and review the problems. Maybe he will want to reschedule some of these items, or he may want to run a small risk of using the planned safety stock.
  2. Expedited orders are orders that are already firm in the schedule, with reference numbers assigned at some earlier planning stage, but for which the need date has moved ahead of the schedule date. The planner can get at any of these items to investigate the problem and decide what to do about it.
  3. With either a minimum lot quantity or a fixed lot quantity, if the new order now planned in the period beyond the freeze will cover the total requirements to the horizon, and leave some projected stock on hand, there is a list of these items to be reviewed for potential obsolescence. The planner may want to cut the order quantity back to avoid ordering more than an all-time supply.

(F) Next the planner usually posts the official dependent demand to the forecast array for forecast reports and for the strategic system.

(G) Finally, the planner may print the detailed schedules for selected items, either at the terminal or on a high-speed line printer.

14.7 SYNTHETIC BILLS OF MATERIALS

The process of exploding top-level requirements through a bill of material can also be exploited to get a forecast of requirements for product lines that have a great deal of variety in the specifications of the product actually delivered to the customer. For example, automobiles can be planned by body style, with a synthetic bill of material that has fractional quantities for each of the optional engines, trim sets, drive lines, and other accessories. That item is never built, of course, with 0.6 of a V-eight engine and 0.4 of a

SYNTHETIC BILLS OF MATERIALS

V-six. But when the forecast for the body style is exploded through such a bill of materials, it does come up with the right requirements for each of the major components and assemblies. The actual product is built to customer specification. So long as there are adequate stocks of each of the components, it is possible to assemble, test, and deliver the product within an acceptable time (see 10.6).

Quite a few different types of capital and consumer durable products can use this concept. Electronic instruments, for example, are built to customer specification, but from a standardized list of components. Cigarette-making machinery is highly standardized. The parts that are affected by the length of the cigarette to be made are specified with one free dimension. Then when a customer orders the machine, a standard bill of materials can call out the right parts list with the right quantities, and for that order the last dimension of the parts affected can be specified for that order.

Alternatively one can set up modular bills of materials for the major subassemblies, with forecasts of requirements one level below the final product. See 10.6 for the safety stock decision rules when the final build schedule is already established.

Whether one has a synthetic bill of materials for prototype end products, or modular bills one level down, it is necessary to capture usage at the module level for statistical forecasting. Specific customer orders in the backlog are exploded and then posted to the assembly level records. For a general discussion of these approaches, see Dave Garwood's article, "Stop: Before You Use the Bill Processor. . . ."

CHAPTER **15**

Shop Floor Control

The principal purpose of all the work on estimating requirements, setting inventory targets, and planning the production schedule is to get goods manufactured on time to be delivered to the customer who is going to pay for them. Therefore an extremely important part of the whole materials management system is the action system that tells the man on the shop floor what he is expected to do towards that goal. There is provision for following the progress of work at every essential step of the process.

15.1 PROCESS ROUTINGS

In most companies there are already three or four process routings. There is the way that the engineer thought a product should be built. There is the way that the accountants accumulate costs. There is the way that the shop actually builds the product. There may even be a different image of reality in the quality control labs. All these descriptions of the process are different, for different purposes. The routing used for production control can be yet another description of the process.

As an example, in one manufacturing company the accountants insist on reports of production at such steps as tumbling, deburring, washing, acid rinse, and plating. So the clerk on the shop floor dutifully fills in standard data in all these slots on the log, every time a lot is through plating and on its way to the next assembly operation. In contrast, my father would buy only one spur, on the grounds that if one side of the horse goes, the other side has to go with it.

The production planning routing can be selective, to identify steps where it is important to plan and measure progress. It can skip over steps that may be in the official procedure for other purposes, which are not necessary for production control. The production process routing should probably include some steps that hardly ever appear on the other types of routing: production control, quality control, receiving, and other operations that do

PROCESS ROUTINGS

not take place on the shop floor but that are nevertheless necessary for the orderly flow of material.

Exhibit 15.1 shows the general format of the information provided in the routing records in the data base for the materials management systems library. There are nine fields to the record, with a separate row for each step to be controlled.

1. Operations sequence number uniquely identifies a step in the process.
2. The department number identifies the group that is to get a daily report of what is wanted and to report actual progress.
3. The setup hours per lot can be used to generate setup costs for economic lot size calculations and for labor standards.
4. The labor grade relates to standard hourly rates for estimating costs and can also summarize the work load by labor grade within department. See, for example, Exhibit 2.8.
5. The direct labor hours per piece develops the total work load for the department by time period, as in Exhibit 2.7.
6. The work center subdivides the work within a department, and could represent a particular machine for loading or a class of similar machines with a more or less interchangeable work force.
7. The days allowed in the operation for move, queue, setup, and run time for a typical lot provide for back scheduling the latest start date at each operation, from either the need date or the schedule date for the job.
8. Five different codes in various combinations are provided to specialize the routing to particular operating environments.
9. The operation can be described briefly to relate it to the more detailed description of the operation on the blue print.

Typical short routings are shown in Exhibit 15.1 for five parts. There can also be standard routing steps before and after the routings for each part number, for example, to allow production planning to release a build order and to verify that the materials have been issued from the stockroom. Since the formal definition of the materials management system is designed to operate in the context of existing systems, sometimes the first and last standard operations are used to allow records from one set of files to be transferred and synchronized with other files.

15.11 Days Allowed

The number of days allowed for an operation is not usually part of a normal manufacturing routing, on the grounds that if one knows the setup hours,

PART NUMBER	DESCRIPTION						DAYS C N P B W	OPERATION
OPNO	DEPT	SETUP	GRADE	HOURS	WKCTR			
49-341-925	PRIMER		FILE INDEX = 138					
10	342	0.00	B	0.006	1020011		1	ELECTRICAL TEST
17	325	0.00	C	0.005	72001611		1	ELECTRICAL TEST
20	325	0.00	C	0.007	72001611		1	ELECTRICAL TEST
50	342	0.00	B	0.162	1020011		1	DISASSEMBLE
60	326	0.00	C	0.025	1020011		1	PACK
70	324	0.00	D	0.014	85029901		1	FINISHED
47-805-263	ROLLER		FILE INDEX = 218					
600	326	0.00	C	0.005	1020011		1	PACK
610	324	0.00	D	0.015	85029901		1	FINISHED
48-115-916	HOUSING		FILE INDEX = 221					
10	342	0.00	B	0.009	1020011		1	SHIM
20	342	1.00	B	0.008	42012684		1	PRESS
30	342	1.00	B	0.016	0		1	ELECTRICAL TEST
40	342	1.00	B	0.035	42012684		1	PRESS
50	326	0.00	C	0.022	1020011		1	PACK
60	324	0.00	D	0.008	85029901		1	FINISHED

41-037-913	WINDSHIELD	| FILE INDEX = 233					
10	326	0.00	C	0.024	1020011	1	PACK
20	324	0.00	D	0.026	85029901	1	FINISHED
45-059-213	WINDSHIELD	| FILE INDEX = 418					
10	326	0.00	C	0.024	1020011	1	PACK
20	324	0.00	D	0.045	85029901	1	FINISHED

OPNO	DEPT	SETUP	GRADE	HOURS	WKCTR	DAYS	CODE	NAME
INITIAL OPERATIONS								
1	320	1	1		10	5	2	RELEASE ORDER
2	320	1	1		20		6	MATLS READY
TERMINAL OPERATIONS								
983	321	1	1		30	2	2	POST STOCK

the lot quantity, and the direct hours per piece, one can compute with great precision to the thousandth of an hour how long it should take to do the job. A great deal of industrial engineering effort has been expended over the years in trying to get similar precision in estimating move and queue times.

There is a practical way to get sufficient accuracy for prodcution planning purpose. Ask the foreman how long he thinks it takes. Use that figure for scheduling initially. After about six months of experience, sit down with the foreman again, with the records of the times that have actually been taken. Increase some of the allowances that have been found to be too short, but decrease most of them in the light of actual experience. After another six months repeat the process.

After a year's experience with such a scheme, the president of the American Thread Company expressed great concern. For years the aisles had been full of cartloads of gaily colored thread and it made the plant rather pretty to look at. The scheduling scheme took out so much work in process that now he could see the floorboards. Some of them would have to be replaced.

There is at all times a check on the total of all the days allowed for the various operations, in that they cannot exceed the lead time that the plant has been using. The man in the shop knows reasonably well how much time is required. Of course he'll ask for more than he really thinks he needs. But once he sees records of the time actually taken, he will usually trust the scheduling system to allow him to work with shorter times, and that will bring the planning process into line with the reduction in work in process that will already have taken place.

As a quick visual check on the consistency of the number of days allowed, Exhibit 15.2 shows the total days allowed for each operation in the routing, with squares representing the accountable time for manufacturing a standard lot quantity, based on the capacity by work center. In the example, operations 10 and 30 have some slack time, but operation 20 requires all of the time allowed to complete a standard lot. If the days allowed were too few, the triangle marking the planned start of the operation would fall somewhere under the line of squares, indicating less than no slack time.

15.12 Codes

The codes provided in the routing, whether for the standard initial and terminal steps or for individual steps for a particular part, customize the procedure to various operating environments. One code suppresses the operation so that while it is in the file, it will not print on the daily work sheet. Other codes indicate nonproduction operations and cost accumulation steps. There is a code for the step at which parts and materials are

Exhibit 15.2

```
ITEM = 2, 39-10-3209; DELUXE WATER FOUNTAIN
FREEZE PERIOD = 13 WEEKS
LOT QUANTITY = 1100 UNITS
SCALE = 3 COIS/DAY
```

```
    IDENT  DESCRIPTION----4----------3----------2----------1----------0

LABOR SCHEDULE:

    999 ORDER COMPLETE                                              ▽
                                                                 △
                                                                 ▽
                                                               [████████]
                                                        |------
    30 INSPECT                                                △
                                                              ▽
                                                      [████████]
    20 PAINT                                        △
                                                    ▽
                                            [████████████]
                                     |------
    10 ASSEMBLE                    △
                                   ▽
                      [████████████████████]
              |-------
   -1 ORDER RELEASE △
                    ▽
                 △
```

LEGEND:
- ▽ OPERATION COMPLETION DATE
- ▨ DAYS LABOR REQUIRED (STD LOT SIZE)
- ooo SETUP DAYS REQUIRED
- |-- SLACK DAYS
- △ SCHEDULED ORDER START TIME

required from the stockroom. Another code allows the daily work sheet to substitute information in the item master for the work center number, so that in the standard production planning operations, for example, the work center can be replaced by the planner or buyer code number.

15.2 DAILY WORK SHEET

The way that the current status of production is shown to each department every day is the work sheet shown in Exhibit 15.3. The report is prepared every morning for each department—the planner can select which departments to include, so there is flexibility in doing special studies. A headline can be printed on each report to convey some special message to the people in the shop or to label a special report.

The list of work to be done can be prepared in quite a number of different sequences. The example shown is sorted by latest start date, so that Mr. Gorham can be sure his people are tackling the most urgent jobs first.

The job is identified by part number and order reference number. The good quantity is the quantity reported as complete from the previous operation. It might be part of a split lot, or the net effect of cumulative yield losses to date. Every once in a while one finds a good quantity that is still equal to the quantity originally scheduled.

What is to be done is indicated by the operation sequence number, together with the standard hours based on the lot quantity and the standard hours per piece. Details of the operation are available to the mechanic in the shop, and have probably been familiar to him for years.

The work sheet shows the latest start date for each operation. However, there may be several operations on the same order in a single department. For example, the 4162 pieces of 33-28-2343 on order reference 10197, the top job on the list, should start operation 10 by 6/28. But operation 20 on the same order is scheduled to start, 9 lines down the report, on 7/05. The real priority for Mr. Gorham is to ensure that operation 30 (16th line) is completed on time, to allow adequate time for other departments. It is not so crucial when operation 10 actually starts.

The name "work sheet" comes from the evolution of this report. Several years ago when development of a complete materials requirements planning system first started, Eric Dammeyer would take a clipboard every day and tour all the departments of Parke-Davis's plant in Detroit. He would note on the work sheet the current status of every open order in the plant: the product identification, the lot number, the current quantity, and the operation now being performed. This report is a direct descendant of that daily tour.

DAILY WORK SHEET

Exhibit 15.3

DEPARTMENT 350   MR GORHAM   SATURDAY, JULY 10, 1976

INCLUDES WORK TO COME FROM OTHER DEPARTMENTS

PART NUMBER	ORDER REFERENCE	GOOD QUANTITY	OPERATIONS SEQUENCE	OPERATIONS NAME	STANDARD HOURS	WORK CENTER	LATEST START
33-28-2343	10197	4,162__	10	ASSEMBLE B	2081.00	1001	6/28/76
33-28-2343	10214	4,096__	10	ASSEMBLE B	2048.00	1001	7/05/76
33-28-2343	10232	6,064__	10	ASSEMBLE B	3032.00	1001	7/06/76
33-28-2343	10249	5,553__	10	ASSEMBLE B	2776.50	1001	7/12/76
33-28-2343	10266		10	ASSEMBLE B	2709.50	1001	7/13/76
33-28-2343	10282		10	ASSEMBLE B	393.00	1001	7/28/76
33-28-2343	10162	34,650__	20	MOUNT GEAR	3465.00	1002	6/22/76
33-28-2343	10180	4,000__	20	MOUNT GEAR	400.00	1002	6/28/76
33-28-2343	10197		20	MOUNT GEAR	416.20	1002	7/05/76
33-28-2343	10214		20	MOUNT GEAR	409.60	1002	7/12/76
33-28-2343	10232		20	MOUNT GEAR	606.40	1002	7/13/76
33-28-2343	10249		20	MOUNT GEAR	555.30	1002	7/19/76
33-28-2343	10266		20	MOUNT GEAR	541.90	1002	7/20/76
33-28-2343	10162		30	FINAL ASSE	3465.00	1050	6/24/76
33-28-2343	10180		30	FINAL ASSE	400.00	1050	6/30/76
33-28-2343	10197		30	FINAL ASSE	416.20	1050	7/07/76
33-28-2343	10214		30	FINAL ASSE	409.60	1050	7/14/76
33-28-2343	10232		30	FINAL ASSE	606.40	1050	7/15/76
33-28-2343	10249		30	FINAL ASSE	555.30	1050	7/21/76
33-28-2343	10266		30	FINAL ASSE	541.90	1050	7/22/76
36-32-6386	10163	4,000__	10	ASSEMBLE	4000.00	2100	6/25/76
36-32-6386	10181	2,000__	10	ASSEMBLE	2000.00	2100	7/01/76
36-32-6386	10198	3,894__	10	ASSEMBLE	3894.00	2100	7/08/76
36-32-6386	10215	3,710__	10	ASSEMBLE	3710.00	2100	7/15/76
36-32-6386	10233	3,870__	10	ASSEMBLE	3870.00	2100	7/16/76
36-32-6386	10250	3,788__	10	ASSEMBLE	3788.00	2100	7/22/76
36-32-6386	10267		10	ASSEMBLE	3815.00	2100	7/23/76
39-82-5503	10192	20,540__	10	ASSEMBLE	10270.00	2150	6/24/76
39-82-5503	10209	15,489__	10	ASSEMBLE	7744.50	2150	7/05/76
39-82-5503	10244	116,799__	10	ASSEMBLE	58399.50	2150	7/09/76
39-82-5503	10226	14,704__	10	ASSEMBLE	7352.00	2150	7/13/76
39-82-5503	10278		10	ASSEMBLE	28358.50	2150	7/16/76
39-82-5503	10261		10	ASSEMBLE	7000.00	2150	7/28/76
37-56-4105	10164	2,000__	10	SOLDER JOI	200.00	3000	7/07/76
37-56-4105	10182	2,431__	10	SOLDER JOI	243.10	3000	7/13/76
37-56-4105	10199	2,000__	10	SOLDER JOI	200.00	3000	7/20/76
37-56-4105	10216	2,282__	10	SOLDER JOI	228.20	3000	7/27/76
37-56-4105	10234	2,103__	10	SOLDER JOI	210.30	3000	7/28/76

During the day a foreman or a scheduler in the department keeps a record of what has been done. He can record an "F" in the blank to indicate that the operation has been finished, and the good quantity is the yield to be reported as available to the next operation.

He can mark a "C" and a quantity to indicate that the order is closed short, and the good quantity has been reduced.

He can mark a "P" and a quantity to indicate that part of the lot is completed and moved to the next operation, but the balance is to be completed on the next report.

If order reference 10197 completes operation 30, then presumably operations 10 and 20 have also been done, and he can mark the "F" down at the sixteenth line of the report.

The idea is that Mr. Gorham for department 350, and the individual people by work center, can see clearly what work they have available to do now, what is coming, and when it should start. In most work centers there is at least one job that should have started before today, and that sort of a job is urgent, to be done as promptly as possible to reserve as much of the time allowed as possible for subsequent operations.

Work center 3000 is nearly caught up, and the subsequent jobs are all for the same part number. In that case one would expect the workman there to run the jobs back to back to save setup costs. But if a work center has several different part numbers, he should be discouraged from running two jobs back to back, if he is pulling forward a noncritical job at the expense of delaying another job that is urgent.

The daily reports provide a credible basis for showing what the schedule is and how much freedom there is to make choices on the shop floor, in a way that most people seem to like. In most instances where people like to run jobs in their own sequence, there simply isn't any believable statement of what the real current urgency is. When they have information about the effect of their work on the rest of the plant, most people will use that information in a positive and constructive way.

15.3 POSTING PROGRESS

At the end of the day, the work sheets are collected and brought back to the production planning office. A clerk can transcribe all the actual progress to the data base quickly through a program that accepts either an order reference number or a reference number and an operations sequence number (Exhibit 1.6). That identifies the job and the place where progress is to be reported. The clerk enters F, P, or C as appropriate to indicate finished, partial, or closed short. In the latter two cases, the computer will also ask for the quantity. Thus the actual progress is reported to the files, and a new work sheet prepared for the next day reflects that progress. If there are any exceptions or problems noted, those cases can be investigated, so that the work shown on the daily report is actually the work that can be seen in the shop.

To post all the work done by several hundred people in the plant in a day, a clerk will usually take less than an hour to bring all the records up to date. The new work sheet, reflecting status as of the close of business yesterday, can be issued within an hour. Hence by the middle of the first shift, the foremen have a complete lineup, reflecting where the work stood as of the end of yesterday's third shift.

OTHER PRIORITY RULES

The production planning department gets a work sheet to see what orders are due to be released and to ensure that the right paper work has been done before the order shows up at the first operation. Quality control should also get a work sheet in order to see what jobs are coming through. There are some plants where quality is a major bottleneck. Because of the expense of the tests, they like to group several lots and run the tests once on all of them. That's fine if the first lot is through testing by the time allowed. But the latest start date, by job by operation, is a good signal as to whether it is reasonable to hold one test to wait for others to be grouped with it.

At the end of posting progress there are two reports prepared for the production planner (Exhibit 1.7). One lists all lots that were reported today as closed short, with the original and current good quantity, and the department and operation on which the loss was reported. If the losses look reasonable they can be accepted. But if anything is seriously wrong, the planner knows immediately that he has a problem to investigate and fix.

The other report lists all jobs that have completed the last operation, and are now posted as on hand ready for use in the files. This report computes a gross yield factor which the planner can use to modify the factor used in planning future lots. At the same time these lots can be flagged for the allocation system (to be discussed in Chapter 17) so that fair shares of the material can be distributed to each stocking location.

The important factor here is rapid feedback of actual progress against plan, so that both the people taking the action in the shop and the planners have the same view of the actual situation. It also means that the data base always reflects current status on all open orders accurately, so that any other reports reflect reality, not just hopes. This procedure also means that the data base reflects the real situation, so new plans will be based on fact.

15.4 OTHER PRIORITY RULES

The work sheet illustrated uses as a priority index the latest start date by operation, back-scheduled from final need or schedule date. It is a fairly stable index that will change as another planning cycle reschedules unlocked orders, but it is also an absolute measure. As time elapses the date automatically becomes more and more urgent. One can see at a glance just how urgent future work will become if the immediate jobs aren't finished to get them out of the way.

There are several other ways of setting priorities on jobs in a shop. Maxwell and Conway at Cornell have done excellent work over the years in investigating a whole range of possible priority rules to see what the consequences are through major simulations (see their *Theory of Scheduling*). Many of the rules tried are based on the value of the job, or the time required at this operation, or the length of the queue ahead of the next operation. All these rules tend to improve one measure of effectiveness, but at the expense of others. Typically measures of effectiveness to be considered include value of work in process, percent of jobs completed on time, maximum time late for jobs not done on time, and labor and machine utilization.

Another set of rules depend on "slack" time (Exhibit 15.2), that is, the difference between the time the job is to be completed and today, less the time that can be accounted for in setup and run times at all uncompleted operations. In a way, the latest start date, based on days allowed at each operation, is a sort of slack-time rule. These rules don't really maximize anything, but they perform well on all measures of effectiveness.

Romeyn Everdale, from Boston, has used a critical ratio index of priority. The numerator of the expression is a measure of availability in terms of the fraction of the work already done to complete the job. The denominator is a measure of need, in terms of stock status related to order point. If the ratio is less than one, the job is urgent. At 1.0 it is on schedule, and over 1 the job could be delayed. It is not obvious quite how much a job should be pulled forward or pushed back, except in relation to other jobs in the shop.

A major difference among all possible kinds of scheduling rules separates those that require feedback of current status from those for which the priority can be established when the job is first released and doesn't change. The simplest, and in many ways the most effective, of these latter rules is "first-come, first-served" as in the case of cars in line for a tollbooth. The operations research profession has built a whole subculture of classifying queues in terms of the discipline for setting relative priorities of different jobs.

There is another large segment of the literature devoted to theoretical models of schedules of N jobs through M machines, arising from an amusing paper by S. M. Johnson, "Optimal Two and Three Stage Production Schedules with Setup Times Included." The results are very pretty when viewed as mathematical theory. However, the case solved so elegantly does not arise often in real factories.

Summary: Computers and People

In a simple business people can hold in their minds all the facts necessary to manage the flow of materials. There is no business so simple that a formal computer system of materials management would be sufficient without people. The role of people is to solve problems, take risks, create answers, and ask questions, out of their store of experience, skill, and judgment. The role of computers is to undertake the calculation according to predefined rules and procedures of various algorithms, including the storage and retrieval of data. If these roles are properly understood then the modern computer can be of enormous benefit in dealing with the computable part of the materials manager's job, to relieve him of tedious calculations so that he will have time and energy to spend on thinking and on dealing with exceptional cases. If these roles are not understood, there is a grave danger of trying to design a computer system that will deal with everything. It is still far beyond our capability to design computer systems with the requisite variety to match the uncertain variation in the environment being controlled. We are making great strides in formalizing great masses of data that can be dealt with by programs. A well-designed library with rich feedback between the computer and the environment can cope with much of the detail. But the computer cannot manage materials flow.

The library being described in this book is based on several principles relevant to the roles of the computer system and the people in the organization. One of them is to provide a modular framework in which various bits and pieces can be modified as necessary to match the real needs of the operating environment. A major advantage of the executable realization is that ideas can be tested in practice. If they are seen to work, use them. Regardless of the theoretical elegance, if they don't help, don't use them.

Another principle is that the formal system should be bent as necessary to appear helpful to people. People are good at matching real variety. This concept involves a whole range of techniques, from ways of trapping bad data on the way into the system in a forgiving method that allows people with judgment to correct it, to flexibility in retrieving and arranging data in reports. Because of the conversational language it is possible to provide for on-line inquiry and editing of any record in the system. However, because of just that freedom of access to the records, there are also provisions for audit trails in all editing functions, so that there is printed copy of what was in the file before it was changed. In the event of a catastrophe, one can always go back to square one before the change was made.

But perhaps the most fundamental concept is that people, given scope for experimenting and risk taking, can be highly creative in dealing with special problems. The more people who contribute creatively to the solution of corporate problems, the more likely it is that the correct answer will be found.

This philosophy should not be interpreted to mean anarchy, with everyone doing his own thing without let or hindrance. It does mean that each echelon of management can define operational objectives and measures of performance, without defining in detail how the work is to be done. People nearer the scene of the action should have scope to try various ways of getting the right job done in the best way at the right time. It helps them enormously to know what measures a good job well done. The wrong measure can maximize accomplishment of unhelpful contributions.

To take a case in point, the daily work sheet does tell, from a more global view, what jobs are available to be done and gives a measure of the relative urgency. It does not dictate an optimum schedule. People in the shop who can see the actual state of the machines, the materials, the tools, and the people can make local decisions within the scope of the priority list. There can be 1001 things that happen in the shop that are relevant to actual delivery of the right product at the right time at the right cost, which cannot in any practical way be captured by a computer. Even if they could be captured, the state of the art has not advanced to the level where we know how to program that information into better decisions.

The theoretical arm of the profession of operations research is refining techniques for many sorts of problems, some of which actually exist in practice. Often the results of this research can be helpful. But in the meantime there are real plants to be run by real people with real products and real problems. The idea of the system is to help those people solve those problems in a practical way. One of the uses of the theory is to discover when it doesn't matter very much which technique is used. If the total system is a balanced attack on the real total situation, there can be immense benefits. If all the effort is put into refining the seventeenth decimal place on one small part of the theory, the flow of materials can get out of control. One theory that is not worth pursuing says a sufficiently elaborate computer can do everything for a company. Creative people with experience and judgment are still needed to take risks and to invent ways of coping with unexpected situations.

SECTION **V**

Physical Distribution

Traditional ways of thinking about the cost of a product include materials, labor, and burden. But that only gets the finished product to the factory door. The cost of getting it to the customer is another appreciable expense. In some consumer products it has been estimated that the physical distribution cost may be as much as the plant cost. Thus there is a growing concern to understand the physical distribution process, in terms that enable a company to manage it well. John Magee, of Arthur D. Little, Inc., has provided an excellent framework for the total system of physical distribution. He points to the inevitability of a service company that combines freight forwarding, warehousing, and inventory management.

Harvey Shycon and John Dowdle of Booz, Allen and Hamilton, have published guidelines for studying the important problem of how many warehouses to have and where to locate them. There are essentially three incompatible functions that field warehouses serve. (*a*) To provide fast service to customers, wholesale druggists have several warehouses in all large metropolitan areas. (*b*) To be able to ship a fair distance at bulk rates, grocery products manufacturers have half a dozen or more regional distribution centers. If there were more such warehouses, the volume through each would be smaller and there wouldn't be the opportunity for bulk shipments. If there were fewer, the distances from the distribution center to the customer, at a higher freight rate, would be too far. (*c*) To accumulate production runs and marshal material for customer needs, many of the machinery manufacturers have plant warehouses. In some cases these warehouses also do some processing, like painting, packaging, and assembling kits.

The National Council of Physical Distribution Management, the Society of Logistics Engineers, and Felix Wentworth in England are very concerned with efficient materials handling, specifically with procedures for selecting—or even negotiating—the best freight rates by various modes of transport. Several operational research groups, especially in England, have been intrigued by optimum routing of trucks and techniques for loading the trucks with the best mix of products.

The United States Navy as well as Robert Camp at Xerox have carried out studies to determine what products can economically be stocked at each location. The results in general show that the greater the rate of usage and the lower the unit price, the greater the number of locations that can afford to stock the item. It also seems to be a general conclusion of this sort of work that although there are logically many combinations of paths through the various available stocking echelons, a relatively small number of standard supply patterns dominate the economics of how to get the item to the ultimate destination (through the three different functional types of warehouses, for example).

Another way of looking at this problem is to turn it around. Instead of asking, "Where can this part be stocked?," ask, "What items can be stocked at this location?"

A feasible way of getting a robust answer to the latter question is to list all stockable parts in descending sequence by the number of calls, or bin trips, per year. The concept is like the distribution by value (Chapter 9) except that the annual usage is expressed not in dollars but in numbers of times that customers have requested the item. There will be a relatively few items at the top of the list which account for a very large fraction of total requests. These items should be stocked at all locations. The argument is based on a marketing concept of service. There is a high probability that when a customer asks for some item, that item is normally stocked at the location nearest him, so that he can get delivery quickly. Since there are costs associated with managing each SKU (stockkeeping unit, a part number in a location), if we can provide that service with the fewest number of discrete items the operating costs will be low.

At the other end of the list there will be a very long list of items that individually have very few calls and in total account for a very small fraction of total customer requests. These items should be stocked (if at all) in only one national location. Since not many customers request them, the delay in getting them from the national location to the customer is not serious. Nor can the transportation and handling costs be significant if there isn't much activity. (We deal in more detail with how to get national parts to local customers in Chapter 16.)

If it makes sense to have regional distribution centers, they can carry the list of items of items in the middle of the range—those with enough activity to warrant stocking in more than one location but not enough to justify the operating costs of managing them in every metropolitan warehouse.

With all the attention that has been placed on the science of physical distribution management, there has been relatively little emphasis on the problem of procedures for replenishing stocks of the standard list of items in the existing chain of field warehouses. Although there may be opportunities to

PHYSICAL DISTRIBUTION

get a better range of products stocked at each location, and to open, close, and move warehouses, those opportunities require major projects and time to accomplish. In the meantime, there are often significant improvements that can be made by managing the flow of material to the warehouses now being used.

Chapter 16 deals with various procedures for replenishing stocks in field warehouses, essentially from the point of view of each regional manager. Chapter 17 considers the merits of techniques that manage the replenishment of all locations from a central knowledge of requirements and stock status. These subjects already offer considerable improvement over naive techniques of inventory control, and the development is proceeding rapidly. That is to say, five years from now this section of the book is more likely to have changed radically than the earlier sections, where the results stem from a great many people's thought over considerable periods of time. But the likelihood that better techniques will be developed should not discourage anyone from exploiting the techniques already developed, to get some pretty impressive improvement of customer service and reduction of investment in field inventories.

CHAPTER **16**

Regional Control

In this chapter we assume there are several field warehouses; these may be company-owned or public warehouses. The range of products to be stocked in each warehouse is established, but the list may change from time to time. The warehouses are considered separately, almost as if they were independent wholesalers or dealers. The replenishment of stocks may be controlled on a central corporate computer, but the logic of the computations considers only the needs of one location at a time. The source of supply for any stocked item is known, and may be either a company plant or an outside vendor.

We want to examine four alternative aspects of the process of getting the right amount of stock of each product into each warehouse at the right time:

Independent orders
Coordinated orders
Planned orders
Search and find

These topics provide a natural progression from the independent wholesaler to a central corporate control over field stocks. Then in Chapter 17 we can consider replenishment methods that are designed to consider the total requirements and stock status of all locations in the decisions of how much and when to ship of what to where.

16.1 INDEPENDENT ORDERS

The simplest case to consider is that of a single item which can be ordered more or less at any time from the source, without regard to the replenishment of other items in the inventory. This is the case of the consumer ordering from Sears, Roebuck, for example, or of the driver filling his car's gas tank. Virtually any of the inventory control techniques described in Chapter 12 could be used. One is the order-point, order-quantity replenishment rule.

16.11 Order Point

Since most of the replenishment techniques require that there be an order point to trigger a new order, let us review the essential elements of that order point. There are three:

1. Forecast of demand. The forecast of requirements for any item can be established by the methods of Section II. The statistical forecast could be an extrapolation of the patterns detected in the past history of demand in that region, or it could be a percentage of a national forecast for the same item. The percentages would probably be based on the recent sales history in all regions and thus would ignore differences in trends and seasonal patterns from region to region. If there is local knowledge of special circumstances, marketing intelligence could be posted to the records to modify the statistical forecast. In a company where the Miami warehouse, for example, ships to South American affiliates as well as to local customers, scheduled demand could be posted to those requirements. In any event, there can be a record of the total expected requirements, item by item, location by location, period by period.
2. The lead time. The lead time from the source to the stocking location is generally known, except for imported materials. If the lead times vary considerably in an unpredictable way, it may be necessary to forecast demand-during-a-lead-time, as described in 8.221. The lead time that is relevant for order points includes the standard allowance for transit time, the administrative time to generate the order and to post receipts after the material arrives, plus the normal interval between shipments or between opportunities to generate new orders. One part of the order point is the forecast of requirements over this lead time.
3. Safety stock. The other component of the order point is the safety stock, as discussed in Chapter 10. Any of the decision rules can be used to compute a safety factor. The safety stock is the product of that safety factor and the standard deviation of the errors in forecasting demand over the lead time. There could, in some circumstances, be justification for setting the safety stock as some quantity of units by management edict. More enlightened thought, however, would explore the exchange of inventory investment for customer service, and pick a tactical choice for the management policy variable that gives a reasonable balance between financial investment and customer service. The decision rule that mini-

INDEPENDENT ORDERS

mizes the aggregate value of back-ordered demand for a given inventory investment (Rule 2) is a logical strategic choice for regional safety stocks. Then the management policy variable is expressed in dimensions of shortages per item per year or, equivalently, the average time between shortage occurrences.

16.12 Reordering

Thus order points can be established for all stocked items. The stock status records keep track of stock on hand, stock due in from the source, any back orders, and hence the available stock. If back orders are treated as a "negative on hand" balance in the records, then the available stock is always the sum of these three components. If the available stock falls to, or below, the order point, it is a signal that a replenishment order should be generated. The test for a new order might be applied whenever demand transactions are posted, which would give the shortest effective lead time. The whole file might be reviewed periodically to report items needing to be replenished. In the latter case, the lead time must be longer by the interval between reviews for reordering. This scheme might be used where the source will accept stock orders only at specified times, or as a crude method for accumulating enough material to order several items from the source at one time, either to earn a quantity discount or to try to achieve some minimum weight to be shipped.

16.13 Order Quantity

When an item is to be reordered, in this independent case, the quantity to order can be computed in either of two ways. The quantity could be fixed, or precomputed like an EOQ, taking account of the concepts covered in Chapter 11 and of any limitations imposed by the source such as minimum order quantities. Alternatively, the decision rules can establish a maximum operating objective, much like the case discussed in Chapter 12 for lumpy demand. Then the current order quantity would be the difference between that objective and the current available stock. Obviously if replenishment orders are always triggered when available stock is precisely equal to the order point, these orders will be the predetermined difference between maximum and minimum levels. But if a single transaction (or all the transactions posted between times when the file is reviewed for ordering) drives the available stock below order point, then the latter procedure restores the deficit. In the long run, somewhat better service is obtained from the max–min type of control than from the fixed order quantity.

You can modify the raw difference between maximum and available stock to get the quantity to be ordered from the source. Round it up to at least the minimum in quantity, time supply, or dollar value. Round it down to stay within maximum limits. Round for reasonable package multiples, like pallets, layers, or cases. If there are quantity discounts, or a special opportunity to buy at a lower price, increase the order quantity as appears economical.

In considering what an economical order quantity is, there is an important difference between material ordered from an outside vendor and material supplied by a plant or factory in the same corporation that owns the field stocks. In the former case, the decision about how much to buy at one time does affect the investment in working stock in the field. Many small orders will increase the annual operating cost to process these orders, but the capital invested in stock as a result of buying for future need will be reduced. Hence the essential assumptions of balancing investment against cost in any of the economical lot size decision rules are pertinent to the environment.

For material being transferred from a corporate plant to a corporate warehouse, however, the corporate investment in working stock was determined when the factory decided on the production quantity. Merely the fact that it has been transferred to a different location does not affect corporate investment. Thus the assumption that more frequent orders reduce inventory investment is not fulfilled in practice.

The argument that there is value added in transporting the material doesn't hold much water either. A year's supply of each product must be shipped to the warehouse over the course of a year, so the cost of transportation will be incurred whether the product is shipped once in total or a dozen times, once a month. Very few corporate accounting systems are sufficiently precise to distinguish the contribution to profits of this difference in the timing of transportation costs.

There is some evidence that the handling costs for straight carloads and straight truckloads (with only one product to be picked, loaded, received, checked, and put away) are less than for cars or trucks containing a mixture of products. It is not clear whether two products per shipment are cheaper to handle than three, but it certainly seems that if there are at least three products in a shipment, the cost of handling a year's supply is very insensitive to the reasonable range of alternatives in the quantity ordered at one time. Although the EOQ formula might look like a convenient way of deciding how much to order at one time, the results are in no sense economical from a corporate point of view, when the same company owns the manufacturing and the field stocks.

For nonstocked items, the base stock system (12.2) is an excellent device for ordering from the source whenever there is a customer demand. The

COORDINATED ORDERS

base stock level is always zero—it defines an item that is not in the range of parts normally stocked. Depending on the environment, the item can be shipped from the source to the remote location either on the next normal shipment or on an immediate emergency shipment. If the demand is sufficiently urgent, the source may ship directly to the customer.

16.2 COORDINATED ORDERS

A more usual situation than independent ordering of individual products is when a whole list of items is supplied from the same source, which again may be either an outside vendor or a company plant. There are three possible schemes for triggering the need for a replenishment order and the list of items to be included on this order.

1. Order points. A naive scheme would be to establish order points, as in the case of independent orders, and accumulate a list of all items for which available stock is below order point, on periodic reviews of the file. The interval between reviews could be established by experience with how long it takes to accumulate an economical shipment.
2. Can-order points. Professor Edward Silver, of the University of Waterloo, has suggested "can-order" points. If the available stock for some item reaches order point, a replenishment order is triggered. Now all other products supplied by the same source are reviewed. For each of them there is a second order point, higher than the normal one. If the available stock for any other item is below this "can-order" point, the item is included in the shipment. Because so many products get ordered earlier than needed, service will be higher (with larger inventory investment) than predicted in the independent case. Hence the normal order point is usually set at a more modest level. The mathematical theory of establishing and evaluating these can-order points has been published by Professor Silver; see the list of articles in the Bibliography.
3. Projected service. A third method, incorporated into IBM's Wholesale IMPACT system, is to project the available stock a lead time into the future. The lead time in this case must include the whole transit lead time, the interval between shipments, and the administrative time between reviews.

We can estimate the expected shortage if we don't order each product now but wait until the next review period. The total shortage for all products can than be accumulated in some standard measure, like dollars, and when that figure exceeds a threshold, the whole list of items is ordered.

In this way a very minor item in the product line is unlikely to trigger a replenishment order, but any potential shortage of a major item will.

For coordinated orders, the interval between shipments from the source can be computed with the joint-order formulas developed in 11.07. Some slow-moving items on the list may be ordered only once every k shipments, to avoid incurring the minor cost of including another line item on the order. The major setup cost in this case would be the costs of processing any order, including receiving inspection and accounts payable. The minor changeover cost would be the nominal amount of cost incurred for marginal additions to the order. If one orders from an outside vendor there is a very important difference in the assumption about inventory investment from the case where the supplier is within the same corporation.

The target for ordering is a supply that will last until the subsequent shipment arrives. For the minor items, it is a supply that will last some multiple of that interval. The net amount to be ordered is the difference between that target and the current available stock. If the available stock is already sufficient to last until the next shipment, the item is not included in the order at all. Hence if a minor item was ordered last time with enough to last for, say, four shipments, the stock on hand now will be large enough that the item is omitted entirely.

For the items that do have to be ordered, the difference is rounded, as before, for time supply, dollar, and quantity limits.

16.3 PLANNED ORDERS

Both the preceding systems have some appeal of simplicity and rationality when considered from the point of view of the manager of an individual regional warehouse. It looks as though he can operate as an independent wholesaler. However, when a corporation looks at the sum total of all the regional warehouses, there are some difficulties with these procedures. For one thing, the total quantity ordered may not be a good shipping quantity. Perhaps the ordering warehouse has carefully considered weight and space for a standard truck, but the carrier has supplied a short trailer, or an extra long one. Or there might be two or more stocking locations along the same route, and the individual warehouses cannot easily plan for drop shipments. Drop shipments may increase the lead time because of longer transit times, but at the same time reduce the total lead time because it is possible to make more frequent shipments to each destination along the route. The point is that individually generated orders from the regions cannot coordinate shipments with some of the practical considerations of planning efficient and economical transporation.

PLANNED ORDERS

Another sort of problem is the load imposed on the supplying plant. If the various regions order whatever they want whenever they want it, the total requirement on the plant can very well be a feast-or-famine situation. Sometimes there are large total orders and at other times nothing at all. A manufacturer who sells to independent dealers who order this way will have some difficulty in forecasting the requirements. Thus either he has to carry substantial investment in finished stocks, or the lead times will occasionally be quite long when he has to stunt through production schedules to meet unusual demand. In either case, in the long run, the cost to the customer increases.

A scheme that is beginning to find some favor in practice is to apply the materials requirements planning concepts of 13.41 at the regional warehouse level. The same procedure applies both to independent dealers ordering from vendors and to company warehouses and distribution centers.

For each product in each stocking location, the time-phased net requirements are established. The gross requirements are the forecasts by period (statistical model, plus marketing intelligence, plus scheduled backlog). Against this one can offset stock on hand (above order point) and stock already on order from the source. From that information one can compute the need date for receipt of the next shipment for that product. The latest ship date is one (transit) lead time earlier.

The quantities to be ordered can be generated as a string of notional orders extending to a reasonable planning horizon. Ideally each customer would send to the source a string of net requirements by period. Then the source can accumulate these requirements into the total need and plan reasonable manufacturing lots. However, if the concepts of the economical balance between ordering and holding costs apply, each region can accumulate its time-phased net requirements into lot quantities, with associated need dates.

The concept of the "blanket order" on a vendor is along these lines. The near-term orders, due within a normal lead time, are considered frozen. When a new order is released each period, one more period is frozen. Beyond that time, the notional orders are for information and planning only and may be changed in subsequent releases. In some cases, limits may be imposed that notional orders will not be changed unless the quantity required changes by more than, say, 10%, or unless the need date changes by at least one planning period. The argument is that cutting down on changes reduces paper work and simplifies planning at the source.

A counter argument is that requirements have in fact changed in the field. If that change is suppressed and not reported to the plant, there may be some long-lead-time consequences that will cause difficulty later when the changed requirement is reported with less time to react to it. With modern data processing the problem of processing current notional orders routinely does not impose the need for limiting change that may have been the case in manual methods. Current accurate information of true needs in the field is very valuable in production planning.

If this procedure is to be followed, the field requirements are posted as scheduled backlog, thus completely eliminating the need for the supplier to forecast at all. Now the source plant has complete information of needs by location, with a proper netting of stock on hand and in transit, and the local order point. The dual accounting scheme described in 13.3 can be exploited to permit the plant the freedom of planning really economical manufacturing runs, whereas the field accounting record of finished goods is more in line with the true marketing needs in the fields. Goods produced in advance of need can be distributed so as to make economical shipments and to exploit the cubic feet available in the field. The investment is still charged to the plant, but the material may actually be in those warehouses.

The meaning of expediting carries over in this case as well. The regional stocks are based on net requirements outside the normal lead time, which is long enough to allow for the preferred mode of shipment, such as rail cars, or even barge to the West Coast. The safety stocks included in the normal order point are sufficient to buffer reasonable variations in customer requirements around the forecast over that lead time. But when an abnormal demand arises, it would be indicated by a need date within the freeze period. This might be a signal for a shipment by some premium mode, like air freight. The user (regional warehouse) would of course be charged with the extra expense of this premium freight to meet a need outside normal forecast.

16.4 SEARCH AND FIND

From time to time the stocks in the field will get out of balance. One location may need more material to meet current demand, and others may have an excess. A central corporate group can monitor the relativel stock position to transfer the excesses to supply the deficiencies in lieu of making more. This concept does, of course, require that there be a single central record at which stock status and requirements are maintained currently. Only a few years ago there was no practical way of getting this information currently and accurately. Now that WATS lines are prevalent for data communication and the concept of distributed processing is creeping into computer systems, it is becoming very practical to maintain such a central record.

The central records of local requirements are easy. In fact one of the jus-

SEARCH AND FIND 341

tifications for a date processing network is to have a rather powerful host computer that can do the mathematical work of statistical forecasting better than can be done practically on the small machines in each region used for order processing. Furthermore, because statistical forecasts are revised at rather long intervals (like a month), there is not much sensitivity to minor delays in accumulating and reporting the demand data.

Stock status is another problem. The reason for search-and-find procedures is that stock status is far from the planned balance, because of unexpected demands and receipts. Such information must be reported from the field. To be useful, it should be reported on a reasonably current basis. In some companies this means a daily feed as of the close of business. In others it may be as of the end of a week, with a delay of a several days in getting it all posted.

There are two methods in common use. One transmits only transactions, to post a perpetual inventory balance at the central computer. There is need periodically to reconcile the inventory balances, not only the book inventory with the physical stock on hand, but also between the two book inventories maintained regionally and centrally. The other extreme is to transmit the region's book inventory periodically, which has accumulated the net effect of all transactions since the last transmission. The latter method has the advantage of being insensitive to delays or even losing a whole transmission. There are some data processing and communications cost trade offs, but it is always surprising to hear the rule of thumb that if revisions are to be posted to more than quite a small percentage of a file, it is just as cheap to post the entire file.

At any rate, let us stipulate that there is available a reasonably current and accurate record that shows the requirements and stock status for every SKU.

16.41 Least-Cost Redistribution

To take a tangible case, let's assume there are six warehouses: a master, Indianapolis, New York, Atlanta, Denver, and Los Angeles. From a comparison of stock status against requirements, the planner has decided that the master could ship 20, New York 20, and Denver 15 pallets. Atlanta needs 5, Indianapolis needs 30, and Los Angeles needs 20.

The methods of computing these relative needs and surpluses are covered in more detail in Chapter 17. For the moment let us assume that the latter three locations have customer orders and no stock, and the first three have stock in excess of normal order point. It is important that the total of the amounts available to ship exactly equal the 55 pallets needed elsewhere.

The ancient practical method is for the locations needing stock of this item to scout around by telephone until they find some. Often the procedures might in fact generate orders to make at least 55 more pallets at the source to fill in the deficiencies.

As managers begin to take a closer look at the consequences of these sorts of action, it has become apparent that it is better to send material from the locations that have too much to the locations that need more. A common practice is to set up a list of alternative locations in a standard sequence, so that Atlanta would always try to get material from Indianapolis before asking Denver or Los Angeles. The ranking of the alternative locations is usually based on the normal transportation cost from the source to the destination—search for the cheapest one first. When only one location needs more stock this approach has a certain intuitive appeal. But for the case in hand, three of the locations need more stock, and three have some to send out.

Exhibit 16.1 shows the six locations and the relative amounts they need or can supply. Clearly Indianapolis should get as much as it can from the master, and Los Angeles should use Denver's surplus. But there isn't enough to go around. If you study the map for a few minutes you can probably work out something that looks reasonable.

In the normal course of events the planner won't have time to draw maps for each problem, and the distances on a map can be misleading. But the objective is clear. Select the sources that are to send material and the desti-

Exhibit 16.1

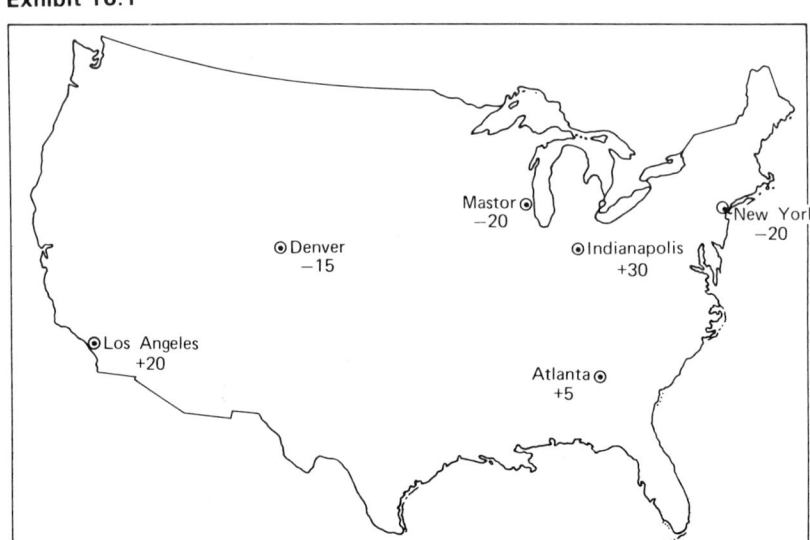

SEARCH AND FIND

Exhibit 16.2

					COST	
Master	0	9	40	35	50	100
Indianapolis	35	0	70	50	90	200
New York	160	70	0	85	185	290
Atlanta	140	50	80	0	140	220
Denver	200	90	190	140	0	110
Los Angeles	420	200	300	220	120	0

S←COST $\underline{LPTRANS}$ −20 30 −20 5 −15 20

Master	0	15	0	0	0	5	20
Indianapolis	0	0	0	0	0	0	0
New York	0	15	0	5	0	0	20
Atlanta	0	0	0	0	0	0	0
Denver	0	0	0	0	0	15	15
Los Angeles	0	0	0	0	0	0	0
	0	30	0	5	0	20	55

nations to which each is to ship in such a way as to minimize the total transportation cost. At the same time, don't plan to ship more than a source has available, nor less than a destination needs (since the total excess precisely balances the total need). The problem is a classical one in linear programming, known as the transportation algorithm.

We need to know the costs per unit of shipping from each possible source to every possible destination. The matrix COST in Exhibit 16.2 shows the costs, in cents per pound.

There is one row for each of the six locations, in a standard order, and one column for each location in the same order. The costs are based on normal shipping practice. Since we are dealing with a single product at a time, the costs can be expressed in any sort of unit, and the total expense will be proportional to the number of pallets shipped.

The function $\underline{LPTRANS}$ takes the cost matrix as its left argument, and a vector of relative requirements as the right argument. Negative quantities correspond to sources, and positive ones to destinations, in the same sequence as the rows of COST. The function produces a matrix of the amounts to be shipped (by rows) to the destinations (by columns).

The programs necessary to do the computations are displayed in Exhibit 16.3. For all their apparent complexity, they are relatively fast to execute.

Exhibit 16.3

```
∇LPTRANS[□]∇

    ∇ S←COST LPTRANS VECT;A;B;C;DELTA;EC;ER;G;H;I;IC;IR;I1;J;J1;K;MAX;N;P;RI;U;V;X
[1]   VECT←L0.5+VECT × IR←ιR+ρA←(ER←VECT<0)/-VECT
[2]   IC←ιC+ρB←(EC←VECT>0)/VECT × COST←ER/EC/COST × MAX←10×⌈+/|VECT
[3]   S←(ρCOST)ρ0 × V←L↑COST-⍟(⍴COST)ρU←L/COST
[4]   RI←ρJ←1+L|(X←((,COST=U∘.+V)/ιR×C)-1)+C × K←1 × J←K+C|X
[5]   L1:S[I[K];J[K]]←⌈/0,L/(A[I[K]]-+/S[I[K]];]),B⌈J[K]]-+/S[;J[K]] × →(RI≥K←K+1)/L1
[6]   G←(2ρN+R+C+2)ρ0 × G[1+IR;1+R+IC]←(MAX×COST=U∘.+V)-S
[7]   G[1+R+IC;1+IR]←⍟S × G[1;1+IR]←A-+/S × G[1+R+IC;N]←B-+/S
[8]   L2:DELTA←LPNETFLOW × →(0=+/1+DELTA)/L3
[9]   H←L/L/COST[I1;J1]-U[I1+(DELTA[1+IR]>0)/IR]∘.+V[J1+(DELTA[R+1+IC]=0)/IC]
[10]  U[I1]←U[I1]+H × V[J1]←V[J1]+(~IC∊J1)/IC]-H × G←G×G≠MAX
[11]  G[I1;J1]←G[I1;J1]+MAX×(G[I1+1+IR;J1+1+R+IC]=0)∧COST=U∘.+V × →L2
[12]  L3:S←S+ER↓EC\L0.5+(MAX×COST=U∘.+V)-G[1+IR;1+R+IC]
    ∇

∇LPNETFLOW[□]∇
    ∇ DELTA←LPNETFLOW;F;FLOW;GAMMA;I;I1;J;K;R;STAGE
[1]   FLOW←0
[2]   L1:DELTA←(⌈/⌈/G),(¯1+ρGAMMA←Nρ(STAGE←(ιN)≤1)[N])ρ0
[3]   L2:I←(ρR←(STAGE=K+⌈/STAGE)/ιN)[1]
[4]   L3:→(0=ρJ←((DELTA=0)∧G[I1+R[I];]>0)/ιN)/L4
[5]   DELTA[J]←G[I1;J]⌊DELTA[I1] × GAMMA[J]←I1
[6]   L4:→((ρR)≥I←I+1)/L3
[7]   →(0=ρI+((DELTA>0)∧STAGE=0)/ιN)/0 × →(DELTA[N]>0)/L5
[8]   STAGE[I]←K+1 × →L2
[9]   L5:FLOW←FLOW+F←DELTA[J+N]
[10]  L6:I←GAMMA[J] × G[I;J]←G[I;J]-F × G[J;I]←G[J;I]+F × →(L1,L6)[1+1<J←I]
    ∇
```

Some of the methods do take advantage of APL which might be hard to transfer to another language. However, there are standard FORTRAN subroutines available from several sources to accomplish the same result.

The results show that the master warehouse should ship 15 pallets to Indianapolis and 5 to Los Angeles. New York should ship 15 to Indianapolis and 5 to Atlanta, and Denver should ship all its excess to Los Angeles.

More to the point, Los Angeles can get 5 from the master warehouse at a unit transportation cost of 100, and 15 from Denver at a unit transportation cost of 110. Indianapolis is entitled to 2 shipments, 15 from the master at 9 cents, and 15 from New York at 70 cents. Clearly it would make sense to ship one of these amounts to cover current needs first, and to choose the cheaper. If the need continues, then a second shipment can use the supply available at the other source. However, conditions may change so that in a few days a different allocation will be preferable.

The same mechanics can be invoked even when the planner does not intend to ship the full quantity to rebalance stocks completely. Orders received from customers at a destination could be referred to the best source to be filled directly from there, until the proper quantity has been used up. Note that the demand should be posted to the warehouse that normally would have served the customer, to record a basis for forecasting

SEARCH AND FIND

future requirements. The shipment will be deducted from stock on hand at the source, but will not show as demand history for forecasting there. How each of the two warehouse managers gets "credit" for the shipments and the sale and the profits is a matter for accounting management, not materials management. The motivation behind all the systems and procedures described in this book is to get the job done properly, not to worry about the artificial ways that accountants keep score. Too often minor officials worry about the score to the exclusion of getting the total job done correctly.

There are some other options when there is an imbalance. If more stock is going to be available from the normal source within a reasonable time, the demand might be back ordered. In some cases it is possible to find in the same location a substitute product that will fill the customer's need. All that the formal analysis can do is to compute quickly the fair shares that could be transshipped, if transshipment is appropriate. In most cases a planner with judgment, experience, and a willingness to take certain risks should make his own decision, based on the facts at his disposal. The analysis of shipping costs is only one of those facts.

CHAPTER **17**

Central Control

In some companies the word "allocation" has an implicit connotation that something has gone wrong. To "put the customers on allocation" means that there isn't enough stock to satisfy everyone, and somehow that means that the production planning process hasn't worked quite right. A less pejorative use of the concept involves three elements: (*a*) some finite resource, (*b*) division among a number of activities, and (*c*) an orderly procedure for making the division. The finite resource can be the stock available for a product, to be divided among stocking locations or customers, which represent the activities. The available stock doesn't have to be in short supply—it could be just at planned levels or even too high. But in any case it is a finite supply. The orderly process of dividing up that stock involves a decision rule of some sort. Some ways of allocating stock have better consequences than others.

In this chapter we consider ways in which a central corporate materials management system can allocate stock routinely among field distribution centers, with the primary objective of getting the best possible total service from the inventory that is in the system. The production planning system controls how much stock there is, on the basis of the requirements and the strategic objectives for various elements of the inventory. There may have been problems in execution so that there is less stock than one wants, or it may have been economical to produce in advance of need so that there is more stock than one needs. But now that the stock is in the system, it should be used to get the best possible service to customers through the stocking locations: field warehouses and distribution centers.

By the end of the chapter we shall apply the same structure of allocation to dividing another finite resource (truck capacity) among different activities (products going to the same destination), and consider several criteria for making that sort of an allocation.

When the regions determine their own requirements independently of each other, there is no assurance that the total of those requirements will match the stock that is available. When the requirements are generated as

NATIONAL SAFETY STOCK

time-phased net requirements, then it is possible for the production plan to cover them with greater precision, but still there is the problem of what to do if the actual stock is greater or less than plan.

This chapter describes procedures that can be used to "push" stock out to the field, instead of allowing the field to "pull" in what they need. The primary purpose of these procedures is to use what is actually available, regardless of whether the plan was good or bad and whether the execution followed the plan or not.

Some of the available stock is reserved centrally as a national safety stock. The remainder is divided among the stocking locations in some equitable way. The process of generating fair shares looks at each product in turn, to divide it among locations. When the list of what can be shipped is known, then one looks at each destination, and makes up economical shipments from among those products. The purpose of the national safety stock is to have more material available later to reallocate (before the next production lot is delivered) since actual usage in each region will be different from the forecast of requirements used in computing the first allocation.

The national safety stock is held at a master warehouse, which could be the plant warehouse, or for purchased materials could be a warehouse more or less in the center of the total market. For each product there is one master warehouse, but the locations may be different for different products.

There are some variations on this theme. For example, the Federal Supply Service and International Harvester Parts Distribution both compute national safety stocks but distribute them among the stocking locations, with provisions for referring orders (see 16.4) when one location runs short.

17.1 NATIONAL SAFETY STOCK

Each regional stocking location will have a reorder point for each of the products it stocks. The method for computing that reorder point was described in 16.11, on the basis of the forecast of local requirements. The relevant lead time for central control is the transit time from the master warehouse to the satellite in question, plus the interval between truck loads (or other form of shipment), plus the administrative times for generating the orders centrally and for posting the stock as on hand after receipt at the satellite. The safety stock in the regional reorder point is the product of the standard deviation and some safety factor. The safety factor can be computed from any of the decision rules discussed in Chapter 10, but Rule 2 is particularly recommended, since it maximizes the value of demand filled from the stock on hand.

The national safety stock is provided to ensure that the satellite can always get what it needs to fill in, if its available stock reaches reorder point before the next production lot. In a sense, the national safety stock protects the production schedule, rather than protecting customer service. In every manufacturing process it is possible to expedite some reasonable number of orders and get them delivered to stock in less than standard lead time. Even with very rigid manufacturing cycles, such as fermentation and heat treating, there are ways of expediting the packaging and inspection processes. The emphasis is on the "reasonable" number of orders. If too many orders are short-dated or expedited, the whole production scheduling process breaks down and one can't be sure of getting anything on time. The work sheets (15.2) provide a very orderly way of changing priorities in all operating departments on the basis of current need. There is some hope of getting the most crucial jobs done early, because the work sheet automatically also moves back work that is no longer needed so urgently. However, even with these procedures, the schedule must not be changed on very many orders.

The national safety stock is established to meet the needs of the field that can't be met by expediting. The safety stock is based on the standard deviation of the errors in forecasting national demand over the production freeze period. That standard deviation is not related in any obvious way to the standard deviations of regional forecast errors, although the national forecast will be very close to the sum of the regional forecasts for any product. The procedures described in Section II allow for a national forecast, based on total demand, and the measurement of the standard deviation of those errors.

The safety factor could be computed from any of the decision rules described in Chapter 10, but Rule 5 is particularly recommended since it minimizes the number of potential shortage occurrences for a given inventory investment. Since the purpose of the national safety stock is to protect enough of the unforeseen variations in requirements so that only a reasonable number of products need be expedited, this rule will generate a given planned number of short-dated orders with the minimum inventory investment.

In a sense this is an "extra" safety stock in the system, in addition to the safety stocks already in the regional reorder points. However, it is not duplicating coverage, since it has a different purpose. Regional safety stocks protect customer service. National safety stock protects the production schedule. If the national safety stock were not there, then the satellite stocking locations could not be sure of getting replenished in the normal lead time—there might be a shortage at the source, which would increase the effective lead time. Even worse, the lead times would appear variable and unpredictable to the stocking locations. That would increase their need for safety stock to achieve any particular desired level of service.

Kenneth F. Simpson showed in his article "In-Process Inventories" that to give a desired level of service to the ultimate customer with the minimum inventory, all risks should be taken at the last stage of distribution. At every intermediate echelon perfect service should be given. That perfect service comes partially from having a safety stock and partially from getting selected orders delivered from earlier stages in less than normal lead time.

17.2 TRIGGERING ALLOCATIONS

There are several ways in which an allocation can be triggered.

1. When new production is received from the source, fair shares can be sent directly to the field. If the manufactured material has to come into a central warehouse location for painting, packaging, and kitting, then the allocation is obviously triggered at the end of that process. Where the vendor can ship directly to the satellite location, then the allocation may have to be computed before the actual delivery time, to allow time for getting instructions to the vendor. In some cases, the allocation may be calculated when the order is sent to the vendor, if his lead times are short. But when the vendor has long lead times, the production planning process can determine the total quantity needed, but the quantity by destination can be computed nearer to the time of distribution, to take account of changes in forecasts and stock status during the intervening period. If the vendor has regional manufacturing or distribution, there may be some advantage to computing the allocation at the time the material is ordered, so that he can deliver from his closest source of supply. Let the vendor get the material transported rather than bringing it in centrally to ship back to a point next door to one of his warehouses.

2. Whenever the available stock (on hand, plus in transit, less back orders) for any product in the field reaches the satellite reorder point, then the stock should again be allocated. Usually there will be some stock at the master warehouse, and a fair share of that material can be sent to the location that needs more. This is a particular instance where central control has some major benefits over local control. If a warehouse orders a standard quantity when it needs more, the central stock may be able to accommodate the first one or two warehouses that order. But soon all the central stock is gone, and locations that reach order point too late may find there is none left.

The process of allocating fair shares from a central view of total stock status and requirements ensures that whenever one location needs more, enough stock is reserved to cover the reasonable requirements at other locations.

3. Ideally one could wait until available stock reaches order point before reallocating. However, in the course of posting the stock status, to compare status against reorder point, one might just as well compute an allocation for every item that has had a demand transaction. As we shall see, part of the allocation process computes a latest ship date, like the need date discussed in 13.21. If a location could have a fair share of what is available, but doesn't need it very urgently, that item will be well down on the priority list for shipment. But if it is useful to make up weight or cube in a truck that is about to be sent with more urgent items, then it is available on the list for the traffic planners to use.

4. Allocations can be computed at regular intervals, as a plan for what will be shipped in the future. In this case the allocation not only considers what is actually in the system, but also certain lots from the production schedule that are due to arrive within the planning period. The planning process is a sort of iterative simulation. The first allocation is based on stock actually available. Then the point in time corresponding to "now" moves ahead, and the production that is scheduled to be completed is added to the available, with a new allocation. One can carry this process on for several periods, but the allocations are more uncertain, because production may differ from schedule and field demand may differ from forecast.

17.3 LATEST SHIP DATE

In Chapter 13 we developed the notion of a need date for the next production lot. Start with the planned target stock, and accumulate the total requirements period by period. Against that cumulative gross requirement offset the stock now on hand, plus the firm orders due period by period. Project the availability as the cumulative production minus the cumulative gross requirements. The need date for the next manufacturing lot is the date when the availability goes from a positive to a negative balance.

The example in Exhibit 17.1 sets up a very simple situation for five locations, each with a constant daily sales rate to represent the forecast of total requirements. The cumulative gross requirements shown are the reverse of projected availability: stock on hand (nothing is assumed to be in transit) is subtracted from the cumulative forecast. Region 1 needs to receive more stock by day 6. Region 2 needs more by day 3.

FAIR SHARES

Exhibit 17.1

```
              FAIR
DAILY FORECAST RATES = 1 2 3 4 5
5 ORDER POINTS = 10 12 14 16 18
5 STOCK ON HAND = 15 16 17 18 19

SAT           CUMULATIVE NET REQUIREMENTS
DAYS =     1   2   3   4   5   6   7   8   9  10  11  12  13  14  15  16  17  18  19  20

   1     ⁻5  ⁻4  ⁻3  ⁻2  ⁻1   0   1   2   3   4   5   6   7   8   9  10  11  12  13  14  15
   2     ⁻4  ⁻2   0   2   4   6   8  10  12  14  16  18  20  22  24  26  28  30  32  34  36
   3     ⁻3   0   3   6   9  12  15  18  21  24  27  30  33  36  39  42  45  48  51  54  57
   4     ⁻2   2   6  10  14  18  22  26  30  34  38  42  46  50  54  58  62  66  70  74  78
   5     ⁻1   4   9  14  19  24  29  34  39  44  49  54  59  64  69  74  79  84  89  94  99

TOT     ⁻15   0  15  30  45  60  75  90 105 120 135 150 165 180 195 210 225 240 255 270 285

LATEST SHIP DATES: 6 3 2 1 1

NATIONAL ON HAND = 80
ALLOCATION COVERS 6 DAYS BEYOND ORDER POINT.
FAIR SHARE QUANTITIES = 1 8 15 22 29

NATIONAL ON HAND = 50
ALLOCATION COVERS 4 DAYS BEYOND ORDER POINT.
FAIR SHARE QUANTITIES = ⁻1 4 9 14 19
DROP OUT SATELLITES 1
ALLOCATION COVERS 4 DAYS BEYOND ORDER POINT.
FAIR SHARE QUANTITIES = 0 4 9 14 19

NATIONAL ON HAND = 15
ALLOCATION COVERS 2 DAYS BEYOND ORDER POINT.
FAIR SHARE QUANTITIES = ⁻3 0 3 6 9
DROP OUT SATELLITES 1 2
ALLOCATION COVERS 1 DAYS BEYOND ORDER POINT.
FAIR SHARE QUANTITIES = 0 0 0 2 4
DROP OUT SATELLITES 1 2 3
ALLOCATION COVERS 1 DAYS BEYOND ORDER POINT.
FAIR SHARE QUANTITIES = 0 0 0 2 4

NATIONAL ON HAND =
```

The latest ship date is one standard lead time earlier than this need date. Hence the first step in any allocation is to compute, for all locations, the latest ship date, offset from the need date. If a location has a great deal of stock, that latest ship date may be far in the future. In normal cases, the need dates will be something like a lead time in the future, so the latest ship dates will be in the next few days or weeks. We shall use that latest ship date as a priority index in planning actual shipments to each location.

17.4 FAIR SHARES

The next step is to compute the fair shares that each location deserves. The example in Exhibit 17.1 is primarily used as a teaching exercise, to explore what happens with different amounts of stock available (for whatever reason). If the national stock on hand is 80 units, it will cover the total field requirements through day 6, but not through day 7. Hence the fair shares would be the list of cumulative gross requirements for day 6.

The program allows one to pick another level of stock to see how that would be allocated. If there are 50 units available to be allocated, they cover through day 4, but not day 5. The first allocation allocates a negative quantity to location 1, which already has enough to cover beyond day 4, and conceptually could give up one piece if that is as far as we want to cover. However, the logic drops location 1 from the exercise, and again finds that the 50 units will cover through day 4.

In the third case, where there are only 15 available, the first step covers two days beyond order point, but two locations already have more than that. They are dropped. The 15 units now cover one day but not two. In this case a third location doesn't need any, so it is dropped, and the allocation covers the other two locations to two days' supply beyond the order point.

The output from one of the programs in the library designed for actual operations is shown in Exhibit 17.2. Based on the same comparison of what is available against what is needed, the program computes a need date and backs it off by the lead time to get a latest ship date. The fair share quantity for the 39-10-3209 fountain will cover each of the three locations to 57 days' supply beyond the order point. In these computations, of course, the forecast is not based on a simple daily average but is interpolated from total requirements using the scheme illustrated in Figure 13.2. The stock on hand and in transit to each location are shown for information, along with the order point.

When some location is already covered to more than the fair share beyond the order point, a note is printed to inform the planner. For example, Denver has 117 pieces more than enough to cover 57 days beyond the order point. Since there is enough to satisfy the other locations, nothing in particular would be done about that excess.

Consider, however, the 37-36-0819 spray at the bottom of Exhibit 17.2. There is very little on hand nationally, which is not enough to bring New York up to its order point quantity. Three other locations have a total of 91 pieces in excess of the fair share supply. For the present New York does have some stock, and they can be given the last 50 pieces available at the master warehouse. But soon Broadview's stock may have to be used to meet New York's demand. The procedures would then be based on the search-and-find techniques for rebalancing described in Chapter 16, and carried out earlier than the distributor would usually start calling his friends when he runs out of stock.

Exhibit 17.2

```
39-10-3209     FOUNTAIN |  FILE INDEX = 2

MASTER ON HAND =              2,536
NATIONAL SAFETY STOCK =       1,421
ALLOCATION COVERS TO 57 DAYS SUPPLY BEYOND THE ORDER POINT.

LOCATION CODE      ON HAND   IN TRANSIT   ORDER PT   QUANTITY   FAIRSHARE   SHIP BEFORE

BROADVIE   110       43                                100          880       7/21/76
NEW YORK   200      221         250          138       60           66        9/20/76
LOS ANGE   500      593                      250      156          163        9/08/76

     TOTAL          857         250          388      316        1,109

LOCATION CODE      EXCESS

DENVER,    400      117

TOTAL               117


37-62-1981     FURNACE |  FILE INDEX = 3

MASTER ON HAND =              426
NATIONAL SAFETY STOCK =       136
ALLOCATION COVERS TO 47 DAYS SUPPLY BEYOND THE ORDER POINT.

LOCATION CODE      ON HAND   IN TRANSIT   ORDER PT   QUANTITY   FAIRSHARE   SHIP BEFORE

BROADVIE   110       -14        200                    100          148       8/20/76
ATLANTA,   300      117                       47       132          139       8/05/76

     TOTAL          103         200           47       232          287

LOCATION CODE      EXCESS

NEW YORK   200       52
LOS ANGE   500       81

TOTAL               133


37-36-0819     SPRAY |  FILE INDEX = 6

MASTER ON HAND =               50
NATIONAL SAFETY STOCK =        915
ALLOCATION COVERS TO 0 DAYS SUPPLY BEYOND THE ORDER POINT.

LOCATION CODE      ON HAND   IN TRANSIT   ORDER PT   QUANTITY   FAIRSHARE   SHIP BEFORE

NEW YORK   200       50                      172       48           50        7/15/76

     TOTAL           50                      172       48           50

LOCATION CODE      EXCESS

BROADVIE   110       50
DENVER,    400       14
LOS ANGE   500       27

TOTAL                91
```

17.5 INSUFFICIENT STOCKS

There will not always be sufficient stock to meet everyone's needs. Let us now consider what happens when the total stock in the system, at all locations, is not enough to bring stock up to order point.

The example in Exhibit 17.3 deliberately picks a quantity of 14, which is less than enough to cover the requirements up to order point, shown in the column corresponding to day 0.

The program now asks for the replenishment lead times. Based on the daily forecast rate and the lead time, the computer can figure out how much of the order point is safety stock. In the first case, the safety stocks were eight pieces at all locations. It next takes 14/15 of each safety stock, which because of rounding gets the same values as before.

The last example takes 10/15 times each safety stock. The fair shares are enough to cover the lead-time requirements, plus the smaller safety stock. As we saw in Chapter 10, to give the maximum service in total from an inventory investment, all items should have the same safety factor. When there isn't enough stock to give the level of service intended by management, the safety stocks are reduced. But all safety stocks are reduced in the same proportion as a means for giving service as good as possible.

Exhibit 17.3

```
            FAIR
DAILY FORECAST RATES = 1 2 3 4 5
5 ORDER POINTS = 10 12 14 16 18
5 STOCK ON HAND = 9 10 11 12 13

SAT          CUMULATIVE NET REQUIREMENTS
DAYS =        1   2   3   4   5   6   7   8   9  10  11  12  13  14  15  16  17  18  19  20

  1     1     2   3   4   5   6   7   8   9  10  11  12  13  14  15  16  17  18  19  20  21
  2     2     4   6   8  10  12  14  16  18  20  22  24  26  28  30  32  34  36  38  40  42
  3     3     6   9  12  15  18  21  24  27  30  33  36  39  42  45  48  51  54  57  60  63
  4     4     8  12  16  20  24  28  32  36  40  44  48  52  56  60  64  68  72  76  80  84
  5     5    10  15  20  25  30  35  40  45  50  55  60  65  70  75  80  85  90  95 100 105

TOT    15    30  45  60  75  90 105 120 135 150 165 180 195 210 225 240 255 270 285 300 315

LATEST SHIP DATES: 0 0 0 0 0

NATIONAL ON HAND = 20
ALLOCATION COVERS 0 DAYS BEYOND ORDER POINT.
FAIR SHARE QUANTITIES = 1 2 3 4 5

NATIONAL ON HAND = 10

5 REPLENISHMENT LEAD TIMES = 2 2 3 3 3
SATELLITE =               1   2   3   4   5
OLD SAFETY STOCK =        8   8   5   4   3
COVER TO SS =             7   7   4   3   2
FAIR SHARES =             0   1   2   3   4
LOCATIONS WITH NEGATIVE FAIR SHARES ARE SOURCES.

NATIONAL ON HAND =
```

INSUFFICIENT STOCKS

Exhibit 17.4

```
39-10-3209      FOUNTAIN | FILE INDEX = 2

ALLOCATION TO 55 DAYS BEYOND ORDER POINT.

SOURCE          DESTINATION        COST FAIRSHARE QUANTITY  SHIP BY

MASTER    100   BROADVIE  110        0     889      100    7/15/76
                NEW YORK  200        4      57       48    9/20/76
                LOS ANGE  500        9     148      144    9/08/76

TOTAL                                     1,094     292


37-62-1981      FURNACE | FILE INDEX = 3

ALLOCATION TO 44 DAYS BEYOND ORDER POINT.

SOURCE          DESTINATION        COST FAIRSHARE QUANTITY  SHIP BY

MASTER    100   BROADVIE  110        0     157      100    8/16/76
                ATLANTA,  300        3     132      132    8/04/76

TOTAL                                      289      232


37-36-0819      SPRAY | FILE INDEX = 6

SOURCE          DESTINATION        COST FAIRSHARE QUANTITY  SHIP BY

DENVER,   400   LOS ANGE  500        4       3        3    7/15/76
NEW YORK  200   BROADVIE  110        4       7        7    7/16/76

TOTAL                                       10       10
```

In actual operations, when stocks are so low as to require reducing the order points, then the program also invokes the rebalancing routines discussed in Chapter 16, to compute how much of the relative excess at other locations could be used to fill what is needed at the locations that are running short. An exception report goes to the planner to warn of an unusual situation. For the first two items in Exhibit 17.4 there are enough at the master warehouse to send material to the satellite locations and cover requirements several days beyond the order point. For the 37-36-0819 spray, there isn't enough stock to cover all order points, and the allocation uses relative excesses at Broadview and Los Angeles to meet requirements at New York and Denver. It does not matter whether New York's requirements are filled from the master warehouse or from Broadview. The planner would probably use the master warehouse stock first. But Denver is better supplied from Los Angeles than from Broadview, so that shipment would be used first if stock is to be transshipped at all.

Note that in times of severe shortages, the safety stocks for the regions may in fact become negative—there isn't even enough to cover lead-time requirements. That is the best service in total that can be achieved with such little stock. Long before that point is reached, however, the product is likely to be frozen, and only legitimate emergency orders from customers will be honored. Stock orders will be held until there is more stock in the system.

17.6 ROUNDING AND LIMITS

Both in Exhibits 17.2 and 17.4 there is a shipping quantity listed beside the fair share. The shipping quantity is less than or equal to the fair share. One difference is that the fair share is rounded down to an integral multiple of the package quantity, which for the examples is 24 pieces per carton. Any excess stock from this rounding is left at the master warehouse, to be used later. If the fair share is less than a full carton, then individual units will be used as the shipping quantity.

The reason for always rounding down is that to round up would send to some location more than its fair share, which runs the risk of later having some other location run short or having to transship.

There is also provision for limiting the maximum quantity to be shipped, recorded by product by location in the item files. This maximum could be set because of storage space or handling problems at the destination. It is also a means for forcing several shipments, over time, for planned allocations based on future schedules. One might apply 11.12 to make the best use of total space available.

The complete flow chart of the essential computations is shown in Figure 17.5. The first calculation for each item processed is the latest ship date for each location. Initially the national safety stock quantity is reserved. If there is enough left to cover all locations beyond the order point, then the fair shares can be computed. If not, the national safety stock is considered to be available for allocation, and again we check to see if that will cover order points.

When stock is sufficient to cover beyond order-point supplies, then the fair shares are computed as in Exhibit 17.1 to cover net requirements to the same number of days' supply for all locations. If any location has more than that already, its stock is reported, the location deleted from the table, and the computation repeated. In this case the source for all shipments is the master warehouse, and the destinations are those stocking locations that do not have excesses.

Figure 17.5

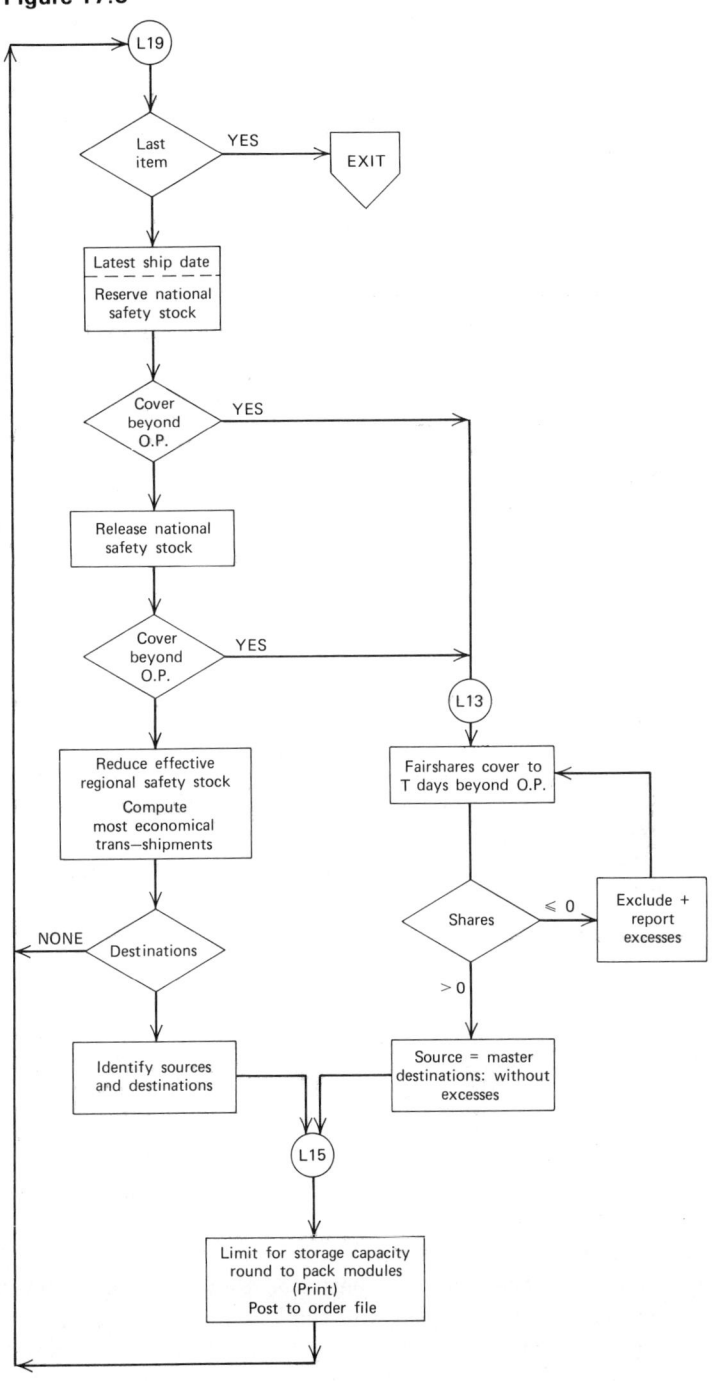

357

If there isn't enough stock to cover order points at all locations, the safety stocks are reduced to match the stock that is available. The fair shares are quantities sufficient to bring stock up to the reduced order points. Some locations may have more than enough to cover such a reduced order point and are considered as potential sources. The program then uses the linear programming technique described in Chapter 16 to find the best match of sources and destinations. This process avoids giving away transportation to the first location in the same spirit that the fair shares allocation avoids giving away stock to the first location that needs something.

At the end the shipping quantities are rounded to package module quantities, limited to a maximum shipping quantity, and stored in a work file. The planner may choose to see the results printed, as in Exhibit 17.4, or to save time the printing can be suppressed.

17.7 OTHER CRITERIA

Two different criteria for allocation are used in this particular system. If there is plenty of stock, the allocation is to a common number of days of supply above order point. If there is a shortage, the allocation is to a revised order point, with a common effective safety factor, to get the maximum possible service out of the stock that is available. These criteria were selected after several years of simulations (not continuous) of quite a wide variety of alternatives. The various criteria were compared on the basis of average stock in the system, number of shipments, service to customers, and remnant stock.

Richard Meyer discovered the concept of remnant stock years ago in the course of designing a production control system for du Pont paints. All the elements of safety stock, working stock, stock in transit, and stabilization stock were carefully documented and budgeted. It turned out that the actual inventory investment was consistently higher than plan. Closer investigation showed what was happening. If the stock, say, of quarts, for a particular paint reached order point, a new production batch of that paint was triggered. (There is no effective way of the equivalent of transshipping from gallons to quarts.) But at that time there was stock still on hand of gallons, drums, and pints. The total of the stock remaining above order point for items that did not trigger the production batch, when some item does trigger it, is called remnant stock.

In *Decision Rules for Inventory Management* I discussed, in Chapter 20, the analogue of this technique as a basis for allocating stock, not among sizes of cans but among stocking locations. Later on I developed some simulations that would test the application in a dynamic situation. These

ALLOCATION OF TRUCK CAPACITY

simulations revealed an unexpected side effect. The rule does tend to reduce remnant stock. The safety stocks are deliberately biased to ensure that the item most likely to trigger the new batch is the fastest-moving item. Then stock may be left over in slower-moving items. The consequence appears to be that when there is a fluctuation in demand for the major item, which has somewhat lower safety stocks, the shortage is serious. Hence this rule tends to give quite poor service in total for the given inventory investment.

17.8 LINING UP SHIPMENTS

The allocation procedure can be run periodically, such as daily or weekly, to generate a list of the products that are available for shipment, with a latest shipping date, fair share and shipping quantity, by location. The results can be printed for review and editing, but the primary output is to a file in the data base.

Exhibit 17.6 shows a summary of the number of lines in the file now set up for consideration to ship from any location to any other location. The information is used when it comes time to line up a shipment to a given destination. In some companies each stocking location gets a shipment on a regular schedule. In others it is appropriate to send a shipment whenever something is needed. In either case the shipment may be a truckload, part of a truckload, a railcar load, or a container for air shipment. For illustration I usually say "truckload," but the same concepts apply for any other quantity.

A report like Exhibit 17.7 can be generated to show all the products allocated to go from a specified source to a specified destination. Both the fair share and the shipping quantity (rounded and limited) are shown for each item, identified by part number and a brief description. The items are listed in sequence by latest shipping date. (There is provision for bypassing the report entirely if the most urgent item at the top of the list doesn't need to be shipped within a specified period, such as the next 10 days.) The computed weight and cubic size of each line item are also shown.

17.9 ALLOCATION OF TRUCK CAPACITY

The preceding examples are based on having small enough quantities of the urgent products so that the shipping quantities will all fit into the truck (or railcar), with some weight or cube left so that products that are available but not needed right now can be pulled ahead to be included on the next shipment.

Exhibit 17.6

TOBESHIPPED

MONDAY, AUGUST 23, 1976
EASTERN DAYLIGHT TIME 17:17:24

85 LINES TO BE SHIPPED.

FROM↓ TO→	100	200	300	400	500	600	TOTAL
MASTER 100							
INDIANAPOLIS, IN 200		24	15	17	16	10	82
NEW YORK, NY 300			2	1			3
ATLANTA, GA 400							
DENVER, CO 500							
LOS ANGELES, CA 600							
TOTAL	0	24	17	18	16	10	85

ELAPSED TIME 27.667S
CPU TIME   0.088S

Exhibit 17.7

SOURCE: 100 MASTER DESTINATION: 400 ATLANTA, GA
17 LINES TO SHIP.

LINE NO	PART NO	DESCRIPTION	QUANTITY FAIR SHARE	QUANTITY TO SHIP	SHIP BEFORE	WEIGHT POUNDS	WEIGHT CUMULATIVE	SIZE CUBIC FEET	SIZE CUMULATIVE
1	50-655-961	DISPLAY	21	21	8/04/76	187	187	13	13
2	44-683-325	GASTANK	7	7	8/04/76	119	306	8	22
3	47-180-523	MOTOR	1	1	8/04/76	21	327	1	23
4	41-182-643	SHROUD	155	155	8/04/76	1,116	1,443	81	104
5	36-183-917	SHROUD	27	27	8/04/76	259	1,702	19	123
6	41-164-588	PROPELLER	838	838	9/30/76	2,514	4,216	184	307
7	33-076-961	SHORT	453	453	10/04/76	3,352	7,568	240	547
8	41-031-505	ADAPTOR	659	659	10/15/76	1,911	9,479	138	685
9	40-696-973	IGNITION	810	810	10/19/76	1,134	10,613	79	764
10	38-027-275	ADAPTOR	1,921	1,921	10/21/76	4,802	15,416	346	1,110
11	34-694-846	IMPULSE-UN	197	197	10/28/76	2,758	18,174	187	1,297
12	49-341-925	PRIMER	730	730	11/02/76	3,285	21,459	241	1,538
13	32-007-035	IGNITION	352	352	11/03/76	278	21,737	20	1,558
14	44-100-824	ADAPTOR	81	81	12/21/76	130	21,867	10	1,568
15	49-029-897	ADAPTOR	82	82	12/21/76	221	22,088	16	1,584
16	49-030-061	ADAPTOR	764	764	12/21/76	1,986	24,074	145	1,729
17	45-059-213	WINDSHIELD	1,600	1,600	12/21/76	4,800	28,874	336	2,065

ACTION: CHANGE, SHIP, NEXT = C
CHANGE QUANTITY ON LINES = 4
1 NEW QUANTITIES = 25
ACTION: CHANGE, SHIP, NEXT = S
SHIP THROUGH LINE NUMBER = 5

When there is a great deal available at the master warehouse, it is possible that the products that have latest ship dates that would put them on the current shipment will also have weight or cube so large that they won't all fit. Then we have another allocation problem. The finite resource is the weight (or cube) of the truck. The activities are the products that must be included on this shipment, because the latest ship date is before the next shipment. One might back off from the total shipping quantity to bring products to equal numbers of days beyond order point. (Of course, this means that for products in general short supply that can't even cover order point, the shipping quantity would not be reduced.)

Another approach, suggested by O. J. Black at IBM several years ago, would be to minimize the total of the expected quantities short by the time the second shipment arrived.

The graph in Figure 17.8 shows the expected dollar value of the shortage for each of four products being sent to the same destination, as a function of the number of units shipped this time. The larger the number of units, the smaller the expected shortage, projected from current stock on hand and the forecast (including the standard deviation of the distribution of forecast errors).

Exhibit 17.9 displays an APL function that goes through the dynamic programming analysis, for either weight or cube constraints, depending on the right argument, to find the best way of allocating the products on this shipment. The left argument for the function is the number of grid units between 1 and the maximum number of units that could be allocated, based on shipping a truck of any one product. The function requires global variables DATA, PAY, and CAP. DATA has one column for each product and rows for available stock, usage, standard deviation, unit cost, and unit weight and cube. CAP is the total weight or cube capacity. PAY has one column per product and one row for each number of units to be shipped. Its values are plotted in Exhibit 17.8. This algorithm is probably much more elaborate than most companies would justify in practice, but in some extreme cases, the logic may be helpful.

17.10 TRANSITION IN ORGANIZATION

The centralized system of balancing field stocks has some advantages, which we summarize a bit later on. In OMC Parts & Accessories Division, and the Federal Supply Service of the General Services Administration, these advantages have appeared large enough to justify a radical change in the organization. Typically the replenishment of field stocks had been under the nominal control of managers in the field, whose performance was

Exhibit 17.8

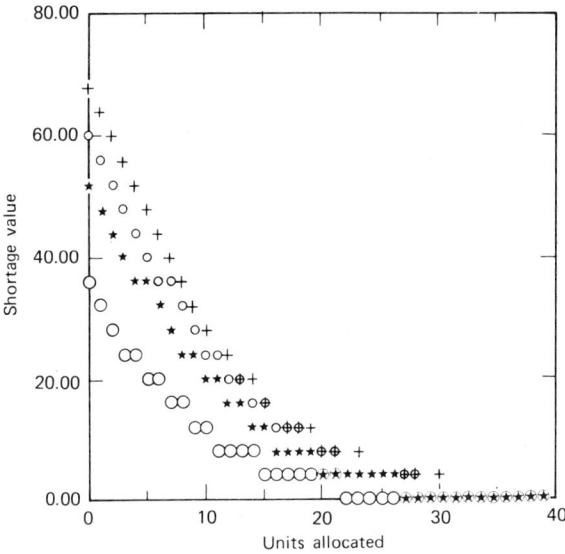

Weekly usage totals	Mean	Std. Dev.
Units	51	27
Dollars	334	184
Weight	340'	185
Volume	246	137

Truck capacity, weight and cube = 500 10000.
The following truck is due to arrive in 1.5 weeks.
The expected shortages are shown in the graph.
Legend:

Item 1
Item 2 *
Item 3 °
Item 4 +

If the truck is loaded optimally for the single constraint on weight the value of the allocation is $23.35
The product quantities are 12 20 20 33

Exhibit 17.9

```
      ∇ N←NGU DYNAMALLOC CASE;G;GU;J;NMAX;T;V;VSA;X
[1]   ⍝ LEFT ARGUMENT IS NUMBER OF GRID UNITS, 25 IS REASONABLE
[2]   ⍝ RIGHT ARGUMENT 1 FOR WEIGHT, 2 FOR CUBE
[3]   ⍝ REQUIRES GLOBAL VARIABLE <DATA> WITH ONE COLUMN FOR EACH PRODUCT
[4]   ⍝ ROWS OF <DATA> ARE:STOCK, USAGE, STD DEV, COST, WEIGHT, CUBE
[5]   ⍝ GLOBAL VARIABLE <CAP> HAS MAXIMUM TRUCK WEIGHT AND CUBE
[6]    '' × 'IF THE TRUCK IS LOADED OPTIMALLY FOR THE SINGLE CONSTRAINT ON
       ',(2 6 ⍴'WEIGHTVOLUME')[CASE;]
[7]    GU←CAP[CASE]÷NGU × J←2
[8]    V←(1,⍴V)⍴V←PAY[(NMAX←1⌈⍴⍴PAY)⌊1+⌊(T←GU×¯1+⍳G←1+NGU)÷DATA[4+CASE;1];1]
[9]   L1:VSA←(((¯1+NGU)⍴10000000000),V[J-1;])[1⌈⌈NGU+⌊(T°.-DATA[4+CASE;J]×
       ¯1+⍳NMAX)÷GU]
[10]   V←V,[1]L/VSA+(G,NMAX)⍴PAY[;J] × →(P≥J←J+1)/L1
[11]   'THE VALUE OF THE ALLOCATION IS ';DLR V[P;G+1+NGU] × N←⍳J-J←''⍴P
[12]  L2:N←N,1⍴¯1+(X≤(1+⍴PAY))/X+PAY[;J]⍳V[J;G]-V[J-1;]
[13]   G←⌊((G×GU)-N[⍴N]×DATA[4+CASE;J])÷GU × →(2≤J←J-1)/L2
[14]   N←N,⌊(CAP[CASE]-+/(⌽N)×1↓DATA[4+CASE;])÷DATA[4+CASE;1]
[15]   'THE PRODUCT QUANTITIES ARE ';⌽N
      ∇
```

appraised partly on the basis of the average inventory investment and the customer service actually rendered. Even when all the decisions were made by programmed decision rules, the fact that the computer resided physically in the manager's building gave him a certain sense of ownership and control.

Under a centralized inventory management system, there may still be some distributed data processing for order entry (and possibly invoicing) in the field, but all the key decisions about who gets how much of what and when are made centrally, taking account of individual stock status and requirements, but allocating short or long stocks so that everyone has a fair share. Obviously in this situation it is not fair to continue to judge the performance of regional managers on the basis of their inventory investment and customer service.

A technique used by Frank Hulswit for making such a transition at ICI Paints Division works well to smooth the transition from one form of organization to another. The eventual system of distribution was designed to be one of centralized allocation. But for the first year, allocations were planned about a week in advance, and the results were sent out to the affected field managers. The report is a preallocation (Exhibit 17.10). Actual values will be based on current stock status, which will change during the review process.

The managers could review the forecasts used in the allocation, the safety stock allowed in the order point, the amount of stock now in transit, and planned allocations period by period out into the future. These factors can be summarized into the projected stock availability.

TRANSITION IN ORGANIZATION

If the manager agreed with the plan, he didn't have to do anything, and in a week the planned allocation would be shipped. If he had any objections, he could override the allocated quantities. He could increase a rounded quantity up to the computed fair share, or reduce it. To get more than the computed fair share he had to change the forecast—introduce marketing intelligence to take account of a special promotion or competitive situation, or post scheduled demand for large planned orders. The new allocations would of course take account of the revised forecast and increase the fair share. But the forecast process itself keeps track of actual sales and gives credit for marketing intelligence that reduced the forecast error (recall Exhibit 3.8).

The idea was that the local managers could retain control, and be seen to retain control, for a period of a year. During that time any problems that arose could be taken into account in the design of the system, so that by the end of the year, it was hoped, the local managers would trust the system and agree to let it operate automatically.

The actual result was that within a few months the universal attitude in the field was, "Why are you bothering me with all this paper work? The system is clearly doing the right thing. Get me out of the loop, and let me tend to other business."

This illustrates the advantage of an executable realization of the formal definition of a new system, which can be used as a pilot test of new concepts. In all cases, the experience with the use of a proposed system helps all sorts of people in the organization to become familiar with the consequences. The advantage of a high-level language like APL is that as suggestions are made, the definition can easily be changed. When people see these first suggestions being acted on promptly, then more and more valuable suggestions start to emerge. In that way, the system evolves to match the real needs of the operating environment.

In all systems development projects, there are problems to be solved, and methods to be thought up to tackle them. Most of the time these problems can be generally defined at the outset, and a plan can be laid out to work on them in an orderly way.

In a few projects, however, some key problem emerged only after the system was operational and was seen not to fit. That is, in spite of careful work to define all the specifications and to solve the identified problems properly, occasionally there was a crucial specification that had not been stated, and that was not missed until it became apparent as a gap in the resulting output.

One example is a pharmaceutical company that forgot to say that lots for new products and for government orders had to have a flag in the identification number to distinguish them from standard products. The file design

Exhibit 17.10

```
32-007-035      IGNITION  |  FILE INDEX = 39

                8/04/76   8/18/76   9/01/76   9/15/76   9/29/76   10/13/76   10/27/76   11/10/76   11/24/76

LOCATION: ATLANTA, GA       400

FORECAST:     SS =   116|      163      161      151      151      313       326       269       247
FAIR SHARE:   IT =   904|      996                                                                1186
AVAILABLE:    OH =   690|     2427     2266     2115     1964     1651      1325      1056       1995

LOCATION: DENVER, CO        500

FORECAST:     SS =   360|      891      890      875      875     1084      1100       931        864
FAIR SHARE:   IT =    |       4178                                                                4974
AVAILABLE:    OH =  3342|     6629     5739     4864     3989     2905      1805       874       4983

44-008-530      IGNITION  |  FILE INDEX = 40

                8/04/76   8/18/76   9/01/76   9/15/76   9/29/76   10/13/76   10/27/76   11/10/76   11/24/76
```

LOCATION: NEW YORK, NY   300

FORECAST: SS =   45| 88   87   98   98   103   103   102   101
FAIR SHARE: IT =   308| 442   794   696   598   392   290   475
AVAILABLE: OH =   219| 881   664

LOCATION: DENVER, CO   500

FORECAST: SS =   159| 373   377   433   433   564   574   508   482
FAIR SHARE: IT = | 1950   856   282   ⁻226   2097
AVAILABLE: OH =   1086| 2663   2286   1853   1420   495   1388

LOCATION: LOS ANGELES, CA   600

FORECAST: SS =   331| 645   670   1002   1002   1249   1268   1144   1094
FAIR SHARE: IT = | 4040   1380   112   ⁻1032   4346
AVAILABLE: OH =   1908| 5303   4633   3631   2629   2220

367

wasn't very hard to change, but the change in file layout affected a great many programs that had to reference that part of the file.

In the Bureau of Supplies and Accounts, the idea of a tracking signal seemed to work fine in all tests, until one month the output produced some 10,000 exception reports, mostly by a good forecast that brought the limit down to the cumulative sum of the errors.

Base index forecasting seemed to work well for seasonal patterns, until we encountered the kind of seasonality for items sold through a department store.

A company that clearly had a very simple production planning situation that was almost a textbook case was doing fine with implementation of standard library programs, until one of the planners said, "What do I do about all these synonyms? For marketing reasons, the salesmen accept orders for the same product under many different part numbers." With some quick work it was possible to build a cross-reference dictionary that made it possible to enter the system with any possible reference, but always retrieve the right master record.

All of these are simple, and rather evident after the fact. But when a new system is developed, it is such things that get left out of the specifications. It is far better to be able to modify the system in a high-level language than in efficient batch code like COBOL or PL/1. And the only way these specifications come to light is by the users seeing actual output under operating conditions.

17.11 "PUSH" VERSUS "PULL"

In a broad sense the techniques discussed in Chapter 16 "pull" stock into a location on the basis of local stock status and requirements, without much regard to what other locations need, or what is available centrally. The procedures in this chapter represent a type of "push" system which starts from total requirements and stock status to determine the fair shares due to each location on the basis of information about requirements and stock status there.

One very clear difference is that a pull system can operate autonomously, with whatever data processing system is available, including men wearing green eyeshades on high stools, writing in ledgers with quill pens (usually called "manual" posting). There is no need for the expense and complexity of integrated communications and data processing networks. The economics of this contrast are changing very rapidly. In the 1950s there was no technical means for effectively sending data from one location to another except in hard copy (or punched cards). Then as telecommunications were developed, the cost of the long lines was prohibitive for the masses of data that would have to be transmitted for an effective centralized system. In the 1970s communications networks are cheap and effective, and often already in place for sales order entry and other purposes. Within another decade, microwave and satellite communications will be cheaper by another order of magnitude.

It has also become apparent within the last two years that the major suppliers of computers are starting to emphasize distributed processing, in which minicomputers can be used for local data processing and also serve as terminals to tie into a central host computer that can carry out the high-powered computations.

Thus it looks as though the cost advantages of the pull system are rapidly disappearing.

The inventory investment advantages would appear to lie all in favor of the push system. Because the national safety stock ensures that satellites can get material whenever they need it, the lead times to the satellite locations are more dependable and may be shorter. Hence the regional safety stocks will be less than under a pull system for the same level of service. The working stock in a push system is based on balancing total requirements against manufacturing setup costs. It represents a smaller quantity and a shorter time supply under a push system than the sum of lot sizes computed for local requirements, region by region, because of the square root effect in any of the formulas that might be used.

The push system guarantees a data base from which it is practical to search for available stock when the whole system is low, to ensure that every piece in the system is used to fill customer demand, not just to adhere to some planning targets for inventory levels.

Even in production planning, the visibility of total requirements and total stock status makes it possible for the production plan to take better account of what really should be produced as well as the current real priorities. A major drawback of some of the simpler versions of pull systems is that the source plant has no advance warning of real needs. A forecast extrapolated from current orders may have a hard time seeing through the lumps to the true consumption. (That is still true of the orders placed by independent dealers, even when the field distribution centers are stocked under a push system.) When it is hard to forecast real needs, there is usually either a much larger central safety stock, or late deliveries that lead to shortages, and commonly both.

Finally, under the push system, when there are relatively long manufacturing lead times, the decision about how much goes to each location can be left open until the product is nearly ready to be distributed. The decision based on stock status and requirements at that time will be better in tune with reality than preplanned orders under a pull system.

Summary: Why Have Inventory?

The total inventory investment shown on the balance sheet, even for a single profit center, tends to lump together requirements for a variety of individual needs. A properly designed system, based on a suitable collection of the modules described in this book, can manage the replenishment of each stockkeeping unit to quite explicit objectives of what the resulting inventory does for the company.

Exhibit V.1 is a much simplified block diagram to summarize the principal elements that must be considered in the decision to change the number of field distribution centers. It can serve as a vehicle to summarize the functional differences among various elements of the total inventory investment. An understanding of each element and what controls it is useful for the successful management of a good materials management system.

If the system is to include more field distribution centers, there are several kinds of operating costs that will be affected. Usually the engineers and accountants have a detailed model of the effect on warehousing, transportation, communications, and data processing. There will be increased costs of inventory control, simply because there are more stockkeeping units to keep track of.

Another major concern with more stocking locations is customer service. Usually the inventory investment can be adjusted so that there is the same probability that an item will be in stock, regardless of the number of stocking locations. The effect on revenue, and hence on profit, from having material stocked closer to more customers still seems to be a matter of marketing judgment. (If you ever plan to close an existing warehouse, set up records to keep track of the volume of sales done before and after with specific customers in the affected region. The experiment doesn't cost anything, and might generate some information about the effect of delivery time on market acceptance of your product.)

There are at least five functional reasons that contribute to the total investment in finished goods inventories. By reviewing the effect of the

SUMMARY: WHY HAVE INVENTORY?

Exhibit V.1

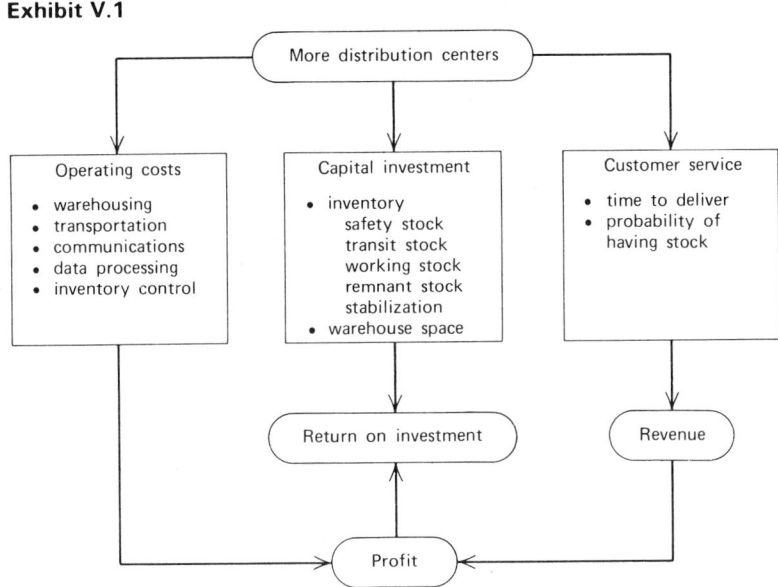

number of stocking locations on each element, we can review the essential concepts that have been developed throughout the book.

1. (*a*) The national safety stock depends on the errors in forecasting national demand over the manufacturing freeze period. Hence it would not be affected by having more or fewer regional distribution centers. It is obviously controlled by the ability to forecast and the length of the freeze period. It can be managed by a strategic selection from among the decision rules and by a tactical choice of the management policy variable. The objective is to exploit whatever ability exists to expedite a reasonable number of replenishment orders, but to have sufficient stock to expedite only a reasonable number of lots.

    (*b*) The regional safety stocks are based on the accuracy of the local forecasts. The total investment can be managed to achieve the same level of service to customers, in the sense of the probability of being in stock, regardless of the number of locations. When total demand is subdivided among several locations, however, it will generally be found that the relative accuracy of the forecasts will be worse. Hence more safety stock would be expected in total as the number of locations increases.

2. The stock in transit is effectively part of the reorder point for each distribution center. It is based on the forecast of requirements over the

transit lead time from the source. If total demand in some region is to be split among two distribution centers, then whether the transit stock increases or decreases depends on the fraction of total usage to be filled from the location with the longer transit lead time.

3. Working stock is the stock that results from producing more than will be consumed by current requirements. It is justified by reducing the setup and ordering costs associated with each new replenishment lot. In Chapter 16 we argued that although a pull system might compute some "economical" shipping quantities, the total working stock is not really affected. The production planning system should control the investment in working stock. Hence more or fewer field distribution centers would not affect the investment. An additional manufacturing facility would, however, increase the total working stock, because each facility would now be balancing setup costs against part of the total usage. If the pull system is designed so that warehouses generate their own order quantities, then more warehouses would probably inflate that portion of the finished goods inventory, roughly in proportion to the square root of the number of stocking locations.

4. Remnant stock is the stock left on hand over order point when the availability for some related SKU triggers a replenishment order. In a push system of distribution that can rebalance field stocks by referring orders or by transshipment, there will be minimal remnant stock. In a pull system, there very well can be large stocks elsewhere when the demand from one location triggers a new manufacturing run. The larger the number of locations, the larger the remnant stock would be under such a system.

5. Stabilization stock is built up by the manufacturing plan to anticipate peaks in requirements for large orders, seasonal sales, and promotions. This part of the total inventory is managed strictly within the production planning process, even if the resulting goods are actually distributed in the field. The amount of stock is not affected by the number of stocking locations, although a good push system will make better use of the field storage space to hold it.

APPENDIX A

File Structure

One of the more frustrating problems of designing complex computer systems can be provision for all the right kinds of information. The application can't very well be developed and tested until the data are available, and one doesn't always know what data to provide. Some of the newer forms of data base management offer a great deal more flexibility in this regard. This appendix identifies the kinds of information that have evolved as useful in the materials management systems library, as a guide to the sorts of information that should be allowed for in other versions.

This library is very short on accounting information, and there is no real provision for order entry files, since these systems usually already exist within the operating environment. It is also assumed that much of the accounting and engineering data are available.

A.1 ITEM FILES

There are a dozen different files used to record data about items on the system for materials management. Some of these files could be combined, but it is useful to comment on each one separately, since they provide different functions.

A.11 Master Record

The item master record as 37 fields identified so far, with room for more as the applications continue to evolve (Exhibit A.1). Each field has a format statement for printing out status records, a standard value that is used to create a new record before the nondefault values for a specific item are loaded, and a mask. The fields where the mask is blank are normally maintained by the system itself. Where the mask has a value 1 the user can change the contents of the field directly. The user has control over the format, the default value, and the mask.

Exhibit A.1

```
FUNCTION = INITIAL

ACTION = D
```

FIELD	FORMAT	STANDARD	MASK	DESCRIPTION
1	I12	0		NUMERICAL DESIGNATION CODE
2	I12	2		TERMS IN FORECAST MODEL
3	I12	0	1	SMOOTHING RATE CODE
4	I12	0		MONTHS ON FAST SMOOTHING
5	F12.4	1.0000	1	TOTAL COST
6	F12.4	0.0500	1	MATERIAL COST
7	F12.4	0.0100	1	LABOR COST
8	F12.4	0.0100	1	BURDEN
9	F12.4	2.0000	1	SELLING PRICE
10	CI12	12		LOT QUANTITY
11	F12.1	12.0		LOTS/YEAR
12	F12.2	25.00	1	SETUP COST
13	I12	1	1	MINIMUM TIME SUPPLY
14	F12.4	1.0000		FACTOR 1-S+P
15	I12	1	1	PACKAGE QUANTITY
16	F12.4	1.0000	1	YIELD FACTOR
17	I12	5	1	SOURCE SAFETY STOCK STRATEGY
18	I12	2	1	LOCATION SAFETY STOCK STRATEGY
19	I12	0	1	SORTING KEY
20	I12	0	1	VENDOR SOURCE CODE
21	I12	1	1	PRODUCT LINE
22	I12	0	1	DISCONTINUE AFTER JULIAN DATE
23	I12	0	1	NEW ITEM AS OF JULIAN DATE
24	I12	2	1	SOURCE PLANNING CONTROL
25	I12	0		LEVEL CODE
26	I12	12	1	PLANNING HORIZON
27	I12	1	1	UNIT WEIGHT LBS/PC
28	I12	1	1	UNIT CUBE CU FT/PC
29	I12	203		LEVEL CODE COMPONENT
30	I12	1	1	FORECAST ERROR SENSITIVITY
31	I12	0	1	MINIMUM LOT QUANTITY
32	I12	0	1	FLAG FOR LOCKED SCHEDULE
33	I12	0	1	BUYER/PLANNER CODE
34	I12	0		TOTAL FINISHED STOCK ON HAND
35	I12	0		FINISHED GOODS TARGET STOCK
36	I12	0		MANUFACTURING FREEZE PERIOD
37	I12	0	1	INVENTORY CLASS

The numerical designation is an encoding of the part number, for sorting, and is a unique reference.

The next three fields have to do with common aspects of the forecast model, the number of terms selected, whether the item is on fast or normal smoothing (or is locked to bypass smoothing entirely), and a counter of the number of periods the item has had the forecast revised by fast smoothing.

FILE STRUCTURE 375

Field 30 contains the code (1 to 3) for the degree of sensitivity to be used in computing tracking signals and demand filters.

Fields 5 through 9 are various ways of stating unit cost components. The analyses within the system are based on standard cost in field 5, but various reports can be expressed in other cost measurements.

Fields 10 through 16 deal with the replenishment lot quantity, expressed in both pieces and lots per year. When the lot quantities are computed, the setup cost, minimum time supply, minimum lot quantity (in field 31), package quantity, and yield factor are used. The factor $(1 - S/P)$ is used to relate the annualized usage rate S to the annualized production rate P (see 11.03).

Fields 17 and 18 accept any of the six codes (Chapter 10) for the safety stock strategy to be used for national safety stock and regional safety stocks.

Field 19 is a special sorting key that can be set up with up to 16 significant digits, to retrieve items based on essentiality, commodity code, source of supply, and so on. Field 20 is a pointer to data in the vendor file about the source of supply. The product line is any code that can be used to group items together for various reports.

Fields 22 and 23 give the effectivity dates, used in forecasting, for any item to be dropped from the files or start to accumulate actual demand. Dates are stored internally as "julian" dates, the total number of days elapsed since December 31, 1900. (A true Julian day calendar refers dates to an astromomical base in 4713 BC.)

Field 24 has one of the six codes discussed in Chapter 13 for covering net requirements with notional orders out to the planning horizon. Field 32 can be set to a nonzero value to lock the scheduled dates so that they are not changed within the freeze period. Field 25 carries the level code, which is automatically maintained by the system as product structures are loaded and edited. The planning horizon, in months, governs the maximum time forecasts are computed into the future (limited to three years).

Fields 27 and 28 give unit weight and cube, for planning shipments from the source to field warehouses. These should represent packed sizes, in the form the product is usually distributed.

Field 29 is peculiar to the way that the APL files are set up to record lists of items by level code.

Field 33 with a buyer or planner code number can be used to organize the daily work sheet for production control, and field 37 contains a number corresponding to the ABC classification (there can be more than three classes).

Fields 34 to 36 store information computed from other sources in the master scheduling run, to be available for reports without having to recompute the values of stock on hand, safety stock targets, and the number of planning periods in the manufacturing freeze period.

A.12 Location Master Record

Additional master item data is specific to each of the stocking locations. The location master record (Exhibit A.2) has 23 fields identified so far, and is stored in an array with one row for each stocking location. There is a convention that the top row of the array (which may be the only row) corresponds to the master warehouse, and is generally interpreted as pertaining to supply from the manufacturing (or purchased) source.

The numerical warehouse code identifies where the item is stocked. The list of locations can be in any sequence for any item.

The stock status is recorded in fields 2, 3, and 22. The last field is a memorandum of fair share quantities computed, but not yet committed to be shipped.

The safety stock is based on the safety factor, times the standard deviation, which in turn is derived from the mean square error and the lead time. The total safety stock in pieces can be the sum of the statistical safety stock

Exhibit A.2
FUNCTION = LOCATIONS

ACTION = D

FIELD	FORMAT	STANDARD	MASK	DESCRIPTION
1	I12	100		NUMERICAL WAREHOUSE CODE
2	CI12	0	1	STOCK ON HAND
3	CI12	0	1	STOCK DUE IN [ON ORDER, IN TRANSIT]
4	F12.2	1.50		SAFETY FACTOR
5	F12.1	0.0	1	WEEKS OF SUPPLY FOR SAFETY STOCK
6	I12	1		STD DEVIATION OVER LEAD TIME
7	CI12	1		SAFETY STOCK [PIECES]
8	I12	0		S.E.T.S
9	CI12	0		MEAN SQUARE ERROR
10	CI12	0		FORECAST FOR NEXT MONTH
11	CI12	0		TOTAL ANNUAL USAGE
12	I12	1	1	LEAD TIME
13	CI12	1	1	REORDER POINT
14	CI12	100,000	1	MAXIMUM STORAGE CAPACITY
15	I12	1	1	1 NORMAL/2 EXPONENTIAL ERROR DISTRIBUTION
16	I12	0	1	DEMAND TO DATE
17	I12	0	1	BIN LOCATION CODE
18	I12	0	1	NUMBER OF PERIODS OF HISTORY
19	CI12	0	1	NO OF MONTHS USED TO FIT THE MODEL
20	I12	0	1	DATE NEW MODEL WAS FIT
21	CI12	0		DEDUCTHIST INTERLOCK
22	CI12	0		ALLOCATED, NOT SHIPPED
23	CI12	0	1	PLUGGED LEVEL

FILE STRUCTURE

(as discussed in Chapter 10) and an arbitrary number of weeks of supply. The reorder point includes all that safety stock, and the forecast over the lead time. The smoothed error tracking signal is recorded in field 8.

The maximum storage capacity is used to limit the maximum quantity to be shipped to any location. For the master warehouse it limits the maximum computed manufacturing lot.

Field 15 carries a code for the form of the distribution of forecast errors.

Demand to date is accumulated by order-entry systems, to be used in revising the statistical forecast at regular intervals. When the forecast is revised, this field is reset to zero.

Field 17 is a location code to find the bin in the warehouse. Most warehousing systems require more than one location.

Fields 18 to 20 have to do with demand history in the statistical forecast model. The number of periods of history identifies when (relative to now) the item was first recorded at each location. Field 19 identifies when less than the total history was used when the model was last fit by multiple regression (Chapter 5), and the date that the model was last fit to history is recorded in field 20. Field 21 indicates whether a demand history at the master warehouse has been reduced because some of the demand has now been reflected at a specific location. Field 23 carries a plugged level that can be used to fit a model, by scaling, when there is insufficient history to fit the model to actual data.

A.13 Forecast Coefficients

As now implemented, the library programs use the same number of terms in the forecast model for all locations for a given part number. The values of the coefficients may vary, of course, to reflect levels, trends, and seasonal patterns. This approach may be the result of some of the power of APL in manipulating matrices. There is an array with one row for each stocking location, and a column for each term in the forecast model (Exhibit 5.18).

The system assumes that forecasts are prepared for each stocking location. Some modification would be necessary to forecast by sales territories, and then accumulate them by different warehouse regions.

A.14 Demand History

The demand history is accumulated in an array that has one row for each stocking location and one column for each period of past history. If some locations have less than the maximum amount of history, the initial periods are filled with zeros, and field 18 of the location master identifies the first actual value. It is recommended that this history be stored off line once a year, to keep the amount of history in the live files between three and four years long. The statistical forecasts can use up to six years of history in selecting and fitting a model, and there is no particular limit to the amount of history that could physically be stored.

A.15 Forecast Array

The forecast array has three dimensions. There is one plane for each stocking location. Within a plane the array has one column for each future period, out to the planning horizon, for the forecast. There are four rows to each plane:

1. The statistical forecast model.
2. Marketing intelligence (net differences to be added to the statistical model).
3. Total amounts in the scheduled backlog of firm orders for future delivery.
4. Dependent demand, posted at the end of the explosion routines (Chapter 14) to have the values available for the strategic system.

The forecast is stored by forecast periods, such as calendar months, or by specified forecast periods in integral numbers of weeks (Exhibit 3.1).

A.16 Open Orders

The details about open replenishment orders are stored in an array with seven columns, and one row for each reference number. The columns contain:

1. The reference number.
2. Original quantity scheduled.
3. Current good quantity as reported by production progress.
4. The schedule date (in internal "julian" form) when the last operation is to be completed.
5. The need date (also "julian") when the last operation would be completed if there were no restrictions.
6. The operations sequence number that identifies the stage of the process where production progress was last reported.
7. Days remaining is the total allowance, from the process routing (see below) for all uncompleted operations.

FILE STRUCTURE

The latest start date for the current operation is then the result of subtracting days allowed from either the need date or the schedule date, as the planner chooses (Exhibit 2.3).

A.17 Product Structure

The product structure is an array with one column for each subordinate item, and from two to five rows. The first row is always a pointer to the file index number of the subordinate. The second row is always the number of pieces of that subordinate required to make one unit of the parent. If the subordinate material is required at one of the later steps in the process routings, the third row provides for a record of what sequence step number corresponds to the time when the item is to be available for the assembly (Exhibit 14.2).

The fourth row of the array will contain exception codes, such as don't smooth, effectivity dates, or phantom bills. If the code corresponds to an effectivity date (to add or delete), then the fifth row of the array contains the date.

It is possible to add and subtract the same subordinate from the bill, for example, to change the quantity each.

A.18 Process Routing

The process routing summarizes the information on how to make the item. The array has one row for each operation, and nine standard columns.

1. Operation sequence numbers. The routings are sorted into ascending sequence, but there can be gaps to allow for adding new steps later.
2. Department number where the operation is performed, to control distribution of the daily work sheet (Chapter 15).
3. Setup time per lot, according to industrial engineering standards. It is used both to generate total setup time for computing economical lots, and for estimating the work load generated by the schedule.
4. Labor grade code (from 1 to 26) is keyed in with labor wage and fringe benefit rates to estimate setup cost, and also to summarize the work load by department by labor grade.
5. Direct operation time per piece is used in estimating the total work load generated by the schedule.
6. Work center number is shown for reference on the daily work sheet.
7. The number of days allowed for move, queue, setup, and run time for a typical lot is used to back schedule to the latest start date for each opera-

tion. In many cases the value would have to be estimated from experience. The total for all operations will be equal to the manufacturing lead time.
8. There are codes to identify what sort of a step this is: pick parts, accounting or engineering reference only, nonproductive operation for which a work sheet is not generated, and so on.
9. A code number that refers to a standard table of names, for a quick identification of the type of operation.

The steps in the routing should be sufficient for production planning and control, and can contain steps for other purposes. Since there is conversational access to the files it is always possible to add new steps if the control process warrants it, or to change the code or delete a step that is found not to be useful for planning and control (Exhibit 15.1).

A.19 Part Number and Description

The unique part numbers used to identify items can be distinguished in the first 10 characters (including significant blanks). To print the standard part number and description on reports, any form of the part number can be recorded here.

A.110 Planning Array

The planning array has four rows to each plane, and one column for each planning period out to the horizon. Since the number of weeks per planning period is generally different from the number of weeks in a forecast review period, the size of this array will differ from the forecast array. The dates corresponding to the first period can be different too. The four rows are as follows:

1. Direct requirements, interpolated from the forecast array for statistical model and marketing intelligence. Scheduled backlog orders are slotted in directly to the proper period.
2. Dependent demand, which is accumulated during the explosion process.
3. Firm open orders, slotted in from the open order array, according to scheduled due date.
4. Notional orders generated by the master scheduling process.

The first column of the array does not really correspond to a period at all. It contains the minimum stock target in the first row and actual stock

FILE STRUCTURE

on hand in the third. The minimum stock target is generally the national safety stock. However, when production is coordinated with field distribution, so that the stock on hand includes stock in transit and on hand in field warehouses, the minimum stock target is national safety stock, plus the sum of the regional reorder points.

If the planning is done only with the official schedule, the array will have only one plane. When a tentative schedule is requested, for exploration of problems, a second plane is added, initially identical to the first (Exhibit 14.2).

A.111 Backlog of Scheduled Orders

The record contains one row for each open order on the part number, with columns for quantity and date promised, and optional columns for other information, such as purchase order number (Exhibit 3.2).

A.112 Where-Used List

The last item file is a simple list of pointers to all parent item file index numbers where a particular item is used as a subordinate on the product structure or bill of materials. This is used for rapid retrieval of master items both for engineering changes and for locating pegged requirements (Exhibit 14.5).

A.2 STATE VARIABLES

To customize the application to a particular operating environment, there are several state variables that describe the environment. Some are selections of bits of codes appropriate to a particular user and some describe the current, on-going state of the system as it is in operation. The following information is indicative of the variety available.

A.21 Switches

There are 10 binary switches that choose alternative paths through the library and hence pick up different parts of the code for individual applications (Exhibit A.3).

Most of the values control whether data are stored in integer or floating form, or whether, for example, forecasts are to be limited to nonnegative quantities. Some indicate whether part numbers and location codes are identified strictly as numerical values or may contain nonnumeric

Exhibit A.3

```
                  SWITCHES

         SUNDAY, AUGUST 15, 1976
         EASTERN DAYLIGHT TIME 15:52:23


         ACTION = D

         OPTION  CONTROLS              VALUE

              1  FORECAST INTEGRAL        1
              2  HISTORY INTEGRAL         1
              3  FORECAST PRORATED        0
              4  FORECAST BY WEEKS        0
              5  REVISION PENDING         0
              6  LITERAL LOCATIONS        0
              7  LITERAL PART NOS         1
              8  STRUCTURE FLOATING       0
              9  FORECAST NONNEGATIVE     0
             10  <WAREHOUSES> RUN         1
```

characters. There are also two interlocks that tell whether the forecast revision has run to completion, and whether the list of warehouse locations has been posted. One of the switches selects calendar months, versus an arbitrary number of weeks, as the forecast revision interval.

A.22 Management Policy Variables

Corresponding to the six safety stock strategies discussed in Chapter 10, there are values for the management policy variables (Exhibit A.4).

The carrying charge used in computing economical lots, and in some safety stock strategies, is carried as the seventh element of this vector. The two parameters of the variance law (Chapter 8) are posted automatically by the system.

The user may weight negative forecast errors more or less seriously than positive forecast errors in evaluating marketing intelligence (Chapter 7), and the relative weight is carried in this vector.

A.23 System Parameters

There are so far 19 different system parameters (Exhibit A.5). Some record current dates when various operations were performed on the files. Others record the maximum number of level codes (for bottom-up searches) and blocking factors to manage the files. There are also default values for the operation at which parts are to be picked, the size of fields, and maximum restrictions on lot quantities and days supply to allocate on one shipment.

Peculiar to the conversational operations in APL, the user can control

FILE STRUCTURE

```
FUNCTION = MANAGEMENT

ACTION = D

STRATEGY   INTERPRETATION                              VALUE

       1   FRACTION OF DEMAND FILLED FROM STOCK       0.9500
       2   EXPECTED TIME BETWEEN SHORTAGES            2.0000
       3   SAFETY FACTOR ITSELF                       1.5000
       4   WEEKS OF SUPPLY                            3.0000
       5   IMPUTED MARGINAL COST OF A SHORTAGE    10000.0000
       6   DOLLARS TIMES SHORTAGES PER YEAR         750.0000
       7   CARRYING CHARGE                            0.2400
       8   <VARIAW> FACTOR                           -1.7687
       9   <VARIAW> EXPONENT                          1.9200
      10   REL WEIGHT TO NEG ERRORS                   0.5000
```

the number of print lines for reports to be produced either at the terminal or on a line printer.

A.24 Production Departments

As a label on the daily work sheet, departments can be identified by either the type of department or the name of the superintendent or foreman who is to receive the report (Exhibit A.6).

Exhibit A.5

```
FUNCTION = PARAMETERS

ACTION = D

ELEMENT       DESCRIPTION                              VALUE

       1   CURRENT MONTH POINTER                           6
       2   NUMBER OF ITEM RECORDS                         29
       3   LAST MONTH OF FISCAL YEAR                      10
       4   LARGEST ORDER REFERENCE NUMBER              10302
       5   LARGEST ACTIVE LEVEL CODE                       3
       6   DATE STOCK POSTED                           27595
       7   FIRST YEAR IN MANUFACTURING CALENDAR           76
       8   MAXIMUM SUBORDINATE PLANNING HORIZON           24
       9   DIGITS IN PART NUMBER                          10
      10   CHARACTERS FOR WAREHOUSE CODE                   5
      11   LEVEL CODE BLOCKING FACTOR                   5000
      12   CURRENT FISCAL YEAR                          1976
      13   DATE OF LAST DEMAND POSTING                 27576
      14   WEEKS BETWEEN PRODUCTION SCHEDULES              2
      15   TERMINAL PRINT LINES PER PAGE                  50
      16   FILEPRINT LINES PER PAGE                       66
      17   KEY OFFSET TIME TO OPERATION NUMBER             2
      18   MAXIMUM LOT SUPPLY [YEARS]                      3
      19   MAXIMUM DAYS SUPPLY TO ALLOCATE               100
```

The list of department numbers also controls the sequence in which the work sheet is printed.

The effective wage rates per hour, for up to 26 different labor grades, can be stored as a vector to accumulate labor costs for various reports.

A.25 Warehouse Locations

The warehouse location can be identified by a short code number or symbol, which is associated with a description, such as the city and state (Exhibit A.7).

There are also two matrices of shipping costs, usually in cents per pound. In each matrix there is one row for each location as source and one column for each location as a potential destination. The entries in the table are the current freight rates. In one plane of the array the costs are based on the normal preferred mode of shipment, and in the other the costs are for the usual premium mode. The planner can select either one when he wants to compute how to rebalance field stocks (Chapter 16).

A.26 Working Days

In the list of "Julian" dates for working days for a three-year period weekends, holidays, and shutdown periods are excluded (Exhibit A.8).

The Julian dates are computed as the total number of days since December 31, 1900. All dates on input and output are represented in standard calendar form, as MM/DD/YY. But for convenience in determining relative dates (either by elapsed calendar days or working days), dates are all stored internally in this sequential form. The calendar can be revised at any time to reflect changes in the working schedule, even to represent a period where the plant may be shut down for labor negotiations. Note that one of the system parameters defines the first year in this calendar at any time.

There is also a vector of the numbers of effective selling weeks per calendar month, to normalize the forecasts when on a monthly basis.

Another list of dates is simply a memorandum of the dates when personal property taxes are assessed on inventory, corresponding to the states in which each of the stocking locations operate.

A.27 Dictionary of Operations

The process routing for each item has a code number that refers to one line of a character array with names of typical processes. This is not intended to be a substitute for the full description which would appear on shop paper.

Exhibit A.6

NUMBER	NAME
117	MR ABRAHAMSON
324	MR ANDERSON
325	MR BECKMAN
326	MR BROCKMAN
328	MR CONNELLY
332	MR DEETS
334	MR DOMNICK
342	MR DREDGE
343	MR ERICKSON
346	MR FABER
354	MR GASINK
369	MR HUTCHINGS
374	MR JONES
383	MR KALETSCH
384	MR KANE
385	MR LEWIS
386	MR MC ILMOYL
391	MR ROBERTS
397	MR RUSSELL
400	MR WARRINER
401	MR STOELTING
406	MR BROWN
407	MR DALEY
408	MR HOLT
409	MR SHERWOOD
410	MR SPINK
411	MR WEST
412	MR LOWELL
413	MR LAWRENCE
416	MR BROOKS
427	MR KAPLAN
432	MR THURBER
433	MR NASH
320	PRODUCTION PLANNING
321	PRODUCTION CONTROL

GRADE		RATE
1	A	10.50
2	B	9.50
3	C	8.50
4	D	7.50
5	E	6.50
6	F	5.50
7	G	4.50

Exhibit A.7
TRANSPORT

MONDAY, AUGUST 23, 1976
EASTERN DAYLIGHT TIME 17:15:44

ACTION = D

NORMAL SHIPMENT COSTS, CENTS/LB:

FROM↓ TO→	100	200	300	400	500	600
MASTER 100|	0	9	40	35	50	100
INDIANAPOLIS, IN 200|	35	0	70	50	90	200
NEW YORK, NY 300|	160	70	0	85	185	290
ATLANTA, GA 400|	140	50	80	0	140	220
DENVER, CO 500|	200	90	190	140	0	110
LOS ANGELES, CA 600|	420	200	300	220	120	0

PREMIUM SHIPMENT COSTS, CENTS/LB:

FROM↓ TO→	100	200	300	400	500	600
MASTER 100|	0	187	893	695	1016	2095
INDIANAPOLIS, IN 200|	270	0	729	508	802	2080
NEW YORK, NY 300|	1680	729	0	855	1851	2915
ATLANTA, GA 400|	1350	508	855	0	1401	2197
DENVER, CO 500|	2030	882	1851	1401	0	1134
LOS ANGELES, CA 600|	4200	2080	2915	2197	1134	0

FILE STRUCTURE

Exhibit A.8

DISPLAY WORKING DAY NUMBERS:
☐:
    30 DAYSFROM 63076

WORKING	JULIAN	CALENDAR	DAY
129	27,576	6/30/76	WED
130	27,577	7/01/76	THU
131	27,578	7/02/76	FRI
132	27,581	7/05/76	MON
133	27,582	7/06/76	TUE
134	27,583	7/07/76	WED
135	27,584	7/08/76	THU
136	27,585	7/09/76	FRI
137	27,588	7/12/76	MON
138	27,589	7/13/76	TUE
139	27,590	7/14/76	WED
140	27,591	7/15/76	THU
141	27,592	7/16/76	FRI
142	27,595	7/19/76	MON
143	27,596	7/20/76	TUE
144	27,597	7/21/76	WED
145	27,598	7/22/76	THU
146	27,599	7/23/76	FRI
147	27,602	7/26/76	MON
148	27,603	7/27/76	TUE
149	27,604	7/28/76	WED
150	27,605	7/29/76	THU
151	27,606	7/30/76	FRI
152	27,609	8/02/76	MON
153	27,610	8/03/76	TUE
154	27,611	8/04/76	WED
155	27,612	8/05/76	THU
156	27,613	8/06/76	FRI
157	27,616	8/09/76	MON
158	27,617	8/10/76	TUE

Rather it is a short memory jogger for "assemble," "paint," "drill," "heat treat," and so on. The idea is that several parts will have operations that can be described by the same brief terms, and it is a pity to waste file space repeating these descriptions over and over again.

There is even a headline message that the planner can change every day to appear on the top of the work sheet, as instructions to the people in the shop in how to use the work sheet or what to look for in particular.

A.28 Standard Operations

There are specific operations in the process routings for individual items. Both to extend the application to production planning, purchasing, and quality control, and to provide for interfaces between the executable realization of a formal definition on a pilot basis with ongoing systems already in place, there is provision for any number of standard initial operations which will automatically be placed at the head of the item routings. Another list of standard terminal operations is automatically placed at the end of the routing (Exhibit 15.1).

The nine columns of the arrays correspond to the standard format for individual process routings.

A.29 Transactions

Finally, there are provisions for defining the names and effects of several standard transaction codes, such as receipt, transfer, issue, demand, and cancellation. In general the effect of any transaction is indicated by $+1$, -1, or 0, for (a) stock on hand, (b) stock due in on order, and (c) demand to date. These balances can be affected in a first-level transaction processing system as individual orders are entered. In general, however, one relies on order-entry systems already in operation.

A.3 DIRECTORIES

One of the major advantages of a conversational system over a batch system is that the planner can retrieve any set of items at any time to work out particular problems. There are three standard ways in which he can retrieve items. (a) Process all items on the file. (b) Supply a list of items. (c) Test each item according to specified criteria and process it if it passes the test.

Items are filed in regular sequence and are uniquely identified within the system by a file index number. When the planner chooses to supply a list of items, one way or another, he has to supply that list in terms of file index numbers. There are several directories, with associated small programs, that help him generate lists of file index numbers from other ways of identifying a group of items.

Items can be identified by ordinary part number, and a directory will translate that into file index numbers. (Some data-base management systems provide this feature automatically.)

FILE STRUCTURE

Since the process of level-by-level master scheduling requires a list of all items at a given active level code, the planner can also use that directory to select items all at the same level code for a report or analysis.

Open replenishment orders are uniquely identified by order reference number, which is used in posting progress on the daily work sheet. The planner can also find the records that pertain to items that have a specified list of order reference numbers.

As items are dropped from the system, slots are opened in the files. (Once an item is loaded, it retains the same file index number until it is dropped.) As new items are loaded, they are first posted to these empty slots. All programs automatically bypass empty slots without testing on retrieval. The planner would not normally want to access the list of empty slots, but it is an important directory for file management by the system.

Finally, there is a general-purpose directory into which the planner may at any time *PUT* lists of particular items of interest. Note, for example, that several programs ask for the name of this directory file, to put lists of exception items for later retrieval. Then in any other program, the planner can specify a particular list simply by *GET*ting the list from that file. The uses of this directory are limited only by the imagination of the planner.

APPENDIX B

Bibliography

The list of references cited here is a small portion of the total literature on materials management and other professional topics involved in the treatment in this book. These references were selected as having the more significant contributions to the state of the art.

The number following the author's name is a file index number for the bibliographical file that is maintained in a public library on Scientific Time Sharing Corporation's APL*Plus system. Additional references can be retrieved from that system by author, title, or subject. There is also a cross-referencing index that suggests other, related classifications to check for books and journal articles that may have been indexed under a different subject heading.

Ackoff, R. L.; Rivett, P. *A Manager's Guide to Operations Research.* John Wiley & Sons, New York, NY, 1963.

Ackoff, R. L. *A Concept of Corporate Planning.* John Wiley & Sons, New York, NY, 1970.

Ammer, D. S. 47 *Materials Management.* Richard D. Irwin, Homewood, IL 1962.

Arrow, K. J.; Karlin, S.; Scarf, H. 255 *Studies in the Mathematical Theory of Inventory and Production.* Stanford University Press, Stanford, CA, 1958.

Beer, Stafford. 122 *Decision and Control.* John Wiley & Sons, New York, NY, 1966.

Beer, Stafford. 1026 *Platform for Change.* John Wiley & Sons, New York, NY, 1975.

Bellman, Richard. 98 *Dynamic Programming.* Princeton University Press, Princeton, NJ, 1957.

Bowersox, D. J.; Smykay, E. W.; LaLonde, B. J. 279 *Physical Distribution Management* Macmillan Company, New York, NY, 1968.

Bowman, E. H.; Fetter, R. B. 210 *Analysis for Production Management,* Richard D. Irwin, Homewood, IL, 1957.

Bowman, E. H.; Fetter, R. B. 199 *Analysis for Production and Operations Management.* 3rd ed. Richard D. Irwin, Homewood, IL, 1967.

Box, G. E. P; Jenkins, G. M. 40 *Time Series Analysis: Forecasting and Control.* Holden-Day, San Francisco, CA, 1970.

Brooks, F. P., Jr. 1025 *The Mythical Man-Month.* Addison-Wesley Publishing Co., Reading, MA, 1975.

BIBLIOGRAPHY

Brown, R. G. 258 *Statistical Forecasting for Inventory Control.* McGraw-Hill Book Company, New York, NY, 1959.

Brown, R. G.; Meyer, R. F. 983 "The Fundamental Theorem of Exponential Smoothing." *Operations Research,* 1961, Vol. 9.

Brown, R. G. 261 *Smoothing, Forecasting and Prediction of Discrete Time Series.* Prentice Hall, Englewood Cliffs, NJ, 1963.

Brown, R. G. 259 *Decision Rules for Inventory Management.* Holt, Rinehart & Winston, New York, NY, 1967.

Brown, R. G. 986 "Simulations to Explore Alternative Sequencing Rules." *Naval Research Logistics Quarterly,* 1968, Vol. 15, No. 2.

Brown, R. G. 260 *Management Decisions for Production Operations.* Dryden Press, Hinsdale, IL, 1970.

Brown, R. G. 1030 "Detection of Turning Points in a Time Series." *Decision Sciences,* 1971, Vol. 2, No. 4, pp. 383-403.

Brown, R. G. 1031 "Improved Customer Service in the HAL Division." *APICS Toronto Conference Proceedings,* 1972, pp. 152-177.

Chambers, J. C.; Mullick, S. K.; Smith, D. D. 111 *An Executive's Guide to Forecasting,* John Wiley & Sons, New York, NY, 1974.

Conway, R. W.; Maxwell, W. L., Miller, L. W. 223 *Theory of Scheduling,* Addison-Wesley Publishing Co., Reading, MA, 1967.

deMatteis, J. J.; Mendoza, A. G. 1027 "The Part Period Algorithm." *IBM Systems Journal,* 1968, Vol. 7, No. 1, pp. 30-46.

Dickie, H. F. 1032 "ABC Inventory Analysis Shoots for Dollars, Not Pennies." *Factory Management and Maintenance,* 1951, Vol. 5.

Driebeek, N. J. 89 *Applied Linear Programming.* Addison-Wesley Publishing Co., Reading, MA, 1969.

Garwood, Dave. 1038 "Stop: Before You Use the Bill Processor." *Production and Inventory Management (APICS),* 1970, Vol. 11, No. 2, pp. 73-79.

Gerson, G.; Brown, R. G. 988 "Decision Rules for Equal Shortage Policies." *Naval Research Logistics Quarterly,* 1970, Vol. 17, No. 3.

Gilman, L.; Rose, A. J. 552 *APL An Interactive Approach.* 2nd ed. John Wiley & Sons, New York, NY, 1974.

Goode, H. H.; Machol, R. E. 102 *System Engineering,* McGraw-Hill Book Company, New York, NY, 1957.

Green, J. H., Ed. 198 *Production and Inventory Control Handbook.* McGraw-Hill Book Company, New York, NY, 1970.

Hadley, G.; Whitin, T. M. 214 *Analysis of Inventory Systems.* Prentice-Hall, Englewood Cliffs, NJ, 1963.

Harrison, P. J.; Stevens, C. F. 1034 "A Bayesian Approach to Short-Term Forecasting," *Operational Research Quarterly,* 1971, Vol. 22, No. 4, pp. 341-362.

Holt, C. C.; Modigliani, F.; Muth, J. F.; Simon, H. A. 219 *Planning Production, Inventories and Work Force.* Prentice-Hall, Englewood Cliffs, NJ, 1960.

Iverson, K. E. 629 *A Programming Language.* John Wiley & Sons, New York, NY, 1962.

Johnson, S. M. 1033 "Optimal Two and Three Stage Production Schedules with Setup Times Included." *Naval Research Logistics Quarterly,* 1954, Vol. 1, pp. 61-68.

Magee, J. F.; Boodman, D. M. 272 *Production Planning and Inventory Control.* 2nd ed. McGraw-Hill Book Company, New York, NY, 1967.

Magee, J. F. 277 *Industrial Logistics.* McGraw-Hill Book Company, New York, NY, 1968.

Mennel, R. F. 1028 "Early History of the Economic Lot Size." *Production and Inventory Management (APICS)*, 1961, Vol. 2, No. 2, pp. 19-22.

Morse, P. M.; Kimball, G. E. 651 *Methods of Operations Research.* Technology Press, Cambridge, MA, 1951.

Orlicky, Joseph. 5 *Material Requirements Planning.* McGraw Hill Book Company, New York, NY, 1975.

Plossl, G. W.; Wright, O. W. 252 *Production and Inventory Control.* Prentice Hall, Englewood Cliffs, NJ, 1967.

Prichard, J. W.; Eagle, R. H. 238 *Modern Inventory Management.* John Wiley & Sons, New York, NY, 1965.

Shelly, M. W.; Gilford, D. M. 284 *Multistage Inventory Models and Techniques.* Stanford University Press, Stanford, CA, 1963.

Silver, E. A. 992 "Some Findings Relative to a Joint Replenishment Inventory Control Strategy." *University of Waterloo Working Paper*, 1971.

Silver, E. A. 991 "A Practical Control System for Coordinated Inventory Replenishment." *University of Waterloo Working Paper*, 1973, Vol. 70.

Simpson, K. F. 1029 "In-Process Inventories." *Operations Research*, 1959, Vol. 7, No. 6, pp. 797-805.

Trigg, D. W.; Leach, A. G. 1035 "Exponential Smoothing with an Adaptive Response Rate." *Operational Research Quarterly*, 1967, Vol. 18, No. 1, pp. 53-60.

van Dobben de Bruyn, C. S. 21 *Cumulative Sum Tests.* Charles Griffin & Co. Ltd., London, 1968.

Welch, W. E. 671 *Tested Scientific Inventory Control.* Management Publishing Corp., Greenwich, CT, 1956.

Wentworth, F. R. L. 285 *Physical Distribution Management.* Gower Press Ltd., London, 1970.

Whitin, T. M. 241 *The Theory of Inventory Management.* Princeton University Press, Princeton, NJ, 1953.

Wiener, Norbert. 49 *Extrapolation, Interpolation and Smoothing of Stationary Time Series.* John Wiley & Sons, New York, NY, 1949.

Wight, O. W. 772 *Production and Inventory Management in the Computer Age.* Cahners Books, Boston, MA, 1974.

Winters, P. R. 1037 "Forecasting Sales by Exponentially Weighted Moving Averages." *Management Science*, 1960, Vol. 6, No. 3, pp. 324-342.

Woodward, R. H.; Goldsmith, P. L. 31 *Cumulative Sum Techniques.* Oliver & Boyd Ltd., Edinburgh, 1964.

APPENDIX C

Glossary

The terminology of materials management is not particularly standard, and the literature contains a lot of jargon that tends to separate members of a particular school of thought from all outsiders. The definitions given here are by no means official or universal. For me, as for Humpty Dumpty, words mean what I choose they shall mean. The glossary is merely an attempt to play fair and let all readers see the particular usage that I employ.

In many cases it has seemed to me preferable to discuss several terms together, so that they can be contrasted. In those cases, there may be a cross reference under word A: "see word B." It makes a little extra work for the reader and a lot of extra work for the author. But the end result should be a clearer discussion of similarities and differences. (Numbers in parentheses refer to sections of the book where the topic is discussed.)

ABC CLASSIFICATION. See DISTRIBUTION BY VALUE.

ACTIVITIES. See ALLOCATION.

ADAPTIVE SMOOTHING. A statistical model of a time series (see FORECAST MODELS) is defined by a collection of fitting functions, with a list of coefficients for each particular series. The forecast, as of any point in time, is computed by multiplying the coefficient vector by the matrix of fitting functions for the (relative) time periods for which the forecast is desired. As new observations of the series are obtained, the values of the coefficients are modified (*a*) to move the origin of time to the period corresponding to the latest observation and (*b*) to make small adjustments in the model because of the new information. Adaptive smoothing in general refers to the process of revising the coefficients where the fitting functions represent models that include level, trend, and seasonal patterns represented by sinusoidal Fourier models. (Chapter 6)

The discount rate (slightly less than 1) affects the relative weights assigned to current and historical data. The weights in all cases decline exponentially with age. The smoothing constants are a vector of values that multiply the forecast error and add the result to each of the coefficients in the model. The smoothing constant vector is derived from the discount rate. A large value (near 1) of the discount rate produces slower smoothing, and a smaller value produces faster smoothing—a more rapid discounting of older information.

The transition matrix corresponds to the list of fitting functions. It has one row and one column for each fitting function. The matrix product of the transition matrix and the vector of values for the fitting function at any point in time produces the vector of values of the fitting functions at the succeeding observation.

ALGORITHM. A general procedure or rule for computing numerical results from a mathematical expression.

ALL-TIME SUPPLY. A quantity that will satisfy all remaining requirements for a product to the end of its life. The end may be defined (*a*) when demand has disappeared, (*b*) when there is no further legal requirement to stock the item, or (*c*) by a marketing decision to discontinue the item. The life of the item can be planned in advance. Sometimes stocks are suddenly made obsolete by an unplanned engineering change, such as for safety reasons.

The last buy of an item is a quantity sufficient to bring the current available stock up to the forecast of an all-time supply. Planning for coverage of all the rest of the requirements for an item can be referred to as "terminal service." (12.7)

ALLOCATION. The general principles of allocation involve (*a*) a finite resource, (*b*) several activities that share in that resource, and (*c*) a rule for dividing the resource among activities. Examples of finite resources would include space or weight in a truck, total available stock of a given product, and a capital budget for safety stock inventory. The activities that share in these resources, respectively, would be all products to be sent to a given destination, locations that stock the given product, and safety stocks planned for all items being considered within the budget.

AMPLITUDE. See FORECAST MODELS.

AVAILABLE STOCK. The stock on hand, plus stock due in (on order or in transit), less any reservations for back orders or scheduled demand due to be shipped but not yet deducted from the inventory balance on hand.

BACKLOG. The item file contains details, by customer order, of the quantity and date due. These quantities can be slotted into the forecast

GLOSSARY

array by forecast period, and are taken into account in production planning by planning period.

BACK ORDERS. See SERVICE.

BACK SCHEDULE. New replenishment orders are due at a need date. Each step in the manufacturing process has a number of days allowed for move, queue, setup, and run time. The latest start date for each operation is back scheduled from the due date by subtracting the total days allowed for all remaining operations.

BALANCE OUT. At the end of a model year, or in anticipation of an engineering change, the stocks of all subordinate items can be reduced in a balanced way. Items that can be carried over to the next model are stocked somewhat above forecast requirements. Items that have no further use can be stocked somewhat below forecast. Items that can be carried over can be stocked to a level somewhat above forecast.

BARYCENTRIC COORDINATES (CENTER OF GRAVITY). The location of a point within a triangle is given by a triplet of distances from the point to each side of the triangle.

BASE INDEX. One way of expressing a seasonal profile is by a set of base index numbers, one for each forecast period of the year. Usually the values express the expected ratio of demand in that period to the demand in an average period. Sometimes base index numbers represent differences. The whole pattern is also called a "profile." If the index numbers are cumulated, they may be expressed as a "percent done," meaning the cumulative percentage of the total season sales done by any period within the season. (5.332)

BILL OF MATERIALS. The recipe or formula for food and drug products or the list of materials required to assemble a piece of machinery. At a minimum the bill of materials identifies each subordinate item and the number of units of that subordinate required to make one unit of the parent item, the "quantity each." Especially when the bill of materials lists only the subordinates used directly on the parent in question, it may be referred to as the "product structure." In some cases the product structure also identifies the step in the manufacturing process where the subordinate is needed and codes for effectivity dates and phantom bills of material. (14.1)

BIN TRIPS. The number of times (per year) that an item is ordered by separate customer transactions, regardless of the number of units ordered.

BLANKET ORDER. An order on the source of supply that specifies quantities by period. Usually the first few periods are frozen and cannot be changed, but orders for later periods are for information and can be changed within reason. Each period the blanket order is extended to a specified horizon, and the requirements for one more period are frozen.

BRANCH AND BOUND. A technique for solving the "traveling salesman" problem. See LINEAR PROGRAMMING.

BRIDGING RUN. The quantity ordered when tooling is to be changed, or the unit cost of the material is to be changed. The quantity ordered will last longer than usual, and will bridge over the period when the source cannot supply more, because the plant is being retooled. (11.05)

BUILD SCHEDULE. The master plan that states the number of units of the product to be assembled by period. The build schedule may identify only the generic product line. Specific configurations may be specified later as customer orders are received.

CAN-ORDER POINT. For several items procured from the same source, one technique of triggering replenishment orders is to compare available stock with an order point. If for any item the available stock is below order point, then a replenishment order is triggered. Included on the list of items to be ordered are all other products for which the available stock is below the can-order point. The can-order point is usually set as a specified time supply above the order point.

CARRYING CHARGE. A management policy variable, with dimensions of dollars per dollar per year, used in economic lot size decision rules to control the exchange of annual operating expense for setups against the capital investment in working stock.

CLOSED SHORT. An order is closed short when less than the quantity ordered will be delivered to stock. It may be the result of scrap losses or unavailability from the vendor.

COEFFICIENTS. See FORECAST MODELS.

COORDINATED DELIVERY. In a time-phased, net-requirements planning system, the arrival of supplies of subordinate items can be coordinated with the schedule for consumption into parents, so that there isn't as much working stock as there would be for continual usage rates. (11.09)

COORDINATED ORDERS. In a family of items obtained from the same source, a single order is placed at one time for a list of items. (See JOINT ORDERS.) Some of the items are ordered in sufficient quantities when they are needed, so that they do not need to be included on every order.

CORRELATION. Two time series are correlated if whenever an observation in one series is on one side of its average (say, above), the corresponding observation in the other series is likely to be on the same side of its

GLOSSARY

average. "Autocorrelation" or "serial" correlation use as the second series the first series offset by some lag or lead time. Usually the degree of correlation is measured by the correlation coefficient, which is normalized by the variances of the two series, to lie between +1 (perfectly correlated) and −1 (always move in exactly the opposite direction from the average). The set of serial correlation coefficients for all possible lags is called a correlogram. (5.331)

COSINE. See FORECAST MODELS.

CRITICAL RATIO. A scheduling priority rule, the ratio of two ratios. The numerator is some measure of need for the item, usually based on time elapsed compared to lead time. The denominator is a measure of availability, usually based on work still to be done and the time in which to do it. If the ratio is larger than one, the job is critical.

CUMULATIVE SUMS. Start with zero. At each forecast revision add the (signed) value of the forecast error. If the forecast is unbiased, the cumulative sum varies around zero (within predictable limits). If there is a consistent bias, the sum grows in one direction. The limits can be expressed simply as a ratio to the standard deviation of forecast errors, or more sensitively, as a V-shaped or parabolic mask that can also detect the time when the process started to go out of control. (8.31)

CYBERNETICS. The science of control, developed initially by Norbert Wiener at MIT. The theory of control systems has evolved to state some very general theorems about the necessary and sufficient conditions for a system to be able to control a complex process.

DAYS ALLOWED. The number of days allowed in the process routing cover move time, queue time, setup time, and operating time for each major step in the process. Setup and run time can be computed precisely from engineering standards, but move and queue time often require judgment and experience. The values are used to back schedule the latest start date for each operation, based on the schedule date for completing the last operation.

DEGREES OF FREEDOM. When a model is fitted to a set of observations, the degrees of freedom available to estimate the error are equal to the number of observations less the number of individual coefficients estimated from the data. The estimate of the variance is the sum of the squares of the residual differences divided by the number of degrees of freedom. Thus the more terms fit to the data, the fewer degrees of freedom. If the reduction in sum of squares does not compensate, the variance may increase, indicating too many terms are being estimated. (5.4)

DEMAND FILTER. As total demand is posted during a forecast review period, it is compared with the most recent forecast for that period. If the difference is large compared to the standard deviation, the demand filter creates an exception report, in case there is something wrong with the value being posted. The objective is to catch very serious errors in entry or in coding special orders as normal. (8.32)

DENSITY. See PROBABILITY DISTRIBUTION.

DEPENDENT REQUIREMENTS. The master schedule for a parent item is exploded using the product structure. The requirement to make a quantity of the parent item in one time period is offset by the time when a subordinate will be required to go into the assembly, and the quantity of the subordinate is the parent quantity times the quantity each. The total of such requirements, by period, is the schedule of dependent requirements, for any subordinate item. (14.3)

DISCONTINUE DATE. The date when no further demand is to be served, as for an engineering change, the end of the season, or the last recorded demand. Controlled by both the planning and forecast horizons.

DISCOUNT RATE. See ADAPTIVE SMOOTHING.

DISTRIBUTION. Physical distribution involves the systems of transportation, warehousing, and data processing to get goods from the producing source into the field to fill customer orders. See also PROBABILITY DISTRIBUTION.

DISTRIBUTION BY VALUE. A list of all items in a stratum of the inventory, arranged in descending sequence by annual value of usage. The usage can be either a forecast or history (and should include a full year, to avoid bias caused by seasonality). The value can be in dollars, cubic feet, weight, or number of bin trips. (9.1)

Class A items are the few items at the top of the list that represent 50% of the total value. Class C items are the last 50% of the items, which account for a small fraction of the total value. Class B items are between, nearly half the items and nearly half the value.

Not only stocked products may be classified this way to focus management attention on the most crucial areas, but also customers, vendors, plants, and other elements of the total system.

DUE DATE. The date when a replenishment order is due into stock. It can be either a need date or a schedule date, depending on the constraints on the schedule.

DUTY CYCLE. The typical interval between execution of a particular part of a system. For example, the duty cycle for the action system is daily to weekly. The planning system is typically weekly to monthly. The

GLOSSARY

requirements system may have a monthly to quarterly duty cycle. Strategic management systems may have quarterly to annual duty cycles.

DYNAMIC PROGRAMMING. A technique of allocating a resource among activities over time, developed by Richard Bellman. The four principal steps are. (*a*) embedding particular problems in a more general framework, (*b*) a principle of optimality to establish a formal model for evaluating any states of the general problem, (*c*) the forward solution, to find a finite set of states that are optimal at least locally, and (*d*) the back solution, to select the set of states that is an overall optimum.

ECHELON. Any stage in a physical distribution system, such as a vendor, the manufacturing plant, finished goods at a master warehouse, regional warehouses, or local stocking outlets.

ECONOMICAL LOT SIZE (ECONOMICAL ORDER QUANTITY EOQ). A quantity to be ordered on each replenishment cycle. In general the lot quantity balances the operating expense of setting up and following the order against the capital investment in the working stock that results from ordering more than enough for current consumption. There are a great many different decision rules, any one of which finds the least total cost of some problem. The design assumptions fall into five categories: (*a*) setup cost, (*b*) usage rate, (*c*) delivery into stock, (*d*) unit cost, and (*e*) premium charged on the investment in money and space. Alternative assumptions under each of these headings formulate different problems, with different optimum solutions. (Chapter 11)

EFFECTIVITY DATE. The date when demand is expected to start being recorded, as when the item is released for sale to customers or when it appears in the bill of materials of some parent item.

EMERGENCY ORDERS. Some companies provide different service, and different payment terms, for "emergency" orders from customers, such as to repair a machine that is out of operation, in contrast to stock orders, which may take longer to fill but have more attractive payment terms.

EMPIRICAL DISTRIBUTION. A probability distribution based on direct observation of data, rather than some mathematical formula to describe the essential nature of the distribution.

EXCESS STOCK. Stock on hand that is more than the largest reasonable level is excess. Typically the largest reasonable stock is based on (*a*) receipt of a full replenishment lot plus (*b*) demand during the preceding lead time as far below forecast as reasonable. (12.5)

In a physical distribution system, one location may have a relative excess when the time that the stock above order point will last is longer than the fair share for all locations. (17.04)

EXCHANGE CURVE (EXCHANGE SURFACE). A representation of the trade off of operating expenses (such as customer service and setup costs) for capital investment in inventory. There is a general curve or surface for any decision rule. Points along the curve are generated by using different values of a management policy variable. The strategic choice among alternative rules can be aided by comparison of the exchange curves. The tactical choice of a value for the management policy variable can be guided by the exchange curve for the rule implemented. Usually management negotiates the current exchange of capital investment for operating expense. (10.3 and 11.042)

EXPECTED DEFICIT. When lumpy demand, or posting the files after several transactions, can move the available stock balance from above an order point to a level well below it, the difference between available stock when an order is triggered and the order point is the "deficit." The expected deficit is a model of the average value of that difference, over many replenishment orders. (12.32)

EXPECTED VALUE. The average of a set of observations. See PROBABILITY DISTRIBUTION.

EXPLOSION. The process of multiplying the master schedule quantities, by time period, for a parent item, and offsetting them to generate dependent demand on the subordinate items in the product structure. (Chapter 14)

EXPONENTIAL DISTRIBUTION. See PROBABILITY DISTRIBUTION.

EXPONENTIAL SMOOTHING. A process of iteratively revising an estimate of a weighted moving average as new observations are obtained. The effective weights decline exponentially with age. See ADAPTIVE SMOOTHING.

"Simple" exponential smoothing estimates the average of the data. "Double" smoothing provides for a secular trend. "Triple" smoothing also estimates an acceleration term, and projects the forecast along a parabolic path, like that of a ballistic missile.

FAIR SHARE. The amount of stock to be shipped to a stocking location to bring the available stock to the same number of days of supply above order point for all locations (or the same number of standard deviations below order point, if the total stock is in short supply). In this book the fair share has already deducted the current available stock. In some usage, the fair share is the stocking objective, from which stock on hand and in transit must be subtracted to determine how much to ship. (17.04)

FAST SMOOTHING. A rate of discounting old information in adaptive or exponential smoothing that places more weight on current observations.

GLOSSARY

FEEDBACK. A general concept of cybernetics and control systems where the difference between actual current output and a desired output is used to generate action within the system that changes the output. Stable, damped, feedback will return to the desired level after reacting to a transient impulse. Undamped feedback may produce oscillations in the output that grow without bound. Real systems as studied by cybernetics and industrial dynamics have recognized that higher levels of control begin to take effect when low-level systems become unstable. Hence a total system may operate effectively even if some of the elements are unstable.

FILE INDEX NUMBER. In the particular APL realization of the formal definition of the materials management system library, each item has a unique internal identification corresponding to the file address for its records. Compare the "Ramac number" used in the grocery trade to identify a particular product.

FIRM ORDER. A replenishment order that is due within the freeze period, for which the quantity is not to be changed by the system, and the due date can be locked not to change. The planner can always change either quantity or due date on an exception basis. In contrast with "notional" orders which are generated to cover requirements beyond the freeze period to the planning horizon. Notional orders can be changed every planning cycle as the net requirements change. (13.5)

FITTING FUNCTIONS. There is one function for each term in the forecast model, such as level, trend, and pairs of seasonal sine waves. The array of fitting functions has one value for each forecast period, potentially extending six years into the past and three years into the future. The forecast for any item is the vector product of its forecast model coefficients with the vector of values of the fitting functions for the period to be forecast. (5.34)

FORECAST ERRORS. The difference between actual demand and a forecast for the same period of time generated earlier. In contrast, the difference between past data and a model fitted to those data is called a "residual" difference. The model assumes that the observed demand was generated by some (unknown) process, with random variation, known as "noise."

FORECAST MODELS. The forecast model for any time series can be expressed as a linear combination of fitting functions where the coefficients are computed to minimize the (weighted) sum of squares of the residuals. The number of terms in the model determines how many of the fitting functions are used, from level, trend, and pairs of seasonal sines and cosines of increasing frequencies (number of complete cycles per year). The Fourier model says that if the pattern repeats cyclicly, a sufficient number of terms will represent the pattern. Nyquist showed that when the observations are sampled at discrete intervals during the fundamental cycle, the highest frequency necessary is a sine wave that goes through one cycle every two observations. The sine waves can be described either by a phase angle (position of the peak relative to the beginning of the year) and amplitude (distance from average either to peak or trough), or by a cosine–sine pair of functions. The latter version is easier to program for computing. (5.34)

The initial conditions are the values of the coefficients obtained by fitting the model to past history. The process of adaptive or exponential smoothing revises the values of the coefficients with additional observations.

Some value will be assigned to the coefficients for every fitting function tried. There may be spurious frequencies, however, where the power (square of the amplitude) is not large enough compared with the variance (square of the standard deviation) when one takes account of the degrees of freedom lost in using more terms in the model.

FOURIER SERIES. Baron Jean Baptiste Joseph Fourier was a French mathematician who showed in 1830 that a sufficient number of sine waves, with increasing frequencies and phase angles and amplitudes to be estimated from the data, could represent a repetitive cyclic pattern of any shape with arbitrary precision.

FREEZE PERIOD. The number of planning periods within which the quantity, and possibly schedule dates, for open replenishment orders are not to be changed automatically by the system. Compare LEAD TIME. Net requirements stated by the user are transferred from the supplier's inventory account into the user's inventory account, under a dual accounting system, one freeze period after they are computed. (13.3)

FREQUENCY. The number of complete cycles of a sine wave within one year. See FORECAST MODELS.

FROZEN ORDER. An order due within the freeze period, which is not to be changed automatically by the system.

GOOD QUANTITY. The quantity currently being produced on a replenishment order. The good quantity will be less than the original scheduled quantity by any scrap that has been reported so far.

GROSS REQUIREMENTS. Include the statistical forecast, marketing intelligence, scheduled backlog, and dependent demand, period by period. If there is provision for safety stock, that value is usually the first "period's" gross requirements. If the safety stock changes with

GLOSSARY

time, then the incremental differences are included in the gross requirements for subsequent planning periods.

Net requirements, by period, apply first stock on hand, and then firm replenishment orders against the gross requirements.

HISTOGRAM. See PROBABILITY DISTRIBUTION.

HORIZON. The number of periods through which requirements are planned, or forecast. The limit may be controlled by the maximum time for which plans and forecasts are generated, or a shorter time for particular items if the item is to be discontinued.

INDEPENDENT ORDERS. Replenishment orders for items where any quantity can be ordered at any time, without reference to the need to replenish the stocks of other items.

"Joint" orders refer to lists of items procured from a single source which are all ordered at one time, usually in supplies that will last until the subsequent order is received. "Coordinated" orders are for items where some of the items are not ordered at every opportunity, but when they are ordered the quantity will last for several replenishment cycles. (11.07)

INITIAL CONDITIONS. See FORECAST MODELS.

INTERPOLATION. A process of finding the value of a function between tabulated values.

INVENTORY MANAGEMENT. A control system that includes second-level decision rules for computing when and how much to order. Usually inventory "control" refers to the first-level system that implements these decisions.

"Inventory" typically implies a list of items carried in stock. "Stock" implies the quantity of a particular item on hand.

ITERATION. In some cases the value of an expression can be computed directly from the formula. In other expressions one must assume some value, evaluate the expression, measure the error in the result, and use that error to modify the assumption. The procedure converges if a result of acceptable accuracy can be obtained within a finite number of steps.

JOB SHOP. A manufacturing process where various products take different routes through the same set if general purpose machinery. Distinguished from a "flow shop" in which all products follow essentially the same sequence of operations.

JOINT ORDERS. See INDEPENDENT ORDERS.

LAGRANGE MULTIPLIER. Joseph L. Lagrange, French geometer, about 1813 developed a technique of minimizing a function subject to constraints on the values of the variables. The Lagrange multiplier is an arbitrary variable multiplying the constraint (expressed as a function whose value is zero when the constraint is satisfied).

LAST BUY. See ALL-TIME SUPPLY.

LATEST SHIP DATE. The transient time is subtracted from the date when present available stock will reach safety stock to obtain the latest ship date. Additional supplies shipped from the source on or before that date will arrive in time to continue service to customers.

LATEST START DATE. The date when a given operation in the manufacturing process must start to leave the allowed time for move, queue, run, and setup for all remaining operations, and still get the whole job done by the schedule date.

LEAD TIME. In general a decision to replenish stocks will result in material on hand a lead time later. When there are finite intervals between opportunities to order, or to deliver, that interval is generally included within the lead time. (In some other usages, replenishment lead time is distinguished from review period, and the total effective lead time is the sum of the two.) Lead times may be established by the vendor, by the manufacturing cycle, or by transit time. Lead times include any administrative time to prepare and issue the order, and to receive and post stock after delivery.

LEARNING CURVE. A new job takes longer to perform than after a similar job has been repeated several times. The time per job frequently is reduced by the same percentage every time the total number of jobs completed has doubled. Hence at the beginning of a new production run there will be some loss in efficiency compared with a standard based on long runs.

LEAST SQUARES. A process for finding the coefficients in a model that minimizes the sum of the squared residual differences between the data and the model. In "weighted least squares" the squared residuals are assigned different weights, depending on when the observation occurred, and the sum of the weighted squared residuals is to be minimized. "Multiple regression" is a similar process where the model involves more than one independent variable, such as time, temperature, and viscosity. (5.34)

LEAST UNIT COST. A technique proposed for finding the size of a replenishment lot quantity with time-varying demand. The period covered is extended until the average unit cost including setup cost per piece in the lot does not decrease by enough to cover the carrying charge on the larger working stock. Contrast with PART-PERIOD BALANCING. (11.103)

GLOSSARY

LEVEL CODE. Top-level items sold to customers with one assembly usage are assigned level code 0. Subordinate items must have level code at least LC + 1 if they are used on any parent with a level code of LC. The purpose is to ensure that as master schedules are exploded, all dependent demand has been posted at level code LC (so that complete requirements are available for scheduling) once level code LC − 1 has been processed.

LEVELS OF SYSTEMS. First-level systems process transactions to maintain files and require efficient and reliable operations. Second-level systems invoke decision rules to manage the exchange of operating costs for capital investment. Middle managers take certain risks based on judgment as part of second-level systems. Third-level systems establish management policy for the whole system, and provide feedback of the exceptions where operations differ significantly from plan. A system that might appear to be "first level" from the corporate headquarters might well be second or third level when viewed from the shop floor.

LINEAR PROGRAMMING. A general mathematical technique of resource allocation. A linear cost expression in several variables is to be minimized, subject to constraints that each of the variables is positive, and usually less than some maximum value. Several classical formulations have special names. The "transportation" problem minimizes the total cost of shipping quantities of a product from several sources to several destinations. The variables are the quantities to be shipped—many of them will turn out to be exactly zero. The constraints ensure that the quantity shipped will not exceed the supply available at any source, and the quantities received do not fall short of the requirements at the destinations.

The "traveling salesman" problem seeks to minimize the total travel cost of a route that passes through every city once and returns to the start. The sequence of setting up for several related products with different changeover costs from one product to any other can be set in this form. The "branch and bound" technique can be used to solve simple traveling salesman problems.

The traveling salesman problem is not properly a linear programming problem. It is an integer programming problem, in which the space of feasible results is restricted to integral values. It is a shock to some students to discover that the optimum integral solution is not obtained by simply rounding the fractional values that may result from linear programming methods. Quite different techniques are required.

LOG-NORMAL DISTRIBUTION. A probability distribution in which the logarithms of the variable are normally distributed. Often a good model of the distribution by value. See PROBABILITY DISTRIBUTION. (9.11)

LOOK AHEAD. For procedures to compute the replenishment lot with time-varying demand, compare the requirements in the last planning period with the average rate of usage. If the requirements in that period are larger than the average, it is well to reduce the coverage by one period. Then the large usage is withdrawn from the first period of the second lot, rather than the last period of the first lot, and that tends to reduce the investment in working stock.

LOT QUANTITIES. See ECONOMICAL LOT SIZE.

LUMPY DEMAND. Demand in which the standard deviation of the residuals from the best forecast model are larger than the mean. (12.3)

MAD. Mean absolute deviation. See PROBABILITY DISTRIBUTION.

MANAGEMENT POLICY VARIABLE. See EXCHANGE CURVE.

MARKETING INTELLIGENCE. Information about changes in the market, in marketing, in products, and in the economy that will indicate that future requirements will be different from a routine statistical forecast.

MASTER SCHEDULE. The time-phased plan for the quantities of an item to be made to cover net requirements. See firm orders. A short-dated order is one that is needed within the freeze period, but was not identified early enough. Expediting refers to existing firm orders where the need date is earlier than the current schedule date.

MASTER WAREHOUSE. The national safety stock is carried in a master warehouse. Satellite warehouses fill orders from customers in their territories. The master warehouse location can coincide with a satellite, in which case the inventory balances are merely a bookkeeping convenience—there is not necessarily any physical segregation. In general a given product has only one master warehouse, but for different products the master warehouse can be at different sites. (17.01)

MATRIX. An array of numbers with rows and columns. APL is particularly convenient for processing all entries of a matrix simultaneously. Matrices have mathematical properties, and several of the operations of materials management can be expressed very conveniently in matrix form.

MAX–MIN. An inventory control procedure. When the available stock falls to or below the minimum level, a replenishment order is triggered. The quantity is the difference between the maximum level and the available stock.

MEAN. The average of a set of numbers. See PROBABILITY DISTRIBUTION.

MEAN ABSOLUTE DEVIATION. See PROBABILITY DISTRIBUTION.

GLOSSARY

MEAN SQUARE ERROR. See PROBABILITY DISTRIBUTION.

MEDIAN. A measure of the center of a set of numbers, such that half the observations are larger and half are smaller than the median. See PROBABILITY DISTRIBUTION.

MODEL SELECTION. See FORECAST MODELS and LEAST SQUARES.

MODULAR BILL OF MATERIALS. Capital products have a large variety of options and accessories, and are usually assembled to order. Each of the stockable subassemblies can be forecast and planned, so that there are reasonable stocks available to meet customer requirements. In that case the end product is made up from modular bills of material, and the particular mix of features is specified as firm orders are received from customers.

A "synthetic bill of material" is a product structure for a typical top-level product in which the quantity each for each stockable module is the fraction of the time that that module is forecast to be used. (14.1)

MONTE CARLO. A process of simulation in which various events are generated at random according to specified probability models. If the models represent reality, the output from the simulation should be realistic. Originally the Monte Carlo concept was used to evaluate complicated models in which it was not practical to explore all possible combinations of values of the independent variables.

MOVING AVERAGE. The average of a fixed number of observations from a continuing time series. As a new observation is added, the average moves along dropping a previous older value.

MRP. Materials requirements planning. Refers to systems that keep track of requirements and plan production in discrete time intervals. Usually the term includes explosion of net requirements from a parent schedule to dependent requirements on subordinate items.

MSE. Mean square error. See PROBABILITY DISTRIBUTION.

MULTINOMIAL DISTRIBUTION. The probability distribution of the outcome of a function of several variables, where each variable takes on two values (usually 0 and 1) with given probabilities.

MULTIPLE REGRESSION. See LEAST SQUARES.

MURPHY'S LAW. If anything can go wrong, it will. Brown's corollary: as soon as you take your eye off it.

NATIONAL SAFETY STOCK. An inventory investment in a physical distribution system to ensure that some stock can be sent to a satellite when its available stock reaches order point, without waiting for more stock to arrive from the source of supply. The national safety stock is based on the errors in forecasting national demand over the replenishment lead time. It serves to prevent short dating and expediting of frozen orders. (17.01)

NEED DATE. The date when net requirements become positive—there is not sufficient stock on hand and on order to cover gross requirements. Contrast schedule date.

NET CHANGE. A production planning process in which any changes in top-level requirements are immediately reflected through all affected subordinate schedules, netting out previous dependent requirements and adding the new ones.

NET REQUIREMENTS. See GROSS REQUIREMENTS.

NOISE. See FORECAST ERRORS.

NORMAL DISTRIBUTION. A Gaussian distribution, which is symmetrical. It can often be generated as the result of the sum of independent random processes. See PROBABILITY DISTRIBUTION.

NORMAL SMOOTHING. See EXPONENTIAL SMOOTHING, ADAPTIVE SMOOTHING, and FAST SMOOTHING.

NOTIONAL ORDER. An order generated to cover requirements past the end of the freeze period. Notional orders give information to vendors about probable requirements and are used in exploding dependent requirements. See FIRM ORDER. (13.4)

NUMBER OF TERMS IN THE MODEL. See FORECAST MODELS.

NYQUIST FREQUENCY. H. Nyquist, in "Certain Topics in Telegraph Transmission Theory" (*Trans. AIEE*, April 1928, pp. 614–644), showed that in a sampled-data system the highest frequency required goes through one cycle every two observations.

OEM. Original equipment manufacturers. Customers who use your product as one of the materials in their own product.

OFFSET TIME. The time between the date when a subordinate item is required and the date when the parent assembly is due to be completed.

ON HAND. The quantity of stock of a product that is now available for sale, less any reservations or commitments for current shipment.

OPEN ORDER. See FIRM ORDER.

OPERATING LEVEL. The maximum level of stock in a max–min system. The order quantity is the difference between the operating level and the available stock when a replenishment order is triggered.

OPERATIONS SEQUENCE. See ROUTING.

OPTIONS. Features in configuring a product that can be specified by a customer. Usually one member of the list is required, but the customer can select from among them. Example: the engine in an automobile.

GLOSSARY

ORDER OF MAGNITUDE.   Factor of 10. If two values do not differ by at least a factor of 10 they are of the same order of magnitude. Values that differ by more than a factor of 100 are two orders of magnitude apart.

ORDER POINT.   A level of stock used in generating signals to replenish the inventory. It provides for the forecast of demand over the next lead time plus some safety stock. Also sometimes called a reorder point. (12.13)

ORDER REFERENCE NUMBER.   A unique number, assigned in sequence, to each replenishment order as it becomes firm or frozen, used to track progress of the work through the production process.

ORIGIN OF TIME.   In forecast models time in the future is measured by positive numbers of periods, and in the past by negative values. The time corresponding to the most recent observation is the origin of time, which moves forward one period with each new observation.

ORTHOGONAL FUNCTIONS.   Sets of fitting functions for forecast models which do not interact with each other. Each additional function from the set contributes new information about the pattern of observations. Fourier series are one example of orthogonal fitting functions.

OUTLIERS.   Observations that differ from the forecast model by more than some large number of standard deviations (such as four).

PARENT.   An assembly is a parent to the subassemblies that appear on its product structure. Any of those subassemblies in turn may be a parent to the parts used to make it.

PARETO CURVE.   Vilfredo Pareto, Marchese di Parigi, an Italian economist, in 1923 showed that wealth is concentrated in a few individuals or institutions, as in an ABC classification, or distribution by value.

PART NUMBER.   A unique identification code for an item in stock. It may contain numbers, characters, and significant blanks. The part number is the identification for users of the system, in contrast to the file index number, which is an internal identification.

PART-PERIOD BALANCING.   J. J. deMatteis and A. G. Mendoza, in "The Part Period Algorithm," developed a technique for determining how much time-varying demand to cover in the first replenishment lot to be scheduled. The procedure attempts to balance the cost to order against the cost to carry the resulting working stock. Like the least unit cost technique, part-period balancing is only an approximation to the exact solution. (11.103)

PARTIAL EXPECTATION.   A function of a probability distribution that is obtained as the area under the probability curve to the right of the value for the argument. It is a measure of the expected quantity that will be on back order for a given safety factor.

PEGGED REQUIREMENTS. Identification of the source of dependent requirements from individual parents. (14.41)

PERCENT DONE. See BASE INDEX.

PERPETUAL INVENTORY. A record in which each receipt and issue is posted to maintain a book value for the quantity on hand.

PHANTOM BILL OF MATERIALS. An indication in the product structure of a collection of parts that are not scheduled and built as a separate stockable subassembly, but that are included in the bill of materials for explosion. The requirements for a customized product would be specified as a short list of phantom bills for modular subassemblies in engineering or customer service. The explosion process would then accumulate the details of all parts that go into these phantom bills. (14.52)

PHASE ANGLE. In a sine wave the relative position of the peak value from the beginning of the period of observation.

PIECE-MONTHS OF STOCK. When requirements and production are represented by cumulative graphs versus time, the area between the two curves is a measure of inventory in piece-months. The average inventory in pieces is the total area divided by the planning horizon.

PIPELINE. The quantity of stock required to set up standard inventory levels at all stocking echelons when a new product is released.

PLANNING HORIZON. See HORIZON.

PLANNING PERIOD. Intervals of time in which dependent demand is accumulated in production planning. For certain scheduling rules, the coverage is to the end of an individual period. Short periods give the appearance of precision in timing dependent requirements but consume a great deal of computer resource. Long periods can lose some significant detail.

PLUGGED LEVEL. When a new product is to be released, the forecast model can be set up initially on the basis of a rate of demand specified by a product planner or marketing manager. That level is "plugged" into the record, as distinguished from an average that later can be estimated from actual demand.

POLICY VARIABLE. See EXCHANGE CURVES.

POLYNOMIAL. A mathematical expression in which the dependent variable is represented by a linear combination of powers of the independent variables. The degree of the polynomial is the highest power appearing

GLOSSARY

in it. For example, a parabola is a second-degree polynomial, because it involves the square.

PRESENT VALUE. Cash to be received or expended in the future has a present value less than its face value, because of the opportunity to have invested that amount between now and then, and the risk that the receipt won't be the same as is now planned. The present value is used in comparing alternative strategies that involve the flow of money over time.

PRIORITY LIST. A list of tasks arranged with the most urgent one at the top. Priorities can be assigned by latest start date, slack time, critical ratio, or any of several other techniques.

PROBABILITY DISTRIBUTION. The chances of an observation (especially of a forecast error) taking on any value within the possible range. The form of the distribution could be normal, log normal, uniform, or exponential if the variable can take on a continuous range of values. If the variable is inherently discrete (integer) valued, then the distribution forms might include Poisson and binomial. (There are a great many other forms.)

Three functions of the distribution are of special interest. The density function is the usual way that the distribution is plotted, and can be symmetrical or skewed. The chance that the next observation will fall into any range of values is proportional to the area under the density curve between those values. The probability function, in this book, is the area under the curve, starting from the largest possible value and integrating the area under the density function from right to left. The probability function expresses the chance that the next observation will be larger than the value of the argument. The partial expectation is the area under the upper tail of the probability function (integrating from right to left). It is proportional to the expected amount short.

A formal model of a probability distribution allows one to generate values of any of these functions from a few parameters. The safety factor is a normalized variable, such that any observation can be expressed as the mean plus a safety factor times the standard deviation. The mean is the same as the average or expected value, but can be different from the median if the distribution is skewed. The standard deviation is a measure of dispersion or spread, and is the square root of the variance. If the distribution should have a zero mean (as for forecast errors) the variance can be reduced to the mean square error (MSE). The mean absolute deviation (MAD) is proportional to the standard deviation, and the ratio depends on the shape of the distribution function. For small samples (of less than a few hundred points) the ratio of the true standard deviation to the estimated mean absolute deviation can be very much different from the theoretical value.

PROCESS ROUTING. See ROUTING.

PRODUCT STRUCTURE. See BILL OF MATERIALS.

PRODUCTION PLANNING. The process of scheduling production to cover net requirements within the constraints on material, labor, and machine capacity.

PRODUCTION RATE. When material is delivered to stock during a production run at a rate that is sufficiently near the usage rate that a considerable portion of the material can be used before the run is over, the annualized production rate (during production runs) should be taken into account in computing economical lot quantities. (11.03)

PROFILE. See BASE INDEX.

PROJECTED AVAILABILITY. The planned stock on hand, over and above the target safety stock, based on the current plans for firm and notional orders against the gross requirements.

PULL AND PUSH SYSTEMS. If replenishment of stocks in one location can be determined without reference to the stock status elsewhere, that is essentially a pull system of field replenishment. In a push system the total stock status is taken into account in computing fair shares for all locations from the stock of a given product. (17.11)

QUANTITY. See ECONOMICAL LOT SIZE.

QUANTITY DISCOUNT. A small quantity of a material can be purchased at list price. If the quantity ordered exceeds a certain "breakpoint" the unit cost can be effectively reduced. In some cases the quantity discount is based on each item's orders. In others it may be based on the total value of all items, or even on a schedule of orders over time. Note that the effect of lower freight rates for shipping in full truckloads, versus less-than truckload, is effectively a quantity discount on total weight of the order. (11.06)

QUANTITY EACH. In a product structure or a bill of materials, the number of pieces of a subordinate required to make one unit of the parent assembly.

QUANTITY TO SHIP. The fair share available to a location may exceed the space available to store it, or the amount that can be handled in one shipment, or a management policy about how much can be sent to the field. Fair shares are also rounded down to full package quantities to get the shipping quantity.

GLOSSARY

QUEUE. A waiting line of jobs available to go through an operation in the shop.

RANGE OF ITEMS STOCKED. The list of items carried in a particular location, without regard to the quantity of each actually or planned to be in stock.

REALLOCATE. Compute the fair shares of material available in the system to bring each location's stock into balance. Usually used when there is no new material coming into the system.

REFERENCE NUMBER. A unique serial number assigned to each replenishment order to aid in tracking its progress.

REGENERATION. Compare NET CHANGE. In a regeneration system, the master schedule is developed at fixed intervals for all items at one level code. The schedule is exploded to generate dependent demand on subordinate items, and then master schedules are developed at the next level code.

RELEASE DATE. New items are released for sale to customers.

REMNANT STOCK. A given bulk commodity (soap, paint, cereal) is packaged in several different ways. When the stock of any end item reaches a certain level a new production lot is required. The remnant stock is the stock, over their order points, of the items that did not trigger a new batch.

REORDER POINT. See ORDER POINT.

REPLENISHMENT LEAD TIME. The time it takes the manufacturing plant or vendor to deliver material, once a replenishment lot has been triggered.

REPLENISHMENT LOT. A quantity of material planned to be brought into stock.

RESERVE BIN. A quantity of stock, equal to an order point, which is set aside in a two-bin system. The rest of the stock is in a working bin. When the working bin is empty, the reserve bin is opened, and that is a signal to order more stock. (12.4)

RESIDUAL DIFFERENCES. See FORECAST ERRORS.

RESOURCE. See ALLOCATION.

REVISE COEFFICIENTS, or REVISE FORECASTS. See ADAPTIVE SMOOTHING.

ROUTING. Also called operations sequence, process routing. A list of the steps required to complete the manufacture of a product. Engineering, accounting, production control, and the shop floor may require different levels of detail in the separate routings. In general a routing step tells what operation is to be done next, where (department and work

SAFETY FACTOR. The safety stock of an item is the production of the safety factor and the standard deviation of the distribution of errors in forecasting demand over the lead time. The order point is the sum of the safety stock and the forecast of requirements during that same lead time, or freeze period. The purpose of safety stock is to serve customer demand above forecast rates, without having to change open replenishment orders. (Chapter 10)

SAMPLING INTERVAL. Demand is observed at regular intervals for forecasting. The interval can be any number of weeks or calendar months. The forecasts are revised once per sampling interval, and are generated as total quantities for future sampling intervals or forecast periods. (5.2)

SATELLITE. See MASTER WAREHOUSE.

SCALING A FORECAST MODEL. The forecast model for an item with short history can be made proportional to the profile or pattern for another item. The ratio is based on the ratio of levels (deseasonalized current rate of demand), and applies to all coefficients in the model. The trend of the new item can be set to zero.

SCHEDULE. See MASTER SCHEDULE.

SCHEDULE DATE. The date when a production lot is due to be completed. It may be the same as the need date, or earlier if lots are released early to stabilize production, or later if there are limitations on material or capacity.

SCHEDULING BACKLOG. The list of firm orders from customers, with quantities and due dates. (3.2)

SCREEN. The process of comparing actual demand to a forecast model to detect outliers that are significantly different from the model. (5.5)

SEARCH AND FIND. The process of using stock at one location that has a relative excess to satisfy demand at another location. Stocks may be transshipped to rebalance the field inventory, or customer orders can be referred to the supplying warehouse. It is not always most economical to ship from the closest location with an excess—its stock may be needed elsewhere soon. (16.4)

SEASONAL PATTERN. See BASE INDEX and FORECAST MODELS.

SECULAR TREND. A long-term trend in which the level of the demand increases (or declines) steadily from period to period.

SEQUENCE NUMBER. See ROUTING. The identification of the sequence of steps in the manufacturing process.

GLOSSARY

SERIAL CORRELATION. See CORRELATION.

SERIOUS GAME. A learning exercise that involves interaction between the computer and the user, designed to teach some principle.

SERVICE. Customer service can be measured in terms of the amount back ordered, the number of times a back order exists, the duration of the back order, the number of customers subject to shortages, and so on. All of the theory of inventory management is based on models of absolute quantities that can be measured. For management reports these values may have to be expressed as ratios or percentages. (10.1)

SETUP COST. The cost associated with placing a single replenishment order. See ECONOMICAL LOT SIZE.

SHORT DATE. A replenishment order that is scheduled for the end of the freeze period but is needed earlier.

SHORTAGES. See SERVICE.

SIMPLE EXPONENTIAL SMOOTHING. See EXPONENTIAL SMOOTHING.

SINE WAVE. A function of time that has a particular shape. See FORECAST MODELS.

SKU. Stockkeeping unit. A particular part number at a particular location. location.

SLACK TIME. The total time remaining until the lot is due to be completed less the planned setup and run times for all uncompleted operations.

SLANTED CHART. A record with one column for each month. A new line is posted whenever the forecast or the production plan is revised, so that forecasts, production, and planned inventory budgets can be compared from month to month as they are revised. (13.6)

SMOOTHED ERROR TRACKING SIGNAL (SETS). Initially set to zero, the value of SETS is modified whenever the forecast is revised by simple exponential smoothing of the forecast errors. If the forecasts have no bias, the errors vary on either side of zero, so SETS has an expected value of zero. When there is bias, SETS grows until the value exceeds some limit (based on the standard deviation of forecast errors) to generate a tracking signal. See also CUMULATIVE SUMS.

SMOOTHED PRODUCTION. The planned production rate is set to cover all gross requirements within the planning horizon. If the requirements do not change, the production rate would not have to change, and the resulting inventory, just after a peak in requirements, will be at planned levels. In the meantime, however, a stabilization stock can be built up during periods of low requirements. (13.42)

SMOOTHING. See ADAPTIVE SMOOTHING and EXPONENTIAL SMOOTHING.

SPLIT LOTS. A replenishment order initially issued under one reference number may be split into smaller pieces to get some material through a bottleneck quickly or to allow for better materials handling in the shop.

SPURIOUS FREQUENCIES. See FORECAST MODELS.

STABILIZATION STOCK. See SMOOTHED PRODUCTION.

STANDARD DEVIATION. A measure of the dispersion of forecast errors, used to set safety stocks. See PROBABILITY DISTRIBUTION.

STANDARD RATIO. A parameter of a log-normal distribution that measures dispersion. The logarithms of the variable are normally distributed with standard deviation s. The standard ratio is the antilog of s.

STATE, as in STATE VARIABLES or STATE OF THE ENVIRONMENT. Real operating environments can exist in a large variety of states from time to time, which can be described in a model by state variables. Some stable variables define what management would like the system to be, and others measure the actual situation. A control system must have at least as many possible states as the environment or process it seeks to control. Otherwise situations will arise that the controls cannot handle.

STATISTICAL FORECAST. See FORECAST MODELS.

STOCK. See INVENTORY MANAGEMENT.

STOCK TARGET. The planned minimum level of stock on hand. It may be simply safety stock or it may include provision for the stock in transit in the physical distribution system and safety stocks at satellite locations.

STOCKING LOCATION. Any warehouse that carries a particular item in its range of products. Distinguished from bin location, which is the place within a warehouse where the item is stored.

STOCKKEEPING UNIT. See SKU.

STRATIFICATION. A process of breaking a long inventory into groups where items within a group are homogeneous in some relevant way. Classification can be different for different purposes of analysis and control. (Chapter 9)

SUBORDINATE PARTS. See PARENT.

SYNTHETIC BILL OF MATERIALS. See MODULAR BILL OF MATERIALS.

TARGET STOCK. The planned stock based on national safety stock, stock in transit, and regional safety stocks.

TAXONOMY. The systematic distinguishing and naming of types that group together similar objects.

TERMINAL SERVICE. See ALL-TIME SUPPLY.

TERMS IN A MODEL. See FORECAST MODELS.

GLOSSARY

TRACKING SIGNAL. A means for detecting systematic bias in the forecasts. See CUMULATIVE SUMS and SMOOTHED ERROR TRACKING SIGNAL.

TRANSACTIONS SHORT. See SERVICE.

TRANSITION MATRIX. See ADAPTIVE SMOOTHING.

TRANSPORTATION ALGORITHM. See LINEAR PROGRAMMING.

TRAVELING SALESMAN. See LINEAR PROGRAMMING.

TREND. See FORECAST MODELS.

TRIPLE SMOOTHING. See EXPONENTIAL SMOOTHING.

TWO-BIN CONTROL. A method of managing the replenishment of stock where a single lot quantity lasts more than a lead time, so that there is never more than one outstanding replenishment order at a time. Material can be withdrawn from the working bin without requisitions. When the reserve bin has to be opened, that is a signal to replenish the stock. (12.4)

VARIANCE. See PROBABILITY DISTRIBUTION.

VARIANCE LAW. A model of the tendency for the mean square error to be related to the forecast level across all items in an inventory. The variance law can be used to set initial estimates of the mean square error for new items, and to increase the levels of protection during promotions.

WEIGHTED LEAST SQUARES. See LEAST SQUARES.

WHERE USED. A method of retrieving all parents that show a given material in their product structures, used for engineering changes and coping with shortages and substitution.

WORK CENTER. A subunit of a production department to indicate either a group of people who are more or less interchangeable or specific machines.

WORK SHEET. A daily priority list for each department in the shop that shows the work available (and to come) in sequence by latest start date. (15.2)

WORKING DAYS. Days on which work can be scheduled, excluding weekends, holidays, and periods when a plant will be shut for inventory, vacation, or strikes.

WORKING STOCK. The average inventory investment that results from a policy of buying or manufacturing material in excess of current needs, to reduce the annual operating costs of setting up replenishment orders.

YIELD FACTOR. The ratio of the average good quantity at the end of the production process to the quantity originally scheduled.

APPENDIX D

Tables of Probability Functions

Exhibit D.2 gives the density, probability, and partial expectation functions of the normal distribution. For negative values of the argument (safety factor), the density is the same as for positive values; the probability is $1 - F(-K)$; and the partial expectation is tabulated.

Exhibit D.3 gives similar functions of the exponential distribution. Since the exponential distribution can be computed exactly it is tabulated for larger increments of the safety factor.

In practice the normal distribution can be evaluated by rational approximations (Exhibit D.1). See *Decision Rules for Inventory Management*, p. 93. The APL formal definition of the method used through the Materials Management Systems Library is the function $R \leftarrow N\ P\underline{P}\ X$ where the left argument N (from 1 to 6) selects which function to compute, and whether to compute the function of the safety factor, or the inverse, safety factor from a value of the function. Exhibit D.4 tabulates values obtained from these approximations.

Exhibit D.1

```
     ∇ R←N PP X
[1]     →(PX,FX,EX,XP,XF,XE)[N]
[2]    PX:R←(*⁻0.5×X*2)÷(○2)*0.5 × →0 ⋒ DENSITY
[3]    XP:R←(⁻2×⍟(((÷○2)*0.5)⌊X⌈*⁻15)×(○2)*0.5)*0.5 × →0 ⋒ INVERSE DENSITY
[4]    EX:R←(1 PP X)-X×2 PP X × →0 ⋒ EXPECTATION
[5]    XE:R←(0.17592241÷X+0.044212641)+0.0012267386÷X+0.00030570313 ⋒ INVERSE EXPECTATION
[6]     R←(X×(0.4442135-0.0706145×X))-1.7529479+R
[7]     R←(4×X<7.1E⁻6)+(⁻X×X>4)+(R×X-0.39894228)×(X≤4)×X≥7.1E⁻6 × →0
[8]    FX:R←6.76151+0.9123×X*2 ⋒ PROBABILITY
[9]     R←R÷21.8468+(X*2)×7.03823+X*2
[10]    R←0.5-X×(6.41979÷75.33103+X*2)+R
[11]    R←(X<⁻4)+R×(X≤4)×X≥⁻4 × →0
[12]   XF:R←(0.5-X)×2.0489+(0.14822401÷0.29670819-(0.5-X)*2)+0.0014532591÷
        0.2505217-(0.5-X)*2 ⋒ INVERSE PROBABILITY
[13]    R←(⁻4×X>0.99996832)+(4×X<3.168E⁻5)+R×(X≤0.99996832)×X≥3.168E⁻5
     ∇
```

Exhibit D.2

SAFETY FACTOR K	DENSITY P(K)	PROBABILITY F(K)	PARTIAL EXPECTATION E(K)	PARTIAL EXPECTATION E(-K)
0.00	0.3989423	0.5000000	0.3989423	0.3989423
0.01	0.3989223	0.4960106	0.3939622	0.4039622
0.02	0.3988625	0.4920217	0.3890221	0.4090221
0.03	0.3987628	0.4880335	0.3841218	0.4141218
0.04	0.3986233	0.4840466	0.3792614	0.4192614
0.05	0.3984439	0.4800612	0.3744409	0.4244409
0.06	0.3982248	0.4760778	0.3696602	0.4296602
0.07	0.3979661	0.4720968	0.3649193	0.4349193
0.08	0.3976677	0.4681186	0.3602182	0.4402182
0.09	0.3973298	0.4641436	0.3555569	0.4455569
0.10	0.3969525	0.4601722	0.3509353	0.4509353
0.11	0.3965360	0.4562047	0.3463535	0.4563535
0.12	0.3960802	0.4522416	0.3418112	0.4618112
0.13	0.3955854	0.4482832	0.3373086	0.4673086
0.14	0.3950517	0.4443300	0.3328455	0.4728455
0.15	0.3944793	0.4403823	0.3284220	0.4784220
0.16	0.3938684	0.4364405	0.3240379	0.4840379
0.17	0.3932190	0.4325051	0.3196932	0.4896932
0.18	0.3925315	0.4285763	0.3153878	0.4953878
0.19	0.3918060	0.4246546	0.3111216	0.5011216
0.20	0.3910427	0.4207403	0.3068946	0.5068946
0.21	0.3902419	0.4168338	0.3027068	0.5127068
0.22	0.3894038	0.4129356	0.2985579	0.5185579
0.23	0.3885286	0.4090459	0.2944480	0.5244480
0.24	0.3876166	0.4051651	0.2903770	0.5303770
0.25	0.3866681	0.4012937	0.2863447	0.5363447
0.26	0.3856834	0.3974319	0.2823511	0.5423511
0.27	0.3846627	0.3935801	0.2783960	0.5483960
0.28	0.3836063	0.3897388	0.2744794	0.5544794
0.29	0.3825146	0.3859081	0.2706012	0.5606012
0.30	0.3813878	0.3820886	0.2667612	0.5667612
0.31	0.3802264	0.3782805	0.2629594	0.5729594
0.32	0.3790305	0.3744842	0.2591956	0.5791956
0.33	0.3778007	0.3707000	0.2554697	0.5854697
0.34	0.3765372	0.3669283	0.2517816	0.5917816
0.35	0.3752403	0.3631693	0.2481311	0.5981311
0.36	0.3739106	0.3594236	0.2445181	0.6045181
0.37	0.3725483	0.3556912	0.2409426	0.6109426
0.38	0.3711539	0.3519727	0.2374043	0.6174043
0.39	0.3697277	0.3482683	0.2339031	0.6239031
0.40	0.3682701	0.3445783	0.2304388	0.6304388
0.41	0.3667817	0.3409030	0.2270114	0.6370114
0.42	0.3652627	0.3372427	0.2236207	0.6436207
0.43	0.3637136	0.3335978	0.2202665	0.6502665
0.44	0.3621349	0.3299686	0.2169487	0.6569487
0.45	0.3605270	0.3263552	0.2136671	0.6636671
0.46	0.3588903	0.3227581	0.2104216	0.6704216
0.47	0.3572253	0.3191775	0.2072119	0.6772119
0.48	0.3555325	0.3156137	0.2040380	0.6840380
0.49	0.3538124	0.3120669	0.2008996	0.6908996
0.50	0.3520653	0.3085375	0.1977966	0.6977966

Exhibit D.2 (Continued)

SAFETY FACTOR K	DENSITY P(K)	PROBABILITY F(K)	PARTIAL EXPECTATION E(K)	PARTIAL EXPECTATION E(-K)
0.50	0.3520653	0.3085375	0.1977966	0.6977966
0.51	0.3502919	0.3050257	0.1947288	0.7047288
0.52	0.3484925	0.3015318	0.1916960	0.7116960
0.53	0.3466677	0.2980560	0.1886981	0.7186981
0.54	0.3448180	0.2945985	0.1857348	0.7257348
0.55	0.3429439	0.2911597	0.1828060	0.7328060
0.56	0.3410458	0.2877397	0.1799115	0.7399115
0.57	0.3391243	0.2843388	0.1770512	0.7470512
0.58	0.3371799	0.2809573	0.1742247	0.7542247
0.59	0.3352132	0.2775953	0.1714320	0.7614320
0.60	0.3332246	0.2742531	0.1686727	0.7686727
0.61	0.3312147	0.2709309	0.1659468	0.7759468
0.62	0.3291840	0.2676289	0.1632540	0.7832540
0.63	0.3271330	0.2643473	0.1605942	0.7905942
0.64	0.3250623	0.2610863	0.1579670	0.7979670
0.65	0.3229724	0.2578461	0.1553724	0.8053724
0.66	0.3208638	0.2546269	0.1528100	0.8128100
0.67	0.3187371	0.2514289	0.1502798	0.8202798
0.68	0.3165929	0.2482522	0.1477814	0.8277814
0.69	0.3144317	0.2450971	0.1453147	0.8353147
0.70	0.3122539	0.2419637	0.1428794	0.8428794
0.71	0.3100603	0.2388521	0.1404753	0.8504753
0.72	0.3078513	0.2357625	0.1381023	0.8581023
0.73	0.3056274	0.2326951	0.1357600	0.8657600
0.74	0.3033893	0.2296500	0.1334483	0.8734483
0.75	0.3011374	0.2266274	0.1311669	0.8811669
0.76	0.2988724	0.2236273	0.1289157	0.8889157
0.77	0.2965948	0.2206499	0.1266943	0.8966943
0.78	0.2943050	0.2176954	0.1245026	0.9045026
0.79	0.2920038	0.2147639	0.1223403	0.9123403
0.80	0.2896916	0.2118554	0.1202072	0.9202072
0.81	0.2873689	0.2089701	0.1181031	0.9281031
0.82	0.2850364	0.2061081	0.1160278	0.9360278
0.83	0.2826945	0.2032694	0.1139809	0.9439809
0.84	0.2803438	0.2004542	0.1119623	0.9519623
0.85	0.2779849	0.1976625	0.1099717	0.9599717
0.86	0.2756182	0.1948945	0.1080090	0.9680090
0.87	0.2732444	0.1921502	0.1060738	0.9760738
0.88	0.2708640	0.1894297	0.1041659	0.9841659
0.89	0.2684774	0.1867329	0.1022851	0.9922851
0.90	0.2660852	0.1840601	0.1004311	1.0004311
0.91	0.2636880	0.1814113	0.0986038	1.0086038
0.92	0.2612863	0.1787864	0.0968028	1.0168028
0.93	0.2588805	0.1761855	0.0950280	1.0250280
0.94	0.2564713	0.1736088	0.0932790	1.0332790
0.95	0.2540591	0.1710561	0.0915557	1.0415557
0.96	0.2516443	0.1685276	0.0898578	1.0498578
0.97	0.2492277	0.1660232	0.0881851	1.0581851
0.98	0.2468095	0.1635431	0.0865373	1.0665373
0.99	0.2443904	0.1610871	0.0849142	1.0749142
1.00	0.2419707	0.1586553	0.0833155	1.0833155

Exhibit D.2 (Continued)

SAFETY FACTOR K	DENSITY P(K)	PROBABILITY F(K)	PARTIAL EXPECTATION E(K)	PARTIAL EXPECTATION E(-K)
1.00	0.2419707	0.1586553	0.0833155	1.0833155
1.01	0.2395511	0.1562476	0.0817410	1.0917410
1.02	0.2371320	0.1538642	0.0801904	1.1001904
1.03	0.2347138	0.1515050	0.0786636	1.1086636
1.04	0.2322970	0.1491700	0.0771603	1.1171603
1.05	0.2298821	0.1468591	0.0756801	1.1256801
1.06	0.2274696	0.1445723	0.0742230	1.1342230
1.07	0.2250599	0.1423097	0.0727886	1.1427886
1.08	0.2226535	0.1400711	0.0713767	1.1513767
1.09	0.2202508	0.1378566	0.0699871	1.1599871
1.10	0.2178522	0.1356661	0.0686195	1.1686195
1.11	0.2154582	0.1334995	0.0672737	1.1772737
1.12	0.2130691	0.1313569	0.0659494	1.1859494
1.13	0.2106856	0.1292381	0.0646465	1.1946465
1.14	0.2083078	0.1271432	0.0633646	1.2033646
1.15	0.2059363	0.1250719	0.0621035	1.2121035
1.16	0.2035714	0.1230244	0.0608631	1.2208631
1.17	0.2012135	0.1210005	0.0596430	1.2296430
1.18	0.1988631	0.1190001	0.0584430	1.2384430
1.19	0.1965205	0.1170232	0.0572629	1.2472629
1.20	0.1941861	0.1150697	0.0561025	1.2561025
1.21	0.1918602	0.1131394	0.0549614	1.2649614
1.22	0.1895432	0.1112324	0.0538396	1.2738396
1.23	0.1872354	0.1093486	0.0527367	1.2827367
1.24	0.1849373	0.1074877	0.0516525	1.2916525
1.25	0.1826491	0.1056498	0.0505869	1.3005869
1.26	0.1803712	0.1038347	0.0495395	1.3095395
1.27	0.1781038	0.1020423	0.0485101	1.3185101
1.28	0.1758474	0.1002726	0.0474985	1.3274985
1.29	0.1736022	0.0985253	0.0465046	1.3365046
1.30	0.1713686	0.0968005	0.0455280	1.3455280
1.31	0.1691468	0.0950979	0.0445685	1.3545685
1.32	0.1669370	0.0934175	0.0436259	1.3636259
1.33	0.1647397	0.0917591	0.0427001	1.3727001
1.34	0.1625551	0.0901227	0.0417907	1.3817907
1.35	0.1603833	0.0885080	0.0408975	1.3908975
1.36	0.1582248	0.0869150	0.0400204	1.4000204
1.37	0.1560797	0.0853435	0.0391592	1.4091592
1.38	0.1539483	0.0837933	0.0383135	1.4183135
1.39	0.1518308	0.0822644	0.0374832	1.4274832
1.40	0.1497275	0.0807567	0.0366681	1.4366681
1.41	0.1476385	0.0792698	0.0358680	1.4458680
1.42	0.1455641	0.0778038	0.0350827	1.4550827
1.43	0.1435046	0.0763585	0.0343119	1.4643119
1.44	0.1414600	0.0749337	0.0335554	1.4735554
1.45	0.1394306	0.0735293	0.0328131	1.4828131
1.46	0.1374165	0.0721450	0.0320848	1.4920848
1.47	0.1354181	0.0707809	0.0313702	1.5013702
1.48	0.1334353	0.0694366	0.0306691	1.5106691
1.49	0.1314684	0.0681121	0.0299814	1.5199814
1.50	0.1295176	0.0668072	0.0293068	1.5293068

Exhibit D.2 (Continued)

SAFETY FACTOR K	DENSITY P(K)	PROBABILITY F(K)	PARTIAL EXPECTATION E(K)	PARTIAL EXPECTATION E(-K)
1.50	0.1295176	0.0668072	0.0293068	1.5293068
1.51	0.1275830	0.0655217	0.0286452	1.5386452
1.52	0.1256646	0.0642555	0.0279963	1.5479963
1.53	0.1237628	0.0630084	0.0273600	1.5573600
1.54	0.1218775	0.0617802	0.0267361	1.5667361
1.55	0.1200090	0.0605708	0.0261243	1.5761243
1.56	0.1181573	0.0593799	0.0255246	1.5855246
1.57	0.1163225	0.0582076	0.0249367	1.5949367
1.58	0.1145048	0.0570534	0.0243604	1.6043604
1.59	0.1127042	0.0559174	0.0237955	1.6137955
1.60	0.1109208	0.0547993	0.0232420	1.6232420
1.61	0.1091548	0.0536989	0.0226995	1.6326995
1.62	0.1074061	0.0526161	0.0221679	1.6421679
1.63	0.1056748	0.0515507	0.0216471	1.6516471
1.64	0.1039611	0.0505026	0.0211369	1.6611369
1.65	0.1022649	0.0494715	0.0206370	1.6706370
1.66	0.1005864	0.0484572	0.0201474	1.6801474
1.67	0.0989255	0.0474597	0.0196678	1.6896678
1.68	0.0972823	0.0464787	0.0191981	1.6991981
1.69	0.0956568	0.0455140	0.0187382	1.7087382
1.70	0.0940491	0.0445655	0.0182878	1.7182878
1.71	0.0924591	0.0436329	0.0178468	1.7278468
1.72	0.0908870	0.0427162	0.0174151	1.7374151
1.73	0.0893326	0.0418151	0.0169924	1.7469924
1.74	0.0877961	0.0409295	0.0165787	1.7565787
1.75	0.0862773	0.0400592	0.0161738	1.7661738
1.76	0.0847764	0.0392039	0.0157775	1.7757775
1.77	0.0832932	0.0383636	0.0153897	1.7853897
1.78	0.0818278	0.0375380	0.0150102	1.7950102
1.79	0.0803801	0.0367270	0.0146389	1.8046389
1.80	0.0789502	0.0359303	0.0142756	1.8142756
1.81	0.0775379	0.0351479	0.0139202	1.8239202
1.82	0.0761433	0.0343795	0.0135726	1.8335726
1.83	0.0747663	0.0336250	0.0132326	1.8432326
1.84	0.0734068	0.0328841	0.0129000	1.8529000
1.85	0.0720649	0.0321568	0.0125748	1.8625748
1.86	0.0707404	0.0314428	0.0122569	1.8722569
1.87	0.0694333	0.0307419	0.0119459	1.8819459
1.88	0.0681436	0.0300540	0.0116420	1.8916420
1.89	0.0668711	0.0293790	0.0113448	1.9013448
1.90	0.0656158	0.0287166	0.0110544	1.9110544
1.91	0.0643777	0.0280666	0.0107704	1.9207704
1.92	0.0631566	0.0274289	0.0104930	1.9304930
1.93	0.0619524	0.0268034	0.0102218	1.9402218
1.94	0.0607652	0.0261898	0.0099569	1.9499569
1.95	0.0595947	0.0255881	0.0096980	1.9596980
1.96	0.0584409	0.0249979	0.0094451	1.9694451
1.97	0.0573038	0.0244192	0.0091980	1.9791980
1.98	0.0561831	0.0238518	0.0089566	1.9889566
1.99	0.0550789	0.0232955	0.0087209	1.9987209
2.00	0.0539910	0.0227501	0.0084907	2.0084907

Exhibit D.2 (Continued)

SAFETY FACTOR K	DENSITY P(K)	PROBABILITY F(K)	PARTIAL EXPECTATION E(K)	PARTIAL EXPECTATION E(-K)
2.00	0.0539910	0.0227501	0.0084907	2.0084907
2.01	0.0529192	0.0222156	0.0082659	2.0182659
2.02	0.0518636	0.0216917	0.0080464	2.0280464
2.03	0.0508239	0.0211783	0.0078320	2.0378320
2.04	0.0498001	0.0206752	0.0076228	2.0476228
2.05	0.0487920	0.0201822	0.0074185	2.0574185
2.06	0.0477996	0.0196993	0.0072191	2.0672191
2.07	0.0468226	0.0192262	0.0070245	2.0770245
2.08	0.0458611	0.0187628	0.0068345	2.0868345
2.09	0.0449148	0.0183089	0.0066492	2.0966492
2.10	0.0439836	0.0178644	0.0064683	2.1064683
2.11	0.0430674	0.0174292	0.0062919	2.1162919
2.12	0.0421661	0.0170030	0.0061197	2.1261197
2.13	0.0412795	0.0165858	0.0059518	2.1359518
2.14	0.0404076	0.0161774	0.0057880	2.1457880
2.15	0.0395500	0.0157776	0.0056282	2.1556282
2.16	0.0387069	0.0153863	0.0054724	2.1654724
2.17	0.0378779	0.0150034	0.0053204	2.1753204
2.18	0.0370629	0.0146287	0.0051723	2.1851723
2.19	0.0362619	0.0142621	0.0050278	2.1950278
2.20	0.0354746	0.0139034	0.0048870	2.2048870
2.21	0.0347009	0.0135526	0.0047497	2.2147497
2.22	0.0339408	0.0132094	0.0046159	2.2246159
2.23	0.0331939	0.0128737	0.0044855	2.2344855
2.24	0.0324603	0.0125455	0.0043584	2.2443584
2.25	0.0317397	0.0122245	0.0042346	2.2542346
2.26	0.0310319	0.0119106	0.0041139	2.2641139
2.27	0.0303370	0.0116038	0.0039964	2.2739964
2.28	0.0296546	0.0113038	0.0038818	2.2838818
2.29	0.0289847	0.0110107	0.0037703	2.2937703
2.30	0.0283270	0.0107241	0.0036616	2.3036616
2.31	0.0276816	0.0104441	0.0035557	2.3135557
2.32	0.0270481	0.0101704	0.0034527	2.3234527
2.33	0.0264265	0.0099031	0.0033523	2.3333523
2.34	0.0258166	0.0096419	0.0032546	2.3432546
2.35	0.0252182	0.0093867	0.0031595	2.3531595
2.36	0.0246313	0.0091375	0.0030668	2.3630668
2.37	0.0240556	0.0088940	0.0029767	2.3729767
2.38	0.0234910	0.0086563	0.0028889	2.3828889
2.39	0.0229374	0.0084242	0.0028035	2.3928035
2.40	0.0223945	0.0081975	0.0027204	2.4027204
2.41	0.0218624	0.0079763	0.0026396	2.4126396
2.42	0.0213407	0.0077603	0.0025609	2.4225609
2.43	0.0208294	0.0075494	0.0024844	2.4324844
2.44	0.0203284	0.0073436	0.0024099	2.4424099
2.45	0.0198374	0.0071428	0.0023375	2.4523375
2.46	0.0193563	0.0069469	0.0022670	2.4622670
2.47	0.0188850	0.0067557	0.0021985	2.4721985
2.48	0.0184233	0.0065691	0.0021319	2.4821319
2.49	0.0179711	0.0063872	0.0020671	2.4920671
2.50	0.0175283	0.0062097	0.0020041	2.5020041

Exhibit D.2 (Continued)

SAFETY FACTOR K	DENSITY P(K)	PROBABILITY F(K)	PARTIAL EXPECTATION E(K)	PARTIAL EXPECTATION E(-K)
2.50	0.0175283	0.0062097	0.0020041	2.5020041
2.51	0.0170947	0.0060366	0.0019429	2.5119429
2.52	0.0166701	0.0058677	0.0018834	2.5218834
2.53	0.0162545	0.0057031	0.0018255	2.5318255
2.54	0.0158476	0.0055426	0.0017693	2.5417693
2.55	0.0154493	0.0053861	0.0017147	2.5517147
2.56	0.0150596	0.0052336	0.0016616	2.5616616
2.57	0.0146782	0.0050849	0.0016100	2.5716100
2.58	0.0143051	0.0049400	0.0015599	2.5815599
2.59	0.0139401	0.0047988	0.0015112	2.5915112
2.60	0.0135830	0.0046612	0.0014639	2.6014639
2.61	0.0132337	0.0045271	0.0014179	2.6114179
2.62	0.0128921	0.0043965	0.0013733	2.6213733
2.63	0.0125581	0.0042692	0.0013300	2.6313300
2.64	0.0122315	0.0041453	0.0012879	2.6412879
2.65	0.0119122	0.0040246	0.0012471	2.6512471
2.66	0.0116001	0.0039070	0.0012074	2.6612074
2.67	0.0112951	0.0037926	0.0011689	2.6711689
2.68	0.0109969	0.0036811	0.0011316	2.6811316
2.69	0.0107056	0.0035726	0.0010953	2.6910953
2.70	0.0104209	0.0034670	0.0010601	2.7010601
2.71	0.0101428	0.0033642	0.0010260	2.7110260
2.72	0.0098712	0.0032641	0.0009928	2.7209928
2.73	0.0096058	0.0031667	0.0009607	2.7309607
2.74	0.0093466	0.0030720	0.0009295	2.7409295
2.75	0.0090936	0.0029798	0.0008992	2.7508992
2.76	0.0088465	0.0028901	0.0008699	2.7608699
2.77	0.0086052	0.0028028	0.0008414	2.7708414
2.78	0.0083697	0.0027179	0.0008138	2.7808138
2.79	0.0081398	0.0026354	0.0007870	2.7907870
2.80	0.0079155	0.0025551	0.0007611	2.8007611
2.81	0.0076965	0.0024771	0.0007359	2.8107359
2.82	0.0074829	0.0024012	0.0007115	2.8207115
2.83	0.0072744	0.0023274	0.0006879	2.8306879
2.84	0.0070711	0.0022557	0.0006650	2.8406650
2.85	0.0068728	0.0021860	0.0006428	2.8506428
2.86	0.0066793	0.0021182	0.0006213	2.8606213
2.87	0.0064907	0.0020524	0.0006004	2.8706004
2.88	0.0063067	0.0019884	0.0005802	2.8805802
2.89	0.0061274	0.0019262	0.0005606	2.8905606
2.90	0.0059525	0.0018658	0.0005417	2.9005417
2.91	0.0057821	0.0018071	0.0005233	2.9105233
2.92	0.0056160	0.0017502	0.0005055	2.9205055
2.93	0.0054541	0.0016948	0.0004883	2.9304883
2.94	0.0052963	0.0016411	0.0004716	2.9404716
2.95	0.0051426	0.0015889	0.0004555	2.9504555
2.96	0.0049929	0.0015382	0.0004398	2.9604398
2.97	0.0048470	0.0014890	0.0004247	2.9704247
2.98	0.0047050	0.0014412	0.0004101	2.9804101
2.99	0.0045666	0.0013949	0.0003959	2.9903959
3.00	0.0044318	0.0013499	0.0003822	3.0003822

Exhibit D.2 (Continued)

SAFETY FACTOR K	DENSITY P(K)	PROBABILITY F(K)	PARTIAL EXPECTATION E(K)	PARTIAL EXPECTATION E(-K)
3.00	0.0044318	0.0013499	0.0003822	3.0003822
3.01	0.0043007	0.0013062	0.0003689	3.0103689
3.02	0.0041729	0.0012639	0.0003560	3.0203560
3.03	0.0040486	0.0012228	0.0003436	3.0303436
3.04	0.0039276	0.0011829	0.0003316	3.0403316
3.05	0.0038098	0.0011442	0.0003199	3.0503199
3.06	0.0036951	0.0011067	0.0003087	3.0603087
3.07	0.0035836	0.0010703	0.0002978	3.0702978
3.08	0.0034751	0.0010350	0.0002873	3.0802873
3.09	0.0033695	0.0010008	0.0002771	3.0902771
3.10	0.0032668	0.0009676	0.0002672	3.1002672
3.11	0.0031669	0.0009354	0.0002577	3.1102577
3.12	0.0030698	0.0009043	0.0002485	3.1202485
3.13	0.0029754	0.0008740	0.0002396	3.1302396
3.14	0.0028835	0.0008447	0.0002311	3.1402311
3.15	0.0027943	0.0008164	0.0002227	3.1502227
3.16	0.0027075	0.0007888	0.0002147	3.1602147
3.17	0.0026231	0.0007622	0.0002070	3.1702070
3.18	0.0025411	0.0007364	0.0001995	3.1801995
3.19	0.0024615	0.0007114	0.0001922	3.1901922
3.20	0.0023841	0.0006871	0.0001852	3.2001852
3.21	0.0023089	0.0006637	0.0001785	3.2101785
3.22	0.0022358	0.0006410	0.0001720	3.2201720
3.23	0.0021649	0.0006190	0.0001657	3.2301657
3.24	0.0020960	0.0005976	0.0001596	3.2401596
3.25	0.0020290	0.0005770	0.0001537	3.2501537
3.26	0.0019641	0.0005571	0.0001480	3.2601480
3.27	0.0019010	0.0005377	0.0001426	3.2701426
3.28	0.0018397	0.0005190	0.0001373	3.2801373
3.29	0.0017803	0.0005009	0.0001322	3.2901322
3.30	0.0017226	0.0004834	0.0001273	3.3001273
3.31	0.0016666	0.0004665	0.0001225	3.3101225
3.32	0.0016122	0.0004501	0.0001179	3.3201179
3.33	0.0015595	0.0004342	0.0001135	3.3301135
3.34	0.0015084	0.0004189	0.0001093	3.3401093
3.35	0.0014587	0.0004041	0.0001051	3.3501051
3.36	0.0014106	0.0003897	0.0001012	3.3601012
3.37	0.0013639	0.0003758	0.0000973	3.3700973
3.38	0.0013187	0.0003624	0.0000937	3.3800937
3.39	0.0012748	0.0003495	0.0000901	3.3900901
3.40	0.0012322	0.0003369	0.0000867	3.4000867
3.41	0.0011910	0.0003248	0.0000834	3.4100834
3.42	0.0011510	0.0003131	0.0000802	3.4200802
3.43	0.0011122	0.0003018	0.0000771	3.4300771
3.44	0.0010747	0.0002909	0.0000741	3.4400741
3.45	0.0010383	0.0002803	0.0000713	3.4500713
3.46	0.0010030	0.0002701	0.0000685	3.4600685
3.47	0.0009689	0.0002602	0.0000659	3.4700659
3.48	0.0009358	0.0002507	0.0000633	3.4800633
3.49	0.0009037	0.0002415	0.0000609	3.4900609
3.50	0.0008727	0.0002326	0.0000585	3.5000585

Exhibit D.2 (Continued)

SAFETY FACTOR K	DENSITY P(K)	PROBABILITY F(K)	PARTIAL EXPECTATION E(K)	PARTIAL EXPECTATION E(-K)
3.50	0.0008727	0.0002326	0.0000585	3.5000585
3.51	0.0008426	0.0002241	0.0000562	3.5100562
3.52	0.0008135	0.0002158	0.0000540	3.5200540
3.53	0.0007853	0.0002078	0.0000519	3.5300519
3.54	0.0007581	0.0002001	0.0000498	3.5400498
3.55	0.0007317	0.0001926	0.0000479	3.5500479
3.56	0.0007061	0.0001854	0.0000460	3.5600460
3.57	0.0006814	0.0001785	0.0000442	3.5700442
3.58	0.0006575	0.0001718	0.0000424	3.5800424
3.59	0.0006343	0.0001653	0.0000407	3.5900407
3.60	0.0006119	0.0001591	0.0000391	3.6000391
3.61	0.0005902	0.0001531	0.0000375	3.6100375
3.62	0.0005693	0.0001473	0.0000360	3.6200360
3.63	0.0005490	0.0001417	0.0000346	3.6300346
3.64	0.0005294	0.0001363	0.0000332	3.6400332
3.65	0.0005105	0.0001311	0.0000319	3.6500319
3.66	0.0004921	0.0001261	0.0000306	3.6600306
3.67	0.0004744	0.0001213	0.0000294	3.6700294
3.68	0.0004573	0.0001166	0.0000282	3.6800282
3.69	0.0004408	0.0001121	0.0000270	3.6900270
3.70	0.0004248	0.0001078	0.0000259	3.7000259
3.71	0.0004093	0.0001036	0.0000249	3.7100249
3.72	0.0003944	0.0000996	0.0000238	3.7200238
3.73	0.0003800	0.0000957	0.0000229	3.7300229
3.74	0.0003661	0.0000920	0.0000219	3.7400219
3.75	0.0003526	0.0000884	0.0000210	3.7500210
3.76	0.0003396	0.0000850	0.0000202	3.7600202
3.77	0.0003271	0.0000816	0.0000193	3.7700193
3.78	0.0003149	0.0000784	0.0000185	3.7800185
3.79	0.0003032	0.0000753	0.0000178	3.7900178
3.80	0.0002919	0.0000723	0.0000170	3.8000170
3.81	0.0002810	0.0000695	0.0000163	3.8100163
3.82	0.0002705	0.0000667	0.0000156	3.8200156
3.83	0.0002604	0.0000641	0.0000150	3.8300150
3.84	0.0002506	0.0000615	0.0000144	3.8400144
3.85	0.0002411	0.0000591	0.0000137	3.8500137
3.86	0.0002320	0.0000567	0.0000132	3.8600132
3.87	0.0002232	0.0000544	0.0000126	3.8700126
3.88	0.0002147	0.0000522	0.0000121	3.8800121
3.89	0.0002065	0.0000501	0.0000116	3.8900116
3.90	0.0001987	0.0000481	0.0000111	3.9000111
3.91	0.0001910	0.0000461	0.0000106	3.9100106
3.92	0.0001837	0.0000443	0.0000102	3.9200102
3.93	0.0001766	0.0000425	0.0000097	3.9300097
3.94	0.0001698	0.0000407	0.0000093	3.9400093
3.95	0.0001633	0.0000391	0.0000089	3.9500089
3.96	0.0001569	0.0000375	0.0000085	3.9600085
3.97	0.0001508	0.0000359	0.0000082	3.9700082
3.98	0.0001449	0.0000345	0.0000078	3.9800078
3.99	0.0001393	0.0000330	0.0000075	3.9900075
4.00	0.0001338	0.0000317	0.0000071	4.0000071

Exhibit D.2 (Continued)

SAFETY FACTOR K	DENSITY $P(K)$	PROBABILITY $F(K)$	PARTIAL EXPECTATION $E(K)$	PARTIAL EXPECTATION $E(-K)$
4.00	0.0001338	0.0000317	0.0000071	4.0000071
4.01	0.0001286	0.0000304	0.0000068	4.0100068
4.02	0.0001235	0.0000291	0.0000065	4.0200065
4.03	0.0001186	0.0000279	0.0000063	4.0300063
4.04	0.0001140	0.0000267	0.0000060	4.0400060
4.05	0.0001094	0.0000256	0.0000057	4.0500057
4.06	0.0001051	0.0000245	0.0000055	4.0600055
4.07	0.0001009	0.0000235	0.0000052	4.0700052
4.08	0.0000969	0.0000225	0.0000050	4.0800050
4.09	0.0000930	0.0000216	0.0000048	4.0900048
4.10	0.0000893	0.0000207	0.0000046	4.1000046
4.11	0.0000857	0.0000198	0.0000044	4.1100044
4.12	0.0000822	0.0000189	0.0000042	4.1200042
4.13	0.0000789	0.0000181	0.0000040	4.1300040
4.14	0.0000757	0.0000174	0.0000038	4.1400038
4.15	0.0000726	0.0000166	0.0000036	4.1500036
4.16	0.0000697	0.0000159	0.0000035	4.1600035
4.17	0.0000668	0.0000152	0.0000033	4.1700033
4.18	0.0000641	0.0000146	0.0000032	4.1800032
4.19	0.0000615	0.0000139	0.0000030	4.1900030
4.20	0.0000589	0.0000133	0.0000029	4.2000029
4.21	0.0000565	0.0000128	0.0000028	4.2100028
4.22	0.0000542	0.0000122	0.0000026	4.2200026
4.23	0.0000519	0.0000117	0.0000025	4.2300025
4.24	0.0000498	0.0000112	0.0000024	4.2400024
4.25	0.0000477	0.0000107	0.0000023	4.2500023
4.26	0.0000457	0.0000102	0.0000022	4.2600022
4.27	0.0000438	0.0000098	0.0000021	4.2700021
4.28	0.0000420	0.0000093	0.0000020	4.2800020
4.29	0.0000402	0.0000089	0.0000019	4.2900019
4.30	0.0000385	0.0000085	0.0000018	4.3000018
4.31	0.0000369	0.0000082	0.0000017	4.3100017
4.32	0.0000354	0.0000078	0.0000017	4.3200017
4.33	0.0000339	0.0000075	0.0000016	4.3300016
4.34	0.0000324	0.0000071	0.0000015	4.3400015
4.35	0.0000310	0.0000068	0.0000014	4.3500014
4.36	0.0000297	0.0000065	0.0000014	4.3600014
4.37	0.0000284	0.0000062	0.0000013	4.3700013
4.38	0.0000272	0.0000059	0.0000012	4.3800012
4.39	0.0000261	0.0000057	0.0000012	4.3900012
4.40	0.0000249	0.0000054	0.0000011	4.4000011
4.41	0.0000239	0.0000052	0.0000011	4.4100011
4.42	0.0000228	0.0000049	0.0000010	4.4200010
4.43	0.0000218	0.0000047	0.0000010	4.4300010
4.44	0.0000209	0.0000045	0.0000009	4.4400009
4.45	0.0000200	0.0000043	0.0000009	4.4500009
4.46	0.0000191	0.0000041	0.0000008	4.4600008
4.47	0.0000183	0.0000039	0.0000008	4.4700008
4.48	0.0000175	0.0000037	0.0000008	4.4800008
4.49	0.0000167	0.0000036	0.0000007	4.4900007
4.50	0.0000160	0.0000034	0.0000007	4.5000007

Exhibit D.2 (Continued)

SAFETY FACTOR K	DENSITY P(K)	PROBABILITY F(K)	PARTIAL EXPECTATION E(K)	PARTIAL EXPECTATION E(-K)
4.50	0.0000160	0.0000034	0.0000007	4.5000007
4.51	0.0000153	0.0000032	0.0000007	4.5100007
4.52	0.0000146	0.0000031	0.0000006	4.5200006
4.53	0.0000140	0.0000029	0.0000006	4.5300006
4.54	0.0000133	0.0000028	0.0000006	4.5400006
4.55	0.0000127	0.0000027	0.0000005	4.5500005
4.56	0.0000122	0.0000026	0.0000005	4.5600005
4.57	0.0000116	0.0000024	0.0000005	4.5700005
4.58	0.0000111	0.0000023	0.0000005	4.5800005
4.59	0.0000106	0.0000022	0.0000004	4.5900004
4.60	0.0000101	0.0000021	0.0000004	4.6000004
4.61	0.0000097	0.0000020	0.0000004	4.6100004
4.62	0.0000092	0.0000019	0.0000004	4.6200004
4.63	0.0000088	0.0000018	0.0000004	4.6300004
4.64	0.0000084	0.0000017	0.0000003	4.6400003
4.65	0.0000080	0.0000017	0.0000003	4.6500003
4.66	0.0000077	0.0000016	0.0000003	4.6600003
4.67	0.0000073	0.0000015	0.0000003	4.6700003
4.68	0.0000070	0.0000014	0.0000003	4.6800003
4.69	0.0000067	0.0000014	0.0000003	4.6900003
4.70	0.0000064	0.0000013	0.0000003	4.7000003
4.71	0.0000061	0.0000012	0.0000002	4.7100002
4.72	0.0000058	0.0000012	0.0000002	4.7200002
4.73	0.0000055	0.0000011	0.0000002	4.7300002
4.74	0.0000053	0.0000011	0.0000002	4.7400002
4.75	0.0000050	0.0000010	0.0000002	4.7500002
4.76	0.0000048	0.0000010	0.0000002	4.7600002
4.77	0.0000046	0.0000009	0.0000002	4.7700002
4.78	0.0000044	0.0000009	0.0000002	4.7800002
4.79	0.0000042	0.0000008	0.0000002	4.7900002
4.80	0.0000040	0.0000008	0.0000002	4.8000002
4.81	0.0000038	0.0000008	0.0000001	4.8100001
4.82	0.0000036	0.0000007	0.0000001	4.8200001
4.83	0.0000034	0.0000007	0.0000001	4.8300001
4.84	0.0000033	0.0000006	0.0000001	4.8400001
4.85	0.0000031	0.0000006	0.0000001	4.8500001
4.86	0.0000030	0.0000006	0.0000001	4.8600001
4.87	0.0000028	0.0000006	0.0000001	4.8700001
4.88	0.0000027	0.0000005	0.0000001	4.8800001
4.89	0.0000026	0.0000005	0.0000001	4.8900001
4.90	0.0000024	0.0000005	0.0000001	4.9000001
4.91	0.0000023	0.0000005	0.0000001	4.9100001
4.92	0.0000022	0.0000004	0.0000001	4.9200001
4.93	0.0000021	0.0000004	0.0000001	4.9300001
4.94	0.0000020	0.0000004	0.0000001	4.9400001
4.95	0.0000019	0.0000004	0.0000001	4.9500001
4.96	0.0000018	0.0000004	0.0000001	4.9600001
4.97	0.0000017	0.0000003	0.0000001	4.9700001
4.98	0.0000016	0.0000003	0.0000001	4.9800001
4.99	0.0000016	0.0000003	0.0000001	4.9900001
5.00	0.0000015	0.0000003	0.0000001	5.0000001

Exhibit D.3

SAFETY FACTOR K	DENSITY P(K)	PROBABILITY F(K)	PARTIAL EXPECTATION $-E(K)$	PARTIAL EXPECTATION $E(-K)$
0.00	0.3679	0.3679	0.3679	0.3679
0.10	0.3329	0.3329	0.3329	0.4066
0.20	0.3012	0.3012	0.3012	0.4493
0.30	0.2725	0.2725	0.2725	0.4966
0.40	0.2466	0.2466	0.2466	0.5488
0.50	0.2231	0.2231	0.2231	0.6065
0.60	0.2019	0.2019	0.2019	0.6703
0.70	0.1827	0.1827	0.1827	0.7408
0.80	0.1653	0.1653	0.1653	0.8187
0.90	0.1496	0.1496	0.1496	0.9048
1.00	0.1353	0.1353	0.1353	1.0000
1.10	0.1225	0.1225	0.1225	1.1000
1.20	0.1108	0.1108	0.1108	1.2000
1.30	0.1003	0.1003	0.1003	1.3000
1.40	0.0907	0.0907	0.0907	1.4000
1.50	0.0821	0.0821	0.0821	1.5000
1.60	0.0743	0.0743	0.0743	1.6000
1.70	0.0672	0.0672	0.0672	1.7000
1.80	0.0608	0.0608	0.0608	1.8000
1.90	0.0550	0.0550	0.0550	1.9000
2.00	0.0498	0.0498	0.0498	2.0000
2.10	0.0450	0.0450	0.0450	2.1000
2.20	0.0408	0.0408	0.0408	2.2000
2.30	0.0369	0.0369	0.0369	2.3000
2.40	0.0334	0.0334	0.0334	2.4000
2.50	0.0302	0.0302	0.0302	2.5000
2.60	0.0273	0.0273	0.0273	2.6000
2.70	0.0247	0.0247	0.0247	2.7000
2.80	0.0224	0.0224	0.0224	2.8000
2.90	0.0202	0.0202	0.0202	2.9000
3.00	0.0183	0.0183	0.0183	3.0000
3.10	0.0166	0.0166	0.0166	3.1000
3.20	0.0150	0.0150	0.0150	3.2000
3.30	0.0136	0.0136	0.0136	3.3000
3.40	0.0123	0.0123	0.0123	3.4000
3.50	0.0111	0.0111	0.0111	3.5000
3.60	0.0101	0.0101	0.0101	3.6000
3.70	0.0091	0.0091	0.0091	3.7000
3.80	0.0082	0.0082	0.0082	3.8000
3.90	0.0074	0.0074	0.0074	3.9000
4.00	0.0067	0.0067	0.0067	4.0000
4.10	0.0061	0.0061	0.0061	4.1000
4.20	0.0055	0.0055	0.0055	4.2000
4.30	0.0050	0.0050	0.0050	4.3000
4.40	0.0045	0.0045	0.0045	4.4000
4.50	0.0041	0.0041	0.0041	4.5000
4.60	0.0037	0.0037	0.0037	4.6000
4.70	0.0033	0.0033	0.0033	4.7000
4.80	0.0030	0.0030	0.0030	4.8000
4.90	0.0027	0.0027	0.0027	4.9000
5.00	0.0025	0.0025	0.0025	5.0000

Exhibit D.4

SAFETY FACTOR K	DENSITY $P(K)$	PROBABILITY $F(K)$	PARTIAL EXPECTATION $E(K)$	PARTIAL EXPECTATION $E(-K)$
0.00	0.3989	0.5000	0.3989	0.3989
0.10	0.3970	0.4606	0.3509	0.4509
0.20	0.3910	0.4215	0.3067	0.5067
0.30	0.3814	0.3832	0.2664	0.5664
0.40	0.3683	0.3458	0.2299	0.6299
0.50	0.3521	0.3099	0.1971	0.6971
0.60	0.3332	0.2756	0.1679	0.7679
0.70	0.3123	0.2431	0.1421	0.8421
0.80	0.2897	0.2128	0.1194	0.9194
0.90	0.2661	0.1848	0.0998	0.9998
1.00	0.2420	0.1591	0.0829	1.0829
1.10	0.2179	0.1359	0.0684	1.1684
1.20	0.1942	0.1151	0.0561	1.2561
1.30	0.1714	0.0967	0.0457	1.3457
1.40	0.1497	0.0806	0.0369	1.4369
1.50	0.1295	0.0666	0.0297	1.5297
1.60	0.1109	0.0546	0.0236	1.6236
1.70	0.0940	0.0444	0.0186	1.7186
1.80	0.0790	0.0358	0.0146	1.8146
1.90	0.0656	0.0286	0.0113	1.9113
2.00	0.0540	0.0227	0.0086	2.0086
2.10	0.0440	0.0178	0.0065	2.1065
2.20	0.0355	0.0139	0.0049	2.2049
2.30	0.0283	0.0107	0.0036	2.3036
2.40	0.0224	0.0082	0.0027	2.4027
2.50	0.0175	0.0062	0.0019	2.5019
2.60	0.0136	0.0047	0.0014	2.6014
2.70	0.0104	0.0035	0.0010	2.7010
2.80	0.0079	0.0026	0.0007	2.8007
2.90	0.0060	0.0019	0.0005	2.9005
3.00	0.0044	0.0014	0.0004	3.0004
3.10	0.0033	0.0010	0.0003	3.1003
3.20	0.0024	0.0007	0.0002	3.2002
3.30	0.0017	0.0005	0.0001	3.3001
3.40	0.0012	0.0003	0.0001	3.4001
3.50	0.0009	0.0002	0.0001	3.5001
3.60	0.0006	0.0002		3.6000
3.70	0.0004	0.0001		3.7000
3.80	0.0003	0.0001		3.8000
3.90	0.0002			3.9000
4.00	0.0001			4.0000

Index

This index lists only references in the main text. Since the Bibliography is alphabetical by author (starting on page 390), and the glossary (starting at page 393) is alphabetical by item, you will also find references there.

ABC classification, 168
ABC list, 55, 125
accessories, 79
accounting, 3
accuracy, 109
action system, 1, 5
adaptive weights, 108
aggregate forecasts, 41, 125
allocation, 7, 243, 346, 349
Amdahl 470, 222
American Thread Company, 320
amplitude, 89, 100
Anheuser Busch, 272
approximation, 235, 418
assortments, 79
automatic sequence, 312
availability, 27
available stock, 241, 256, 349

Babcock and Wilcox, 272
Babcock, George D., 202
backlog, 36, 37, 134, 340, 381
back orders, 58, 64, 175, 335
balance out, 199
balance sheet, 69, 161
Barnard, George, 155
barycentric coordinates, 230
base case, 204, 210
base index, 85, 368
base stock, 245
Beer, Stafford, 67
bibliography, 390
bill of materials, 298
binomial distribution, 200
Black and Decker, 124
Black, O. J., 362

blanket orders, 339
Box, G. E. P., 108, 158
breakpoints, 225
bridging runs, 207, 223
budgets, 27, 291
bulky products, 209, 238
Bureau of Supplies and Accounts, 368
buy ahead, 129

calendars, 88, 271
Camp, Robert, 330
Campbell Soup, 124
can-order point, 337
Carborundum, 168
carrying charge, 70, 208
Caterpillar Tractor Company, 4, 174
centered moving average, 97
central control, 346
central file, 3
central limit theorem, 146
changeover costs, 227
changes in demand, 129
Chase Manhattan Bank, 124
chi-square test, 146
Class A items, 169
classification, 163
closed short, 323
codes, 320
coefficient, 48, 89, 94, 377
coefficient of variation, 142
commercial printing, 13
computers, 327
Conway, R. L., 325
coordinated delivery, 207, 231
coordinated orders, 337
correlation, 84

432 INDEX

criteria, 358
critical ratio, 326
culling the inventory, 171
cumulative sums, 154
current/noncurrent, 54
current parts, 174
customer demand, 77
customer service, 70, 370
cybernetics, 53
cycled production, 228

data base, 4
days allowed, 317
decision rules, 58, 173, 262
Decision Rules for Inventory Management, 111, 118, 155, 224, 358, 418
default values, 240
degrees of freedom, 151
delivery rate, 207
demand, 77, 107
  during lead time, 173, 247
demand filter, 48, 120, 156
demand history, 377
demand transactions, 248
demand year to date, 151, 247
deMatteis, J. J., 237
density, 140
dependent demand, 35
dependent requirements, 21, 301, 303
descriptive forecasts, 73, 128
design assumptions, 202
Dickie, H. Ford, 169
direct labor, 14
directories, 388
direct requirements, 301
distribution, 6, 138
distribution by value, 165
Dowdle, John, 329
dual accounting, 276
due dates, 269, 273
duPont, 170, 208
duration of shortage, 177
duty cycle, 69
dynamic lot sizes, 45
dynamic programming, 232, 261

economical order quantity, 202
effectivity date, 308
end of season, 199
engineering, 3
error, 107
evaluating marketing intelligence, 49
evaluation, 128, 131
Everdale, Romeyn, 326
exception, 26
exception report, 122
excess stock, 255
exchange curves, 69, 191, 214

exchange surface, 222
expected deficit, 246
expected number of shortages, 176
expediting, 26, 64, 314, 348
explanatory forecasts, 73
explosion, 21, 35, 267, 298
exponential distribution, 140, 142, 430
exponentially declining weights, 108
exponential smoothing, 109, 160
extrapolating, 196

failure rates, 79
fair shares, 7, 350
families of items, 227
feasibility, 304
Federal Supply Service, 193, 347, 362
feedback, 5, 53, 64, 75, 158, 326
file structure, 373
finished production, 15
finite delivery rate, 215
firm orders, 21, 286
firm requirements, 36
first-come, first-served, 326
first-level system, 69
fitting functions, 89
fixed interval, 242
fixed lot quantity, 283
fixed time supply, 283
Food and Drug Administration, 22
Ford Motor Company, 168
forecast of demand, 334
forecast errors, 45, 120, 136
forecasting, 73, 94, 118
foregone conclusions, 160
form of distribution, 136
formal definition, 71
formal system, 263
Fortune, 70, 161
Fourier series, 89
freeze period, 21, 26, 273
freight costs, 10
freight rates, 329
function of distribution, 140
functional parts, 174

Garwood, Dave, 315
General Electric Company, 124, 169
General Foods, 127
Gerson, George, 181, 219
glossary, 393
good quantity, 14, 325
government orders, 365
gross requirements, 279

Hamner, John, 4
Harrison, P. J., 109
hierarchy, 5
histogram, 138

INDEX

433

Honeywell, 126, 159, 169
horizon, 21
horizontal, 81
hot list, 26
Hulswit, Frank, 364
human judgement, 52

ICI Paints Division, 364
IMPACT, 150, 178, 242, 337
independent orders, 333
initial buy, 258
initial forecast, 43
insufficient stock, 354
interaction, 217
International Business Machines, 124
International Harvester, 347
interpolation, 271
inventory, 54, 370
inventory control, 241
inventory management, 161
investment, 194
Iverson, Ken, 111

Jackson, Ed, 174
Jenkins, Gwilym, 108
job shop, 13
Johnson, S. M., 326
joint orders, 227, 242
judgement, 5
julian calendar, 378

Kimball, George E., 199, 245

labor grade, 31
Lagrange multiplier, 190
last buy, 206
last operation, 16, 325
latest ship date, 7, 350
latest start date, 13
lead time, 21, 149, 151, 334
least-cost redistribution, 341
least squares, 94, 102
least unit cost, 237
level, 43, 81
level code, 20, 26, 302
levels of systems, 67
limits, 356
linear programming, 10
liquidity, 209
list of items, 164
location status, 18
lognormal distribution, 142, 196
lognormal model, 165
lot for lot, 279
lot quantity, 202
lot size and safety stock, 217
LPTRANS, 343
lumpy demand, 100, 231, 245

MAD, 45, 148
Magee, John F., 69, 329
make/buy, 54
Management Decisions for Production Operations, 230
management policy variables, 58, 190, 382
management science, 161
manufacturing calendar, 276
manufacturing cycle, 273
Mariner, Kenneth, 133
marketing intelligence, 36, 41, 122, 123
master schedule, 19, 35, 269, 300
master warehouse, 6, 37
materials requirements planning, 176, 266
maximum lot quantity, 212
maximum operating level, 243
maximum stocking objective, 286
Maxwell, W. L., 325
mean, 140, 147
mean absolute deviation, 45, 142, 148
mean square error, 148, 151
measurement, 11
measures of service, 58, 176
median, 148
Mendoza, A. J., 237
Mennell, Roy F., 202
Meyer, Richard F., 358
minimum back orders, 181
minimum lot quantity, 283
minimum time supply, 212
model, 77
  of time series, 81
model selection, 94
model year, 207
modular bill of materials, 78
modular library, 158
months of supply, 66
Morse, Philip M., 199
moving average, 97, 110
Murphy's Law, 154

National Council of Physical Distribution
  Management, 329
national safety stock, 64, 347, 371
need date, 274
net change, 304
net forecast, 37
net plus business, 128
net requirements, 279
new items, 43, 104
new product, 365
  introduction, 127
newsboy problem, 199
New York Stock Exchange, 152
Nile River, 152
no history, 104
noise, 88
normal distribution, 140, 419

normal probability, 138
notional orders, 21, 279
number of shortages, 185
number of warehouses, 370
Nyquist, J., 89

obsolescence, 238, 314
obsolete stock, 206
official schedule, 304
offset time, 21
OMC Parts and Accessories, 362
open orders, 378
operating costs, 370
operation name, 14
operations sequence, 317
options, 79
 accessories, 200
order entry, 3, 69
order point, 241, 242, 334, 337
order quantity, 243, 244, 335
order, 77
order status, 21
organization, 362
original quantity, 325
outliers, 100
overhauls, 250

packaging, 13
parabolic mask, 155
parent items, 35
partial completion, 323
partial expectation, 140, 147, 176
part number, 54, 380
part-period balancing, 237
pegged requirements, 22, 305
people, 5, 31, 279, 327
performance, 11
permanent changes, 126
phantom bill, 310
pharmaceuticals, 13
phase angle, 89
Phillips Lamp, 152
photographic film, 13
physical distribution, 329
PICS, 53
pipeline fill, 126
planned orders, 338
planner, 304
planning array, 269, 380
planning periods, 272
planning system, 1, 18
planning table, 252
plugged level, 102
policy variables, 221
polynomials, 83
practical approach, 220, 235
precision, 109
premium on investment, 208

price rise, 207
priority report, 13
priority rules, 325
probability, 137, 140
probability density, 147
probability functions, 418
process routings, 316, 379
product line, 125
production control, 12
production planning, 265
product structure, 298, 379
profile, 97
PROGCONST, 111
programmed decisions, 71
progress, 14, 324
projected service, 337
promotions, 128, 207
pull, 347, 368
purchasing, 3
push, 347, 368

quantity discounts, 206, 225
quarterly profile, 100

rational approximation, 418
razor blades, 129
reference numbers, 26, 287
regeneration, 303
regional control, 333
regional distribution, 330
regional safety stocks, 371
regional stock, 64
regression, 94
remnant stock, 372
reordering, 335
replenishment, 244, 246
requirements system, 1, 35
requisite variety, 72
reserve bin, 251
response to change, 170
retrieval, 164
return on investment, 208
revise coefficients, 120
revising, forecast, 47, 107
risk, 209
rounding, 122, 212, 336, 356
routing, 316
rule of thumb, 226

safety factors, 58, 183
safety stock, 45, 55
 strategies, 173, 334
sample, 196
sampling interval, 80
satellites, 6, 348
scaling, 104
schedule date, 26, 274
scheduled backlog, 36, 134

INDEX

schedule quantity, 17
scrap loss, 15
screen, 100
search and find, 340
seasonal cycles, 83
seasonal patterns, 43
second-level system, 69, 162
sensitivity, 211
service, 222
service parts, 79
setups, 14
  costs, 203
shipments, 77, 359
Ships Parts Control Center, 171
shop floor control, 316
shortage duration, 60
shortage occurrences, 58, 185
short dated orders, 26, 314
short history, 45
Shycon, Harvey, 329
significance, 81
significant digits, 212
significant part numbers, 163
Silver, Edward A., 242, 249, 337
Simpson, K. F., 177, 349
simulations, 70, 72, 159
sine wave, 89
skewed distribution, 146
SKU, 78
slack time, 326
slanted chart, 31, 291
smoothed error tracking signal, 155
smoothed production, 281
smoothing calculations, 110
smoothing constants, 111
Smoothing Forecasting and Prediction, 111, 150
Society of Logistics Engineers, 329
sorting key, 375
space occupied, 209, 238
specifications, 365
specified service, 178
stabilization stock, 373
standard deviation, 45, 58, 140, 147, 148, 221
standard hours, 14
Stanley, Emory, Jr., 156
state variables, 381
stationary time series, 108
statistical forecast, 36, 43
Statistical Forecasting for Inventory Control, 148, 154, 178
Stevens, C. F., 109
stimulus, 128
stock, 54
stock on hand, 27, 256
stock-keeping unit, 78, 163
stock in transit, 371

strategic choice, 58, 70, 192
strategic system, 1, 53
stratification, 54, 163
subassembly, 20
sublots, 16
subordinate parts, 21, 35, 265, 298
summary reports, 27
sunspots, 152
supplier's inventory, 277
symmetrical distribution, 146
synonyms, 368
synthetic bill of materials, 314
synthetic product, 78
systems development, 365

tactical choice, 58, 70, 193
talent, 159
taxonomy, 67
Taylor, Frederick, 70
temporary changes, 125
tentative schedule, 304
terminal service, 259
Theil, H., 158
thinking, 123
third-level system, 70
time-phased requirements, 265
time-varying demand, 231
tracking signals, 49, 120, 133, 154
transactions, filled, 178
  short, 60
transition matrix, 110, 362
transport, 329
transportation algorithm, 10
travelling requisition, 251
trend, 43, 81
Trigg, Derek, 108, 133
trim/functional, 54
triple smoothing, 83
truck capacity, 359
turning points, 126, 155
two-bin system, 250
two populations, 168

uniform distribution, 139, 142
uniform weights, 108
unit costs, 206
United States Rubber, 126
United States Steel, 168
Upjohn, 194
usage rates, 204
user's inventory, 277
U. S. Navy, 250, 259, 330

van Dobben de Bruyn, C. S., 108
variable lead times, 150
variance, 47, 147
variance law, 47,
  152

Wagner, Harvey, 205, 232
Wall Street Journal, 70
warehouse, 6
warehouse locations, 384
warehouseman, 161
WATS line, 340
wedding gifts, 79
weeks of supply, 185
weighted least-squares, 107
weights, 108
Welch, W. Evert, 169
Wentworth, Felix, 329
Wharton School, 124
when to order, 242
where-used, 381
Whiten, T. M., 205, 232

Wiener, Norbert, 108
Winters, Peter, 108
work center, 14
working bin, 251
working days, 384
working stock, 27, 64, 372
workload, 34
work in process, 34
work sheet, 14, 322

Xerox, 79, 330

yield, 301
yield factor, 325
yield ratio, 17